D1526836

ATLANTIC STUDIES ON SOCIETY IN CHANGE

NO. 78

Editor-in-Chief, Béla K. Király

Associate Editor-in-Chief, Peter Pastor

Assistant Editor, Edit Völgyesi

War and Society in East Central Europe
Volume XXXI

Graydon A. Tunstall, Jr.

PLANNING FOR WAR AGAINST RUSSIA AND SERBIA

AUSTRO-HUNGARIAN AND GERMAN MILITARY STRATEGIES, 1871-1914

Social Science Monographs, Boulder, Colorado
Atlantic Research and Publications,
Highland Lakes, New Jersey

Distributed by Columbia University Press, New York
1993

EAST EUROPEAN MONOGRAPHS, NO. CCCLXXIV

Copyright © 1993
by Atlantic Research and Publications, Inc.

Library of Congress Catalog Card Number 93-71876
ISBN 0-88033-271-9

Printed in the United States of America

Table of Contents

INVENTORY CONTROL

Mo. _f. /_   Quan ___/___   u,

Subject _£2 4,_

Author _TUN STALL_

Title _PLANNING FOR_

WAR, ETC...

☐ paperback ☑ cloth

Price $_53.00_

* * * * * * * * * * * * *

Date Sold ___/ /__

Other _____

Table of Contents

Preface to the Series

The present volume is a component of a series which, when completed, will constitute a comprehensive survey of the many aspects of East European society. The books in the series deal with the peoples whose homelands lie between the Germans to the west, the Russians to the east and the Mediterranean and Adriatic seas to the south. They constitute a particular civilization, one that is at once an integral part of Europe, yet substantially different from the West. The area is characterized by a rich diversity in language, religion, and government. The study of such a complex subject demands a multidisciplinary approach and, accordingly, our contributors to the series represent several academic disciplines. They have been drawn from the universities and other scholarly institutions in the United States and Western Europe, as well as East and Central Europe. The author of the present volume is Assistant Professor of History at Cedar Crest College and International Executive Secretary-Treasurer of Phi Alpha Theta.

The editors, of course, take full responsibility for ensuring the comprehensiveness, cohesion, internal balance, and scholarly quality of the series. We cheerfully accept this responsibility and intend this work to be neither a justification nor condemnation of the policies, attitudes, and activities of any persons involved. At the same time, because the contributors represent so many different disciplines, interpretations, and schools of thought, our policy in this, as in the past and future volumes, is to present their contributions without major modifications.

Acknowledgments

Many people have been generous in lending me support and encouragement while I wrote this book. It is a pleasure to be able to thank them now. The first ones to be mentioned are my mother, Valance T. Tunstall, my wife, Nancy, and my graduate school advisor, the late Dr. Robert A. Kann, without whose encouragement this book would never have been possible. All three have provided a major influence on my academic life.

Special thanks go to Ann Gorman, who provided inestimable aid in reading through the proofs, and to Hilda Cooper, who typed the manuscript.

Mention should also be made of two special colleagues and friends, Peter Pastor and Robert I. Weiner. Peter for years has encouraged my endeavors in writing this monograph, and Bob has been a constant and true friend.

While researching for the monograph particular assistance was provided by Peter Broucek of the Vienna War Archives, and Leopold Moser, formerly of the War Archives library.

Introduction

Since the time of Frederick the Great, Prussia and then a united Germany had moved to the center of the European diplomatic and military stage. If at first not on a par with France and Russia, after 1871 Germany displaced those two nations as the leading, and even predominant, continental power. Such status, however, brought with it serious problems, particularly the menace of some sort of anti-German coalition which might involve Germany in a two-front war.

After 1871, Bismarck saw that Germany must be protected from diplomatic isolation in order to avert having to fight on the battlefield to preserve her position. As a champion of Prussia (now the dominant part of the German Empire), he could not neglect the near-disastrous lesson taught by the Seven Years' War when Prussia was nearly crushed by the forces of France, Russia, and the Habsburg empire striking from the west, east, and south. After Austria-Hungary had become an ally in 1879, the greatest danger lay unquestionably in a two-front war with France and Russia.

The Franco-Prussian War had poisoned Franco-German relations for the foreseeable future so that there was always a threat in the west. But there were possibilities with Russia. Since the Napoleonic era, Prussia and Russia had been friendly, although not diplomatic brothers, and Bismarck tried very energetically to maintain at least Russia's acquiescence in German continental predominance. Such diplomatic initiatives as the Three Emperors' Alliance with Russia and Austria-Hungary exemplified his efforts to prevent the formation of an east-west alliance against Germany.

But Bismarck, and especially his successors, failed in this mission. If Franco-German hostility was one of the facts of diplomatic history between 1871 and 1914, the dispute between Austria-Hungary and Russia in the Balkans was another. By the middle of the nineteenth century, Austro-Hungarian interests and Russian expansion in that region had come close to an open clash. The Crimean War and Austria-Hungary's vacillation therein undoubtedly heightened the antagonism between the two.

Another factor was the constant Russian Pan-slavic propaganda directed at the Slavs under Habsburg rule.

The Austro-Hungarian and Russian situations were different, however. Whereas Russia desired to expand her influence in pursuit of a unified national policy, Austria-Hungary's problem was that of holding herself together. Austria-Hungary, a multi-national empire, found herself in difficulties in an age of increasingly virulent nationalism and had almost been broken down into her component units in 1848 and 1849. Some of her own nationality groups had compatriots across the frontier who were free and independent, and any expansion of this phenomenon definitely encouraged disintegrative forces within the empire. In this respect, the unification of Italy and the independence of Serbia and Romania in 1878 represented the beginning of a variety of diplomatic, as well as internal, difficulties, manifesting itself with the diplomatic and military shifting of power after the Balkan Wars of 1912-1913.

Russia, in the meantime, was expanding her sphere of interests in the Balkans. In particular, her support of Serbia endangered Austria-Hungary's hold on her own Southern Slav population. The situation was seriously aggravated in 1908 when Austria-Hungary occupied Bosnia-Herzegovina without consulting the other great powers. The instability in Europe because of this Austro-Russian rivalry was heightened because Bismarck's successors were unable to maintain a controlling influence over Austria-Hungary's Balkan policy.

We will investigate the general question of how Germany, without sacrificing her predominance on the continent, and Austria-Hungary, fighting to survive as a great power with her territorial integrity intact, tried to coordinate their roles in the strategy of a two-front war. German leadership in military planning was virtually unquestioned; consequently, the ideas of the Elder Moltke and of Waldersee are presented here as a background to the Schlieffen period when the strategy employed by the Central Powers in the First World War was devised. The focus of this study will be on the frequently overlooked role of Austria-Hungary in that strategy.

For Austria-Hungary to be an effective ally of Germany, at least one of her potential enemies had to be brought into the Dual Alliance as Italy was in 1882, thereby creating the Triple Alliance. As further guarantee, Austria-Hungary concluded another, albeit secret, alliance with Romania, which was subsequently joined by Germany and Italy. Serbia, Austria-Hungary's future chief adversary in the Balkans, made a secret agreement with the Habsburg Empire in 1881 concerning the coordination of her foreign policy with that of Austria-Hungary. The overthrow of the Obrenovic dynasty in 1903, however, placed Serbia definitely in the camp of Austria-Hungary's enemies. Since Austro-German military strategy required that Austria-Hungary field her main forces against Russia, the Serbian switch and the growing unreliability of Italian and Romanian support endangered planning for a two-front war as envisioned in the Schlieffen plan on the eve of 1914.

We will examine in considerable detail the military planning and proposed troop deployments worked out by the general staffs of Austria-Hungary and Germany, from 1882 through the summer of 1914. The roles to be played by Italy and Romania in overall strategy will also be studied, since their defection in 1914 seemed to point up a number of the weaknesses in Austro-German planning.

Also to be considered is the nature and extent of the military agreements or understandings between Germany and Austria-Hungary that are believed to have come into existence in the pre-war period. It will be shown that despite whatever formal ties linked the two powers, both had strategic preferences that vitiated the possibility of a victory on the eastern front within the timetable envisaged by the Schlieffen plan and almost brought about the defeat of Austria-Hungary. Considering developments within the Triple Entente, the Schlieffen plan may well have been obsolete, but errors and mutual misrepresentations by the military leaders of the Central Powers, Moltke and Conrad, certainly aggravated the situation.

Since diplomacy played a key role in the events leading to the clash of armies in 1914, close attention will be paid in particular to the events surrounding the Bosnian Crisis and the Balkan Wars. By upsetting the delicate diplomatic and military balance that existed in southeastern Europe, by aggravating Austro-Russian tension, and by helping to alienate Italy and Romania, these events led to considerable re-thinking, especially for Austria-Hungary, concerning military planning for a possible confrontation with Russia.

Another topic to be studied is the interaction between the military and diplomatic leadership within and between Germany and Austria-Hungary. As will be seen, diplomatic and military leaders often did not understand each other's priorities and programs; and in the fateful July crisis in 1914, the diplomats succumbed to the "military necessities" of the moment. In addition to this lack of coordination and consultation, the General Staffs of Germany and Austria-Hungary did not maintain the close contact or cooperation that they might have even after the fighting had begun in August of 1914.

The present study will carry the military planning of the pre-war period into the battlefield reality of the First World War in order to assess the adequacy of Central Power — especially Austro-Hungarian — military strategy and preparation on the eastern front in connection with the Schlieffen plan. In a sense, the fighting in the east during August and September proved to be a tragic and costly laboratory test which betrayed both the Central Powers' overestimation of themselves and their underestimation of their opponent, Russia. As will be seen, this general miscalculation was translated into certain actual troop deployments that led to an initial victory for Russia, at least over Austria-Hungary.

Chapters I and II will discuss German and then Austro-German military planning from 1871 through 1905, the year when the Schlieffen plan was devised. Chapter III will examine events from 1906 through 1909, the Bosnian Crisis and its ramifications, and the Austro-German agreements of 1909. The general strategic principles from 1909 through 1914 will be studied in Chapter IV, and the Balkan Wars (1912-1913) and their effect on this strategy will be examined in Chapter V. Chapter VI encompasses developments from January 1914 through the July crisis of that year, Chapter VII the Austro-Hungarian mobilization, and Chapter VIII the historiographical picture of the mobilization. An overview of the initial military campaigns will portray the actual battles — Chapter IX in August 1914, and Chapter X, September.

In order to collect the materials needed to investigate this topic, it was necessary to work in the appropriate archives in Vienna. Relative to the military aspects, the Kriegsarchiv has received particular attention. Documents from the Operations Bureau, Railroad Bureau, Etappen Bureau, Intelligence Bureau, from the Army High Command, and liaison officers' reports have been studied. Army field records, map collections, and documents from the military chanceries of Franz Ferdinand and Franz Joseph and from the War Ministry have also been extensively consulted as have the personal papers of Generals Beck, Conrad, and Urbanski. Recent acquisitions of private papers round out the military sources. The Haus-, Hof-, und Staatsarchiv provided the primary materials for diplomatic matters connected with the Triple Alliance, Russia, the Balkan countries, and the opening campaigns.

In military terms, this war would be one for which Austria-Hungary proved totally unprepared. The troops found their training consumed in offensive exercises with no attention to defensive maneuvers, least of all preparing defensive positions. The artillery, low in number and quality, proved grossly inferior to those of the Russians; the airplanes too primitive and unreliable to provide crucial reconnaissance information. The cavalry went to war with troopers inadequately armed and garbed in easily targeted colors, as well as equipped with impractical saddles. The cavalry completely failed to provide essential intelligence information, and, because of misuse at the frontiers, suffered heavy losses and exhaustion before major battles commenced. Their worth by then had become negligible.

The Austro-Hungarian two-front war against Serbia-Montenegro and Russia found Vienna launching uncoordinated, ill-prepared offensives, with little or no artillery preparation.

Miscalculating that Russia would not enter the war initially, over forty percent of Habsburg forces would be hurled against Serbia for a knock-out blow before the lumbering giant of Russia could mobilize her troops. The gamble, however, became disaster.

Russia not only gained valuable days' advantage by an earlier mobilization, but also mobilized much more rapidly than anticipated. In addition, Habsburg troops slated to deploy in Galicia became bogged down in battle in Serbia or were held up by railroad technicians' miscalculations.

An entire army, the Second, was deployed against Serbia because of calculations by the Railroad Bureau Commanders and the High Command that Serbia could be dealt with rapidly. This army finally departed from the Serbian front partially beaten in battle to arrive in Galicia in time to join a retreat from eastern Galicia.

Vienna would launch an offensive, as foreseen for years, to seize the initiative from the Russian enemy before she could combine her staggering numerical superiority for a thrust into the bow-shaped configuration of Galicia. But, in addition to the advantage of an overpowering superiority in troops, Russia's railroads could transport troops at almost twice the rate of the Habsburgs.

Meanwhile, the northern offensive between the Bug and Vistula Rivers required the Austro-Hungarian eastern flank forces in Galicia to assume a defensive stance, protecting the flank and rear of the attacking armies in the north.

The defending east flank forces would be routed in a devastating battle because their intelligence and reconnaissance failed them miserably. The Army High Command also ignored warnings to this exposed flank in its haste to launch offensives inside Russian territory towards Lublin and Cholm.

At no crucial point on the front would the required mass of troops be deployed. This again could be traced back to an entire army, the Second, being deployed against Serbia despite a late mobilization against Russia. The Railroad Bureau, foreseeing chaos otherwise, refused to halt the Balkan mobilization to hurl all necessary, albeit numerically deficient, forces against the colossal northern rival.

Instead of forty infantry divisions being deployed in War Case Russia as planned, only twenty-eight would be initially fielded against Russia, while twenty-three would be deployed in the Balkans.

Add to this that St. Petersburg had initiated mobilization measures at the time of the rejection of the Austro-Hungarian "ultimatum" to Serbia, and the Railroad Bureau in Vienna requested, and received, 4 August as the first mobilization day against Russia. The Russians thereby gained a week's advantage over Austria-Hungary, although Conrad's strategy had as its basis the advantage of time and a more rapid mobilization to counter the more slowly mobilizing Tsarist masses.

In pre-war agreements, the German High Command had agreed to launch an offensive over the Narev River to support the sorely needed northern Habsburg advance, which served to tie down enemy troops while the main German armies crushed France Schlieffen-style.

It didn't help matters that in all Conrad's flexible military planning, nothing had been calculated for a simultaneous war against Serbia-Montenegro and Russia. Operations Bureau work had been spent on the possibility of Russia entering a fray after Serbia, or vice versa. The Railroad Bureau, however, had no plans for a War Case B followed immediately by a War Case R.

Conrad von Hötzendorf's armies also suffered because their armaments program lagged far behind their neighbors'.

Technologically, Vienna suffered severe handicaps. Airplanes, as mentioned, had been ignored for war service. Artillery, lacking in numbers, also was obsolete compared to that of other Major Powers.

Add the often-overlooked Habsburg disadvantage that Russia had gained by her experiences in the Russo-Japanese War, and Serbia could hurl battle-proven veterans from the Balkan Wars to meet any advance (Vienna's last major conflict dated back to 1866).

And finally, Austria-Hungary's official history of World War I, and memoirs written by leading generals at the time, portray events of the early weeks of the war in a different light from reality; thus the "Command Conspiracy."

CHAPTER I

Elder Moltke 1871-1888

From 1882 through 1914, a series of strategic plans for an eastern war was negotiated between the General Staffs of the German Empire and the Austro-Hungarian Monarchy. The precedents for the August 1914 deployment plans in the east had been set as early as the 1870's.

These precedents were established during three chronological periods. The first period, from 1871 to 1888, saw the service to Germany of General Field Marshal Count Helmuth von Moltke (the Elder Moltke). On the Austro-Hungarian side, General Frederick Beck-Rzikowsky began his tenure as Chief of the General Staff in 1881. The second period, from 1888 to 1906, witnessed the collaboration of the German Chiefs of Staff, Count Alfred Waldersee and Count Alfred von Schlieffen, with Beck-Rzikowsky. The final period (1906-1914) to be discussed later in greater detail, involved the plans of the Younger Moltke (nephew of the Elder Moltke) and the Austro-Hungarian General Conrad von Hötzendorf.

The German generals dominated the first two periods. The reason for the dominance of the Germans was that the Austro-Hungarians had been politically and militarily weakened by their defeat in 1866 in the Austro-Prussian War. The weak personalities of the Austro-Hungarian leaders also contributed to the problems of this period. Only after Count Schlieffen retired in 1905 did Conrad von Hötzendorf place the Habsburg military machine at the center of allied military planning.

The strategic plan suggested by General Conrad in 1909, a modification of Beck's plan, became the basic allied strategy for the eastern front until the outbreak of World War I. To understand this plan, it is necessary to review the earlier strategic contributions of the Elder Moltke and General Beck. Their agreements provided the background for the 1909 — and thus the 1914 — agreement on eastern strategy.

The dominant military theorist of the earliest period, Helmuth von Moltke, was the military unifier of Germany in 1871. Moltke, already sixty-five years old when appointed Chief of the General Staff, had masterminded the Prussian campaigns of 1866 and 1870-1871. Through a series of successful wars, he substantially increased the power of Prussia which then was able to unify Germany. Moltke, a man of tremendous strategic insight, also realized the effect of industrial power on military policy. Before a single railroad network existed in Germany, he already recognized the military potential of the railroad and later he utilized this new technological factor with the greatest precision.

Moltke did not map out actual day-to-day campaigns, as would General Alfred von Schlieffen later. As a loyal pupil of the military theorist Karl von Clausewitz, Moltke believed that no one could anticipate all the tactical problems of war and that battles were spontaneous actions directed by military circumstances.[1]

Unlike Beck, Moltke did not emphasize staff and army maneuvers as the panacea for strategic problems. He believed that such maneuvers did not realistically represent actual battlefield circumstances and their requisite solutions. Moltke regarded strategy as a system of ad hoc expedients, the art of acting under the pressure of the most difficult conditions.

Moltke realized the value of the strategic envelopment campaign, the outflanking of the enemy and annihilation of his forces by striking the rear or weakest point of his main body. Moltke attempted this strategy at the battles of Sadova in 1866 and Sedan in 1870. Later, Schlieffen adopted the strategic envelopment principle, enlarging it into a strategy which he expected would bring victory after one gigantic battle of annihilation.

The Elder Moltke, as early as 1859, feared a two-front war in which Germany would be engaged with both Russia and France. Moltke planned to capitalize on Germany's central position in Europe and its excellent railroad network, using interior lines to shift troops and supplies from one front to another. Yet he also had reservations because the same advantage of the inner line of operations could become the tactical disadvantage of an encirclement during the battle.

In Moltke's day, the Russians could not be expected to mount an offensive as quickly as the French, because of their lack of railroads and slowness in mobilization. Moltke's strategy, in a two-front war, would be to utilize the advantage of interior lines, striking first at the weaker of two enemies — Russia. Looking at the 1914 strategic plan, one is reminded of Moltke's 1859 thoughts defining a two-front war:

Establishment of one front with a minimum of resources; as rapid and effective a campaign as possible on the other; finally recovery of whatever may have been lost in the first theater.[2]

The basic military principle became the containment of one enemy (France) with as few troops as possible and the simultaneous deployment of a massive force to crush the other (Russia). This resembled the later Schlieffen plan, but with the priority of the initial opponent reversed. Moltke did not delude himself about the "conclusive" victory over France in 1871:

Germany cannot hope in a short time to free herself of one opponent through a rapid and lucky offensive towards the west, in order then to turn against another one. We have just seen how hard it is even to complete the victorious struggle against France.[3]

At the peace negotiations in 1871, Moltke emphasized Germany's demand that France relinquish a part of French-speaking Lorraine and the major fortress at Metz. These positions would serve as the containment keystones of a strong German defensive buffer. The terms of the 1871 Treaty of Frankfurt had secured a major strategic advantage for the Germans.

By April 1871, Moltke had altered his strategy. In an operational draft, he called for an offensive against both the French and the Russians. The concept established a defensive posture because Moltke could not visualize an offensive campaign that could cripple Russia, due to her enormous size and formidably rough terrain. Germany, in addition, would have to face France alone in the west. Against Russia, Moltke prophesied that it would be in Austria-Hungary's self-interest to aid Germany.

If Germany were confronted with an eastern war, she had to be defended against attack in three distinct areas: Königsberg, the vital fortress protecting the German northern flank; the province of Posen; and the route to Breslau. Moltke, considering the influence of distance upon strategy, realized that a Russian main thrust to seize Berlin would most likely come from Warsaw, the former Polish capital and now a military bastion. The distance from Prussia to Warsaw was half that from Posen or Silesia to Warsaw.[4] A German thrust from the north into Poland would accordingly disrupt any Russian advance westward towards Silesia.

German mobilization became a crucial factor in Moltke's plans for an eastern campaign. Moltke, counting on an earlier mobilization and deployment, hoped that advancing German troops could completely disrupt initial Russian troop concentrations by encircling and forcing them to retreat into their interior.

Moltke anticipated that, in an eastern war, the main Russian army concentration would be behind the great fortress triangle in the Vistula, Bug, and Narev River area. With Austro-Hungarian cooperation, he deemed it feasible to attempt an allied pincer movement between the Prussian and Galician frontiers to seize the western half of Poland from Russian control. With Habsburg aid in mind, Moltke evolved a plan by which nine German army corps would cross the Vistula River from East Prussia to attack in the direction of Warsaw, thereby concentrating his forces in Polish soil. The Austro-Hungarians, merely by assembling troops in the vicinity of Cracow, would automatically provide a certain amount of security for both the unprotected German industrial province of Silesia and the entire Prussian frontier.[5]

Moltke's thoughts on the military threats to Germany were similar to those of Bismarck, the diplomatic mastermind of unification. Bismarck fully realized that as a result of her defeat in 1866, Austria-Hungary had begun to focus attention on the Balkans. Bismarck's goal was to preserve the diplomatic isolation he had imposed upon France in 1871. His concept of European order, like that of Metternich before him, was based on the common interests of the conservative eastern monarchies. The result of his machinations at this time led to the creation of an alliance of Austria-Hungary, Germany, and Russia.

A joint military convention was signed in May 1873. The following month, a "political agreement to join in consultation in the event of differences" came into existence. A "German underwriting" of this Austro-Hungarian-Russian agreement, which vicariously sought to prevent a Franco-Russian alliance, led to the actual founding of the first League of the Three Emperors on 22 October 1873.

All went well for Bismarck until the "war scare" of 1875, when the French Foreign Minister made it appear that Germany was preparing to launch a preventive war against France. Immediate Russian and British promises to intervene on France's behalf produced the first fissure in the edifice of the Three Emperors' League.

Then, in July 1875, an uprising against Turkish misrule in the province of Herzegovina quickly spread to neighboring Bosnia, where local conditions of abuse and maladministration had also fanned the flames of revolt.

This situation introduced the Eastern Question of 1875-1878, which profoundly affected the future relations of the three eastern monarchies.

In September 1875, Bulgaria had joined the turmoil; further violence in May 1876 resulted in a Bulgarian bloodbath. Bulgaria's defeat led both Serbia and Montenegro to declare war on Turkey on 30 June 1876. The chief powers in the Balkan area, Austria-Hungary and Russia, sought a mutually satisfactory solution to this Balkan explosion, which pitted them against each other. Accordingly, in July 1876, the foreign ministers signed a secret convention at Reichstadt in Bohemia. The "agreement" surveyed the various possibilities for both powers in case of either a Serbian or Turkish victory, but had the weakness of a definition of terms neither clear nor formal.[6]

In September 1876, the Serbs suffered a crushing military defeat which led to Russian intervention against Turkey, her age-old rival. Russia thus entered the struggle, in spite of the Reichstadt agreement promising her non-intervention, on behalf of oppressed Orthodox Christian Slavs.

Prior to commencing hostilities with Turkey, however, the Russians had negotiated and arrived at a mutually agreeable settlement with the Austro-Hungarians, since circumstances had negated the old agreements of Reichstadt and necessitated new contracts. On 15 January 1877, the Budapest Convention would be signed, and it would be supplemented by further agreements on 18 March 1877. These secret agreements established Austro-Hungarian neutrality and opposition to any collective mediation. In return, the Habsburgs would be permitted to occupy the provinces of Bosnia-Herzegovina,[7] a point which would become a focus of contention between Austria-Hungary and Russia decades later.

Russia declared war on Turkey on 24 April 1877. The military campaign proved long and difficult, but in the end Russia imposed upon Turkey the Treaty of San Stefano. Contrary to the terms of the secret Austro-Hungarian-Russian agreements at Budapest, a Greater Bulgarian state was created by the treaty. This act was tantamount to the establishment of dominant Russian influence in the Balkans and over Constantinople. Also, by the San Stefano treaty, Bosnia-Herzegovina was to become autonomous under joint Austro-Hungarian-Russian supervision.

In the meantime, concerned with the Russo-Turkish War and its implications, Central Power military planners began to consider their alternatives. In a memorandum of 3 February 1877, Moltke, considering it unlikely that Russia would attack Germany unilaterally in 1877, reviewed the various scenarios of a German two-front war. Moltke calculated that

France would side with Russia in the event of an armed conflict. He decided that the main German forces would be unleashed initially against France, leaving only minor units in the east. But the real basis for German war planning proved to be France's more rapid operational readiness and that she provided a more immediate military threat in the event of a two-front war. A great decisive battle against France in the west within three weeks would free troops for transfer to the east in order to counter the more slowly mobilizing Russian troops.[8]

If the battle turned against Germany in the west, the Rhine River formed an excellent defensive barrier. In any case, German railroad lines had the capacity to transport eight army corps from the Rhine to the Vistula River area in a ten-day period. Until these units could arrive in the east, Moltke judged the Vistula River defensive line adequate to contain the Russian forces for a period of one month. Consequently, in the initial massive attack planned for 1877-1878, in the event of war, the main forces of Germany would be aimed at France.

The Elder Moltke rejected these ideas. His future operational planning would consist of a powerful opening offensive against the Russian regime and a subsequent offensive-defensive holding action in the western theater. The reason for this shift of emphasis was that the French had initiated excellent defensive military measures between the years 1871-1878. In carrying out this scheme of a great offensive against Russia, the German western frontier would be perfectly suited for defense against French invasion; gigantic fortifications barred incursions on major roads, while the Rhine River provided a formidable obstacle to entering the heartland of the empire.

On the other hand, vast expanses of land in the east offered the possibility for successful large-scale operations, and Prussia itself offered an excellent forward bastion for an initial assault. Moltke considered that the only way to defend the 750-kilometer-long eastern frontier was by military formations dispersed over a wide arc and later advancing in an offensive movement to link up on enemy soil.[9]

Because of the 1877-78 Balkan crisis, the Austro-Hungarian military planners also prepared for a military situation in the east. Twenty-three and one-half infantry divisions and four cavalry divisions would be deployed against Russia in case of hostilities. If the Russians fielded two separate army groups against the Habsburgs, the main Austro-Hungarian military thrust would be launched into Russian Poland; if this invasion was successful, the Austro-Hungarian main forces would then turn to the eastern enemy forces.[10]

With the Treaty of San Stefano signed on 3 March 1878, different interpretations arose of the Austro-Hungarian-Russian political agreements arranged before the outbreak of the Russo-Turkish War and the Treaty of San Stefano. The disagreement can be explained by the fact that the Russian representatives drafting the post-war treaty were ignorant of the previous obligations accepted by their government at Budapest.

To the chagrin of the Russians, both Austria-Hungary and England opposed the treaty. Russia had to accede to the convening of the Congress of Berlin in 1878. The most important results of this Congress included Turkey's loss of one-half of her European territory; Bulgaria's reduction to one-half the size called for in the Treaty of San Stefano and the subsequent creation of a semi-autonomous Turkish province, Eastern Rumelia, south of Bulgaria; Romania's loss of Bessarabia to her ally, Russia; Austria-Hungary's "temporary" right to govern the provinces of Bosnia-Herzegovina (she could have annexed them, but was content with the more ambiguous status of occupation); and the provision that the Sanjak of Novibazar could be garrisoned by Austria-Hungary to prevent the union of Serbia and Montenegro.

After the Congress of Berlin, Russian resentment increased towards both Germany and Austria-Hungary. Bismarck therefore decided that he could no longer depend solely on the friendship of Russia and must consolidate his position with Austria-Hungary and Britain. Since the Congress, it had also been discovered that Russia had been sounding out both France and Italy for possible closer connections. These factors encouraged the formation of an Austro-Hungarian-German alliance.

A further catalyst to the German approach to relations with Austria-Hungary was the end of German-Russian harmony and cooperation with Bismarck's diplomatic cornerstone, the League of the Three Emperors. At the same time, reports began arriving that Russia had begun to increase her troop strength in western Poland at the Austro-Hungarian-German frontier. However, the Russo-Turkish war had revealed glaring deficiencies in the Russian army, so these transfers proved merely disquieting.

The maneuver did not prevent the Elder Moltke from re-examining his alternatives in the event of a two-front war. France no longer offered the prospect for the early German offensive victory that had seemed plausible a year before. Thus the Elder Moltke decided that:

> If we must fight two wars 150 miles apart . . . we should exploit
> in the west the great advantages which the Rhine and our powerful
> fortifications offer to the defensive and should employ all the fight-
> ing forces not absolutely indispensable for an offensive against the
> east.[11]

In an eastern war against Russia, Germany anticipated at least Austro-
Hungarian neutrality. This neutrality would draw Russian troops from the
German to the Galician frontier. If the Dual Monarchy actively entered
into an eastern conflict allied with Berlin, the odds for a German victory
would naturally increase. The main Russian advance, in case of active
Habsburg participation in such a conflict, could be anticipated against the
Dual Monarchy.[12]

In strategic planning for an eastern conflict, Moltke would deploy four
German armies, consisting of thirteen army corps. These corps could be
operational and ready between the twentieth and twenty-third mobilization
day, compared to Russia's need for forty-five days. The immensity of their
projected deployment posed a major problem for the German planners.
Because of the Prussian railroad configurations, it would be impossible to
assemble all four German armies together on Prussian soil without a
considerable loss of time. This consideration prompted Moltke's plan to
link up his forces in Russian Poland, which would actually permit more
rapid concentration of troops. The objective of the projected German
offensive was Warsaw, the central bastion in Poland. A key advantage in
such a strategy was that an offensive action into Poland would provide
the best defense for the entire Prussian frontier.

If they were successful in taking Russia's Polish possessions, German
forces would be re-transferred by rail to the western frontier rather than
advancing into the Russian interior. As Moltke himself stated: "We would
have no interest in following up a victory in Poland with an advance into
the interior of Russia, but it would enable us to send the greatest part of
our armies to the Rhine."[13]

It was decided that in the west in a two-front war, only four German
army corps would initially defend against France. Because of the great
numerical disadvantage in the west which this situation would pose, fortresses assumed a significant role in halting the threat of an enemy invasion.

In a memorandum composed for Kaiser Wilhelm I on 10 October 1879,
the Elder Moltke reinforced his arguments for an initial thrust into Poland

in a two-front war. He emphasized that France had doubled her army strength and built many frontier forts since her defeat in 1871. Moltke concluded that the successful 1870 strategy was no longer viable.[14]

Meanwhile, in 1878, Moltke influenced the realization of the Austro-Hungarian and German alliance which was finally signed in 1879. Moltke deeply distrusted the Russians; coupled with reports of a major buildup of Russian troops at the Polish frontier, his suspicion led the German Chief of Staff to expound upon the advantages of an alliance with the Dual Monarchy.

Moltke, in fact, considered the Austro-Hungarian Monarchy the only useful ally for the German Reich in the case of a two-front struggle. A simultaneous Austro-Hungarian military call-up would be particularly advantageous for Germany because it would draw enemy formations from the Prussian frontier. Austria-Hungary would also attract a first Russian offensive, and, in the interim, would allow the allied eastern strike forces to smash the slower-mobilizing Russian formations. With this space to maneuver, German troops could quickly be transferred to the western front in order to strike the militarily more dangerous French before a Russian recovery. When and where help could be sent to the Rhine remained the key to Moltke's planning.[15]

The Elder Moltke, however, harbored no illusions and had serious doubts about Austro-Hungarian military capabilities. Accordingly, the Dual Alliance did not radically alter German operational planning for the east. Moltke's views were clearly presented in his important memorandum of January 1880. In it, one of his main points remained that a major Russian assault would be aimed against the Habsburg Monarchy, not Germany. In other words, both Russia and Germany, in a two-front struggle, would strike the weaker of two potential enemies.

The strategy Moltke wished to assign his Habsburg ally included an immediate offensive with 600,000 troops deployed from the area between Cracow and Lemberg in Galicia on the twenty-fourth mobilization day. Such a thrust into Russian Poland, following a two-day march, would place the Austro-Hungarian armies before the key Russian bastions of Dubno. From this vantage point, troops could disrupt the southern Russian railroad system, precluding any large, rapid enemy concentration of forces. Yet, Moltke was still afraid that his new ally would assume a defensive stance in the Carpathian Mountains rather than advance from Galicia. In the case of the Carpathian position, the German eastern forces would obviously have to battle a much larger Russian contingent.

Significant for the future war planning was the blueprint for a "pincers" deployment emanating from both Prussia and Galicia to destroy Russian troop concentrations in Poland. The strategy, modified under Schlieffen, became the core of the eastern strategy for 1914. This plan of encirclement or strategic envelopment capitalized on the Dual Alliance's numerical advantage through the sixteenth mobilization day. At this point, the combined Austro-Hungarian-German forces would, according to plan, attack the lumbering and slowly deploying Russian armies.[16]

Returning to the diplomatic origins of the Dual Alliance, the background to the signing of the treaty included the effects of the Austro-Hungarian Foreign Minister Gyula Andrássy's illness and imminent resignation. Bismarck wished to conclude an alliance agreement with Andrássy. His goal became an agreement in which both powers would support each other in the event of a third-party military attack.

Several factors supported Bismarck's arguments for selecting Austria-Hungary, not Russia, as an ally. Foremost was that Russia, being a stronger power than Austria-Hungary, would naturally seek to control any alliance with Germany.

The articles of the Dual Alliance stipulated that if one of the signatories should be attacked by Russia, the other pledged full military aid. If either signatory were to be attacked by a power other than Russia (i.e., Germany by France; Austria-Hungary by Italy), the other would observe benevolent neutrality. If, however, the attacking power were aided by Russia, both parties would place all their fighting forces in the field. Germany's commitments were more comprehensive than Austria-Hungary's. In addition, the two parties agreed that no separate peace treaties could be ratified. The Dual Alliance would be valid for five years and would be kept secret.

This Austro-Hungarian-German agreement introduced the alliance systems which would become so significant in the days leading up to the World War I, but it would not be until 1882 that Germany and Austria-Hungary, in their initial cooperative military discussions, would establish the basic military strategy which they would test in Poland and Prussia in August 1914.

The cornerstone of Bismarck's foreign policy from 1879 remained the alliance with the Austro-Hungarian Empire. To him, the Dual Monarchy had to remain at all costs an independent great power and a figure in the European balance of power. Bismarck described its maintenance as a life and death question for Germany, and he was willing to go to war to protect Austria-Hungary if, and only if, she were attacked by Russia. Bismarck also strove for maintenance of the *status quo* in the Balkans and for an Austro-Hungarian-Russian settlement of problems in that volatile area. Another guiding principle for Bismarck's foreign policy was that France should be completely isolated and prevented from forming a hostile coalition.

The Dual Alliance of October 1879 thus did not preclude friendly ties with Russia. Starting in 1880, German diplomats attempted to re-establish the traditional Russo-German ties. The overall aim of the Germans and particularly of Bismarck was to re-establish the Three Emperors' League. Meanwhile, the Russians, semi-isolated by the disruption of the Three Emperors' League of 1872-1875, strove for a return to normalcy in German-Russian relations.

In 1881, Tsar Alexander II was assassinated. His successor, Alexander III, approved the formation of a new Three Emperors' connection on 18 June 1881. This new agreement proved more extensive than the earlier League of the Three Emperors, providing for the case of a Russo-Turkish war. By the terms of the agreement, any alteration in the *status quo* regarding European Turkey had to be agreed upon by the three powers. A protocol appended to the treaty reserved for Austria-Hungary the right to annex the provinces of Bosnia-Herzegovina at whatever moment she deemed opportune. Thus, the Russian concessions to Austria-Hungary in the Reichstadt Agreement and Budapest Convention were reaffirmed. Another development which addressed the possibility of future Austro-Hungarian-Russian conflict divided the Balkan peninsula into zones. A western sector under Habsburg influence encompassed Bosnia, Serbia, and Macedonia; the eastern sector, consisting of Bulgaria, East Rumelia and Turkey, fell under Russian influence. This division, though implicit in the text of the treaty and in harmony with the spirit, did not appear in the actual wording. The treaty did serve one major purpose for Bismarck: it prevented an Austro-Hungarian-Russian conflict and thus diverted Russian attention from the Balkans to Central Asia, where Britain would be Russia's antagonist.

The new Three Emperor's Alliance, in substance a mere consultation pact, did not supersede the terms of the Austro-Hungarian-German Dual Alliance of 1879.

A further diplomatic event in 1881 was the ratification of an Austro-Hungarian-Serbian treaty on 21 June 1881. Serbia, for all purposes, became an appendage of the Dual Monarchy. The treaty was renewed on 15 June 1889 and remained in force until 1895.

In the military spheres, except for a "War Case Russia," strategic planning by the Habsburg General Staff for 1880 did not yet count on full German military assistance, even though the alliance had been ratified in 1879. In 1881, therefore, the Habsburg General Staff studied the possibility of their own two-front struggle against Italy and Russia. In the event of a Franco-Russian two-front war, it was assumed that Germany would probably deploy her main forces in the east.[17]

For 1881, in a projected war against Russia, Austro-Hungarian military planners would deploy two armies (the First and Third) in the area between the fortress cities of Przemyśl and Cracow; the Second Army would be deployed in the critical Lemberg area; and the Fourth Army was to guard the Italian frontier. Due to insufficient rail networks, the troops deploying in Galicia would have long marches and a deployment duration of thirty-three to forty days, compared to twenty-one days for the allied German eastern army.

The Habsburg military leadership recognized that Austria-Hungary could never defeat Russia without the assistance of allies. In particular, the alliance of Germany with the Dual Monarchy would provide the necessary difference in numbers even if Italy joined Russia in a war against Austria-Hungary. But it was understood that if France entered an armed conflict against Germany, the German General Staff would counter the French with significant forces, considering them the most dangerous opponent next to Russia. In this situation, the German troop strengths designated for the east would decline substantially. Further, a Franco-German campaign in the west would require much more time because of the system of French forts across the common frontier. According to the Austro-Hungarian General Staff, the Viennese diplomats would have the task of keeping Serbia-Montenegro and Romania neutral in the Balkans if a war between the Great Powers erupted. Turkey was to provide a military balance against these Balkan states.

In the event of an eastern war, the main Austro-Hungarian army group would assemble at the San River line to launch an offensive on the right Vistula River bank, initially in the direction of the Russian fortress city of Lublin and then towards either Warsaw or Siedlce. An additional major group would protect the right flank of the deploying armies. As the years passed, this exposed right-flank position in eastern Galicia became increasingly significant. The Austro-Hungarian General Staff remained concerned that massed Russian cavalry would sweep across the Galician frontier to disturb their deployment.[18] Both fears remained factors in Habsburg military planning until 1914.

In the following year, 1882, the Triple Alliance came into existence by the addition of Italy to the Austro-Hungarian-German Alliance. The new alliance benefited all three participants in some way. For Austria-Hungary, the alliance meant that in an eastern war her southwestern frontier with Italy might be cleared of defending troops and freed for utilization against Russia; her rear flank would thus be protected. Germany might gain from a shift of these Austro-Hungarian forces to the east in a two-front war and was assured that since Italy would not ally with France and Russia, she would be forced to concentrate more of her troops in the Alps. Bismarck's goal in the alliance is best summarized by the phrase "sparing the Austro-Hungarian forces, rather than winning those of Italy."[19] The Austro-Hungarians nevertheless continued preparations for a "War Case I" (Italy), but held Italian fighting abilities in low esteem.

Meanwhile, the initial discussion between the General Staffs of Germany and Austria-Hungary occurred in August 1882. Field Marshal Beck conferred with the German Quartermaster General Count Alfred Waldersee. Waldersee agreed that Germany, in the event of a two-front confrontation, would launch her major offensive in the east in coordination with that of the Dual Monarchy in order to achieve a strategic double envelopment, thereby forcing the Russians to come out of their fortified positions.[20] A question not resolved in 1882 involved the matter of a joint command of allied forces. Delayed consideration of this matter proved to be a decided disadvantage in the opening months of the campaigns of 1914.

The final 1882 allied military agreement provided for Beck's forces to deploy in three main groups. Thirty-two of his thirty-nine Habsburg divisions would be assembled to advance north from between the Bug and Vistula Rivers. Two additional flanking groups would advance from their original positions around Cracow and Lemberg to protect the main army's flanks as it advanced.

Following a twin Austro-Hungarian-German advance into Poland, the allied forces would link up east of Warsaw, thus taking possession of Russian Poland, while neutralizing the Russian middle Warsaw army. Further allied coordination would follow after the above objective had been met.

Because of the peculiarities of geography, the half-bow configuration of the Galician frontier in the deployment area, the slowness of Austria-

Hungary's deployment compared to Germany's, and the increasing Russian threat to his right flank in eastern Galicia, Beck feared that he would initially have to clear this right-flank area to the east, or in a northeasterly direction (Proskurov) before his main forces could launch their offensive between the Bug and Vistula Rivers. Beck recognized that this flank-clearing operation, required by the frontier configuration, could result in a delay of two to three weeks in the attack of the main group.

Beck mentioned to his allies the possible improvements to his strategic railroad network, a recurring bone of contention between them. Germany had the railroad capability of fielding thirty-one infantry and eight cavalry divisions in the east by a twentieth mobilization day. An offensive could be launched the following day. Austria-Hungary could not launch her own main offensive until ten days after that, at the earliest.[21] Actually, Austro-Hungarian forces would not be fully operational until the forty-fifth mobilization day, while the Russians would be ready on their forty-second.

In December 1882, Beck prepared a memorandum emphasizing the above agreements as a basis for his further deployment planning. These agreements would remain the basis for Austro-Hungarian military planning until World War I.[22]

During the General Staff discussions, Waldersee promised a German deployment of twenty infantry and six reserve divisions (400,000 men), or more than half of the first-line German formations, to the east in the event of a war. The main force would advance between the Vistula and Niemen Rivers with the goal of moving from the right Vistula bank across the Narev River. If France declared herself neutral in an eastern war, a total of forty German infantry and nine cavalry divisions could be sent into Poland. For this simple "War Case R" (Russia), a German main force would advance out of East and West Prussia (between the Vistula and Niemen Rivers). Crossing the right bank of the Vistula River, the German force would advance with protective cover against the Russian fortress of Kovno towards the Narev River in the direction of Bialystok and Warsaw. It had become obvious that France and the western theater had now become the most important considerations for Germany, a change which led General Beck to inquire whether Germany would actually field the promised twenty divisions in the east in the event of a two-front war. Moltke replied that with the natural defensive strength of the German western frontier, "many forces" could indeed be assembled in the east.[23]

At the same time, the Austro-Hungarian-German agreements provided a daring solution to the geographical disadvantage of the excessively long allied frontiers with Russian Poland. The major threat to such a strategy would be that the Russian High Command would initially send its forces against one of the allies, resulting in the encirclement of its deployed attack formations. The Russian deployment was anticipated in three large army groups, the major one being in the Warsaw-Bialystok-Ivangorod area and consisting of thirty-one infantry, eleven reserve, and seventeen cavalry divisions.[24] Right-flank security groups could also appear in the Vilna area and in the Podolian region of Radzivillov-Proskurov.

But friction in military planning between Germany and Austria-Hungary appeared almost immediately. The more sophisticated German General Staff began to exert pressure on its Habsburg ally to improve its military capabilities and to speed-up its mobilization timetables. Since the Russians could seriously threaten his right-flank military positions in eastern Galicia, Beck had reason to consider these suggestions. The major hamper to Habsburg deployment timetables was the chronic lack of strategic railroad lines. The most important line, the Karl Ludwig Railway, extended from fortress Cracow to east of the major depot at Lemberg, but its occasional proximity to enemy territory made it vulnerable to disruption in a mobilization movement.

The railroad problem became obvious in 1883 when Beck decided to shift the main weight of his deployment from western Galicia to the San River area in order to capitalize further on the early operations readiness of the Dual Alliance. Beck's decision reflected the effect of the 1882 agreement with Germany. Yet, it was in eastern Galicia that the Russians could pose their gravest threat to a Habsburg deployment, by striking at the Habsburg right-flank position.[25]

On 22 March 1883, the Dual Alliance was renewed and was henceforth to be automatically renewable. In the same year, other agreements provided strategic advantages for the Central Powers. An Austro-Hungarian-Italian accord relieved Habsburg troop commitments on their southwestern frontier, while, in the east, a secret Austro-Hungarian-Romanian treaty — which Germany, and subsequently Italy, adhered to — was ratified on 30 October 1883.

According to the terms of the Romanian treaty, the Romanian armed forces would prevent the advance of Russian troops towards Constantinople and the Straits in the event of an eastern confrontation. A series of fortresses would also be constructed Prussian-style, one behind the other, both at the Carpathian Mountain woods in Transylvania and near the Danube River.

Romanian participation with the Triple Alliance in a war with Russia
provided several other advantages for Austria-Hungary: the removal of
any military threat to the Hungarian province of Transylvania; more Austro-Hungarian troops available than if some were tied down by a neutral
Romania; the drawing of Russian troops from the Austro-Hungarian to
the Romanian front, most probably from the endangered Habsburg right-
flank position; and the strengthening of this weak Habsburg flank position
by extending the allies' right flank to Romania.[26]

At the same time in the diplomatic realm the Three Emperors' Alliance
was renewed in 1884. Renewal did not allay concern about Russia in
military planning, however, as General Waldersee no longer expected
Russia to withdraw her troops into her vast interior if the Central Powers
invaded Poland. The German General Staff desired, as before, to defeat
these forces while they assembled. Also, it appeared conceivable that if
the Germans failed to dispatch a sufficient fighting force to the east for
an offensive effort, the Austro-Hungarians would merely hold back at their
best defensive position in the Carpathian Mountains instead of launching
an offensive.

The Austro-Hungarian-Italian military agreement and Romanian
Treaty of the preceding year meanwhile manifested themselves in the
Habsburg war plans for 1884. The previous plan for a two-front war
against Italy and Russia could now be modified, allowing Beck to allot
only defense troops for the Italian frontier, while directing the mass of his
troops to attack Russia. Twenty-six divisions would be mobilized in the
northeast against Russia and eleven against Italy. At the same time, he
had been promised a deployment of over one-half of the German army in
the east.[27]

Allied Austro-Hungarian-German military planning for 1883 and 1884
remained conceptually much the same. By 1884, the First and Third
Armies could conceivably launch the main Habsburg advance on the
twenty-first mobilization day, a marked improvement in timetables.[28]

One fear continued to haunt the Habsburg military planners. If Germany and Austria-Hungary became involved in a war with Russia, and
France later entered such a conflict, allied plans could be seriously affected. France would draw substantial German units to the western frontier, which would then release Russian forces to be sent against Austria-
Hungary. Habsburg planners also questioned whether Germany could then
launch her promised offensive in the east. In either case, Austria-Hungary
would have the unpleasant duty of meeting the brunt of the Russian enemy.

The nagging problem of the inferior strategic railroad situation at the Austro-Polish frontier was lessened in 1885. Railroad improvements resulted in an estimation for a more rapid Austro-Hungarian deployment — twenty-one days. With the improved railroad situation, Vienna, in 1886, could deploy thirty-one infantry and eight cavalry divisions on the evening of the twenty-third mobilization day. On the evening of the twenty-eighth mobilization day, all Habsburg army corps would be operations-ready.[29]

Due to these positive changes, the first significant revision in years of planning for "War Case R" occurred; simultaneously, the pressure caused by events resulting from the 1885 Serbo-Bulgarian War and by intelligence reports of Russian military activity led to attempts to speed up Austro-Hungarian deployment timetables further. The military Intelligence Bureau in Vienna calculated at this time that in a war, Russia would deploy sixty-two infantry and twenty-one cavalry divisions in three main groups. Because almost all Russian strategic railroad lines led in the direction of Lublin and Proskurov, two main concentrations could be anticipated. If the main enemy fighting forces were to be fielded at the Austro-Hungarian right flank in the Proskurov area (eastern Galicia), a serious threat would be posed to the conceived Austro-Hungarian deployment. It was obvious both that the strategic Habsburg railroad lines in that direction would have to be increased in number and that the capacity of the old ones would have to be improved in order to counter this mounting threat.[30]

In France, General Georges Boulanger's appointment as war minister in May 1886 raised a furor. The resulting war scare and saber-rattling disheartened the German General Staff, because the French were capable of launching an offensive much more rapidly than were the Russians. The French situation encouraged Waldersee to expound the virtues of a quick military triumph in the west as the most secure defense of the eastern theater in a two-front struggle. In response to this new strategic concept, only fourteen German infantry divisions might now be deployed in East Prussia. This reduction of forces in favor of a western initiative appears very similar to the Schlieffen strategy of ten years later. But even as word of modifications reached German military planners, Waldersee, without any qualms, promised Vienna that half of all German forces would be dispatched to the east in the event of a two-front war. Beck, however, doubted seriously whether the promise would be kept.

The Balkans had been relatively quiet since the Congress of Berlin, but this tranquility was shattered by events in Bulgaria in 1885. The previous terms of the 1878 Treaty of Berlin, which ended the Russo-Turkish War of that year, created a Bulgarian state and established autonomy for the Turkish province of Eastern Rumelia. In the meantime, a revolutionary movement in the province of Eastern Rumelia, which would have been united with Bulgaria if the Treaty of San Stefano had remained in force, pressed for union with Bulgaria.

Serbia strongly protested the possible union of Bulgaria and Eastern Rumelia. Her leaders, who hoped to expand southward, sought Austro-Hungarian support for the Serbian position under Article VII of their 1881 treaty of alliance. After King Milan's trip to Vienna for consultation, a Serbian general mobilization against Bulgaria resulted in the crushing defeat of the aggressor. At this point, Austria-Hungary threatened to march into Serbia on the pretext of a Russian intention to occupy Bulgaria. The Russians disclaimed any such intention, calling the Austro-Hungarian move a breach of the Three Emperor's League. Tsar Alexander III, considering Bulgaria to be in Russia's sphere of interest, later refused to renew the Three Emperor's League upon its expiration in 1887. Thus, the Balkans once again threatened Austro-Hungarian-Russian relations.

In January 1886, as the crisis intensified, Bismarck informed the Habsburg Ambassador in Berlin that if Russia attacked Austria-Hungary, Germany would assist her, but that Germany would not play the role of auxiliary army in order to increase Austro-Hungarian influence on the Danube.[31] Such German support had always been a cardinal point in Bismarck's diplomatic web.

The joint Austro-Hungarian-German military plans were now increasingly brought into question. Waldersee wrote in March 1886 that in the event of a two-front conflict, German forces would be fielded almost equally between the eastern and western theaters of operation. Thus, in order to relieve pressure on the German eastern forces, the Austro-Hungarians would have to move as quickly as possible against Russia. According to Waldersee's calculations, if the western German forces proved strong enough, it would be possible to engage in a "decisive battle" against France within three weeks — or so he thought. While this great western battle progressed, a simultaneous threat was posed to the eastern Prussian frontiers. It was estimated that the mobilization of four army corps, two cavalry divisions, one cavalry brigade, and three reserve divisions would be sufficient to protect these eastern regions. If Russia had not committed herself militarily in a Franco-German war by the fourteenth German mobilization day, most of these few units would be transferred by railroad to the west. In this event, only meager forces would be available for Prussia to counter a Russian threat.[32]

Reputed Russian arms preparations in the winter of 1886 caused growing consternation in the two General Staffs. In Vienna, such reports resulted in increased unit strengths, improved defensive structures and fortresses, and renewed attempts to upgrade the capacity of rail lines leading to the Galician frontiers. Russian improvements in their own military capabilities also stimulated the Austro-Hungarian General Staff to plan the complete assembly of their combat troops for the twentieth mobilization day in a conflict. With the construction of new railroads and the improvement of existing lines, supporting columns also had to step up mobilization timetables. Intelligence sources calculated that on the same day the Austro-Hungarians had mobilized eight cavalry and thirty-five infantry divisions, the enemy would field fourteen cavalry, twenty-six infantry divisions, and three infantry brigades.[33]

The next year, 1887, proved to be significant: in addition to the war scare in the east, the Triple Alliance was renewed on 21 May. As the Three Emperors' Alliance was allowed to lapse, the Russian Tsar was "inclined" towards a treaty with Germany alone. The Tsar's objective fit into Bismarck's plans, although his main obstacles to a Russo-German pact remained the existence of the Dual Alliance and the need for a Russian pledge of neutrality in the event of a Franco-German war. Negotiations finally produced a joint Russo-German agreement, the Reinsurance Treaty, which established that benevolent neutrality would be observed if either Austria-Hungary should attack Russia or France attack Germany. A significant exception stated that this benevolent neutrality did not apply in the case of an aggressive war of Germany against France, or Russia against Austria-Hungary. Bismarck also recognized Russia's "historic rights" in the Balkans and the legitimacy of her influence in Bulgaria and Eastern Rumelia. In addition, the Reinsurance Treaty stipulated that no alterations in the *status quo* of the Balkans would be allowed without previous Russo-German agreement. The agreements in the defunct Three Emperors' Alliance relating to Constantinople and the Straits remained in force; Germany did not directly oppose Russian control of these areas. Bismarck, however, did assume that other powers, e.g., England, would oppose such a move. This was resolved on December 12, 1887, with the conclusion of negotiations among Austria-Hungary, England, Spain and Italy. The signed treaty was the result of Bismarck's behind-the-scenes brokering.

This type of Bismarckian secret diplomacy did not remain unopposed at home. The Reinsurance Treaty was actually concluded without the notification or consultation of the German military chiefs. Thus, when intelligence reports indicated increased Russian armaments, Waldersee demanded a preventive attack on Russia for 1888. He considered Austria-Hungary to be directly threatened by Russian machinations and thus insisted that Germany fulfill her military treaty obligations to her ally. To add to the confusion, it became known that France and Russia had begun to expand their diplomatic contacts. This information increased the pessimism and anxiety of high-ranking officers in the German General Staff.

Using the Elder Moltke's influence, Waldersee immediately waged a spirited campaign to convince both Emperor Wilhelm I and Prince Wilhelm that an immediate preventive war against Russia was necessary.[34]

During this process, Waldersee also irritated Bismarck by allowing certain leaks to the Austro-Hungarian Ambassador and military attaché and made suggestions in Vienna concerning possible Austro-Hungarian troop movements for an actual deployment toward the Habsburg northeastern frontier; raised the question of discarding restrictions on the *casus foederis* as defined in the Dual Alliance Treaty; and even gave the impression that the German government desired a joint Austro-Hungarian-German attack on Russia. Bismarck, after learning of the matter, clearly stipulated that German military might would not be utilized to achieve Hungarian and Catholic ambitions in the Balkans.[35]

The military question evolving from the wording of the Austro-Hungarian-German treaty of 1879 really entailed who would be the attacked party and who the attacker. Bismarck would make the final decision: as long as the Iron Chancellor stood at the helm of German diplomacy, the General Staffs would not supplant the politicians in such crucial matters. Bismarck did, however, encourage the Austro-Hungarians to advance their defensive preparatory measures.

War fever pervaded the two General Staffs in 1887-1888. Reports detailing Russian actions which were reputedly preparatory for war continued to flow in. The allied military leaders favored an attack on Russia, but Bismarck maintained his position that Russia must provoke such a war by attacking Austria-Hungary first.

The Austro-Hungarian General Staff, in the meantime, prepared for any eventuality. The threat posed by Russian armaments in the winter of 1886 led to a revision of the existing deployment plan.[36] During this crisis, General Beck's desire for a definite answer to the question of whether

Germany would divide her forces equally between the eastern and western theaters in a two-front conflict led to friction between German and Austro-Hungarian military authorities. Beck was obviously concerned that anything less than an equal dispersement of German fighting men would allow the Russians to dispatch additional units against his Austro-Hungarian armies, as well as endanger the Austro-German double encirclement offensive strategy.

Habsburg military calculations suggested that at least thirty-two of the Russian contingent of divisions had to be diverted from Austria-Hungary's northeastern (Galician) frontier, as it would be impossible for Austria-Hungary to battle Russia alone. If this latter possibility were to occur, thirty-two to thirty-four Austro-Hungarian divisions would be pitted against sixty-four Russian divisions, and Vienna would face an insurmountable two-to-one disadvantage. If, however, the enemy had to mobilize at both the Galician and Prussian frontiers, the situation would obviously prove more militarily favorable to Austria-Hungary.

A significant document in this war-scare period, illustrating the German military viewpoint, was a report written by Waldersee. According to Waldersee, the Russians now possessed the capability of fielding 1,164 cavalry squadrons against Germany's 464. If reserve-cadre battalions were utilized, twenty-four additional Russian divisions could also be made combat-ready. Waldersee noted that strategic railroads in Russia had also been expanded to the west.

A further important indicator of military preparedness in this period involved the building or improving of fortresses. Waldersee emphasized, prior to 1878, notably effective Russian forts could be found only at Brest-Litovsk, Ivangorod, Novogeorgiesk, and Warsaw. Since that time, others had been developed at Kovno and Dubno in Volhynia. The major Warsaw bastion had also been improved, while the fort at Brest-Litovsk had been transformed into a "highly significant" arms depot center. In addition, railroad connections to these centers had multiplied. *In toto*, Russian military improvements gave Waldersee the impression that Russia indeed intended to launch a war.

In the report, Waldersee also demanded that Germany support her ally Austria-Hungary. Because the Germans feared that the Dual Monarchy remained too weak and unprepared for war, the Dual Monarchy should not be allowed to suffer armed defeat at Russian hands under any circumstances. Such an eventuality would present a distinct threat to the industrially important Prussian-Silesian region. At the same time, Waldersee feared that an Austro-Hungarian defeat in Galicia would knock the ally out of a war, and that Germany would then be left to face a future Russian onslaught alone. Waldersee concluded that only if Germany and Austria-Hungary advanced immediately against Russia would matters turn out favorably.

Beck's intelligence reports at the time led him to the same conclusion Waldersee made: there could be no doubt that Russia was preparing openly for war. To help remove the narrow Bismarckian interpretation of the 1879 Dual Alliance, Russian military measures were represented as being serious enough to warrant an immediate Austro-Hungarian military intervention in order to prevent an overpowering surprise attack in the future. Such a preventive thrust, intended for defensive purposes, should now present Germany with grounds for the *casus foederis*.[37]

In all this flurry of activity, there existed a distinct Austro-Hungarian distrust of German intentions. Leading Austro-Hungarian military authorities believed that their German ally would, in the event of a war, dispatch a meager four corps, or 100,000 men, to the east. Such a poor show of force would be tantamount to the Dual Monarchy's having to face Russia alone. Such suspicions revealed the frustration of a military leadership which continually received conflicting reports from the German diplomatic and military sources concerning deployment data for the German eastern theater.

Austro-Hungarian concern was partly due to Waldersee's repeated promise that the allied military agreements of 1882 still bound one-half of the German army to the east in a two-front conflagration. The German Foreign Secretary and son of Chancellor Bismarck, on the other hand, clearly stated in 1886 that Germany would deploy her main forces at the Rhine River in the west in such circumstances — a clear contradiction to Waldersee's assurances.[38]

Extreme diplomatic and military tension continued into 1888. A Habsburg Crown Council, convened on 8 December 1887, resolved to extend security measures in Galicia. Troop unit manpower, including artillery and cavalry regiments, was increased; forts were improved; and blocking positions were established. Additional troops were earmarked, if necessary, for transfer to the northeastern frontier while railroad improvements were accelerated. These measures corresponded to the intentions of both Bismarck and Moltke to have their Austro-Hungarian ally strengthen herself.[39]

In April 1888, General Beck learned that Germany intended to assemble twenty-two infantry divisions in Prussia in the event of a two-front conflagration. These divisions would force a crossing of the Narev River to unite with Austro-Hungarian forces east of Warsaw. Romania, it was assumed, would field an 80,000-man army on the extreme Habsburg right flank. With three Austro-Hungarian armies to be fielded, the advantage appeared to lie with the Central Powers in case of an eastern campaign.

In an actual conflict, Austro-Hungarian-Romanian forces would advance towards Lublin after clearing the area of Proskurov and Dubno, which threatened the right flank. The allied German fighting forces advancing from the Vistula River area would, after bypassing the fortified Russian Vistula front, force the Russians to fight.[40]

The same year, 1888, witnessed Moltke's retirement. Through his years as Chief of the German General Staff, strategic principles had remained basically constant. The Elder Moltke's last operational plans, in effect until February 1888, provided for the same simultaneous offensive both from Germany's eastern frontier and from Austro-Hungarian Galicia. In the center of Russian Poland, the main Russian armies would be encircled as they assembled. This coordinated allied advance would force the Russians to come out of their fortified positions behind the Vistula and Bug Rivers, and in one direction or the other, to seek a decision in the open.

To summarize Moltke's strategy: contrary to Schlieffen's later plans, Moltke would split his armies into two almost equal portions. He would not seek a "battle of annihilation" by concentrating the mass of his armies for one decisive blow at either France or Russia, as Schlieffen sought to in his own plan, which evolved between 1891-1905. Moltke did not count on achieving a total victory in a two-front war, i.e., on being able to defeat each opponent in turn. The major German offensive would be against the Russian forces in coordination with Austria-Hungary, except briefly in 1877. Overall, Moltke desired a victory over the enemy armies and a German victory, but not so overwhelming a success to lead in the future to further difficulties. For Vienna, the product of the Moltke era was an acceptable plan for its armies in the event of an eastern war. This plan stipulated a Habsburg advance into Russian Poland. The Austro-Hungarian Second Army, assembled in the area of Lemberg, would provide right-flank protection for this movement. Except for certain details, the same basic concept would be utilized in 1914. Conrad von Hötzendorf, Austro-Hungarian Chief of the General Staff (1906-1911 and 1912-1917), retained the Moltke-Beck strategical concept. Between 1891 and 1906, however, a dramatic change would occur in Austro-Hungarian-German strategic planning. This period has aptly been termed the Schlieffen era. Until this period, the major military thrust of the Dual Alliance would be directed against Russia in a two-front war. Waldersee would serve as Chief of the German General Staff only for a brief period (1888-1891), and General Alfred von Schlieffen would serve until 1905.

CHAPTER II

Military Planning 1888-1905

War clouds continued to loom over the horizon as the new year, 1888, commenced. Waldersee, soon to be the Chief of the German General Staff, foresaw a war with Russia. He pondered whether Germany should initiate the inevitable preventive war since future crises would surely favor the Russians. But Kaiser Wilhelm I neither desired war with Russia nor trusted his Austro-Hungarian and Romanian allies. Waldersee also worried because Viennese mistrust of German intentions appeared to be increasing.[1] He personally sought an open and solid relationship with the Austro-Hungarian General Staff.

Waldersee, second-in-command in the German General Staff since 1882, had high political ambitions which were encouraged by his supposed friendship with the future Kaiser, Wilhelm II. He had initiated a campaign of sniping at Bismarck's "see-saw" policy. The discovery that Crown Prince Frederick was mortally ill with throat cancer further raised Waldersee's ambitions. Kaiser Wilhelm I died in March, 1888, and Frederick succeeded him for a one-hundred day reign. In fulfillment of his hopes, on 10 August 1888, Waldersee was appointed Chief of the German General Staff. His term of office was to be brief but significant as a transitional period between the Elder Moltke and Count von Schlieffen.

Waldersee possessed both charm and a quick wit, but several defects in his personality helped bring about his downfall. Namely, these were an inability to assess his own limitations, a natural appetite for intrigue, and an inability to judge character. Most significantly, he judged Prince Wilhelm to be a kindred spirit, with the consequence that all his political hopes began to rest on his personal connection to the new Kaiser.

During Waldersee's period, 1888-1891, there can be no question that allied military relations attained a new intimacy. The relationship would ripen to such an extent that, in 1891, when Waldersee was dismissed,

Franz Joseph and Beck considered his replacement a catastrophe for the Dual Monarchy.

Waldersee's command period produced no great alteration in German military planning. Accordingly, in a two-front war, the German strategy called for a rapid offensive in the east in conjunction with Austro-Hungarian forces. In the western theater, a defensive stance would be assumed.

Deployment planning for 1888-1889 still mirrored a fear of future Russian military capabilities, particularly the possibility that enemy cavalry might make an initial quick thrust to discoordinate an Austro-Hungarian-German deployment. Distrusting Russian intentions, Waldersee developed a flexible plan. A weak army group would be retained in its assembly area until the twelfth day of mobilization. If Russia did not commence military operations by then, this reserve army (the Fourth) would be immediately dispatched by rail to the French frontier.

One problem that concerned the German Operations Bureau was that German precautionary military measures at the Russian frontier could easily elicit an unwanted reaction from St. Petersburg. At the same time, without such precautions, Russian cavalry forces could strike into Prussia unopposed. If, however, enemy cavalry masses did not cross the frontier on the second mobilization day, German precautionary steps would protect the mobilization.

The crux of Waldersee's eastern planning remained the full utilization of Germany's rapid mobilization and deployment, while hiding the initial weakness of the German eastern forces. Accordingly, cavalry formations would be increased to shield German movements and to give courage to the Austro-Hungarian allies.[2]

While Russia continued to transfer troop units towards her western frontiers, discussions began between Bismarck and the Italian Premier concerning the possibility of dispatching an Italian army north of the Alps to fight at the Rhine River against France, even though the Italian army was considered almost worthless. Vienna, not interested in direct Italian activity in the Balkans, declared that no advantage would accrue from it.[3]

The allied Romanian army was meanwhile considered incapable of launching an offensive into Bessarabia against Russia. Its forces could, at most, be expected to deploy in the south of Moldavia where they would await a Russian thrust.

Austro-Hungarian war plans for the northeast against Russia still counted on a joint German-Austro-Hungarian encirclement of enemy forces in Poland with only small defensive units being deployed at the Serbian frontier. The Austro-Hungarian Operations Bureau remained concerned about German intentions, however, and again tried to obtain a more explicit and binding agreement from Berlin.[4] Bismarck thereupon reiterated the defensive intention of the Dual Alliance Treaty. For the political leadership, the mere massing of Russian troops at the frontiers did not produce the *casus foederis* for Germany.

The Elder Moltke's final eastern strategy for a two-front war remained a joint offensive into Russian Poland. The smaller portion of the German armies would be deployed in two army groups in the eastern theater. In the event of a two-front war, seven German Corps would launch an offensive against the Russian enemy.

The German deployment would consist of two corps being transported directly to Gumbinnen and Luck on the eastern frontier of Prussia. The remaining five corps would assume positions along a thirty-mile front extending from Inovrazlav (Hohensalza) to Ortelsburg. Both groups would advance to reassemble on enemy territory, then continue in the direction of the lower Narev River to the area of Pultusk-Ostrolenka to force battle.[5]

The German General Staff, immediately after 1888, expected France to enter an eastern conflict. With a German deployment in both the east and the west, and with these new circumstances, the number of troops designated for the protection of Prussia's eastern frontiers became fourteen German infantry and five cavalry divisions. If, as agreed, Italy fielded troops at the Rhine, additional German troops would be released for the east.[6] The major Russian offensive would be anticipated against Austria-Hungary.

Waldersee's first memorandum as Chief of the German General Staff, February 1888, is dominated by consideration of his Austro-Hungarian allies. Waldersee felt that previous German troop strengths, promised for an eastern campaign in a two-front war, would be insufficient to obtain a rapid and decisive victory. Moltke's allotment of fourteen infantry and five cavalry divisions was increased to twenty-two infantry and five cavalry divisions with additional reserve divisions.[7]

The Austro-Hungarians also revised their deployment plans in 1889. The new deployment, providing unusual flexibility, took into account of three distinct alternatives. Enemy tactics would determine which one would be used. A swing force of twelve infantry divisions that could be thrown into the balance with any of the three was created.[8] Beck, meanwhile, maintained his earlier concept of having a powerful army at the San River.

Between 1886 and 1890, three days were removed from the Austro-Hungarian deployment timetables. By 1889-1890 only twenty-three mobilization days were considered necessary to deploy twenty-eight infantry, eight cavalry, and nine militia divisions.[9]

Meanwhile, Serbia, bound by secret treaty to the Dual Monarchy since 1881, caused concern at the end of the rule of King Milan, the Austro-Hungarian "tool." For the future, Vienna's military planners would assemble more troops at the Serbian frontier in the event of a war. Romania, on the other hand, appeared to strengthen her military ties to the Dual Alliance.

Russia's continued shift of army units westward toward the frontiers resulted in further reassessment of the allied deployment plans.

The previous German plan of attacking across the Narev River toward Pultusk-Ostrolenka now no longer seemed advantageous because the Russians could assemble their forces to the east, thereby drawing the Germans progressively further from their sources of supply. Such an extensive march would increase the necessity of flank protection for the advancing army as it approached its objective, the fortified heights at Lomscha.

Accordingly, Waldersee decided to shift the German deployment eastward, so that the Russians would not anticipate such a stroke and would thus be unprepared to counter it. With a simultaneous German thrust across the Niemen River towards Bialystok, the enemy's assembling of troops and use of crucial railroads would be disturbed, while the Russians would be forced out of their Polish fortress triangle and into battle. The weather factor came increasingly under scrutiny. An offensive thrust across the Narev River would be unthinkable during the wet-weather season in April and May-and possibly in June and November-since the river might rise over its banks and make the land impassable. While weather factors were a deterrent to an offensive in the east, this was not the case in the west.[10] This factor carried more weight in the plans of General Schlieffen later.

By 1890, German pressure for a speedier Austro-Hungarian deployment had reaped some benefit. The Austro-Hungarian forces would be operation-ready at their right-flank group in eastern Galicia, and the five to six corps main grouping at the middle San River area would be ready on the twenty-third mobilization day.

It appeared that the Russians, as a counter, could move eighteen to twenty divisions against the weak eastern Galician frontier. The only way to prevent a potential disaster there would be to expand the capacity of the very sparse railroad lines to that region. Due to the threat of invasions by large Russian cavalry forces to disturb Austro-Hungarian mobilization, railroads and deployment remained a crucial factor in Austro-Hungarian military planning until the outbreak of war in 1914.[11]

The following year saw Waldersee removed as Chief of the General Staff. In his last war plans for 1890-1891, a dual Austro-Hungarian-Hohenzollern attack would be launched from east of the lower Narev and Vistula Rivers. If this attack was successful, the Russian railroad connections to St. Petersburg, Moscow, and Kiev would be cut off, which would force their emergence from the fortress triangle to offer battle. In anticipation of this new plan, the German General Staff would have to improve and extend the eastern Prussian railway network.[12]

Meanwhile, in August 1889, Franz Joseph and Beck went to Berlin, where the new Kaiser, Wilhelm II (1888-1918) promised that an Austro-Hungarian mobilization would be the signal for a German mobilization.[13]

Overall, Waldersee had only modified Moltke's strategy slightly, shifting the German deployment eastward and southward. The Elder Moltke's offensive had been aimed at the Russian Narev Army; Waldersee's offensive had been at both the Narev and Niemen Armies to prevent the latter from aiding the former in battle. With the increased scope of Waldersee's proposed action, the number of German units for the east would have had to be increased.

One decisive consideration in planning remained for Waldersee, as it had for the Elder Moltke. That factor was the more rapid operational-readiness of the Austro-Hungarian-German armed forces, coupled with the assumed slowness of Russian deployment. Because of inadequate railroad connections near the Prussian frontier, it was thought that at least four weeks were needed for the Russians to assemble their forces around their central Warsaw bastion.

Also to be considered was the fact that Romania's army cemented the allied right flank position. By attacking into Russian territory, Romania could divert enemy formations from the main theaters of operation. With Italy in the Triple Alliance, the Dual Monarchy could also shift troops from their southwestern frontier to the northeastern.

1888-1891 saw close coordination and cooperation between the allied General Staffs, contrary to the later Schlieffen period. The 1882 military agreements remained the basis of military planning. The overall concept of a joint envelopment of Russian formations in Poland by means of a dual thrust from Prussia to Galicia remained.

In addition to the conclusion of the Austro-Hungarian-German alliance of 1879, the decisive considerations in this strategic plan were the recent strengthening of the French army, the build-up of France's frontier fortresses, the deficiencies of the Russian Polish railroad network, and the comparative slowness of Russian mobilization.

Since appointment as Quartermaster General in 1882, Waldersee had striven for railroad and road improvements, particularly in the region leading to the right bank of the Vistula River. By 1891, these improvements had been accomplished.[14]

The crucial diplomatic event during Waldersee's short tenure as Chief of the General Staff was the non-renewal of the Reinsurance Treaty of 1887. On 18 March 1890, Bismarck was forced to resign from his position, causing Germany to let the treaty lapse on 18 June 1890. Kaiser Wilhelm initially favored a renewal of the treaty, but upon receipt of reports concerning Russian military activity, he changed his mind.[15] He then accepted the advice of certain key advisors urging non-renewal.

Until Bismarck's fall, Tsar Alexander III and his Germanophile foreign minister's pro-German tendencies did much to prevent the formation of a Franco-Russian alliance. However, with the uncertainty and apparent re-orientation of German policy, Alexander III began to gravitate toward just such a French connection.

German arguments supporting the nonrenewal of the treaty included the following: that it was incompatible with the Dual Alliance; that Bismarck's system of alliances involved a much too complicated facade; and, further, that the treaty committed Germany to a definite policy on Russia. Without the treaty, it was argued, Germany would be able to balance the two rival Empires, England and Russia.

In St. Petersburg, fears quickly arose that Germany had launched a "new course" with the nonrenewal of the Reinsurance Treaty and apparent conclusion of an Anglo-German agreement. Leading Russian statesmen feared that these activities indicated that Germany favored a connection with England over one with Russia.

The German Kaiser and the Foreign Office failed to realize that with the expiration of the treaty, a future two-front war for Germany was now very possible. For Bismarck, one of the cardinal principles of the Reinsurance Treaty had been that it prevented Russia from concluding an agreement with France against Germany. France, in her weakened and isolated condition, could not contemplate war against Germany without the support of Russia or another ally. With the expiration of the Rein-surance Treaty, the lines of contact between the two "free agents"-Russia and France-had now been opened .

In military affairs, Waldersee was succeeded by a more devoted military strategist, Count Alfred von Schlieffen. After the death of his wife, Schlieffen had buried himself in military study and problems. In the process, between 1892-1905, he gradually created a plan which involved the shifting of the main German deployment in a two-front war from the east to the west. This plan became the basis for a German two-front conflagration, and indeed served as the model for the Central Power's opening campaigns in World War I. The plan involved a daring risk: A massed force of German troops would wheel through neutral Belgium in an attempt to outflank French armies, then strike an annihilating blow against the French and Swiss frontiers.

This strategy ran counter to the strategy of both the Elder Moltke and Waldersee. Schlieffen also not only calculated the deployment and first concentrations of his forces, but, contrary to the practice of his predecessors, also mapped out the great decisive battles themselves on a day-to-day basis.[16]

Schlieffen constantly studied both the eastern and western frontier regions in the yearly summer and winter "Great General Staff Trips." During these excursions, he evaluated all strategical and tactical variants. Since the advent of the machine gun and improved artillery prevented a decisive frontal attack against the enemy's central positions, total victory over a numerically superior foe necessitated a stroke at his flank and rear-cutting off the enemy's avenues of retreat-which would result in its destruction. This concept was considered imperative by Schlieffen for the victory of a numerically weaker nation over two flanking enemy powers.[17]

Schlieffen considered a two-front war inevitable, and, if it was long and drawn out, disastrous for Germany. Only a military strategy of rapid annihilation of opponents would serve to preserve the German system. Schlieffen's lack of concern for political concepts led him to ignore in his strategy such factors as the neutrality of nations like Belgium. This line of reasoning resulted from Schlieffen's rating of France as the strongest and most dangerous of his potential two-front antagonists. As Schlieffen himself stated, a victory "results...only through the most rapid destruction first of the one, then of the other opponent."[18]

Accordingly, an opening offensive campaign against Russia could not produce the necessary total victory for the following reasons: it would be too time-consuming, considering the enormous extent of territory and the inferior Prussian railroad system's inability to handle the rapid deployment of a million-man army; and the Moltke-Beck plan of a dual offensive from separated areas (Prussia and Galicia) could no longer achieve the advantage of surprise. The crossing of the Narev River would now be extremely difficult because the Russians had strongly fortified Lomscha, the key objective of such an assault. The swampy lowland terrain would also retard the movement of large armies. Even if the Narev River could be easily forded before Russian formations had assembled, the Russians could simply retreat eastward, drawing German armies inland to rob them of the chance for a battle of annihilation while allowing France to prepare for her stroke. Further, weather factors at certain times of the year limited hope for a total success.

The advantages of first striking France included the nearness and completeness of the German rail networks at the Franco-German border; the possibility of a decisive battle within a short period of time; and the neutralization of the most immediately dangerous opponent. Moreover, the French deployment was more rapid and effective than that of the Russians, and the elimination of the direct French threat to the key industrial areas of the Ruhr, Saar, etc., was important.

Schlieffen's preoccupation with a great decisive battle in the west, led the Prussian war theater to recede into the background. Although Vienna would be expected to cover the German rear flank from the very beginning, Schlieffen treated his ally as a second-rate power incapable of sustained action. The nonchalance and condescension with which he treated his Viennese counterparts resulted in an almost complete rupture of contact between the two General Staffs by 1896.

This does not imply that an eastern campaign received no attention. Each year, a plan for a "Great Eastern Deployment" was mapped out alongside a plan for western deployment. The vital assumptions for such a "Great Eastern Deployment", however, were a neutral France, and Russia as a sole opponent. If this situation did arise, almost the entire German army would be hurled against the Russian front. Four armies would be deployed on a front extending from Thorn to Memel. The flank position would be expanded much further northeast than envisioned by Waldersee, with a major stroke being unleashed across the Narev River in the direction of Bialystok. The plan called for the encirclement, then annihilation, of the anticipated major Russian concentration between the Bug and Vistula Rivers. The enveloping movement would be launched from a point further north than the Elder Moltke and Waldersee had planned.[19]

Schlieffen's thoughts were revealed in his first memorandum in April 1891. First and foremost, he stated categorically that the agreements between his predecessors and the Austro-Hungarian General Staff, by necessity, retained their validity. In particular, however, Schlieffen feared that the Austro-Hungarian front in Galicia could not be sustained without German aid.

Already Schlieffen doubted that a German offensive at the Narev and Niemen Rivers could succeed because of likely Russian counter defensive measures. Also, the geographical problems of crossing the swampy lowlands of Poland had to be overcome. For Schlieffen, a rapid and decisive battle seemed precluded,[20] and a German offensive launched from East or West Prussia seemed to present increasingly more difficulties.

Schlieffen finally came to the conclusion that the planned offensive — over the Narev River against Lomscha — must be abandoned. Such an effort would require at least twenty-two divisions, which would be far beyond the capacity of the inadequate railway system south of the Vistula River. But, more importantly, troops could not be spared from the western theater.[21]

Schlieffen began to abandon the previously accepted notion of separated Austro-Hungarian-German offensives, but this contradicted the agreements with the Austro-Hungarian General Staff.

A major influence on Schlieffen's revised planning was that the Austro-Hungarian troops required a longer time to mobilize. Thus, he decided that the German eastern forces should advance not from Prussia but from Upper Silesia, and then to the Vistula River to unite with Austro-Hungarian units.[22]

When he assumed office in 1891, therefore, Schlieffen had not yet embraced the idea of an initial attack in the west. He had only altered the direction from which the German offensive into Poland could be launched. A defensive western posture would be maintained, because of Schlieffen's early belief that before the French came out of their excellent fortified positions for a decisive battle, German troops would have to be transported eastward.[23]

Schlieffen suggested that until 1893, the mass of German eastern forces (four corps, seven reserve, and three cavalry divisions) would advance towards the Vistula River to the Zavichost-Annopol stretch, where they would unite with Austro-Hungarian forces. Only four infantry and one cavalry division would cover East Prussia. However, this plan did not meet with Beck's approval.

Austro-Hungarian-German relations soon suffered. At the first personal encounter between Schlieffen and Beck, 27 August 1891, the Austro-Hungarian came away with a bad impression of his German counterpart. At their next meeting, Schlieffen proved unwilling to discuss strategic planning with his Austro-Hungarian colleagues.

An August 1892 memorandum produced a sharper break from earlier German planning. Greater emphasis was now placed upon the growing French threat in the west. The Austrians were judged by Schlieffen to be a match for Russian units in Poland where it was estimated that twenty-eight Austro-Hungarian divisions would counter twenty Russian divisions. In this memorandum, Schlieffen, for the first time, openly opposed the Elder Moltke's division of forces against France and Russia. One enemy should be dealt with at a time. France now became the initial opponent. Thirty-seven divisions would be earmarked for the west, against her, while the allied Italians might insert ten additional divisions at the Rhine. Eighteen divisions were destined for the east.[24]

Schlieffen's first major effort in 1892 to change strategical planning appeared in a December memorandum. According to this memorandum, the Moltke-Waldersee plans could not succeed because military conditions had changed by 1892. Concentrated Russian armies could now be expected at the German frontiers, particularly near Lomscha. The German army could no longer be expected to surprise the Russians in the early stages of deployment — in fact, Schlieffen was certain that the Russians probably had information concerning the German plans in the east.[25]

Ignoring that factor, the argument continued, even if the Narev River could be crossed and the Vistula River forts bypassed, it would be highly unlikely that the Russians would retreat southward toward Beck's forces. More likely, the enemy would withdraw eastward into Russia where railroads could be utilized to great advantage.

In summary, the memorandum stated that it would neither be possible to gain a decisive victory against, or destruction of, the Russian armies. At most, a series of frontal battles could have some success. Early and effective Austro-Hungarian aid could be discounted because of the distance separating the Prussian and Galician Campaign areas, some 375 to 450 kilometers. Yet, despite the weakening of German eastern troop strengths, a plan for an offensive across the Narev River was retained. If the Russians attempted to invade East Prussia during such an offensive, they could not unite their armies (Narev and Niemen) until they had reached a position to the west of the Masurian Lakes. In that case, Schlieffen would strike first one and then the other of the Russian army groups separated by the lakes. This idea remained the basis for the eastern campaign in Prussia in August and September, 1914. At the same time, Schlieffen conceived a total victory resulting from a grand offensive against France.

In both his 1891 and 1892 memoranda, Schlieffen emphasized his fear that the Austro-Hungarian armed forces would not be able to fulfill their obligations in Galicia, and his low estimate of them continued throughout his term as Chief of the General Staff. At the same time, he recognized the distinct necessity of Austro-Hungarian aid — Germany needed her ally. If Beck's forces did not advance from Galicia, the German troops would be forced to retreat-or worse, be destroyed in East Prussia. Yet he did not attempt to improve relations with Beck or encourage mutual cooperation.[26]

The major problem for the Austro-Hungarian General Staff, meanwhile, remained the relative lag of its army's mobilization. A contributing factor was the still insufficient number and low capacity of railroads over the Carpathian mountains into Galicia. In 1892, some improvements in that area had allowed for an eastward shifting of the assembly of Austro-Hungarian troops. A new threat to the right flank positions led to demands for the reinforcing of troops in that area.[27] In the following year, 1893, Schlieffen wrote a memorandum seeking a cooperative offensive with his Austro-Hungarian allies, but with German forces advancing from Silesia rather than from East Prussia. He termed Moltke's earlier plan for a dual offensive from Galicia and East Prussia as "disastrous," so the plan for a Narev offensive was abandoned. The German plan for the east entailed a deployment of only four infantry divisions and one cavalry division in East and West Prussia. The main eastern force, ten infantry and three cavalry divisions, was to cross the Vistula River after proceeding from Silesia.[28]

Beck, however, was not enthusiastic about this development. Basically, he continued to focus his attention on the problem of eliminating the enemy threat to his right flank. Any offensive advance from Galicia into Poland could be seriously threatened. He feared that the enemy might immediately lunge into Galicia, before that exposed flank could be protected. The assembly of enemy cavalry particularly worried him, but also on his mind was that the Russian Volhynian and Podolian groups had the capability of uniting their forces for a sustained drive towards Zloczóv before they could be countered. To check this threat, and to accelerate Beck's deployment plans, the completion of a new rail connection into eastern Galicia was required by 1895.[29] This improvement would make more rapid the assembly of formations in eastern Galicia, but this would occur at the expense of the deployment in western Galicia.

Schlieffen, planning for a small German force in the east, desired that the Austro-Hungarian forces draw major Russian formations from the Prussian frontier southward. As Conrad stated in 1914, Austria-Hungary was to "bleed to death" for her ally. By drawing Russian troops to the south, the Austrians would also reduce the threat to German flank positions, the main threat being against the German left flank.

Returning to the diplomatic stage, in the background of Schlieffen's appointment in 1890 was, above all, the nonrenewal of the Russo-German Reinsurance Treaty of 1887, which hampered Germany's free hand in the Anglo-Russian rivalry. "Noisy" renewal of the Triple Alliance on 17 May 1891 finally resulted in the first serious diplomatic exchanges between France and Russia. The era of the Bismarckian order was over.

During this period in the early 1890s, Russian activity began to focus on the Far East, as indicated by the construction of the Trans-Siberian railroad. For support and protection of their machinations, the Russians began seriously to favor France's position in the Far East. The Chief of the French General Staff attended the 1891 Russian army maneuvers. The first concrete steps toward an alliance between the nations occurred 21-27 August 1891 when a political entente came into existence.

In 1890, Kaiser Wilhelm and his chancellor visited Vienna, where they established an oral agreement stating that any solution to the Straits question could not be reached according to Russian guidelines. German concessions to St. Petersburg concerning the Near East would be arranged only with the consent of Vienna. This agreement demonstrated that Germany had reversed Bismarck's Balkan policy, at least temporarily.

Russo-French ties solidified with the conclusion of their military convention of 17 August 1892. They agreed that the bulk of their forces would counter Germany in a war. The convention meant that Germany would face a two-front war, and that France had escaped from her diplomatic and military isolation. In the future, the French would provide more financial aid for the build-up of Russian railroads and the strengthening of her armies. For Germany greater dependence on Austria-Hungary en-

sued. Berlin, however, rapidly returned to Bismarck's safer Balkan policies of holding Vienna in check, easing the possibility of a Russo-German
rupture.

As soon as the Franco-Russian Treaty had been concluded in January,
1894, German foreign policy tried to disrupt it. Kaiser Wilhelm heralded
the return to Bismarck's policy of friendship with Russia, enthusiastic
about the division of spheres of influence in the Balkans. Even Schlieffen
agreed.

Chancellor George Leo Caprivi, who had followed a basically anti-
Russian policy, stepped aside for Chlodwig Hohenlohe, who based his
policy upon friendship with St. Petersburg. Meanwhile, Wilhelm attempted to create a Continental League, consisting of Germany, France,
and Russia.

The Kaiser's plans failed. In the interim, the Franco-Russian military
convention, although technically only a military convention, assumed the
full force of a treaty on 4 January 1894. The first article of this secret
alliance promised a French military force of 1,300,000 men and 700,000
to 800,000 Russians to confront Germany in an armed conflict. A German
mobilization would be immediately countered by a Franco-Russian one.[30]

A new era in European diplomatic history was born. The new Franco-
Russian tie disturbed the previous German continental system, while establishing a fairly balanced grouping of powers in its place. This change,
in turn, encouraged the Great Powers to shift their attention away from
Europe by pursuing their imperialistic adventures in the remainder of the
world.

In the years 1893-1895 there occurred a shuffling in key diplomatic
personnel. In addition to the rise of Hohenlohe, Alexander III died in 1894
and Nicholas II became the new Tsar. Giers was replaced as Foreign
Minister. In Vienna, Agenor Goluchowski replaced Gustav Kalnoky as
Foreign Minister.

Russian attention transferred to the Far East, a move which was encouraged by German policy. The 10 February 1894 Russo-German tariff
treaty improved Berlin-St. Petersburg relations and encouraged Berlin's
efforts to sap the vitality of the Franco-Russian combination.

The Sino-Japanese War of 1894-1895 presented further opportunity
for Wilhelm to push his ideas of cooperation with France and Russia. The
chances of a Franco-German war – or of trouble breaking out – in the
Balkan area decreased, while St. Petersburg awaited further events in the

Far East.   Kaiser Wilhelm considered it unwise to oppose a Russian
acquisition of Constantinople, and he even suggested the old Bismarckian
policy of a partitioning of the Balkans.[31]

In 1895, Vienna did not seek territorial extension in the Balkans but
intended, at all costs, to prevent an expansion of Russian influence there.
Austro-Hungarian policy thus favored the status quo in the Balkans, and
would naturally exclude any chance of Constantinople falling into the
hands of Tsar Nicholas.

If, however, Russia should occupy Constantinople and England should
acquiesce, Berlin's position was that Austro-Hungarian intervention was
entirely at her own risk. It was assumed that, if Germany were to enter an
Austro-Hungarian-Russian conflict, France would follow suit. Germany
thus affirmed her intention of supporting Austria-Hungary only if the
latter's existence were threatened. The basic principles of German foreign
policy now depended upon Russia's entanglement in the Far East.

An additional event of 1895 is worthy of note. Serbia's ruler, King
Alexander, did not renew the secret 1881 treaty with AustriaHungary, last
renewed in 1889 by King Milan. Rather, Serbia looked to Russia for an
alliance.

In the military sphere, Schlieffen's plans for a battle of annihilation
against France took shape between the years 1894-1899. In the process,
relations worsened between the German and Austro-Hungarian General
Staffs. Indicative of this trend, Schlieffen informed the Austro-Hungarian
military attaché on 8 February 1894 that he could no longer be as com-
municative concerning his plans as was his predecessor. Therefore, Beck
instructed his own military attaché in Berlin to discontinue any discussions
concerning deployment details.[32]

The change in German strategic planning became apparent in April
1894. Because the promised Italian deployment of troop formations on
the Rhine appeared very unlikely, Germany would have to face France
alone in the west. The number of German forces designated for the Prussian theater would thus have to be reduced.[33] A segment of these units
would assemble and march toward the San River mouth to the Annopol
region to meet Austria's troops. Eventually the entire German eastern army
would probably wheel in the direction of Warsaw. Schlieffen, meanwhile,
counted on Russia's use of two geographically separated armies, the Niemen and Narev Armies.

Accordingly, the Masurian Lakes would provide the opportunity to
strike the left flank of the advancing Niemen Army. Schlieffen's calcula-

tions would prove accurate and useful in the battles of Tannenberg and the Masurian Lakes in 1914.

The rising threat to Austria-Hungary's right flank position continued to occupy the Dual Monarchy's tactical and strategical planning.[34] The assumption that the Habsburg deployment would create problems, among which were the large enemy troop concentrations within a few days' march of the frontier, increased these fears.

Meanwhile, in his impulsive manner, Schlieffen dramatically reverted to the original 1882 plan of deploying German troops in East Prussia for 1895. In relaying this *volte face* to Vienna, he made suggestions for Austria-Hungary to consider. But on 30 May 1895, Beck rejected these proposals with valid arguments.[35]

The result was that the allied plan would remain, at least briefly, a German offensive from Silesia in the south to the Vistula River stretch Zavichost-Annopol and an Austro-Hungarian thrust from western Galicia.

Schlieffen would, if necessary, allow Russian forces to occupy East Prussia while the offensive in the south unfolded. If the Russians were to invade East Prussia, it could be anticipated that they would have so outpositioned themselves that they would not be able to regroup in time to participate in the major battle being waged east of the Vistula River. The German offensive would be launched from a southerly (Silesian) rather than a northerly (East Prussian) direction; and this offensive would consist of fewer German troops - eighteen divisions, to link up with Austria's advancing forces.[36]

In April, Beck informed the German High Command that before the mass of his armies began its thrust, he would probably have to field five to seven corps at his right flank to create room for maneuvering in the direction of Rovna. At the same time, to accelerate deployment in eastern Galicia, more railroad trackage was an obvious necessity.[37]

Suddenly, on 12 July 1895, Schlieffen wrote to Beck, that he thought that executing the allied operations plan for a common offensive from Silesia was fraught with danger. He also criticized proposed Austro-Hungarian military measures to strengthen their right flank positions by saying that too few troops were destined for the main objective in Poland.[38]

Then, in December 1895, Schlieffen reported to Beck that he had returned to the Elder Moltke's plan of advancing from East Prussia, crossing the Narev River, and then advancing against the main enemy force. Fewer German troops (four corps) would be utilized, so the final objective

could not be as ambitious as the earlier plan. Essentially, Schlieffen no
longer felt that he could abandon East and West Prussia to a Russian
invasion, because it could now be expected that the major enemy drive
would be directed against Germany rather than against the Dual Monarchy.[39]

The Austro-Hungarian deployment would still consist of two main, but
separately assembling forces. The Third Army's mission was to eliminate
the threat to the Austro-Hungarian extreme right flank. The remaining
Austro-Hungarian forces in Galicia, the eight corps of the First and Second
Armies would advance northward between the Bug and Vistula Rivers.
This overall military concept remained the nucleus for Austro-Hungarian
planning through 1907-1908. But glaring deficiencies continued to exist
in the eastern Galician railroad connections and the capacity of the
single-track Hungarian rail lines.[40]

For 1896, the Austro-Hungarian deployment plans remained basically
unchanged, but the German plan once again was centered around a main
force to be assembled to the south of Insterburg. This task force would
advance against the Russian Niemen Army, defeat it, then turn toward the
Narev River – much as the earlier plan had directed. However, German
eastern units would now deploy in western rather than eastern Prussia.
The main force would now advance to Rozan, rather than Lomscha as
earlier planned.[41]

Schlieffen, in the meantime, still worried that the Austrians might be
delayed in their war offensive. The inevitable result of his concern was a
serious strain in Austro-Hungarian-German relations.[42] Operational planning and coordination of deployments were terminated for almost a full
decade.

Schlieffen now became increasingly concerned with the western war
theater. In a letter of March 1896 to his military attaché in Vienna,
Schlieffen complained of Beck's request for details about German deployment plans and lamented the Elder Moltke's promise to dispatch eighteen
divisions to the eastern theater. Schlieffen, while continuing to lament the
slowness of Austro-Hungarian mobilization, resolved to include a higher
proportion of reserve units with these line units in the future.[43]

The diplomatic crisis that unfolded in the Near East between 1895-
1897 encouraged Kaiser Wilhelm again to propose creation of a Continental League consisting of Germany, France, and Russia. In the long run,
it was reasoned, such a league would also force England to join the Triple
Alliance.

About the same time, the Russian Foreign Minister announced his policy to be based on Far Eastern priorities. For the Balkans, this proclamation signified that Russia would support the status quo in regard to Turkey.

Improved relations between Austria-Hungary and Russia also resulted from the ratification of an 8 May 1897 Balkan agreement, which lasted ten years. Because of Berlin's diplomacy, the Austro-Hungarian government saw no alternative to such an Austro-Russian tie. A deep Austro-Hungarian mistrust of continuing German-Russian rapprochement was also an issue.

The Russians, however, expressed the most significant reservations concerning Vienna's policy. The Treaty of Berlin of 1879 assured to Austria-Hungary the right of military occupation of Bosnia-Herzegovina. The annexation of these two provinces would raise a more extensive question.

For the Dual Monarchy, St. Petersburg's reservations naturally removed some value from the Austro-Russian agreement, because Russia retained a free hand regarding Turkish territories in Europe as well as to the provinces of Bosnia-Herzegovina. Franz Joseph's government had no choice but to be satisfied, because pressure from Berlin had helped to produce the understanding with the Russian regime.[44]

Two new appointees in Germany in 1897 would have great influence upon events in the near future. Bernard von Bülow was named Foreign Secretary and Admiral Alfred von Tirpitz top naval commander. The latter appointment would lead to a naval race between England and Germany after a new German navy would be created.

In military and strategic planning, Schlieffen was now occupying himself mainly with the tactical assignments of his proposed right-wing hammer thrust into France and the composition of those forces. This planning continued from 1897 to 1905. During this period, the German government, and General Staff, accepted the political implications including the violation of Belgium's and Holland's neutrality.[45]

The major diplomatic events of 1898 included an Anglo-French confrontation over the Sudan and English advances to Berlin as an attempt to discuss formation of an alliance. Activities outside of Europe, meanwhile, strained the former groupings of the major states. For example, Russia, preoccupied with the Far East, displayed no hostility towards Vienna; at the same time, the allied Austrians and Germans began to drift slowly apart. Italy was also becoming increasingly unreliable in Austro-

Hungarian-German Triple Alliance schemes, for she had begun to gravitate towards France.

In August 1899, France and Russia began to enlarge the scope of their 1894 alliance. Their original military convention would now remain in force for as long as the Franco-Russian agreement applied. In the Balkans, on 25 November 1899, the Turkish Sultan signed the preliminary papers for a German company to construct a railroad extending from Constantinople to Baghdad. A line had been opened between Germany and Constantinople in 1888. Russo-German relations deteriorated increasingly as German economic interests in Turkey appeared to develop into political hegemony.

During this entire period, 1896-1901, the contacts between the German and Austro-Hungarian General staffs remained tenuous. Schlieffen's low esteem of the Austro-Hungarians was unchanged.[46]

Schlieffen continued to expand the scope of his strategic planning for an annihilating military blow against France. From 1900, in a two-front war, six German armies - almost the entire German military machine - would be hurled into France. In any conflict against Russia, the smaller German forces would probably have to retreat behind the Vistula River line. After a total victory had been obtained against France in the west, troops would then be transported eastward, where lost territory could be regained and a battle of annihilation could be conducted.[47]

To Schlieffen, the major difficulty in his planning was the possibility that an eastern war might develop in which France might not initially offer military commitment. In such an event, over one-half of the German army would be deployed in the east to cooperate with their Austro-Hungarian allies. A strong army, its left flank extending to Bialystok, would advance from East Prussia to the Narev River at Pultusk-Lomscha. The smaller portion of the German army would be maintained in deployment stations, ready to surprise the French striking their left flank positions if the French attempted to advance into Germany.[48]

In 1901, St. Petersburg's attention, following the Boxer Rebellion, once again was riveted on China. Militarily, the rebellion meant that new Russian formations would be mobilized for service in Manchuria. With this necessity in mind, Schlieffen planned to field only small numbers of troops at the Prussian frontier in the case of an eastern war threat. One army corps would guard the enemy approaches from the Masurian Lakes, while the main body of the small eastern force would be deployed between Allenstein and Vehlau. Schlieffen assumed that two Russian armies, twice the strength of his troops, would be assembled in the Niemen and Narev areas.[49] As battle plans stood for these circumstances, reinforcements being shifted from the west could not be expected, regardless of what the military situation might have become in the east.

In the meantime, English attempts at reaching some form of an agreement with Germany continued from 1898 to 1901, but the German Foreign Office did not react positively, badly misjudging the situation and overestimating England's "necessity" for concluding diplomatic ties with Berlin.

In the Balkans, Romania's connection with the Triple Alliance was ratified for the third time in 1902. A military agreement with Austria-Hungary in 1901 had already provided for a Romanian deployment in the upper Moldavian area, in the event of a war with Russia, to achieve close union with Austro-Hungarian forces. Romanian forces after mobilization and deployment would launch an offensive in the direction of Mohilev.[50]

England meanwhile jettisoned her "splendid" isolation and concluded a treaty with Japan, Russia's antagonist in the Far East. During the same period, relations among the Triple Alliance powers continued to worsen. In 1896, the Austro-Hungarian General Staff had already begun preparing measures for a "War Case I" (Italy). Two years later, Italian-French relations improved, but in July 1900 King Umberto Humbert was assassinated, and his successor, Victor Emmanuel III, treated his allies coolly. His reserve did not preclude the ratification of a Triple Alliance naval agreement for a "War Case F + R" (France and Russia), which was concluded on 5 December 1900. But relations between the allies, Vienna and Rome, continued to worsen after 1900 over the question of Balkan matters.[51]

The Triple Alliance itself was renewed 28 June 1902, but a Franco-Italian agreement of November 1902 actually negated Italy's earlier obligations.

Austria-Hungary also suffered a serious worsening of her Balkan position in 1903. In Serbia, on the night of 10-11 June, King Alexander, his wife, and several ministers were brutally murdered. A shift away from Austro-Hungarian tutelage had already occurred in 1889 when King Milan had abdicated. After 1903, relations between the two countries steadily deteriorated, chiefly because the new king, Peter I, from the rival Karageorgevic dynasty, promoted the idea of a Greater Serbia.

For Viennese military leaders, these events meant that war measures would now have to be drafted against Serbia. Attention was also focused on Bulgaria as a military counterweight to the potentially hostile Serbia. In addition to a now possible "War Case S" (Serbia), Italian diplomatic activity also resulted in Vienna's attention to "War Case I", which received further attention.[52]

These concessions did not preclude the signing on 1 December 1903 of a military accord which provided for the transport of the Italian Third Army to the Rhine to fight with the German army against France in the event of a war.[53] The effect of this agreement, however, was partially negated by the aforementioned Franco-Italian agreement of 1902.

Two years later, England and France concluded their *Entente Cordiale*, but France's position became critical after the Russo-Japanese war erupted. German diplomatic pressures of 1905-1906, which were intended to weaken the Franco-Russian and Anglo-French ties, resulted in closer contact between these same groupings, and political cooperation commenced.

The conclusion of the *Entente Cordiale* also had an effect on Italy. Rapprochement between Italy and France had really begun in earnest in 1902, but with France's new agreement with England it increased. Italian public opinion, on the other hand, turned increasingly against Austria-Hungary and by 1904, Serbia, as Russia had suggested, had swung to a definite policy of friendship with Russia and hostility to Austria-Hungary. Russian ill will toward Austria-Hungary was not mitigated by the fact that in 1904, the Russian Government successfully obtained the promise of Austro-Hungarian neutrality in the event of a Russo-Japanese struggle. Kaiser Wilhelm fully supported the accord.[54] Unresolved Russo-Japanese frictions soon resulted in a Japanese attack on Port Arthur on 8 February 1904, without ultimatum or declaration of war. The bloody fighting ended with the Treaty of Portsmouth, which was concluded on 5 September 1905.

The Russo-Japanese war provided an opportunity for Germany to pose as a friend of Russia. In October 1904, the German government even offered an alliance to Russia. The ultimate German aim was obviously either to rupture the Franco-Russian alliance or to push France to enter into a Russo-German agreement. The attempt failed.

French aspirations over Morocco became a center of German concern in 1905. By March, this led to a Franco-German crisis that induced further German attempts in July 1905 at Björkö to secure a personal agreement between the Kaiser and the Tsar. The Björkö meeting came in the wake of the crushing defeat of the Russian fleet in the Tsushima Straits, after which Russia's last faint hope of victory over Japan vanished. Wilhelm, therefore, utilizing the Russian defeat, pressed for a Russo-German defensive alliance - which, according to the Kaiser, should be presented to Paris, where the Russians should influence the French to adhere to it. The plan crumbled, however, when following Björkö the Tsar's advisers counseled that the French should be consulted beforehand. It was obvious that France would not join such an alignment.

Worse still, Russia, repulsed in her Asian ambitions, refocused her attention on the European arena and the flammable Balkans. For years, Russia had not been considered a military threat to either Germany or Austria-Hungary, and her power was not considered serious by Central European military planners during that period.

Estimates by Berlin and Vienna General Staff planners of the fighting quality of the Russian forces were not high because no major Russian military success had been achieved in the first eleven months of Russo-Japanese hostilities. The Russian ineptness attributed to poor Russian commanders, deficiencies in equipment and armaments, and also to the enormous logistical problems.[55] German and Austro-Hungarian military planners also expected that as a result of the conflict, Russian arms would be in disarray for years to come.

For the short term, at least, the Austro-Hungarian General Staff saw Italy as the main threat to Austro-Hungarian interests. The military also refocused its attention on Romania and its Hohenzollern King Carol as being important in strategical considerations. An important assumption, and Romania's natural basis for opposition to Russia, was that the Russian overland route to Constantinople would cross Romanian territory.[56]

Schlieffen, in his last year as Chief of the German General Staff, had issued an important memorandum in which he considered the Russo-Japanese War and the Morocco crisis. Those events had confirmed his opinion that in the event of a war, an initial quick defeat of France would be essential. *In toto*, according to a "finalized" Schlieffen Plan, part of eight German armies would be hurled in an outflanking maneuver through neutral Belgium and deep into France. Only ten German infantry divisions would be deployed in eastern Germany, as a defensive force to counter a possible Russian threat.

These final operational plans had evolved as a result of the annual General Staff ride in June 1904. From the moment the plan was spelled out in this form, it became the basis for all German operational planning until the First World War. Schlieffen, it must be noted, did not actually plot out a definite campaign because the troop units necessary for his formulations did not exist. The final Schlieffen blueprint, therefore, admitted a number of intangibles.[57]

In December 1905, during the Morocco crisis, Schlieffen had put the final touches on his master plan. Schlieffen felt that "the present moment would be undoubtedly favorable" for German military action.[58] From 1897-1905, German operational planning had swung toward the concept of a great enveloping battle of annihilation to be launched through Belgium and Holland into northern France, with the goal of neutralizing Paris and then crushing the French armies against the Swiss and German frontiers. Crucial to Schlieffen's plan was his assumption that the French would probably first assume a defensive stance, because after 1905 they could not count on effective Russian aid. At the same time, he wondered whether France might not herself attempt to outflank the German troops by advancing through Luxembourg, Belgium, and the Netherlands.[59]

Some major complications did exist. For Schlieffen's plans, eight additional army corps would have to be created for use with his attacking forces. The general doubted that his country had, or could obtain, the superior forces necessary for a favorable outcome on the battlefield.[60]

With Schlieffen's forced retirement in 1905, a distinct and significant phase of German military history came to an end. Schlieffen's legacy would be played out in the opening campaigns of World War I, but in circumstances far different from those he had envisioned during final drafting of his plan in 1905. At the time of Schlieffen's retirement, Russia had been prostrated by the 1905 war and could not pose a serious threat to the Central Powers for years to come. France would thus be the focus of any German war.

The weaknesses of the Schlieffen plan included inadequate allowance for the defense of the frontiers against a rapid Russian thrust if Russia began to recover from her military debacle of 1904-1905. All would be staked on the massive annihilating blow against France, where even the German reserve units would be combined with first-line units in the invasion through Belgium into France. The period from 1906 to 1914, however, only served to highlight the weaknesses of the France-centered stratagem.

CHAPTER III

The Bosnian Crisis, 1908-1909

The year 1906 was a watershed in Central European military and diplomatic history. Both Germany and Austria-Hungary, reacting to the fears generated by the events of 1905, appointed new men to the posts of Chief of the General Staff. For the Dual Monarchy, Conrad von Hötzendorf replaced Frederick Beck-Rzikowsky; in Germany, Helmuth von Moltke the Younger succeeded Count Alfred von Schlieffen. Also, new faces appeared in the diplomatic arena: Baron Alois Aehrenthal was appointed Austro-Hungarian Minister of Foreign Affairs, and Aleksandr Petrovich Izvolskii was appointed Minister of Foreign Affairs in Russia. The staff changes were momentous as closer links between the military hierarchies of Austria-Hungary and Germany were ultimately established.

Conrad von Hötzendorf, who would lead the Danubian Monarchy into the First World War, has been depicted as a warmonger. He has been portrayed as ardently demanding that accounts be settled by preventive war with Italy and Serbia before it was too late for the Austro-Hungarians to win such a war and before Russia had recovered from the 1905 revolution.[1] Considered a brilliant strategist and called the Schlieffen of Austria, von Hötzendorf was very intelligent and inexhaustibly energetic. Although he has borne the reputation of being a troublemaker, he was truly aware of Austria-Hungary's many problems.[2] By the time Conrad assumed the position of Chief of the General Staff, Austria's diplomacy had been cemented solidly in the Dual Alliance of 1879. Italy, a doubtful partner at best, rounded out the Triple Alliance founded in 1882.

Austro-Hungarian diplomatic relations with Russia in 1906 were based on the 1903 Mürzsteg Treaty. This treaty aimed to provide a cover for Russia's European border during her war with Japan. The situation on the Austro-Hungarian southeastern frontier in Serbia and Montenegro had gradually but increasingly become embittered after the 1903 assassination of the Serbian King Alexander. Conrad's response to the deepening Bal-

kan crisis was to call for the absorption of Serbia and Montenegro into
the Dual Monarchy.

The two newly appointed Chiefs of the General Staffs, Conrad and
Moltke, first met face-to-face in Berlin in May 1907. Conrad summed up
the meeting as "entirely worthwhile,"[3] particularly since it closed the
ten-year gap of non-intercourse between the two General Staffs.

The change in diplomatic leadership in Russia had an effect upon the
overall military and diplomatic situation. The selection of Izvolskii —
formerly minister in Belgrade, Munich, Tokyo, and Copenhagen — as
minister of foreign affairs proved disquieting for the Central Powers. By
1907, after Izvolskii had secured agreements with both England and
France (the Triple Entente), he then proceeded to reopen the question of
the Straits and Constantinople. His diplomacy signaled the shift of Russian
interests back to the Balkans.

Aehrenthal's attention focused on the Balkan peninsula as well. The
new foreign minister set as his first goal the restoration of Austro-Hungarian prestige in the Balkans. Considering the growing unrest among the
empire's nationalities, he felt that success in the realm of foreign affairs
would be a most advantageous development. He hoped that it would also
gain him greater freedom of action within the Triple Alliance.[4]

Aehrenthal, like Conrad, cast his eyes on the provinces of Bosnia-Herzegovina, and the goal of their annexation became the central theme of
his foreign policy. Although they were nominally under Turkish suze-
rainty, the Dual Monarchy had administered the provinces since the Congress of Berlin in 1878: and, in Aehrenthal's view, the Turkish government
was too weak to offer resistance to any intervention in this area. But with
the revolution of the Young Turks in 1908, he feared that the new government of Turkey would attempt to modernize and strengthen the grip on
its empire.

The Austro-Hungarian army's operational plans for the Galician-Rus-
sian frontier in 1905 remained basically unchanged from those of 1897-
1902. Only two organizational changes were initiated. Of primary importance was the creation of a fourth army to cover the northeastern border.
At the same time, the *Jäger* (mountain) battalions stationed in Galicia
were to be transferred to the southwest for use against Italy. In the event
of mobilization, the territorial reserve units were to be added to the northeast theater to secure the railroad lines at the Austro-Russian frontier.

Three contingency plans for war in 1905-1908 provided for "War Case
I" (Italy), which assumed a simultaneous war against Italy and Serbia-

Montenegro; "War Case B," against the Serbian Kingdom alone; and "War Case R," based on a combined Austro-Hungarian-German war against Russia.

Plans for "War Case R" for 1907-1908 indeed demonstrated General Beck's influence, but General Conrad's changes to Beck's plans would be assimilated into the Operation Bureau's plans for 1908-1909 and 1909-1910. These alterations were based primarily on intelligence reports and captured material detailing Russian war plans against the Dual Monarchy. These reports led to the conclusion in 1907-1908 that in case of mobilization, enemy forces deployed in the area west of the Vistula River would consist only of cavalry and small infantry units, while major formations would be deployed only east of the Vistula River. The main Russian forces were expected to operate in the Russo-Polish provinces of Volhynia and Podolia.

This new information led to a 1907 revision of Conrad's "War Case R" strategy.[5] Political assumptions for war planning against the Russian empire were solidly based upon the alliance with Germany; Romania was expected, at best, to be an active ally or, at worst, to remain neutral. Italy, another ally, might be expected to remain neutral. France would most likely attack in an Austro-Hungarian war with Russia.

According to Austro-Hungarian intelligence reports, the Russians would field an army comprised of at least twenty corps. Nine of these would undoubtedly be sent against Austria-Hungary and the remaining eleven would be directed against Germany. This figure did not include four additional enemy corps which could be shifted against either of the Central Powers. Assuming that the Russian V Corps in Warsaw would be used against the Germans, a maximum of three additional corps, a total of twelve, would face the Austro-Hungarian army - three more than anticipated in 1902.[6] Conrad's operational plans called for the deployment of fourteen corps to be directed against Russia. The key assumption in Conrad's thinking was that Germany would enter the fray by the terms of the Dual Alliance. If Germany would intervene, she might have to conduct a two-front war against France and Russia. The military agreements supposedly still in force between the allied general staffs in 1907 were those devised in the days of Beck and Schlieffen. These agreements had committed Germany to field five corps and eight reserve divisions against the Russian Empire. It must be recalled, however, that there had been no direct contact between the two commanders since 1897. The validity of these figures was therefore questionable.

Three possible Russian military deployments were examined by the Operations Bureau. The Austro-Hungarian General Staff calculated in 1907 that the most likely possibility was the same one anticipated by General Beck in 1902, in "Variant A." Variant A pointed to a major enemy offensive south into Galicia from the Luck-Rovno-Dubno area where seven Russian corps were deployed. In coordination with these troops, a smaller Russian force was expected to strike from Lublin southward between the Bug and Vistula Rivers. From the Proskurov area at the eastern portion of the Bug River, an additional enemy force of two corps might be launched westward into eastern Galicia.[7]

"Variant B" consisted of a potential major enemy advance of eight or nine corps pushing southward into the region between the Bug and Vistula Rivers. Supporting offensives might then be initiated both from the area east of the Bug River and westward from Proskurov. This particular variant, because it required more time for deployment, posed a serious disadvantage to the Russians.

The third variant (C) was considered least likely because it would require the longest deployment time of the three. In this case eight or nine enemy corps would strike westward into eastern Galicia from the Proskurov area. An additional covering force of two corps could be anticipated to the north between the Bug and Vistula Rivers, and one to two corps could be anticipated from the Luck-Dubno-Rovno area.

To counter these three alternatives, Conrad favored the combination of German and Austro-Hungarian armies on the battlefield. The projected union of allied forces would occur as both armies advanced to the area between Warsaw and Brest-Litovsk. Conrad recognized the danger of a Russian attempt to outflank either ally. The threat to the Austro-Hungarian-German flank would have to be eliminated immediately. Overall operational planning, at the same time, would have to be flexible enough to meet any likely contingency. For Conrad, the solution to these problems was the establishment of army task forces to ward off the enemy units in the Proskurov area (Podolia) east of the Bug River (right flank), and from the Cracow area (left flank). The main Austro-Hungarian attack would then be launched between the Bug and Vistula Rivers after an initial assault eastward against Russian flanking forces in the Proskurov area. According to "Variant B," only if the enemy deployed between the Bug and Vistula Rivers would the main Austro-Hungarian thrust northward between the rivers commence immediately.

By necessity, Conrad's strategic planning against Russia was devised with an eye on developing enough flexibility to launch his major offensive northward between the Bug and Vistula Rivers as described; to push from further eastward in Galicia in a northerly direction against the Dubno-Luck area; or to allow for a major eastern flank thrust against Proskurov into Podolia.

Austro-Hungarian strategic planning for 1908-1909 and later years retained this emphasis on flexibility. In all three enemy variants, a weak Austro-Hungarian army would assemble at the middle San River region, and another army would assemble south of Tarnopol. These two army groups would provide the eastern flank security for the anticipated main offensive being deployed at Lemberg and east of Lemberg, an area embracing Lemberg-Kamionka-Strumilova-Zloczóv-Zborov.[8]

The advantage of such a grouping was that it simultaneously offered three choices for the direction in which a major offensive could move and counter Russian flanking possibilities. Thus, major offensives could be launched against the enemy in the Dubno-Luck-Rovno area, in the process being able to respond to "Russian Variant A." A main advance between the Bug and Vistula Rivers would nullify the enemy's "Variant B," while an advance eastward into Podolia against Proskurov would check "Variant C".

At this early date, Conrad introduced only two specific changes in General Beck's earlier plans. First, by shifting three infantry divisions from the left flank at Cracow to his First Army, he focused on a new maneuver area which ranged from Cracow to east of Tarnow. One cavalry and one militia division remained for the left flank operations in the western Vistula River area (adjacent to Cracow). The second, an organizational change, would expand the original three Austro-Hungarian armies at the Galician frontier into four. These were to be designated, left to right, the First, Fourth, Third, and Second Armies.

The assigned mission of these four Austro-Hungarian armies was chiefly a joint offensive by the First and Fourth Armies northward towards Lublin between the Bug and Vistula Rivers. The geographical location of these new groupings would enable the armies, when deployed, to advance either in a northern or northeastern direction. The newly-created Third Army (formed from one-half of the old Third Army) would move towards Rovno, while the new Second Army (approximately the other half of the old Third Army) would provide flank security to the east. The Second

Army would beat back the anticipated enemy attack from the Proskurov area and then join in the Third Army's battle.[9]

The uncertainty concerning Russian intentions had produced the Austro-Hungarian strategic necessity of forming a strong middle army group and weaker flank security forces. With German aid, these formations were supposed to counter first-line Russian forces totaling twenty-six corps, eight infantry brigades, and twenty-three cavalry divisions, supported by a second-line force of twenty-nine infantry and nine Cossack divisions.[10]

The flexibility of Conrad's strategic plans is noteworthy. Three distinct strike forces were made available for a two-front war. In a "War Case R+B" (Russia and Balkan), a reserve twelve-division swing group would be capable of launching a powerful offensive against Russia. A minimal Balkan defense force, called the Minimal Group Balkan, would safeguard possession of Austria-Hungary's Southern Slav provinces. This Minimal Group force, the Austro-Hungarian Fifth and Sixth Armies, contained about eight divisions. The major Galician defense force, thirty divisions strong, was to be known as the A-Group, while the twelve remaining divisions (the reserve swing group mentioned above) became the B-Group.

The A-Group, the B-Group, and the Minimal Group Balkan could be mobilized either independently or collectively. Thus, the Dual Monarchy could, if necessary, conduct partial mobilization against Serbia alone without mobilizing against Russia or Italy.

But while the flexibility of Conrad's arrangements was evident on paper, certain limitations restricted actual implementation of the plans. The key factor was the weakness of the Austro-Hungarian rail network. For example, if the partial mobilization against Serbia was effected and Russia threatened to intervene, insufficient rail transport lines would prevent the twelve-division B-Group (basically the Second Army) from reaching Galicia without a significant loss of time; the thirty-division A-Group would then have to counter a Russian offensive without reinforcements from the Balkan Theater for several weeks.

In spite of the rail network's obvious effects on troop flexibility, Conrad made no serious attempts to enlarge Austro-Hungarian rail capacity before 1911, and then only after the infusion of French funds allowed Russia to expand her own strategic rail network in the critical border areas. Instead, Conrad pursued his goal of confirming German assistance in the east, a crucial factor in all his operational planning. He believed that a German attack southward into Russian Poland would force Russia to divert enough troops from Galicia so as to render his A-Group capable of dealing with the remaining Russian forces alone. To this end, Conrad directed his correspondence to Moltke beginning in January 1909. The breakdown of Austro-Hungarian troop strengths in the potential 1908-1909 conflicts included "War Case B" (Balkan), with the B-Group (Second Army) and Minimal Group Balkan fielded that would contain twenty infantry and three cavalry divisions. Two cavalry divisions of the Galician A-Group added to the force would bring the total of involved forces to a little more than one-third of Conrad's forces. In a "War Case R+B" (Russia and Balkan), forty and one-half infantry and eleven cavalry divisions, the A and B Groups, would face Russia, while only eight divisions the Minimal Group Balkan, would fight Serbia and Montenegro.[11]

In the political realm, Aehrenthal, an ambitious diplomat, believed that "under the prudent quietism of his predecessor, Austria-Hungary had not played the role in Europe which was her due." He was well aware that to strengthen the position of Austria-Hungary in the Balkans by way of annexing the provinces of Bosnia-Herzegovina, he had to have Russian acquiescence.

In the meantime, Russian Foreign Minister Izvolskii visited Vienna from 25 September to 7 October 1907 in an attempt to find a favorable solution to the Straits question, which was vital to Russian interests. Aehrenthal's schemes to annex Bosnia-Herzegovina thus became linked with the Straits question. Pursuing this goal, Aehrenthal presented his view on the Bosnia-Herzegovina question on 1 December 1907 in a Joint Ministers' conference. The result was that the participants drafted conditions for an eventual annexation.

To allay European — and particularly Russian — fears of Austro-Hungarian expansion (expressed in the phrase "march to Salonika"), Aehrenthal, in return for toleration of the annexation of the two Balkan provinces, offered to give up the claims based on Article 25 of the Treaty of Berlin of 1878. This article granted the Dual Monarchy permission to maintain garrisons and to possess military and trading roads over the entire area of the Sanjak of Novibazar, which separated Serbia from Montenegro.

Before moving forward on Bosnia-Herzegovina and relinquishing the Sanjak rights, Aehrenthal approached Conrad on 17 December 1907. Conrad wholeheartedly supported the annexation of the two provinces and even called for the affiliation of Serbia with Austria, much as Bavaria was associated with the German Empire.[12] Max von Bülow, the German Chancellor since 1900, also supported Aehrenthal's plans. Izvolskii, the Russian Foreign Minister, was troubled, however, since Russia could no more tolerate a peaceful Austro-Hungarian penetration of the Balkans than a forceful takeover. Therefore, Izvolskii quickly announced that such an annexation would be contrary to the Austro-Russian agreements of 1897 and 1903. On the other hand, the Austro-Hungarian position was that Russia had conceded to the annexation in principle by the agreements of 1876, 1877, and 1881. Izvolskii then suggested to Aehrenthal in a memorandum dated 2 July 1908 that Austro-Hungarian acquiescence to the reopening of the Straits, closed to Russian warships since the Crimean War, might serve as *quid pro quo.*[13]

Aehrenthal leaped at the opportunity presented by his Russian counterpart to achieve his goal of annexation. The "Young Turk" revolution of 6 July 1908 precluded a great deal of diplomatic haggling between the two ministers since it raised the very real possibility that the new Turkish government would move to block Aehrenthal's aims. Prodded by the revolution, Aehrenthal decided that annexation must not be delayed, and he moved quickly to finalize the arrangement with Izvolskii and declare Austro-Hungarian sovereignty over the two provinces.

In a meeting of the Austro-Hungarian Ministers held on 19 August 1908, Aehrenthal presented his position and questioned Conrad regarding Austria's military situation. Conrad replied that Germany was secure as an ally and that Russia and Serbia were not prepared for war. He considered Italy the only potential military threat, but assured Aehrenthal that she could be handled.[14] The participants at the Joint Ministers' Council thereupon declared the proposed annexation of Bosnia-Herzegovina to be necessary in principle. At this juncture Aehrenthal relayed a positive reply to Izvolskii's memorandum of 2 July.

Upon receipt of the above communication, the Russian minister sought to meet with Aehrenthal at Buchlau, using his July memorandum as a basis for the meeting.

Although no written records exist, at the Buchlau meeting Izvolskii apparently agreed to the annexation. Russian compensation would certainly have been demanded in the form of the opening of the Straits. Aehrenthal, meanwhile, had encouraged the Bulgarians to proclaim complete independence from Turkey, in obvious violation of the 1878 Treaty of Berlin. Bulgaria's independence was announced on 5 October 1908, and Austria-Hungary proclaimed the annexation of Bosnia-Herzegovina a day later.

The Bosnian Annexation Proclamation raised a storm of indignation in Russia, where it was viewed as an arbitrary and unilateral action by the

Austro-Hungarian government. Because Russian public opinion had no inkling of Izvolskii's diplomatic activities and of what had transpired at Buchlau, the proclamation appeared to be aimed against the Slavic people.

The strongest reaction to the proclamation occurred in Serbia, when a military call-up of first-and second-line troops was ordered on 9 October. The result of the call-up was the mobilization of 120,000 Serbians and the creation of the *Narodna Obrana* [National Defense] society, which would later be mistakenly held responsible for the assassination of the Habsburg heir Franz Ferdinand.[15]

Izvolskii found himself in a very awkward position. Because his note of 2 July directly implicated him, there was no way he could deny active participation in the planning of the annexation. His English and French allies did, however, demand a conference of the Great Powers on the matter of the annexation and so provided Izvolskii with an opportunity to extricate himself from the predicament.

German Chancellor Bülow now threw Berlin's full weight onto the scale in Vienna's favor in order to prevent a solidification of the Triple Entente, to maintain the Austro-German Dual Alliance, and to humiliate Izvolskii, the primary figure in the formulation of the Anglo-Russian Entente of 31 August 1907. But Chancellor Bülow's efforts on behalf of Austria-Hungary irreparably damaged the relations between the Central Powers and Russia, which Bismarck had striven to render more cordial. Indeed, Bülow has been accused of laying the foundations of the 1914 catastrophe.

Bismarck, as previously mentioned, had authored the cardinal German diplomatic policy to prevent Austro-Russian conflict in the Balkans. In 1909, Bülow, contrary to Bismarck's plans, supported a proposed Austro-Hungarian attack on Serbia. He was convinced that such a war would remain localized due to Russia's military "unpreparedness" and political difficulties. Consequently, on 30 October 1908, Bülow handed a "blank check" to Aehrenthal by stating that "I shall regard any decision taken by you as imposed by circumstances"[16] — ironically, these words came from a professed admirer of Bismarck.

General Conrad, on several occasions in 1908, had insisted that he had to coordinate military planning with Moltke, since their previous brief encounters had not succeeded in establishing close cooperation or joint planning. Every one of Conrad's requests to cement this collaboration had been frustrated by the foreign office because Aehrenthal felt that the matter was not urgent.[17] But his attitude changed in 1908. In a letter of 8

December, Aehrenthal suggested to Chancellor Bülow that the Chiefs of
the General Staffs of both countries should have "a written exchange of
ideas on such an eventuality of war and should examine the hypothesis
of Italian neutrality" or "in the case of a Russian attack on Austria-Hungary, Italy would break her word and join our enemies." Bülow accepted
the suggestion and the proper instructions were exchanged.[18] By approv-
ing Moltke's reply to Conrad, dated 21 January 1909, both Bülow and the
Kaiser, in effect, endorsed a plan for German mobilization if Russia should
intervene against Austria-Hungary after the latter had attacked Serbia.

In the meantime, Serbo-Montenegrin-Austro-Hungarian friction concerning the annexation produced the threat of war in January 1909. In the
Dual Monarchy, the question arose as to when the time would be right to
settle accounts with the troublesome South Slav kingdoms. The pressure
of the military for an immediate war allowed the belief that Russia and
Italy would be less prepared for hostilities in 1909 than a few years later.
Conrad himself believed that the final resolution of the South Slav question would be a means of revitalizing Austria-Hungary after a thirty-year
period of stagnation.

With any military action before 1 March 1909 unthinkable, Archduke
Franz Ferdinand, heir apparent to the Austro-Hungarian thrones, received
a letter from Tsar Nicholas II on 7 December 1908. The Tsar stated that
Russia would not enter a military conflict over Bosnia. But the Tsar's
stated position failed to deter Conrad's insistence on joint consultations
with the German military leaders. In pursuit of this very objective,
Aehrenthal had contacted his German counterpart, Bülow, about opening
channels for military exchanges.[19]

Conrad therefore commenced correspondence with his German counterpart Moltke in a letter dated 1 January 1909. Conrad stressed the
necessity for mutual consultation, particularly if Russia should intervene
in the Balkans against Austria. Since Russian intervention would presumably constitute the *casus foederis* for Germany (by the terms of the Dual
Alliance of 1879), Conrad sought clarification of the military measures
Germany would take if she launched a preventive war against France or
if she were attacked by France. Conrad considered it of the utmost importance to know what Germany's attitude would be and what military cover
she would provide for the Monarchy in such circumstances.[20] Conrad
wanted to know the precise number of troops which Moltke would use to
strike both France and Russia in an allied conflict. He regarded this
information as vital to Austro-Hungarian decisions regarding their own

potential two-front struggle and would, in fact, decide which of two possible courses of action Austria-Hungary should take.

One alternative was to strike a decisive blow against Serbia in the Balkans while holding Russia off until German forces were freed from the French war theater. The other alternative was to position only a minimal force against Serbia while fighting in the Dual Monarchy's decisive battle against Russia. Conrad also mentioned that Romania was a very desirable ally since she might tie down the Russian Fifth (Bessarabian) Army and thus protect the Monarchy's extreme eastern right flank.

Conrad informed Moltke that he had prepared the military details for two possible alternatives. In a "War Case R," forty Austro-Hungarian infantry divisions would be fielded against Russian Poland as early as the twenty-second mobilization day. A small covering force of eight infantry divisions would be assigned to guard the Serbian frontier. In the event that Russia waited for Austro-Hungarian action, "War Case R" might be preceded by a "War Case B" against Serbia. This case proposed that if Austria-Hungary became committed in the southeast and was then threatened in Galicia, at least thirty infantry divisions would be immediately dispatched to the northeastern theater. Conrad assured an Austro-Hungarian offensive into Russian territory on the same twenty-second mobilization day, *if* Moltke would promise a corresponding German attack. If Austria-Hungary received notice to this effect, Conrad would then coordinate his deployment and strategy with Moltke's. Conrad also hinted that three months after his first mobilization day, he would be able to transfer eight to ten additional divisions to the Galician battle front. Of course, emphasis was placed on the necessity for German military support against Russia if Austria-Hungary was engaged in a two-front struggle against both Serbia and the Russian colossus.[21]

Two days after the dispatch of his letter to Berlin (i.e. on 2 January), Conrad pressured Aehrenthal to make a final settlement with Serbia immediately. He argued that within a two to four year period, the Italians and Russians would be strong enough to aid the Serbians and that war against all three powers would be impossible. On 23 January, Conrad announced preparations for a mobilization and for "War Case B."[22]

Written with the approval of Kaiser Wilhelm II and Chancellor Bülow, Moltke's reply to Conrad's letter of 1 January arrived on 21 January. Moltke supported Austro-Hungarian action and accepted Conrad's written concepts:

It is to be foreseen that the time will come when the equanimity
of the Monarchy in face of Serb provocation will come to an end.
Then nothing will remain but for her to enter Serbia. I think that
only an invasion of Serbia could, in the event, lead to active intervention by Russia. This would provide the *casus foederis* for
Germany. The ensuing military operations would be based on the
information given by Your Excellency that Austria-Hungary at the
beginning could not muster more than thirty divisions in Galicia
against Russia. The moment Russia mobilizes, Germany also will
mobilize, and will unquestionably mobilize her whole army.[23]

Moltke further emphasized that because of Russia's military and financial weaknesses and the threat of revolution, the Russian government
would likely avoid a conflict, although Russian public opinion might force
the Tsar's hand. Reassuring Conrad concerning their Italian ally, Moltke
stated that Italy would not intervene militarily in the Balkans, but if she
did, "I can assure you that Germany will consider the protection of the
rear of its ally as a self-evident duty." France, in Moltke's consideration,
was inclined to go to war. The Kaiser agreed with him.[24]

Because of the alliance of 1879, according to Moltke, Germany would
fulfill her treaty obligation to aid the Dual Monarchy in an Austro-Russian
war. If France remained neutral in an Austro-Russian conflict, Moltke felt
that no difficulties would arise in regard to Russia even if Austro-Hungarian forces should initially be committed to Serbia. He emphasized that
the main overall allied goal remained the annihilation of the Russian
armies.[25] If, however, France intervened, Moltke would strike one opponent with a massive concentrated attack, leaving only minimal forces to
defend against the second foe; a rapid decision on one front was the
objective. But a defensive posture against France would require so many
troops that sufficient forces would not then be available to obtain a decision against Russia. The vastness of the eastern operational areas, the
unfavorable Polish terrain, and the enemy's opportunity to withdraw into
her interior all favored an initial German assault in the west. Therefore,
consistent with Schlieffen's plan, the German strategy in a two-front war
was an overpowering flanking maneuver against France.

On the eastern front, Moltke estimated that the Russians would field
twenty-five infantry divisions (including seven reserve divisions), two
infantry brigades, and about twelve cavalry divisions against Austria-Hungary. Since the total Russian strength was calculated at fifty-four infantry

divisions, four infantry brigades, and twenty-one and two-thirds cavalry divisions, Moltke calculated that twenty-nine infantry divisions, nine cavalry divisions and two infantry brigades would face Prussia. With great confidence, General Moltke predicted that his armies would defeat France before the situation became critical on the Austro-Hungarian-Russian frontier. This confidence was based partly upon the anticipated slowness of Russian mobilization and Russia's difficulties in fighting on two fronts against both Germany and Austria-Hungary. Therefore, until the French were crushed, only small German contingents would be allotted to contain the Russians in the east. Believing that the French and Russians would not go to war over the Bosnian affair, Moltke accepted Conrad's proposed deployment of thirty divisions in Galicia in the unlikely case of a war against Russia alone.

Moltke confined himself to generalizations in this introductory letter. His main goal was to reassure Conrad of German cooperation in the event of a war with Russia. In no case was Conrad to deploy defensively in the Carpathian Mountains. Because the Schlieffen Plan called for a massive invasion of France, the small German forces in Prussia would be insufficient to prevent a determined Russian advance towards Berlin or industrially important Silesia; thus Austro-Hungarian aid was vital. Moltke calculated that an Austro-Hungarian invasion of Russian Poland would draw off large Russian contingents, thus providing Germany with the breathing space necessary for the defeat of France. But if Conrad assumed a defensive stance, the invasion routes into Germany's eastern provinces would be open to Russian forces. An Austro-Hungarian offensive was therefore an absolute necessity for Germany.

Moltke had, however, committed Germany to Austria-Hungary in case of a Habsburg war against Serbia. If Russia mobilized her forces, the *casus foederis* was created for the German nation as well. Such clear-cut assurances of support under the alliance as those contained in Moltke's reply were precisely calculated to assure Conrad of German support.[26] But in no way did the Conrad-Moltke correspondence result in the conclusion of a formal military convention. In the future, Moltke would refrain from outlining specific details, although he was pressured by Conrad to do so.

Some historians, examining the question of war guilt, faulted Moltke for extending German treaty obligations to the extent that he promised military support for Austro-Hungarian machinations in the Balkans; Gerhard Ritter, on the contrary, argued that Moltke's correspondence "didn't really constitute the kind of carte blanche for any and every Balkan venture such as was given the Austrians in Potsdam on 6 July 1914." Ritter further noted that if anyone should be held responsible for the political commitment to Vienna, it would be Bülow. According to some historians, a General Staff agreement was concluded in January 1909, committing Germany to battle in case of an Austro-Hungarian-Russian conflict resulting from a war against Serbia. However, this agreement does not apply to Moltke's position in 1909, when there was no real threat of the weakened Russian military machine conducting war.

For Conrad, however, the letters were considered binding, as seen by his request for a confirmation by Moltke of the Austro-Hungarian-German plans in the first letter of each following year. It is questionable whether Moltke saw the letters as binding; they assured him of an Austro-Hungarian offensive which would tie down as many Russian troops as possible.

Aehrenthal was satisfied with Moltke's reply. Most significant to Aehrenthal was the assurance that Germany would support Austro-Hungarian actions in the Balkans. He thus felt confident that if Russia was threatened by Germany, she would not now interfere in the Bosnian crisis. Aehrenthal concluded that Izvolskii's threat of a Russian mobilization was merely a bluff, particularly since Germany had declared its intention to mobilize. The German Kaiser also expressed satisfaction with the first exchange of letters, stating that he hoped Moltke's first letter "would produce the desired impression in Vienna."

According to Conrad's calculations, communicated in a letter to Moltke on 21 January 1909, on their twentieth mobilization day, the Russians would send their First and Second Armies against Germany and their Third and Fourth Armies to check Austria. The Russians smaller Fifth Army would counter Romania. Twenty-seven infantry plus two reserve divisions would counter Germany; twenty-four infantry and three reserve would be sent against Austria-Hungary, and five and one-half infantry plus one reserve would face Romania.

Conrad's initial military strategy would be to strike the enemy armies northward between the Bug and Vistula Rivers with his major attack force. For the Balkans, he would station forces only sufficient to maintain Austro-Hungarian territorial possessions.

A second possibility assumed a neutral France with Russia restraining herself until Austria-Hungary became engaged militarily with Serbia, so that Austro-Hungarian troops could not be transferred immediately to the northeastern theater. To remedy this particular situation twenty-eight to thirty Austro-Hungarian infantry divisions would be deployed in Galicia

— assuming that Germany would field her main forces, which totaled more than thirty divisions, in the east. The result of this deployment would be an allied pincer movement into Russian Poland for which Conrad would deploy his forces between Tarnopol and the San River area.

A more difficult situation would find both France and Russia simultaneously going to war against Germany and Austria-Hungary. In this situation, Conrad would accept Germany's conducting its initial major operation, in Schlieffen fashion, against France. This situation naturally would leave additional enemy corps to be turned against Conrad's forces once the Russians ascertained the German grand strategy of rapid victory in the west.

Conrad further considered two different situations. An immediate deployment by the French and Russians was possible, or both armies could hold back until the Dual Monarchy had committed strong forces against Serbia in the Balkans. Conrad estimated that the first possibility, that of an immediate Russian deployment, would lead to success if Austro-Hungarian deployment could be accomplished by the twenty-fourth mobilization day and if the nineteen and one-half divisions of the Russian First and Second Armies were checked at the Prussian frontier by his ally, Germany.

Conrad reemphasized that the most hazardous situation would be Russia's holding off deliberately "until Austria-Hungary engaged considerable forces in Serbia without being able to withdraw them for use in Galicia." With only twenty-eight to thirty divisions then available for deployment in Galicia, no extra German aid could be expected while the German invasion of France was in progress.

This situation would become progressively more dangerous as years passed and Russia recouped the military damage suffered during the Russo-Japanese war. Numerical ratios at that time, 1908-1909, also showed that an Austro-Hungarian offensive northward would be conducted under unfavorable conditions, with a Russian superiority of from two and one-half to seven and one-half divisions. These calculations assumed that Germany's forces in East Prussia would tie down nineteen and one-half Russian field divisions and the three-division garrison of Warsaw. Conrad, considering these unpleasant contingencies and trying to force Moltke to commit more troops to the east, suggested that, under the circumstances, he would initially postpone an offensive from Galicia because his troops were committed to the Serbian front. Should he, Conrad, not wait until the cooperation of German forces was assured *after* their early victory over France before he invaded Russian territory?

Conrad inquired as to when, in the event of a two-front war, Moltke anticipated transferring troops from France to the Prussian frontier. Conrad sought to have at least twenty German divisions shifted by the thirty-fifth mobilization day, leaving fifty-one divisions to fight against France. If these additional infantry units were not available until the fortieth mobilization day, he intimated that he would draw back his own initial deployment to the line Bochnia-Neu Sandec-Bartfeld, with a weaker subsidiary force east of the Dukla pass in the Carpathian Mountains or at the San-Dniester line.[27] This threat to pull back the deployment of Austro-Hungarian troops was intended to displease Moltke - Conrad hoped that it would extract a German commitment favorable to his plans. Conrad further suggested the deployment of Austro-Hungarian troops at the San River mouth-Rudki line. From there, a surprise attack could be launched by his forces as the enemy began its own offensive thrust. The prospects of success for such an attack might well be improved by the participation of allied Romania. If Romania were to field her eight infantry divisions at Jassy, these divisions could strike the Russian Fifth Army and then wheel around to engage the Russian Fourth Army at its southern flank and rear.

Conrad's second letter closed with some crucial questions: exactly which German units would be utilized in the east during the major strike into France? Where would they be deployed, and how? Would they actually tie down nineteen and one-half Russian divisions? Where would German troops transferred from the west be deployed and how strong would they be?[28]

This letter was no more satisfactory to Moltke than Conrad's first letter. As in the earlier letter, Conrad sought to formulate a precise allied operational plan that would guarantee his own offensive success. Moltke's answer, like his earlier reply, avoided providing exact details, but encouraged Conrad to find an offensive solution to a Russian mobilization. Moltke constantly tried to forestall any agreement that would commit him to a fixed number of troops in the east or a precise plan of operations. In fact, the first concrete information supplied by Moltke was that his eastern Prussian Eighth Army would field a total of thirteen infantry divisions rather than the eighteen Conrad expected.

Accepting Conrad's data, Moltke replied to Conrad's second letter on 24 February. Moltke then stated that if France did not declare war and

Russia did, in a "War Case R," he would deploy thirty-seven German infantry divisions east of the Vistula River between Thorn and Gumbinnen by the twentieth mobilization day, whereupon an offensive would be launched immediately against both the Russian Niemen and Narev Armies. Noting that there was little likelihood of a war only with Russia, he nevertheless promised some additional troops in the event of such a war and proposed the Breslau-Ivangorod area as the most effective direction of German advance.

In the more likely circumstance of a two-front war against France and Russia, Moltke committed himself in writing to deploy thirteen divisions east of the Vistula River. This promise would be repeated often to placate Conrad, who was sure that these troops would be sufficient to engage nineteen and one-half enemy divisions. At the same time, an expected Russian invasion of Prussia would be countered by German offensives. Moltke agreed that the most difficult, but most likely, war case involved Russian intervention *after* the Dual Monarchy became entangled in Serbia. This scenario would be even worse if the German armies had already launched an invasion of France in accordance with the Schlieffen Plan, which would preclude effective aid against the Russian forces in Poland.

Answering Conrad's direct question about the shifting of German troops to the east, Moltke declared that, "here the enemy is also a determining factor," so, obviously, no precise formula could be determined. If France launched her own offensive, a German victory could be expected three weeks after mobilization. On the other hand, if the French assumed a defensive posture behind their fortress lines, a victory would take four weeks. Nine to ten days would have to be added to these figures to allow for troops to be transported to the east.

Moltke withheld from Conrad the exact location of German deployment in the east because of the "unknown factor" of enemy positions. Deployment might occur in Prussia, at the Vistula River, or in Posen. Conrad was assured, however, that "Austria-Hungary would not be let down." Moltke reaffirmed his view that in a two-front war the most pressing objective should be the defeat of Russia and France; in this way "the Serbian affair will solve itself as a matter of course." In the original copy of Moltke's letter, Conrad penciled the following remark: "certainly, but what am I to do if already tied down in Serbia?"[29] Moltke's purpose was obviously to inform Conrad that Germany had not forgotten the east and to placate him with assurances of confidence and support. Moltke realized that Germany's eastern rear flank had to be covered at all costs, but he hoped that protection would be at Austria's expense while Germany was battling in France. Moltke's notification that the decision in the west could be anticipated in three to four weeks, with the expected ten days for railroad transport of troops to the eastern front, provided a general timetable for Conrad, but Moltke had again avoided giving precise details. Until 1914, the only significant change in Moltke's calculations would be that he would estimate longer transport times as French military power grew — from four weeks initially to six weeks now — for significant German forces to be shifted to the east (sixtieth mobilization day when one added transport time).

Conrad must have been displeased with Moltke's reticence. He had intended to control the strategy in the eastern theater, and he had planned on launching an offensive against Russia even if Austria-Hungary was embroiled in a Balkan war. For Conrad's plans to be successful, German forces had to launch an offensive across the Narev River to tie down the First and Second Russian Armies. This German assault across the Narev River was intended merely to pin down enemy units, and not to initiate a major offensive into Poland as the Elder Moltke had planned. Nor would there have to be a direct connection between the allied Austro-Hungarian and German forces.

Conrad's answer to Moltke's letter, written on 3 March, sought more acceptable answers to his questions. The potential allied war cases were rehashed and Conrad accepted Moltke's 24 February promise of the dispatch of thirty-seven of the seventy-one German divisions in the east between Thorn and Gumbinnen in the event of a pure "War Case R." A German offensive could be expected on the twentieth mobilization day, and it was assumed that twenty-nine and one-half enemy divisions would be thus engaged, leaving only twenty-seven to encounter the deployed forty Austro-Hungarian divisions. The originally designated eight Austro-Hungarian divisions would serve as a "minimal" security force in the Balkans. Thirty-six Austro-Hungarian divisions could strike from Galicia on the important twentieth mobilization day. Conrad's expectation of Romanian participation remained unchanged: Romanian forces should neutralize the Russian Fifth (Bessarabian) Army. The Austrians would launch their main attack between the Bug and Vistula Rivers, anticipating a German thrust against the Narev Army.

Conrad reaffirmed his and Moltke's belief that a military decision against Russia would resolve his Balkan problems. He also acknowledged the figure of thirteen German divisions, which were earmarked for the east in the event of a two-front war. He stated that intelligence sources had indicated that of the presumed twenty-seven Russian divisions to be directed against Prussia, perhaps eight would be transferred to the Galician frontier once it was discovered how few German divisions had been fielded in the east. Conrad's forty divisions would then have to fend off thirty-five Russian divisions, while the thirteen German divisions would face nineteen and one-half.

In promising an Austro-Hungarian offensive from Galicia between the twentieth and twenty-fourth mobilization day, Conrad also urged Moltke to advance against the Russian Second (Narev) Army and thus cooperate with his own advance. Conrad also proposed that three German divisions be stationed at Insterburg to hold off the entire Russian First Army, and that the remaining ten divisions be launched across the Narev River to link up with his offensive. Moltke was not pleased with these suggestions.

In the most dangerous of all two-front war cases, that of Russia and France holding back until Austria-Hungary was involved in the Balkans, Conrad informed Moltke in his 3 March letter that he still planned to direct twenty-eight divisions offensively into Poland. He again acknowledged the German decision to earmark thirteen divisions for Prussia in such an event and to transfer troops from the west only after the thirty-eighth day of war.

Conrad further informed Moltke that an opening offensive was vital to a military success in the east, but that he would draw his troops back to the San-Dniester line unless Germany committed strong units in Prussia. His "decided dislike of any hesitancy" and his "conviction of the great value of the initiative" are cited by Conrad as reasons causing him to personally favor an offensive action. Most vital to his decision were Moltke's assurances of a German eastern offensive with a main thrust, ten divisions strong, aimed at the enemy's Second (Narev) Army. Conrad knew that the more the Russians were bogged down in northern Poland by the Germans and in Bessarabia by the Romanians, the fewer could be aimed against his own formations. If the Russians were so occupied, Austro-Hungarian success would be more likely.[30]

On the same day that Conrad sent this letter (3 March 1909), Moltke dispatched to Conrad a technical study on troop dispositions. In the case of a war with Russia, Moltke anticipated that twenty-one enemy infantry, ten reserve, and nine and one-half cavalry divisions plus two infantry brigades would be sent toward Prussia; and twenty infantry, six reserve, and twelve and one-half cavalry divisions plus two infantry brigades would be sent against Austria-Hungary. The Russian VII and VIII Corps (four infantry divisions), four reserve divisions (the 52., 53., 69., and 70.), and one cavalry division would probably be inserted at the Romanian frontier.

If the Russians indeed transferred troops from the Prussian frontier to the Galician, when they realized the Schlieffen Plan strategy, Moltke calculated that the total transferred would be thirteen and one-half infantry and three and one-half cavalry divisions. Eighteen and one-half infantry and six and one-half cavalry divisions would then be left to attack the German Eighth Army force of thirteen divisions. Moltke expected that the total Russian numbers needed to invade Galicia would be forty and one-half infantry and sixteen cavalry divisions. Reflecting upon the Bosnian crisis, Moltke reiterated his belief that France did not want war and that only Pan-Slavic pressures could force Tsar Nicholas II's government to intervene.[31]

Conrad's written acknowledgement of the Moltke technical study contained his repeated and adamant insistence that an offensive of ten German divisions be sent against the enemy's Narev Army to prevent significant Russian troop shifts to the Austro-Hungarian front. A joint allied advance would, Conrad insisted, certainly prevent large enemy undertakings across the left bank of the Vistula River. German strategy, therefore, would dictate where Conrad's units would be assembled: either forward of the San and Dniester Rivers, and near the frontier, or, less favorably, behind these rivers.

The central issue in the Conrad-Moltke correspondence had thus been broached. If the German eastern forces were to launch an early offensive across the Narev River, Conrad could attack from Galicia without regard to a simultaneous fight with Serbia. If Moltke chose not to attack in the north, Conrad threatened, the Austro-Hungarian fighting forces would assume a defensive stance along the Carpathian Mountains and the San-Dniester River line, encouraging the Russians to launch a massive drive along the open routes to Berlin and Silesia.

In a letter dated 19 March 1909, Moltke finally capitulated to Conrad's demand for an offensive. In a simple "War Case R," he promised an offensive with forty-five German divisions against the Russian Niemen and Narev Armies. To clarify his own position in the case of a two-front confrontation with France and Russia, Moltke wrote that the disposition of his Eighth Army in Prussia "was to be as the first line for the protection of the provinces east of the Vistula River." Whether the mission would be completed in an offensive or defensive manner would be the decision of the local commander. Since it was known that France had exacted obligations from Russia, Moltke assured his Austro-Hungarian counterpart that the Russian commanders would be incapable of shifting a large number of troops from the Prussian to the Galician frontier; the French would obviously want as many German troops as possible to be tied down in the east. Moltke then promised:

> I will not hesitate to make the attack to support the simultaneous Austro-Hungarian offensive. Your Excellency can count absolutely upon this assurance, which has been extensively considered . . . should the allies' intention be disturbed by enemy action, immediate reciprocal information is required.[32]

The German promise would also be valid if France and Russia initially held back from a war. Conrad's proposed northern offensive between the Bug and Vistula Rivers against the Third Russian Army could therefore count on German support in any eventuality. Yet such a German venture across the Narev River against enormous enemy numerical supremacy could be suicidal, and no advantage was likely to be gained from an offensive by a numerically deficient force. Moltke emphasized this fact in his letter to Conrad. He reiterated that the Eighth Prussian Army had a defensive mission to protect Prussian provinces. He added that recent Russian railroad construction indicated the probability of a major enemy attack into Prussia. Although Moltke knew that it was unrealistic to promise to invade Russian territory with ten divisions - retaining only three to ward off the entire Russian Niemen Army - he would do it anyway: "such an attack by weak forces must at all events overcome severe difficulties, it would be threatened on the right flank from Warsaw, on the left from Lomscha. I shall not hesitate to launch such an attack in support of the simultaneous Austro-Hungarian offensive."[33]

Moltke made this promise despite the fact that the chances for success of such undertakings were virtually nil. His acquiescence partially reflected the inability of both the allied diplomats and the military leaders to solve the problem of a two-front war. Certainly, Conrad was more concerned with the eastern front than was Moltke. For Moltke, the entire fate of any great continental war would be settled in the west. To promise an offensive across the Narev River, and even later to withdraw the offensive on the eve of war, mattered little to him, since he believed that the war would not be decided on that front in any case. But Conrad chose to base all future military planning decisions on the Moltke letter of 19 March and was surely surprised when, in 1914, Moltke decided against the Narev offensive.

Conrad's acknowledgement on 10 April 1909 of Moltke's promise for the German offensive brought his reciprocal word that he would deploy the preponderant weight of Austria-Hungary's armies against Russia, even if he was involved in a war against Serbia-Montenegro.[34]

In the meantime, the intensifying Bosnian crisis had caused Tsar Nicholas II to telegraph to the German Kaiser the prediction that any final estrangement between Russia and Austria-Hungary would certainly influence Russian relations with Germany. But the telegraph arrived too late. Bülow, the German chancellor, had resolved to achieve a great diplomatic victory even at the cost of irreparable damage to the relations between his country and Russia. On 21 March, the day before the Tsar's telegram arrived, Alfred von Kiderlen-Wächter, the acting Foreign Secretary, dispatched the famous "yes or no" telegram to his ambassador in St. Petersburg, that appeared to be a German war threat. The telegram included the following:

> We must be certain that Russia will return an affirmative answer to the Austro-Hungarian note and declare, unreservedly, her agreement to the abrogation of Article 25. Your Excellency will make clear to M. Izvolskii that we expect a definite answer: Yes or No; any evasive, involved, or vague answer would have to be regarded by us as a refusal. We would then withdraw and let things take their course; the responsibility for all further eventualities would fall entirely on M. Izvolskii after our making a last, sincere effort to be of service to M. Izvolskii in clearing up the situation in a manner acceptable to him.[35]

When Izvolskii received the démarche on 22 March 1909, he told his subordinates that the note would have to be accepted. The reasoning was simple: a rejection would leave Serbia at the mercy of Austria-Hungary. In addition, Russia's allies, France and England, were not prepared to fight, and Russia might face attack herself. Therefore, the Tsar had no recourse but to approve Izvolskii's decision, and he did so on 23 March.[36]

In Berlin, Russia was not expected to act, even though an Austro-Hungarian invasion of Serbia seemed imminent. On 27 March, Kaiser Wilhelm II wrote Tsar Nicholas II that Serbia's provocative stance might force Austria-Hungary to take military measures against Serbia and that the

German government would not be able to exert pressure on the Austro-Hungarian government.

Also on 27 March, Conrad, in a discussion with Franz Joseph, insisted on taking military action against Serbia. He asserted that Italy, Russia, and France were militarily unprepared, that England did not favor war, and that Romania was an ally. Conrad concluded with the familiar argument that Austro-Hungarian military inactivity would be to Russia's advantage. At a Council of Ministers meeting on 29 March, presided over by Aehrenthal, Conrad was granted a partial mobilization for "War Case B." Obviously, even Aehrenthal now expected war.[37]

Aehrenthal, however, quickly changed his course when he realized fully the degree to which Franz Joseph and Franz Ferdinand opposed conflict. The foreign minister was also forced to admit that the Austro-Hungarian national differences in the empire precluded a drastic solution to the South Slav problem. But recognizing this problem did not prevent him from stepping on Izvolskii's toes by his circulation of a brief memorandum to London, Paris, Rome and Berlin. This memorandum contained the very documents exchanged between Vienna and St. Petersburg in November and December 1908.

On 10 March the government of Serbia declared that it had no intention of causing a war. Belgrade promised to maintain good neighbor relations with Vienna on reciprocal terms. On 31 March, Serbia accepted the course of events, undertaking to halt her opposition to the annexation of Bosnia-Herzegovina.[38]

The Bosnian Crisis was now, for all practical purposes, concluded. The Central Powers had achieved a decisive diplomatic victory. Izvolskii had not only been personally humiliated, but Russia had also been forced to back down while her allies, England and France, did nothing. The Austro-Hungarian and German Kaisers exchanged congratulatory letters.

An unwelcome after-effect of the crisis was the distinct worsening of Austro-Hungarian-Russian relations. Between them, Aehrenthal and Izvolskii had destroyed the Austro-Hungarian-Russian "détente" which had preserved a kind of diplomatic balance in the Balkans since 1897; they had brought their countries face to face in what proved to be a mortal duel, and they had poisoned their future personal relations with bitter personal antagonism.

Growing Russo-German antagonism was a further development of the Bosnian Crisis. Bülow's bullying of Izvolskii had led to unforeseen and serious consequences. According to the German Ambassador to Russia, "the legend [that] Germany threatened her (Russia) with the 'mailed fist' finds credence in wide circles and has for the moment made feeling run high against us, even in circles usually well disposed towards us."[39] Another step had been taken on the long road to German-Russian hostility.

As to whether the Bosnian Crisis had been a truly astounding victory, both Conrad and Moltke had serious misgivings on this point. Conrad, in particular, felt that the moment for decisive action had slipped through his fingers. Although an apparent diplomatic success had been won, the last chance to settle accounts with Serbia had been lost. He therefore looked towards the future with great anxiety.[40]

Conrad's argument during the crisis had been that Russia, France and Italy had not been prepared for military action in 1909, but that with each year the advantage would swing further to their side. Vienna had thus missed a chance to settle the matter once and for all. Now the future pointed to the danger of a multi-front war "all because of the diplomats!"[41]

Moltke, too, foresaw the future in this fashion. In a letter to Conrad on 14 September 1909, he regretted that a chance had been lost for what he considered a successful local conflict between Austria-Hungary and Serbia. Settling the conflict would have strengthened the monarch internally and achieved a supremacy in the Balkans. Further, Moltke asserted that even if Russia were to enter an Austro-Serbian conflict producing a European war, the Central Powers' chances for a favorable outcome had been better in 1908-1909 than they would be in a few years.[42]

The exchange of letters between the Austro-Hungarian and German general staffs during the Bosnian Crisis, meanwhile, had ended the previous lack of communication between Generals Schlieffen and Beck. Closer military ties were established, political assumptions and military possibilities reviewed, and salient points agreed upon — at least on the surface. But a Austro-Hungarian-Serbian conflict in which Russia was actively involved seemed destined for some time in the future. France and Germany could be ensnared by treaty into participation in such a war, while Italian neutrality and Romanian support were anticipated.

Militarily, Austria-Hungary and Germany had agreed that Germany would initially seek the major battlefield decision against France, deploying only thirteen divisions in the east to support her ally's planned offensive, thus tying down nineteen and one-half Russian divisions by launching an offensive across the Narev River.

In Russia, the immediate effect of the Bosnian crisis was to encourage a crash program to rebuild the military so weakened by the Russo-Japanese war. Further humiliation could only be prevented by military power. The emphasis on strengthening the Russian military machine would have an undue influence on July 1914 events. A later showdown might have a different climax. Although England and France had not duly supported Russia in the crisis, Germany's uncompromising attitude had produced the Austro-Hungarian diplomatic victory. This, the Russians could not forget.

Serbian ambitions in Bosnia-Herzegovina were also temporarily curtailed because Serbia had not received support from Russia. A circular from the July 1909 Pan-Slavic conference in St. Petersburg suggested that Russia reorganize her military forces and internal structure, so as to prepare to "take up energetically her mission as protectress of the Slav world . . . certainly in two or three years at the most the time will come when the Slav world, under the leadership of Russia, must strike the great blow."[43] The future would decide the next round; Serbia prepared for her chance, while it could be expected that in a future "War Case B", Russia would enter the conflict.

The Bosnian Crisis had also witnessed another serious blow to the territorial integrity of Turkey. At the same time, a deep rift had been created in Austro-Hungarian-Italian relations. This rift was widened by the Racconigi Agreements between Italy and Russia, according to which Italy would support Russia's aspirations in the Straits in return for Russia's acquiescence to Italy's planned conquest of Tripoli.

CHAPTER IV

Strategic Planning and Military Agreements 1909-1914

Between the Bosnian Crisis of 1908-1909 and the outbreak of the Balkan Wars of 1912-1913, few extraordinary diplomatic events affecting eastern European affairs occurred. The only exceptions were the Russo-German meeting in Potsdam in 1910, and the Tripoli War in 1911-1912. Both events were overshadowed by the Autumn 1912 Balkan eruptions, which constituted the second step towards a major war in eastern Europe.

There was a great deal of activity, however, in the realm of military planning and preparations. In theory, Conrad's thoughts for a two-front eastern war, i.e., "War Case R+B," would continue to incorporate the Schlieffen idea of initially advancing with a preponderant force against one enemy, while stationing only the most necessary subordinate units to counter the second. After the main enemy armies (Russian) had been annihilated, the bulk of the forces would be sent to fight the secondary opponent (Serbia-Montenegro). The rapid growth of railroads had inaugurated this concept of shifting entire armies from one battle front to another.

At the same time, the military dogma had evolved that rapid deployment was the most vital factor for achieving an initial military success. In this strategy, the major problems to be resolved in a two-front confrontation were which of the two enemy forces would be the most dangerous; which should be countered first; how many troops would be sufficient to guarantee success against the major opponent; how many should parry the second one; what role fortresses should assume; and how best to protect deployment railroads in the event of enemy advances.

It could be foreseen that in a major war the Russians would launch forays over the frontier to disrupt the mobilization of Austro-Hungarian units. Conrad strove for more rapid operations readiness in order to launch an early Austro-Hungarian offensive before the enemy had the capability to maneuver in large numbers and to preclude massive Russian cavalry raids across the Galician frontier.

As Russia was by far the most powerful potential Austro-Hungarian foe, Conrad's reasoning suggested that a success against her would lead to an overall victory in any two-front war. Favoring Austro-Hungarian chances for a victory in a war conducted in 1909-1910 was the continuing slow Russian rebound from the devastating military effects of the defeat in the Russo-Japanese War.

Several factors, however, might forestall a contemplated success for Conrad — foremost was the ability of the Russians to avoid a decision in Russian Poland simply by withdrawing into Russia's vast interior. In the event of war against Russia, Conrad's cardinal strategic principle was a rapid thrust into Poland before enemy mobilization could be completed and the enemy's unlimited manpower inserted.

Also difficult was the probability that Germany, herself engaged in a two-front war with France and Russia, would commit only a small number of troops to the east. The Russian armies facing Austria-Hungary could then total forty to forty-three divisions, while the Monarchy could field only twenty-eight to counter them if also initially engaged against Serbia-Montenegro in the Balkans.[1]

These considerations prompted Conrad to suggest to Moltke that it was possible in a two-front conflict he (Conrad) might have to delay an initial advance into enemy territory because of the obvious numerical disadvantage against the Russians. Conrad had also developed a plan for the German and Austro-Hungarian armies in the east in the event that France did not intervene in a war which involved Russia — to immediately hurl an assault deep into enemy territory to destroy her armies.

Although a restriction of Austro-Hungarian strategic aims appeared necessary, in order to spare troops Conrad remained firm in his conviction that only an opening offensive against Russia would both prevent the danger of encirclement by enemy forces numerically superior to his own, and ensure that he retained the military initiative. In any event, he reasoned realistically that without an Austro-Hungarian offensive, the numerically small German eastern army would be completely overpowered.

The Austro-Hungarian strategy for "War Case R" that evolved in the summer of 1908, based partially on captured Russian war plans, would remain the basis for Conrad's war planning until 1912-1913. It involved the deployment in Galicia of the following four armies: a left-flank army of four corps (twelve divisions), the First Army; a left middle army of approximately three corps (nine divisions), the Fourth Army; a right middle army of four corps (twelve divisions), the Third Army; and a right-flank army of at least two corps (six divisions), the Second Army.[2]

At the outbreak of a conflict, a strong left-flank force, the Austro-Hungarian First and Fourth Armies, would advance north as rapidly as possible between the Bug and Vistula Rivers towards the fortress of Lublin. The advantages to be gained by such an initial offensive included the assurance of providing security for the important land routes to Vienna, Budapest, Berlin, Breslau and Posen; it also would draw enemy formations southward into battle, providing freedom of movement for a possible retreat of Austro-Hungarian forces westward if it became necessary, it assured easy liaison with German forces; and it would help reduce the enemy's potential enormous numerical advantage by creating a united allied front.

The two right-flank Austro-Hungarian armies, the Third and Second, would initially ward off flanking threats from the easternmost frontiers of Galicia. They would then proceed northward and attempt to encircle the Russian divisions deploying in the vicinity of Rovno.

The Second Army, whose units composed the majority of the twelve-division strong swing force or B-Group, would initially be deployed in the Balkans in the event of a pure "War Case B." The Second Army was also designated to provide the vital right-flank security in Galicia for threats from the Luck-Kovel area in a pure "War Case R," but this scenario would leave a significant power vacuum at the Galician right flank if the Second Army became committed in battle in the Balkans at the outset of a simultaneous Russian conflagration.

In the most likely case during this period of a war with Russia and Serbia-Montenegro, only twenty-eight to thirty Austro-Hungarian infantry divisions and seven and one-half cavalry divisions (the A Group) could be deployed in Galicia. Eight or nine additional divisions could be made available from the Balkan theater approximately three months after a victory over Serbia-Montenegro had been attained. In this particular military situation, Germany would undoubtedly have to cope with both France and Russia.

According to the Schlieffen Plan, a covering force of thirteen German infantry divisions could be retained in the east with the mission of tying down nineteen and one-half enemy divisions. Five additional reserve divisions, dependent upon promised Italian aid actually being deployed at the Rhine, might be deployed in the east. General Moltke had earlier informed Conrad that he anticipated a military decision in the battle against France on the twenty-first mobilization day *if* France launched her own offensive into Germany, or on the twenty-eighth mobilization day if the French armies defended themselves behind their border fortresses. Calculating railroad transport time into Moltke's equation, it was impossible that German forces being retransported to the eastern front could arrive in Prussia before the forty-first mobilization day.

An Austro-Hungarian military consideration was that if the only enemy formations assembled between the Bug and Vistula Rivers were subordinate ones, then Conrad's two left-flank armies, after defeating the Russians in that area, would be released to advance northeastward against the Russian troops at Rovno. The right middle army (the Third) would then launch an offensive to counteract the Russian Rovno Army as soon as the cooperation of the left middle army (the Fourth) had been secured. The far right-flank deployed Second Army, fielded at the Sereth River, had the assignment of right-flank security for the entire inaugural operation. If this army was capable of dispersing threats from the enemy bastion in the vicinity of Proskurov, it would join forces with the other three armies advancing northward.

Romania, an ally since 1883, would, it was assumed, assemble her forces which were eight divisions strong in the region of Jassy, to prepare an offensive against the Russian Fifth (Bessarabian) Army. At the same time, Conrad hoped that the Romanian advance he anticipated might also tie down the enemy VII (Crimea) Corps. Optimistic Austro-Hungarian speculation also envisioned these same Romanian units intervening against the Russian Proskurov Army at the easternmost Austro-Hungarian flank, while further of the allied second-line units would protect the Danube River (towards Serbia) to prevent any enemy sallies from the lower Danube region.[3] A German deployment in East Prussia and a Romanian one in Moldavia, by providing protection on both extreme Austro-Hungarian flanks, would enable Conrad to assemble his deploying armies forward of the positions otherwise possible. Major Russian deployment concentrations countering the Austro-Hungarian armed forces could be anticipated in the Russian provinces of Volhynia and Podolia. The peculiar configuration of the Galician frontier presented the Russian generals with a tactical advantage: Galicia curved in a semicircle from the mouth of the San River to the Zbrucz River, which would enable the Russians to attack the province from two directions and so possibly encircle the Austro-Hungarian forces.

It was calculated that the Russians could field fifty-four to sixty-two infantry divisions, four infantry brigades, and twenty-one and two-thirds cavalry divisions against both Germany and Austria-Hungary. The Russian generals, it was postulated, would probably relegate twenty-nine infantry divisions, two infantry brigades, and nine cavalry divisions to counter Germany, while the remaining twenty-five to thirty-three divisions, two infantry brigades, and twelve to eighteen cavalry divisions would be pitted against the Austro-Hungarian Empire.[4]

Meanwhile, Austro-Hungarian intelligence sources indicated a possible rearward (to the north) and southward shifting of Russian troop concentrations. These reports were substantiated by both the build-up of Russian railroad lines leading to the Austro-Hungarian frontier areas and the improvement of the fortresses Rovno-Dubno-Luck. Completion of the rail line connecting Szepitiovka and Kamieniec-Podolsk might possibly facilitate the transfer of major Russian forces to their important southern flank. This would ultimately increase the already serious threat to Conrad's easternmost flank. Ascertaining whether enemy troop concentrations would continue in the surmised areas or be shifted as indicated became a vital concern of Conrad's Operations Bureau's planning. If the Russian railroads in Podolia continued to be improved significantly, it would pose an increasingly serious military threat to any right-flank grouping of an Austro-Hungarian deployment.[5]

Following the conclusion of the Bosnian crisis, Conrad reopened contacts with his German counterpart, General Moltke, in a letter on 8 January 1910. His introductory remarks expressed confidence that the allied "agreements" of the preceding year had retained their validity.

Conrad related that in the case of a military conflict, he counted on Romania as an ally, while he anticipated Turkey and Bulgaria would neutralize each other. Conrad's old fear of his ally Italy also reappeared: for a potential War Case "I & R" (Italy and Russia), he planned that only subordinate units would be assigned to counter Russia and Serbia.[6] Conrad still assumed that Russia could not pose a major military threat yet, so he concentrated on allied Italy to be the major potential opponent in a war.

That Conrad was so obsessed with defeating Italy first in an armed conflict was indicated by his willingness temporarily to sacrifice even the heartland of the Empire to a Russian advance. He continued to assume that Germany would field thirteen divisions in East Prussia to guard her exposed eastern flank while the bulk of her armies invaded France. After both Italy and France had been disposed of in a two-front conflict, Conrad reasoned that the Central Powers would turn their combined forces to the east against Russia in order to regain whatever territories might have been lost in the interim.

Moltke began his reply to Conrad's correspondence of 30 January 1910 with assurances of the viability of the 1909 allied agreements: "I regard these agreements as binding; they retain their validity until they are changed or replaced by the consent of both parties. They have been made the basis of this year's mobilization arrangement."[7]

Moltke also accepted Conrad's written affirmation of Romanian fidelity, noted the increasingly important role Turkey would play in the Balkans in the future, and recognized Conrad's calculations for a "War Case R+I+B." Moltke then turned his attention to France. He stated that if a war broke out in the east and France initially held back, then the German government would demand from the French government a comprehensive and clear declaration as to how France would react. The "immediately given" answer would provide the decision as to which front the German army's main forces would initially advance. Moltke further asserted that "an evasive or ambiguous answer would be considered tantamount to a declaration of war," however, in the case of a declaration of French neutrality, it would be respected.

Conrad, in each succeeding year, would require Moltke to acknowledge the previous communications regarding military planning. In 1910, in his annual memorandum, Conrad specifically referred to "binding written agreements" with the German ally. These "agreements," he asserted, constituted the *casus foederis* for Germany even if the situation should arise that the Dual Monarchy initially attacked Serbia, which would lead to the mobilization of Russia. Conrad's actions in July 1914 would be based on the above assumption, and on the fact that the German military would have to accept the risk of a war with Russia if they encouraged Austria-Hungary to attack Serbia.

Conrad transmitted information concerning these letter exchanges with Moltke to Aehrenthal on 7 February 1910. The foreign minister thus learned that the commanding generals had agreed that in a war in which Austria-Hungary, Germany, and Romania were opposed by France, Russia, Italy, and Serbia-Montenegro (War Case "R+I+B"), Austro-Hungarian troops would attack Italy first. Conrad also informed Count Aehrenthal that he welcomed an understanding with Russia in order to cover his rear flank and so free him to act against Italy, which he saw as a greater threat to the Empire than Russia itself.

In a letter written on 23 February 1910, Conrad then accepted the points that Moltke enumerated in his 30 January letter. On 30 March, in reply, Moltke expressed satisfaction that Romania would, in a war, assume the offensive into Bessarabia; and on 9 April, Conrad reaffirmed to him a commitment by the Romanian Chief of Staff to deploy his own forces in the Moldova region in the event of an eastern war.

In diplomatic circles, changes in key personnel after the Bosnian Crisis of 1908-1909 included the selection of Theobald von Bethmann Hollweg as successor to Prince Bülow (July 1909) in the German Foreign Office and Chancellery, and that of Sergei Sazonov (September 1910) as replacement for Russian Foreign Minister Izvolskii. The only serious contact between diplomats from major eastern powers relative to the Balkans occurred in 1910 when Bethmann Hollweg and Kiderlen-Wächter of Germany participated in discussions at Potsdam with Sazonov. Bethmann Hollweg, desiring a closer tie to St. Petersburg, stated that if Austria-Hungary harbored actual expansionist plans in the Balkans, Germany was neither bound nor inclined to support her.[8] Sazonov thus left from the meeting convinced that Germany had no obligation to support Vienna in any expansion policy in the Balkans. Aehrenthal, learning of Germany's reluctance only after the fact of the Potsdam meeting, immediately recognized that the Germans were attempting to impress the Russians with the fact that they did not unconditionally support Austria-Hungary in the Balkans.

In military circles, concrete Austro-Hungarian war preparations for 1910-1911 included "War Case R" — a war against Russia with Germany and Romania as allies, Italy neutral, and minimal forces arrayed against Serbia and Montenegro; "War Case I" — a war against "allied" Italy with Germany and Russia neutral and only minimal forces facing Serbia-Montenegro; and "War Case B" — a war against Serbia and Montenegro with the neutrality of all remaining states and the maintenance of defensive forces against Italy or Russia. If Russia intervened in a "War Case B," it was felt that Italy could be an additional opponent; thus "War Case I+R," the most unfavorable conflict possibility for Vienna, was to be avoided at all costs. The Austrians obviously did not have the necessary forces to counter the possible three-front "War Case R+I+B,"; thus the chief Austro-Hungarian diplomatic goal became the avoidance of such a constellation.[9]

In the strategic planning for "War Case R," it was decided that only minimal forces would be dispatched to the Balkans. Moltke and Conrad agreed that if Russia were eliminated as a foe, the Austro-Hungarian Balkan problem could easily be solved. At this time, Conrad realistically admitted the sheer impossibility of simultaneously attaining a favorable decision in the Russian and Balkan war theaters, since Austria-Hungary simply lacked the military means. An action instituted first against Russia, on the other hand, might incur an instantaneous Serbo-Montenegrin reaction, which is exactly what the Operations Bureau expected; yet no concrete plans existed for such a simultaneous outbreak of hostilities with Russia and Serbia-Montenegro, nor for a war in the Balkans culminating in an immediate Russian intervention. Though examined by the Operations Bureau, these specific strategic problems would not be satisfactorily resolved by August 1914, a delay which would create the catastrophic military situation that will be examined in detail later.

In the Operations Bureau, meanwhile, intelligence reports suggested that a new Russian Central Army, composed of five corps, had been created by the strengthening of the military districts of Kazan and Moscow with troops drawn from other areas. If the reports proved correct, approximately six infantry and two cavalry divisions had been transferred to this central army. All indications thus led to the Operations Bureau's conclusion that in the event of the outbreak of war there would be a withdrawal of the Russian deployment deeper into Russian Poland away from the region west of the Vistula River to the Bug River area.[10]

If accurate, these reports further signified to Viennese Operations Bureau planners that in a mobilization period, the Russians would evacuate the area west of the Vistula River, leaving only cavalry and infantry brigade size units, while withdrawing their major infantry concentrations further into the interior of Russian Poland. The same intelligence sources indicated that Russian troop strengths at the northeastern Galician frontier, in the area extending from Sokol to Tarnopol southward along the eastern borders, continued to be significantly increased. This increase indicated a further threat to Conrad's easternmost flank. These potential changes in Russian troop locations and the possibility of a withdrawal from the area of their Vistula forts also caused Conrad to anticipate a two-pronged enemy advance in a war.

The Dual Monarchy's military planners, accepting the above possibilities, realized the necessity of creating and expanding railroad connections to eastern Galicia in order to hasten the assembly of their troops on their right flank. Year by year the lack of a sufficient rail network to the badly exposed eastern Galician flank became more obvious, but nothing was ever done to satisfactorily alleviate the situation.

Since the disastrous and humiliating Russo-Japanese War, a great re-organization had meanwhile been initiated in the Russian military machine. A new tendency, which emphasized quality rather than quantity, evolved in the Russian General Staff. Thus Russia's twenty-four reserve divisions reputedly had been consolidated into seven compact first-line infantry divisions, which signified that Russia now possessed seventy-eight first-line infantry divisions. Although not actually representing a numerical increase in manpower, the overall quality of her fighting forces had significantly improved.

Russia had not, however, recovered sufficiently from the war against Japan to participate actively in a Balkan war in 1910-1911. But Austro-Hungarian intelligence sources appeared to confirm a possible Russian deployment for 1910-1911 against the Dual Monarchy, comprised of thirty-two infantry and seventeen and one-half cavalry, eleven reserve, two and one-half third-line divisions, and perhaps the VII Crimean Corps. Twenty-nine and one half-infantry, fifteen and one-half cavalry, three reserve and one third-line infantry division could be expected to be inserted against Germany.[11]

In strategic planning terms for an eastern war, geography favored the Russian planners. If Conrad's armies invaded Poland from eastern Galicia, they would be entering solid enemy territory with obvious threats to his flanking positions. Russian generals would also have the opportunity to encircle attacking Austro-Hungarian forces if the three assumed enemy groupings in the Cholm-Dubno-Proskurov line advanced in the direction of the Galician citadel at Lemberg. Because of the bow-like shape of the Galician frontier, the mass of the three Russian groups could unite on a common battlefield within seven to eight days after deployment. To counter this potential threat, Conrad devised a plan to initially launch a brief main battle between the Bug and Vistula Rivers against one of these groupings, while staving off the remaining two. Success for this strategy depended entirely upon a more rapid Austro-Hungarian operational readiness that would be more rapid than that of the Russians.

In the Austro-Hungarian strategic planning for 1911, a special directive reviewing possible Russian military alternatives became a keystone in future Operations Bureau calculations.[12] Whether the Russians planned to assemble the major portion of their armies in the area of Kovel-Rovno-Ostrog to the northeast with secondary forces around Proskurov, or whether they would place their major forces around Proskurov at the easternmost Austro-Hungarian flank with secondary units at Luck-Dubno-Rovno-Ostrog, remained the vital question. In the latter situation, as a counter move, the Austro-Hungarian commanders would deploy the bulk of their armies on the Sereth River around Tarnopol with the remaining formations opposing the attack directions from Dubno, Luck, Brody and Radziechóv. The key for planning purposes now and in the future would be a rapid and reliable assessment of Russian intentions and deployment plans.

If, however, available intelligence reports proved incorrect — with the main enemy deployment actually being assembled in the Dubno-Rovno region — a quite risky northern Austro-Hungarian offensive would be necessary against the areas of Luck-Dubno-Rovno-Ostrog. If such an offensive occurred and proved successful, then all or a portion of Austria's forces would then perform a giant wheeling movement in an eastern direction to continue military operations against Russia.

Regardless, it had become obvious that Austro-Hungarian railroad capacities had to be upgraded. The deployment lines in eastern Galicia could handle the transport of nine divisions through a twenty-fifth mobilization day. Pressing additional trunk lines into service could raise the total to sixteen and one-half divisions to meet the anticipated deployment of twenty-seven enemy divisions. Further adjustment of track usages for transport of troops could increase the transport ratio ratio to 21:27 divisions, but even this ratio was viewed as unacceptable by Conrad and his Operations Bureau.[13]

The main Austro-Hungarian offensive plan for a war in 1910-1911 (after examining the above possibilities) remained the advance of the two left-flank armies, the First and the Fourth, between the Bug and Vistula Rivers. The First Army would strike northward towards the objective of Lublin and the Fourth Army towards that of Cholm. The Third Army, middle right in the attack formations, would protect the main assault by parrying any enemy thrust towards it from the east. This mission would require the Third Army to attack towards Luck and Dubno, with its strong left-flank group forcing the opponent back into the Polosie swamps, thus separating this enemy force from the enemy Proskurov group in the process.

Further to the east, the Second Army's task required an offensive towards the area of Proskurov to prevent enemy advances from this easternmost flank region. The Romanian Army would guard the extreme

Austro-Hungarian right flank.[14] In detail, in "War Case R" forty infantry and nine and one-half cavalry divisions would counter Russian forces, and in "War Case R+B" twenty-six infantry and seven and one-half cavalry divisions would counter St. Petersburg's military moves. The difference in numbers in the two war cases of fourteen infantry and two cavalry divisions facing the Russians would be the result of a Balkan conflict coinciding with a war against Russia necessitating that fewer troops be dispatched initially against the northern adversary.

In the event of a Balkan war alone, fielding a military force strong enough both to guarantee a rapid success against Serbia and Montenegro and to create a free hand for possible further action was essential. But if a Balkan war were to be followed immediately by a military confrontation with Russia after a "War Case B" deployment, the swing B-Group troops would have to be withdrawn from the southern theater and immediately dispatched to the northeast. In this situation, time became the crucial factor. Also to be taken into consideration was the potential political effect of military events in the Balkan arena upon the internal situation in the Dual Monarchy. A defeat at the hands of Serbia could have a disastrous effect upon Austro-Hungarian prestige and power in the Balkans. Taking this factor into consideration, a total of fourteen infantry divisions would be deployed for a war in the Balkans in 1910-1911. These unit numbers were judged adequate both to protect Austro-Hungarian Balkan territorial possessions and to prevent a potential military reversal. The problem of a two-front war in the Balkans and with Russia would plague Conrad and his Operations Bureau until the mobilizations had been completed in 1914, when this most likely but dreaded war situation had actually become a reality.

On 26 May 1911, Conrad forwarded to Moltke a routine inquiry about the possibility of war with Russia, explaining that his decision for a left-flank, two-army offensive northward from Galicia was a result of his desire to prevent Russia from severing his (Conrad's) forces from possible retreat routes to the main portions of the empire, and to preclude the threat of a Russian encirclement of his deploying armies. He also emphasized his intent to assemble his main forces in the middle of eastern Galicia (east of the San River) in order to launch a left-flank offensive. To support this intended action, he wanted a corresponding German force to advance into the region where the Bug and Narev Rivers meet. He wrote that he anticipated that Germany would field forty to forty-five divisions and Austria-Hungary forty in the unlikely case of a war breaking out only with

Russia. In the event of a two-front war, he expected that Germany would field only thirteen divisions in the east, while the mass of the remaining troops would be utilized to follow the Schlieffen plan's concept of a mass envelopment of the French armies.

Moltke's reply to Conrad's correspondence, dated 3 June 1911, affirmed his intention to field his eastern forces in the Narev-Niemen River region in order to tie down much of what was believed to be the Russian central army. But Moltke also expressed the fear that in the event of an allied advance, this central army might simply retreat into the Polish interior. Moltke also raised the possibility of an Austro-Hungarian right-flank advance (from eastern Galicia) to push Russian forces into the Pripjet marshes,[15] which would also serve to neutralize the threat to Conrad's right flank.

In a letter of 10 June 1911, Conrad reemphasized to Moltke the various problems involved in his deployment plans. Amongst these, Conrad cited a growing threat to his right flank positions in eastern Galicia and in addition, two separate enemy fronts now seemed likely in that portion of the war theater. Anticipated Russian troop concentrations also appeared directly to threaten the central bastion of Lemberg and the Tarnopol area as well.

Central Europe's key diplomatic event in 1910-1911 proved to be the Tripoli War. Tripoli, the last portion of North Africa open to conquest, became the goal of Italian foreign policy and imperialism. On 5 November 1911, following the outbreak of war between Italy and Turkey, Italian annexation of Tripoli was announced, creating a *fait accompli*. Germany's resentment toward allied Italy following this action was clear because of Berlin's growing concern over Turkish and Balkan affairs. The Balkan question had suddenly and violently been reopened.

Conrad, seizing an opportune moment for what he saw as the chance to settle accounts with both Italy and Serbia, raised a cry for the immediate military chastisement of both. He calculated that Russia's internal problems and her diplomatic controversy with England made her a doubtful participant in such a conflict. To achieve his aggressive ends, Conrad began more and more to meddle in Aehrenthal's jurisdiction — the Foreign Office. But what Conrad as military strategist had failed to realize was that the diplomats, both in Vienna and Berlin, were looking at these developments in an entirely different light. These men realized that African complications resulting from the Tripoli War would tend to divert Italian interests away from the Balkans and, in the process, arouse the ire of

England and France, thereby actually resulting in Italy's closer association with the Triple Alliance. Conrad's miscalculation and his annoying interference in diplomacy, as well as his insistence on a preventive war against Italy, led to his dismissal as Chief of the General Staff on 30 November 1911.

The new Chief of the General Staff, Blasius Schemua, immediately established contact with his counterpart Moltke. General Schemua, not deviating from Conrad's military planning, accepted the fact that the present allied military "agreements" would be binding for the future and indicated that the Austro-Hungarian preparations for "War Case R" for 1912-1913 would involve the most rapid preparation of the two armies of the Austro-Hungarian left flank for the launching of an immediate offensive. Schemua also acknowledged his own acceptance of Moltke's earlier promise to Conrad to dispatch thirteen infantry and two cavalry divisions to the east for their anticipated combined eastern offensive.[16]

In the following year, because the Balkan Wars had produced such a tense European situation, General Schemua and Archduke Franz Ferdinand traveled to Berlin to sound out possible German intentions. According to Schemua, Moltke assured him at an interview on 22 November 1912: "not of any hesitant offensive, but a powerful one parallel to ours.... he said repeatedly that we can rely absolutely upon Germany's support...if we are threatened by Russia."[17]

Moltke further claimed that in the event of an eastern war German troops would arrive in the east in four to five weeks, or by the fortieth mobilization day. He did not question or object to the contents of Schemua's earlier letter requesting his confirmation of all previous plans. On his return to Vienna, Franz Ferdinand reported that in Berlin he had met with great understanding and cooperation.

In the meantime, war planning preparations for a potential armed conflict in 1911-1912 generally followed the same pattern as 1910-1911. The Austro-Hungarian deployment planning for "War Case R" in 1911-1912, and the battle projection for 1912-1913, would be greatly influenced by the earlier mentioned anticipated Russian rearward deployment of its main military units from the western Vistula River area; by the reputed creation of the central army in the Moscow area; and by concurrent enemy railroad construction activity. These multiple considerations gave strong support to the desirability of altering Conrad's earlier preparations for a "swinging-up" of his First and Fourth Armies to the north and to the northeast.

Operations Bureau calculations for "War Case R" in 1911-1912 were based on these enemy contingencies, but they allowed room for some tactical elasticity. Thus the intended Austro-Hungarian offensive strike northward could also be adjusted toward the northeast in order to counter a possible enemy deployment there.[18] New objectives for the four armies' offensives became: for the First Army — Vladimir-Volynski; the Fourth Army — the Luck area; the Third Army — the area of Dubno; and the Second Army — the right flank region at Proskurov.

A rapid offensive would commence when the First, Fourth, and Third Austro-Hungarian Armies had reached the same tactical perimeter line in the area of Tarnopol-Brody-Hrubieszov. The timing for the attack depended on the First Army's travel time because it had to move the farthest before reaching its assault line, thus requiring seven more days than the other armies. It had also been calculated that by this time, the right-flank Second Army, its units possibly conveyed to the Balkan front in the event of a mobilization there and before a mobilization could have occurred against Russia, would have to have already been retransported to the northeastern theater to counter the more dangerous Russian enemy.

The most important alterations in the 1910-1911 deployment plan included a return to the earlier concept of establishing strong flank groups at the expense of the two central armies. Especially noteworthy was the assignment of stronger cavalry units (four divisions) to the left-flank First Army, in order to pinpoint the foe's right-flank positions and also to reconnoiter the area into which the First Army would actually advance. A further planning change resulted in the entire First Army's main forces now being fielded east of the San River, leaving only cavalry units west of the river. An offensive could then be launched northward, or northeastward, without the troops having to cross the river.[19]

The most significant anticipated enemy effect on Austro-Hungarian operational planning in this period was the possible shifting of significant numbers of Russian forces to be deployed at the extreme eastern Galician flank. This possibility arose from intelligence reports of the construction of further Russian deployment railroads toward eastern and northeastern Galicia which, according to sources, could be completed in 1913.[20] Additional intelligence reports of June 1911 also suggested that the overall Russian deployment might be shifted further southward, or as far as Kamieniec-Podolsk, a shift which would increase the threat to the right-flank area in the case of any of Conrad's deployment possibilities.

In Austro-Hungarian strategic war planning for 1912-1913, the main concerns had been the possibility of a "War Case R," or "War Case B," or both combined ("R+B"). The deployment calculations for a war only with Russia assumed that a conflict would commence without any preceding partial mobilization of forces in the Balkan theater. At the same time, the possibility had to be muted by Operations Bureau planners that a Balkan war could precipitate a war with Russia. According to both the Operations and Railroad Bureaus, this potential occurrence of "War Case B" followed by "War Case R" could be accomplished without disturbing the overall planned deployment scheme.[21] In other words, a Balkan mobilization could be followed by a "War Case R" mobilization without seriously disrupting either separate mobilization activity.

The Railroad Bureau further claimed that their war preparations were so thorough that the Balkan mobilization could be stopped "at any time" and a full mobilization against Russia begun. Russian armed interference, on the other hand, they assured, would not hinder a settling of accounts with Serbia-Montenegro, but would merely force certain measures to be initiated, the extent of which would depend on the range of Russian military activities at the time. Further, Railroad Bureau assertions at the time included the statement that deployment of the three Galician frontier corps, or even a full deployment against the Russian forces could occur while fighting units of the B-Group continued to roll by rail towards the Balkans.[22]

Serbia and Montenegro as potential antagonists also obviously required serious attention. Plans to fight an isolated war, against them, "War Case B," continued to be reviewed, but it became increasingly more likely that a war involving the Dual Monarchy against these two Southern Slav states would result in a Russian military intervention, or vice versa. Operations Bureau plans called for a total of eight infantry divisions to comprise the Minimal Group Balkan in the event of a "War Case R" preceding "War Case B." If, however, a "War Case B" preceded "War Case R," eleven infantry and three cavalry divisions would be directed against the two Slavic states. Russia, obviously the vastly more powerful and dangerous foe, had top priority in the event of such a two-front military confrontation. It seemed only common sense that if Russia suffered a severe military setback, the Dual Monarchy could "settle accounts" in the Balkans at will.

Russian efforts to accelerate their military deployment timetables by calling a trial mobilization in 1912, coupled with an intensifying Balkan crisis, meanwhile created consternation in Austro-Hungarian General Staff circles. Increasing improvements in Russian military proficiency, which were becoming more and more apparent, could seriously affect any Austro-Hungarian mobilization at the Galician frontier. Perhaps of greatest concern was that Austria's most vital detraining areas continued to be increasingly exposed to potential enemy strikes. If the Russians somehow succeeded in gaining a time advantage before the opening of a war, there could be no guarantee that the Austro-Hungarian mobilization and deployment could be carried out successfully.[23] General Schemua's war planning for "War Case R," as had Conrad's, assumed that Vienna would indeed have the necessary time advantage.

Earlier, as mentioned, Conrad had dreaded the threat that in the event of an order for a general mobilization masses of Russian cavalry would be hurled over the Galician frontier at seriously exposed Austro-Hungarian deployment railroads near the borders. Partly due to this concern, General Schemua ordered a study of, and preparation for, a strategic redeployment, or a drawing back of Austro-Hungarian deployment areas in the case of a mobilization. This was the planning for the *Rückverlegung* that would become increasingly a factor in Austro-Hungarian military planning.

The strategic redeployment, as envisioned later by Conrad, entailed a reduction in the size or extent of the overall Austro-Hungarian deployment area and, consequently, a significant change in the mission of the military for a war with Russia. The new deployment mission, if actually decided upon, would be to have initially the Austro-Hungarian armed forces proceed to the defensive line encompassing Oswiecim-Cracow-Tarnov-Jaroslau-Przemyśl-Lemberg and to the San-Dniester bridges at Mikolayov, Zydaczov, and Yezupol. This deployment plan obviously ran counter to Conrad's earlier concept of a rapid northward offensive strategy, which was drawn from a more forward placement of troop locations.

For the Austro-Hungarian General Staff, this potential strategic redeployment simply meant that compared to the earlier deployment planning in which the battlefront area extended some four hundred and forty kilometers — the new strategic redeployment area, on the other hand, would now embrace a smaller front to the rearward of the original one — encompassing now only three hundred and forty kilometers, with three fewer infantry divisions placed in the new forward lines.[24]

In concrete terms, the Railroad Bureau determined that the latest time possible for a decision to switch from the normal planned forward deployment to the possible strategic redeployment would have to be the third mobilization day for the A-Group units to be fielded in Galicia as a counter to Russia. The main advantage to this *Rückverlegung* plan was that the choice could be made as late as the fifteenth mobilization day of the "War Case B" as to whether the Second Army, which basically comprised the B-Group forces, should be hurled against Serbia-Montenegro to ensure a complete victory in conjunction with the Minimal Group Balkan in a war beginning as a simple "War Case B," or whether this twelve division B-Group should be thrown into the scales in conjunction with the A-Group against Russia in a combined "War Case R+B."[25]

With respect to the increasing Russian threat at the extreme Austro-Hungarian right-flank positions, the Railroad Bureau reported that it would be impossible to deploy major Austro-Hungarian forces in eastern Galicia if the main deployment railroad, the Karl Ludwig, should fall into enemy hands.[26] The Karl Ludwig railroad line ran parallel to the Russian frontier and, at certain points within twenty-five kilometers of the border thus providing a tempting target for enemy cavalry and Cossack raids. The general weakness of the layout and extent of Austro-Hungarian deployment railroads was never eliminated as a significant block to effective military planning.

The effects of the Balkan crisis created by the 1912-1913 Balkan Wars, and the Russian military measures initiated in the autumn of 1912, to be studied in more detail in the following chapter, can be seen in the frantic way in which the Austro-Hungarian General Staff examined both the various factors involved in the planning for strategic redeployment of the Austro-Hungarian forces, and the necessity to order the revision of deployment plans for the 1913-1914 campaign year.

In March 1913, with the Balkan Wars crisis still smoldering, General Schemua again traveled to Berlin to clarify the confusing German position assumed before the Balkan Wars began. Moltke once again promised to launch an offensive parallel to Austria's in the case of a war against Russia. Reporting back to Vienna, Schemua stated that Vienna could count absolutely on German armed support if Russia threatened the Empire, in accordance with the earlier 1909 military agreements. Moltke had insisted in March that it would take four to five weeks for Germany to settle accounts militarily with France in the west; then strong additional forces would be immediately transported to the eastern theater. In order further to ensure that a full Austro-Hungarian deployment against Russia ensued, Moltke agreed that sometime after the regular divisions had been assembled in Prussia, some reserve divisions would be added; but Moltke stressed that the Schlieffen Plan itself must remain unaltered.

Two significant attempts to create closer and more viable military cooperation within the Triple Alliance reached fruition late in 1912. The more important venture concerned common allied military measures to be conducted in the area west of the Vistula River, where it could be assumed that the Russians would not deploy significant troops. This area encompassed the Prussian Silesia and Cracow region. This new agreement became necessary to some extent because of the lack of information or intelligence reports on Russian intentions in that strategically and industrially significant area. Signed on 20 December 1912, the agreement became the joint General Staff's written foundation for a limited allied offensive to commence in that area immediately upon the outbreak of hostilities. The object of this military venture, to be launched along the western banks of the Vistula River, would be to protect both the coal regions in Silesia and the Austro-Hungarian deployment railroads extending from Oderberg to Cracow.[27]

The second attempt to achieve cohesion in allied military affairs succeeded in its immediate purpose but was outdated within the next calendar year due to events in the Balkan Wars. Conrad, temporarily Inspector General of the Austro-Hungarian armies after being removed as Chief of the General Staff in 1911, assumed the responsibilities for a mission to retain and strengthen Romania as an active ally in case of an Austro-Hungarian-Russian conflict.

Conrad indeed returned to Vienna with a written agreement signed by the Chief of the Romanian General Staff, who reassured him that Bucharest would remain true to the Triple Alliance. Austria-Hungary now possessed a written military pact with Romania similar to the one Conrad felt existed between Berlin and Viennese military officials.[28]

According to the agreement, Romania's military cooperation would entail a major operation against the Russian positions at Kishinev in Moldavia. Conrad explained that he expected the Romanian formations to assemble *en masse* in the area of Jassy in order to encounter and tie down the entire Russian Fifth Army. He doubted, however, that Romania could accomplish this ambitious mission, since he knew that if Austria-Hungary appeared to be the aggressor in a war with Russia, then the Romanian obligations would not be honored — which could spell disaster for the Austro-Hungarian positions at their extreme right flank.

The question of the viability of the Triple Alliance treaty itself came to the fore in the latter half of 1912, as negotiations began for its early renewal. Following months of painstaking diplomatic haggling between

Austria-Hungary and Italy over the question of mutual territorial compensation in the event of a realignment in the situation in the Balkan peninsula, the treaty was ratified on 5 December 1912. The Austro-Hungarian officer corps, however, led by Conrad, advised against reaffirmation of the tie with Italy; but Franz Joseph and Aehrenthal rejected their opposition to renewal of the Triple Alliance Treaty.

Then, on 18 December 1912, bad news was received from Rome. The German government received official notification that as a result of the Tripoli War, Rome could not dispatch her earlier promised three army corps and two cavalry divisions to Germany to be utilized against France in the event of a war. Speculation even suggested that Italy would declare her neutrality if a war broke out. General Alberti Pollio, Chief of the Italian General Staff and an advocate of the Triple Alliance, assured the Germans, on the other hand, that Italy would mobilize if indeed the *casus foederis* did arise.[29] This promise did not reassure Moltke, who now thought that Germany would once again have to plan to carry on the fight with France alone, although Italy claimed a desire to transport troops to the German-French border as soon as possible after a conflict commenced.

The following day, 19 December 1912, the German ambassador in Italy reported to Berlin that the King and Crown Prince of Italy had reassured him that their country unconditionally supported the Triple Alliance alignment. On 21 December 1912, General Pollio, claiming governmental authorization, informed Moltke that if the *casus foederis* should arise, Italy would launch an immediate offensive against France.

Coinciding with these activities concerning Italy's army obligations to her allies, naval questions also came to the forefront. Despite some very touchy moments in Austro-Hungarian-Italian relations during the joint negotiations, a naval pact was concluded on 23 June 1913 that stipulated that in the event of a war by the Alliance, the Austro-Hungarian and Italian fleets would be united for common action. This new agreement revised the earlier 1900 naval pact which kept commands separate.[30]

The apparent good relations between Austria-Hungary and Italy allowed Conrad, who had been reappointed Chief of the General Staff in December 1912 because of the intensifying Balkan crisis, to revise his deployment plans to counter the increasing threat raised both by the Balkan Wars and by the apparent improvements in the capabilities of the Russian armed forces. Accordingly, the III and XIV Austro-Hungarian Corps, originally designated to protect the Italian frontier in a pure "War Case R," would now be deployed in Galicia to increase the numerical odds against the Russian enemy. Now only reserve and police units would defend the Graz and the Tyrol areas in the above circumstances.[31]

On 24 January 1913, General Waldersee, Chief of the Operational Group of the German General Staff, journeyed to Italy to clarify her position in Triple Alliance military calculations. Later stopping in Vienna to discuss "War Case R" matters, he conveyed to Conrad's staff that previous "agreements" between Austria-Hungary and Germany had "generally" remained in effect. (These "agreements" provided for thirteen German divisions to be fielded east of the lower Vistula River in an eastern conflict. The possibility of an additional four to six reserve divisions being sent was also mentioned.[32])

Correspondence between Conrad and Moltke was renewed in January and February 1913. Moltke, in a letter dated 10 February, attempted to confirm the results of the Waldersee mission to Italy and Austria. He therefore described Italy as an ally to be trusted and, to overcome any of Conrad's doubts, clearly stated that even if Italy did not dispatch her Third Army to the Rhine theater, during a mobilization the number of German fighting forces designated for the eastern campaign would not be reduced.

Moltke also reemphasized his belief that a European war was inevitable and that the forthcoming struggle would settle the issue between Slavs and Germans.[33] Conrad's reply to this letter of 15 February 1913 opened with a word of gratitude for the possibility of further second-line German troops being dispatched to the east to increase the German forces opposing Russia. But in replying to Moltke's statements regarding an inevitable showdown between the Germans and Slavs, Conrad emphasized that a large concentration of Slavs resided in the Dual Monarchy. The remainder of this particular letter was devoted to the Monarchy's problem with Serbia. Conrad insisted that the creation of a greater Serbia as a result of the Balkan Wars had to be prevented, since the morale of the victorious Balkan states had already been boosted significantly and their territorial boundaries extended as a result of the recent wars in the area. These same states, particularly Serbia, had potentially doubled their military strength.[34] Conrad then summarized his arguments by stressing the absolute necessity of German and Romanian military support if an Austro-Hungarian offensive launched from Galicia was to have any chance of success.

Meanwhile, the General Staff Operations Bureau prepared its military strategy for 1913-1914. When it was completed, the basic concepts remained generally the same as Conrad's initial plans of 1908-1909. However, three new developments did affect the detailed planning. First, stemming directly from the Balkan situation, especially the Third Balkan War, came the increasing awareness of the unreliability of Romania as a Triple Alliance ally, despite the written military agreement signed in December 1912. A second complication resulted from the effect of French diplomacy and money. Paris had been particularly concerned that, in the event of a two-front war, Russia would not put sufficient military pressure on Germany in the east to help relieve the anticipated pressure on France on the western front. Consequently, the French had begun to pressure Russia to extend and build new strategic railroads to the Austro-Hungarian-German frontiers. This extension and improvement of Russian strategic rail lines could be used to transport the recently improved Russian army in a much shorter time.

In earlier General Staff calculations, as mentioned, it had been expected that in the eventuality of a war with Russia, the regions west of the Vistula River would be evacuated of major Russian armed forces. Now it could once again be anticipated that significant Russian forces might be deployed there, as well as an additional secondary group at the eastern flank to the south of the Dniester River. This scenario would help fulfill French expectations of a rapid Russian offensive against the Central Powers as defined in the Franco-Russian military alliance.[35]

Conrad's major suppositions for his war planning against Russia in 1913-1914 included the possibility of an Austro-Hungarian strategic rearward redeployment — *the Rückverlegung* — because of the advanced extent of the Russian war preparations; and the reputed creation of a central army in the Moscow region. From a thorough study of the railroad configurations in Russian Poland, it was anticipated that an enemy deployment of main forces would occur in the extended area of Vladmir-Volynski, Luck, Dubno, Rovno, and Jaroslau. Vienna's scheme to counter enemy moves for the time period 1913-1914 retained the same basic outlines as those for 1912-1913. The most obvious alteration of previous planning involved the redeployment of five cavalry divisions toward the proposed army strategic rearward redeployment positions, and the transference of the Austro-Hungarian XII Corps to the Czortkov region in case of a mobilization against Russia. Both measures were designed to prevent Russian encirclement of the endangered right-flank deployment positions and, in turn, to provide the opportunity to attempt an encirclement of the Russian left-flank positions.[36]

The key to the Dual Monarchy's evolving strategy remained the early operations readiness of their left-flank First and Fourth Armies. With this crucial advantage, an offensive operation by these two armies could be conducted either in a northward or northeast direction. This early advance had the advantage that while it would supposedly clarify the enemy situation at the Austro-Hungarian left flank, it would simultaneously preclude an enemy encirclement of their own forces in this critical area.

The overall Austro-Hungarian strategy continued to entail the launching of a major First and Fourth Army offensive between the Bug and Vistula Rivers which, if successful, would eventually encompass portions of the Third Army as well. Initially, the Second and Third Armies would provide right-flank protection eastward in the event that Russia directed strong military forces toward the eastern Galician frontier. If, on the other hand, only small concentrations of Russian forces would be deployed between the Bug and Vistula Rivers, where the major offensive was planned, then the extreme left-flank Austro-Hungarian First Army would force these lesser troops to retreat, thus shielding their remaining units from the threat of being outflanked. The other three armies would then wheel eastward to launch a major offensive. In this scenario, the main assault would be performed by the Second and Third Armies. The Fourth Army would meanwhile launch a decisive thrust northward, to be joined by the First Army on its left after it had completed its own defensive attack.

The Fourth, Third, and Second Armies, twenty-five to thirty divisions strong, would advance along a front extending approximately one hundred kilometers. In the forty kilometer wide area in the vicinity of Sokol-Hrubieszov, a further nine to ten divisions would be fielded. Thus along an overall one hundred and forty kilometer front extending from Halicz to Ravaruska, thirty-five Austro-Hungarian divisions would be aligned with the First Army fielded north of this position. In either scenario, if necessary, a further army group would be placed south of the Dniester River to forestall a Russian advance between the Dniester and the Carpathian foothills.[37]

In a very detailed operations study of projected Russian military deployment areas, the following three in particular received emphasis: the Vistula River area; the fortress triangle at Rovno-Dubno-Luck; and the east-flank positions in the Proskurov-Novosielica region. These areas were selected to be emphasized for study because of the proximity of Russian railroad lines to the mutual frontiers. It was assumed that there would be

a major Russian military endeavor launched from the Vistula River area
and fortress triangle. After reviewing the various military possibilities, no
serious revision appeared to be necessary for Austro-Hungarian deployment planning because railroad connections to the east of Lemberg remained poor, thus the main forces in Galicia would have to be deployed
rearward in the Lemberg area and not further east.

In 1913, as a result of the Balkan crisis, Moltke made a momentous
decision when he decided to terminate future yearly plans in favor of a
sole Great German Eastern Deployment. Assuming that Great Britain and
France would immediately enter a war between Germany and Russia,
Moltke considered to be out of the questions any alteration of the Schlieffen Plan which would call for an overwhelming stroke against France. The
assumption that there would no longer be a one-front war in the east would
have serious consequences in 1914. Germany thus retained the concept
that her major forces would initially encounter France. For the eastern
front, twelve to fourteen divisions were left to be fielded in East Prussia
while a militia corps would cooperate with Austro-Hungarian extreme
left-flank forces around Prussian Silesia or Posen according to the terms
of the 1912 allied agreement. Only after France had been thoroughly
crushed would additional German troops be transferred to the eastern front.

In the Austro-Hungarian Operations Bureau, other concerns held the
spotlight. For example, there was absolutely no plan to counter the threat
of a potential major enemy deployment on the Austro-Hungarian right
flank. If, in fact, major Russian formations were deployed in the Russian
provinces of Volhynia and Podolia and this escaped the detection of the
General Staff, the designated Austro-Hungarian major offensive between
the Bug and Vistula Rivers would be launched in the wrong direction.
Obviously the result could be catastrophic. The attacking Austro-Hungarian main forces, striking "into the air" and threatened at their now exposed
flanks, could be forced to retreat hastily behind the San-Dniester River
line to regroup their armies there and counter the "unexpected" enemy
thrust from the eastern flank.

The main Austro-Hungarian plan, however, remained the opening
stroke between the Bug and Vistula Rivers. The advantages anticipated
from this final strategic plan for 1913-1914 were that it was well-suited
to the overall Austro-Hungarian strategic railroad network; that it provided
sound protection for the Empire's crucial center area; and that it corresponded to the "planned" joint Austro-Hungarian-German pincer offensive

from their respective territories toward Warsaw to cut off and destroy assembling enemy formations.[38]

The strategic railroad configurations began to increase in significance in war planning. The daily railroad deployment capacity for Galicia totaled 153 trains, of which 108 led to the Tarnov-Lemberg region. Only forty-five trains could thus be transported daily east of Lemberg toward the frontiers, so the most natural deployment area for the main forces remained that between Tarnov and Lemberg.

The General Staff strategic planning for the following year (1914-1915) continued to reflect the varied effects of the 1911 Tripoli War, the 1912 renewal of the Triple Alliance, and the conclusion of the 1912-1913 Balkan crisis without Great Power involvement. In the operations planning, owing partly to the renewed Italian agreements, contingency plans for a "War Case I+R" would, for the first time, be omitted from detailed calculation.

The Austro-Hungarian strategists were also convinced that as a result of the Balkan Wars, victorious Serbia would need years to assimilate her new land acquisitions which totaled 34,000 square miles, and mold her newly acquired population of 1.5 million, into an effective military instrument. Therefore, they decided, at this time, that the troop-strength commitments for the Minimal Group Balkan should not be revised in 1914-1915 planning. This decision was also apparently influenced by the belief of Vienna's military leadership that Serbia's military position would be temporarily weakened while she adjusted to her successes in the Balkan Wars.

But the deployment plans for a "War Case R" received major modification between the winter of 1913-1914 and the opening battles in August 1914. Perhaps the most crucial strategic decision in early July 1914 was the order to initiate the strategic redeployment back to the San-Dniester River line.

A contributing factor for new revisions in the plans was the increasingly doubtful posture of Romania as a reliable ally from 1913 on. This was due in part to negative Romanian public opinion when it was realized that Vienna had not wholeheartedly supported Bucharest's diplomatic position and claims against Bulgaria following Romania's entrance into the last phase of the Third Balkan War. Vienna had also sought revision of the favorable Treaty of Bucharest terminating the war. The result of the increasing Romanian irredentism in the Hungarian province of Transylvania was that Bucharest not only became a most doubtful military factor for the Triple Alliance in a future war, but now even appeared to be rapidly drifting toward the Triple Entente coalition.

Another decisive factor affecting the decision to accept the strategic redeployment planning was that it was now much more likely that Russia would intervene militarily if the Dual Monarchy chose to attack Serbia. This raised both the difficult question of how to react to the various possibilities of such a Russian intervention, and the frustrating exasperation of knowing that it was impossible to pinpoint the exact moment of that probable Russian intervention. In particular, Conrad realized that his forces would be at a disastrous military disadvantage if he dispatched the twelve-division B-Group swing force (the Second Army) in conjunction with the Minimal Group Balkan to crush Serbia-Montenegro in a "War Case B" and then had to react to a Russian mobilization while his deployment troops were in rail transport to the Serbian frontier.

To prevent this potential catastrophe, greater security for the troops that would be fielded in Galicia following a "War Case B" mobilization and deployment could be obtained by withdrawing their deployment bases to the rear. This was the *Rückverlegung*, or rearward deployment. Such action would not only significantly shorten the initial army front but also would force the enemy to risk heavier losses in any attempt to disturb an Austro-Hungarian mobilization and deployment. The strategic redeployment would also provide greater overall security so that unwelcome military surprises could be prevented. On the other hand, the rearward deployment presented the disadvantage of providing the enemy with the ability to link together numerically superior forces for battle by gaining additional time in the mobilization and deployment phase. It would also take the key factor of the initiative out of Conrad's hands, at least temporarily. Both factors were totally foreign to Conrad's earlier strategic principles.

It should also be stressed that in Austro-Hungarian strategic planning for both 1913-1914 and 1914-1915, the divisional strength of Russian combat forces had been seriously underestimated. If Conrad indeed fielded both the A- and B-Groups in Galicia as planned in a "War Case R," he could have at his disposal at most forty infantry and eleven cavalry divisions with twenty-seven additional reserve and replacement brigades. He could, therefore, find his forces at a great numerical disadvantage. This indeed would be one of the results of the Intelligence Bureau's miscalculations of potential enemy strength.

Railroad networks and communications had become vital considerations for modern warfare since the wars of German unification. Due greatly to substantial French financial support, Russian railroads by 1914 had become far superior in troop carrying capacity to the Austro-Hungarian network. For deployment purposes, Russia could utilize five two-rail and four one-rail lines, which had the additional significant advantage that, unlike Vienna's, they did not have to overcome, in a mobilization and deployment, such serious geographical difficulties as traversing the Carpathian Mountains. Vienna possessed seven one-line railroad stretches leading to their main deployment area, two of which had to cross extremely mountainous terrain. Russia had the capacity to transport a total of 260 trains per day to the battlefront, the Austrians only 153. This Russian advantage could be detrimental to the "linchpin" of Conrad's planning: his earlier operations readiness if, indeed, St. Petersburg gained time to mobilize and deploy her armed forces before Austria-Hungary could react.

In addition to these cited difficulties, a particularly embarrassing event in 1913 affected Conrad's decision to quickly revise 1914 military planning. In June 1913, the Colonel Alfred Redl espionage affair came to light. Colonel Redl allegedly betrayed military information to Russia, France, Serbia, and Italy. The Chief of the Russian Intelligence bureau in Warsaw had discovered Redl to be homosexual, he utilized this information to Russian advantage. As a result of being discovered to be a major spy, Redl was offered the opportunity to commit suicide by the personal order of Conrad. By taking his own life, Redl obviously made thorough questioning about the espionage affair impossible. Most unsettling, particularly for the German allies, was that Redl had served in the Intelligence Bureau of the Austro-Hungarian General Staff, and the extent of his treasonous activity remained unclear because of Vienna's reluctance to disclose the extent of his activities.

After Redl's suicide, an extensive investigation by the Austro-Hungarian Intelligence bureau resulted in the report that the following materials had been "officially" discovered to have been compromised: the General Staff Reserve handbook; the Austro-Hungarians' *Kriegs Ordre de bataille*, with supplements revealing frontier and railroad security measures; material explaining the armaments of the Dual Monarchy's fortresses; overviews of minefield positions surrounding communication and other significant military objects; and "possibly" the mobilization orders for the VIII (Prague) Corps.

Conrad and his General Staff never revealed whether the latest Austro-Hungarian war preparations and deployment plans had also been compromised. In fact, General Staff representatives claimed that under no circumstances could Redl have betrayed such secrets, because he had no access to the relevant documents. Russian documents indicate, however, that the Austro-Hungarian military leaders engaged in a cover-up.[39] The private papers of the Chief of the Austro-Hungarian Intelligence Service in 1914 also indicate that it was known that Redl had revealed overall deployment plans to Russia. In any case, the Redl case certainly influenced Conrad's deployment plans for 1914-1915 against both Russia and Serbia.

To sum up, the activities of Austro-Hungarian and German General Staffs contributed to Europe coming dangerously close to the brink of war between 1909-1914, especially during the 1912-1913 Balkan Wars. The military consequences of the wars caused extreme consternation in the military command channels. For one thing, Romania suddenly seemed lost as a military ally for Austria-Hungary. Russia had also used the crisis to improve her armed forces significantly, and Serbia had doubled the size of her territory. On the other hand, Bulgaria and Turkey had been badly weakened by their recent struggles and could no longer be expected to hold the balance of military power in the Balkans on behalf of the Central Powers. Italy appeared to have drifted closer to the Central Powers, but allied military authorities had serious doubts about her true intentions in the event of an actual war-time situation.

CHAPTER V

The Balkan Wars, 1912-1913

The effects of the Tripoli War of 1911 encouraged the various Balkan states to believe that Turkey's weakened condition would allow them to absorb the remaining Turkish territory in Europe. A Balkan League composed of Serbia, Montenegro, Bulgaria, and Greece was therefore established under Russian tutelage. This Balkan alliance launched attacks against Turkey in October 1912 and by December had taken all Turkish lands adjacent to the western side of the Dardanelle Straits. A planned London peace conference was delayed by a brief Second Balkan War, which forced Turkey to cede still more territory.

At the London conference, Austria-Hungary sought and won the creation of an Albanian state which would block both Serbian expansion to the west and access to the Adriatic Sea. Serbia was thus forced to seek a Saloniki Sea economic outlet at the expense of her former ally Bulgaria. Austria-Hungary opposed this action and encouraged Bulgaria likewise to prevent it. Bulgaria attacked Serbia in June 1913, launching a Second Balkan War. In this war, Bulgaria was soundly defeated by its erstwhile allies and Romania — and even Turkey took the opportunity to side with Bulgaria's new enemies.

As a result of the Balkan Wars, Serbia, Greece, Albania, and Romania gained additional territory, but Serbia felt shortchanged and Bulgaria, though enlarged to some extent, felt that its full territorial ambitions had been cut short by defeat. Serbia became especially irritated that Austria-Hungary, by supporting the creation of Albania, had prevented her from gaining an outlet to the sea. Continuing Austro-Hungarian-Russian tension was partly a reflection of this resentment.

In examining the diplomatic developments of the crucial years of the Balkan Wars, 1912 and 1913, it becomes evident that the Central Powers had to cope with several new major problems. First, Russia not only continued to improve the capabilities of her armed forces, but accelerated these efforts in order to become an even greater military power than she had been during the Bosnian Crisis.

Secondly, Germany appeared to misunderstand Austria-Hungary's difficult position relative to the Balkans until as late as Autumn 1913. While Vienna sought a Romanian-Bulgarian rapprochment, Kaiser Wilhelm argued instead for a wholly unrealistic Austro-Hungarian-Serb *detente*. By the summer of 1913, as Romania continued to drift further away from the Triple Alliance, Vienna felt that Germany was making little effort to prevent Romania's defection. Then, in October 1913, Germany abruptly switched her line and supported, in the strongest terms, the Austro-Hungarian position relative to Serbia and Bulgaria. Nevertheless, Germany did not want Austria-Hungary to take her support in the Balkans for granted.

Thirdly, the intensifying Austro-Hungarian-Russian dispute over the Balkans, a potential source of open conflict, had become a tinder box by the end of 1913. Indirectly, this dispute was manifested in a growing Austro-Hungarian fear of Serbia, Russia's proxy in the Balkans and one of the major winners of the Balkan Wars. During the wars, both Austria-Hungary and Russia engaged in considerable posturing in order to test each other's present and future intentions and capabilities. The Hohenlohe mission to St. Petersburg in early 1913 only temporarily smoothed over the relations between the two powers.

Fourthly, relations between Austria-Hungary and Italy, always strained, now fluctuated greatly. Italy became quite receptive to the creation of Albania, since this prevented Serbia — and, perhaps indirectly, Russia — from gaining direct access to the Adriatic Sea; but, at the same time, Rome in 1913 was so suspicious of Austria's intentions in the Balkans that her own membership in the Triple Alliance was often in question, particularly by Vienna.

A fifth problem was Foreign Minister Leopold Berchtold's attempt to establish at least some semblance of order in the Balkans through the creation of a Romanian-Bulgarian understanding and the adherence of Bulgaria in some way to the Triple Alliance. According to Berchtold, who was named to his position after Aehrenthal's death in 1912, such an agreement would presumably make Romania a more reliable ally in case of a war with Russia and would also advance Austria's position *vis-á-vis* Serbia. But in actuality, Berchtold's policy supported Berlin's accurate perception that such a policy would only drive Romania away from the Triple Alliance. Also, Romanian-Bulgarian relations had become further embittered during the course of the Balkan Wars, particularly after Romania mobilized and attacked Bulgaria in the Third Balkan War.

In 1913, Germany contributed to military tensions, due to an increase of German war-preparedness signaled by an Army Bill, and General Liman von Sanders's mission to Turkey to reorganize the Sultan's defeated army. Germany was viewed as an increasing threat by a Russia determined to obtain the Dardanelle Straits and Constantinople.

Just prior to the outbreak of the Balkan hostilities in 1912, the German Chancellor Bethmann Hollweg visited Vienna. His encounters there demonstrated the allies' mutual lack of trust concerning Balkan politics. A Kiderlen Wächter memorandum dated 2 September 1912 had emphasized that Berlin had no desire to toe Vienna's Balkan policy line,[1] but that Germany, supposedly possessing only a secondary interest in Balkan questions, would strive to support Vienna's position if informed of her intentions in advance.

Berchtold thereupon reassured Berlin that his government had no aims for expansion in the Balkans but, on the other hand, he said that there were certain territorial alterations in the Balkans which it could not allow, e.g., Serbian expansion. Bethmann Hollweg thus felt assured that Berchtold intended no aggressive policy in that area, but might be forced into it by Serbo-Montenegrin machinations. The new Austro-Hungarian Chief of the General Staff, Blasius Schemua, also appeared to be much less aggressive than his bellicose predecessor Conrad.

Meanwhile, as early as 1910, Foreign Minister Sazonov had been working on the creation of a Balkan League comprised of Serbia, Montenegro, and Bulgaria to reputedly preserve the *status quo* in the Balkans and to help Russia in a future war against Austria. The League concluded an actual treaty in March 1912. Despite obvious Russian intentions, the individual Balkan states had their own objectives and pursued them, allied with Greece, in the First Balkan War of October 1912.

Trouble between the major powers began when Russia herself initiated a series of provocative military measures. St. Petersburg first announced that she would conduct a trial mobilization timed to coincide with an approaching confrontation between the Balkan states and Turkey. At a Russian military conference which was convened on 10 September 1912, the decision to extend military service terms by six months was approved, thus in one swoop essentially increasing Russian manpower numbers by twenty-five percent.[2]

As a potential military adversary of Vienna, the Russian army had been immensely improved since the Russo-Japanese war, but particularly since the Bosnian Crisis. During the Balkan Wars, through the mechanism of the trial mobilization, whereby second-line forces were prepared for rapid assimilation into the regular army formations, the Russian army overcame many difficulties which would have retarded an actual wartime mobilization. St. Petersburg, following the outbreak of the Tripoli War, had begun partial mobilization measures as early as March 1912.[3]

The Russian trial mobilization announced for September 1912 was obviously intended to prevent Austro-Hungarian military intervention in an upcoming Balkan conflict. When, at the beginning of October 1912, Vienna did not react, Russia extended the service time of her reserves called up for "maneuvers." The intended trial mobilization was then postponed until a calculated first decision in the Balkan Wars would be made. This move was also designed to thwart Austro-Hungarian action. These significant Russian troop call-ups meant that the danger to Austria-Hungary now involved the possibility that Russian cavalry masses could now disturb any Austro-Hungarian deployment and mobilization in Galicia.

From the very beginning of the Balkan crisis in 1912, Berchtold and the Foreign Office could not control the course of events which ultimately resulted in tragedy for Vienna. No steady or purposeful Austro-Hungarian policy was formulated during the early phase of the Balkan conflict, although Berchtold did manage to make the following outline: under no circumstances could Serbia be allowed to reach the Adriatic coast; an Albania capable of independent existence must be created to preclude the emergence of a great power in that area; the Romanian claims for territorial adjustments must be accepted; and Vienna must have freedom of trade in former Turkish territory. However, it quickly became apparent that these guidelines did not represent a fixed program; rather, they provided general principles to be adapted to events. The question of a possible Serbian port on the Adriatic coastline and the creation of a viable Albania would raise the greatest difficulties, but the military events of the Balkan Wars quickly came to the forefront.

By 7 October 1912, the day the First Balkan War broke out, Russian preparatory military measures included the calling up of reservists for four weeks' training and of individual reserve divisions stationed in Russian Poland; the retention of the third-year levy of men; preparations for a trial mobilization and the attainment of peacetime military unit strengths; and a partial troop increase in the Warsaw region. The trial mobilization occurred in a large section of Russian Poland which included German frontier areas as well as the vicinity of Vilna and Moscow. Continuation of such mobilizations, and initiation of further Russian military measures, would obviously necessitate urgent Austro-Hungarian countermeasures, perhaps even the mobilization of the three Galician frontier Corps.[4] Russian military measures, after all, had resulted in a numerical increase in the Russian army of 50,000-60,000 reserves and 170,000 men for the trial mobilization. These combined troops, as well as the normal enemy troop strength, confronted an Austro-Hungarian defensive force of a mere 21,000 men in Galicia. Thus, Russian armed manpower on active duty now extended far beyond the normal requirements of the five corps force normally assigned to the Warsaw military district.

The trial mobilization raised grave concern in Vienna. Its meaning became clearer on 4 October 1912 when the Russian military attaché in Berlin informed Kiderlen Wächter that if Austria-Hungary should attack Serbia, public opinion would obligate his government to intervene in the conflict. This forceful posture would be maintained by Sazonov throughout the entire crisis in 1912-1913, although the Foreign Minister repeatedly stated that he desired a peaceful settlement of all Balkan issues.[5]

Unknown to military and civilian leaders of the Central Powers, political complications on the frontiers triggered a significant order to the Russian Warsaw military district on 30 September 1912. According to this command, a telegram order to begin mobilization in Russia's European military districts should be interpreted also as the order for the opening of armed hostilities.[6] Russia did not actually consider herself ready to intervene in a military conflict against Austria-Hungary, but the possibility of becoming involved in such a war in 1912 was certainly contemplated. A "war party" in St. Petersburg foresaw and awaited an "unavoidable" day of reckoning with the Dual Monarchy.

While all these events were transpiring in Russia, German authorities attempted to reassure Vienna. On 10 October, Kiderlen Wächter promised that Austria-Hungary could count on unconditional German support during this crisis as at the time of the annexation of Bosnia-Herzegovina. It was emphasized that, above all, Berlin desired that Austria-Hungary should make herself appear to be the provoked party, not the aggressor in her activities. As Russian military measures intensified in Poland, the German line mellowed towards Vienna. Wilhelm himself finally became convinced that Austria-Hungary had been provoked, and he became willing to accept the *casus foederis* with all its concomitant consequences.[7]

In actuality, German policy merely sought the localization of any Balkan conflict. True to its 1910 Potsdam stand with St. Petersburg, Berlin would attempt to prevent any active Austro-Hungarian intervention in the Balkans. Berlin, fearing that she would be faced with an Austro-Hungarian *fait accompli* but at the same time wishing to support her ally, above all, did not want to be left in the dark as to Austria's true intentions in the escalating crisis.

On 11 October, the Russian trial mobilization in Poland terminated as scheduled, but in Warsaw and in Russia itself, frantic military activities continued. By the end of October, the Austro-Hungarian military leadership recommended that Count Berchtold contact Berlin concerning possible military countermeasures because of the extent of Russian military activity along both the German and Austro-Hungarian frontiers.[8]

Moltke had meanwhile taken the position that the numerous military preparations in Russia had allowed her to facilitate the mobilization of her key military districts, i.e., Warsaw, Kiev, and Odessa; and that any additional measures, e.g., a new trial mobilization accompanied by strong troop transfers to the west, or even reserves being called up, must be construed as a Russian mobilization. It began to appear that Russia would not allow a repetition of the 1909 Bosnian Crisis.[9] Reports of Russian military activity pervaded the Austro-Hungarian intelligence documents of November 1912. For the Vienna Operations Bureau, these varied measures seemed to indicate a planned attempt to destroy Austria's most strategic deployment railroad (the Karl Ludwig) in the event of the outbreak of hostilities. Consequently, orders would be issued to initiate railroad security measures and to commence improvements of Austro-Hungarian fortresses.[10]

Russia had thus succeeded in provoking the initial Austro-Hungarian-Russian confrontation by inaugurating numerous military measures on the eve of the outbreak of hostilities in the First Balkan War. St. Petersburg and Vienna later exchanged charges of responsibility for the initiation of the ensuing mobilization measures assumed by the two powers.

The continuing westward transfer of Russian troops toward the frontiers also caused the Austro-Hungarian military planners to consider the possibility that, contrary to earlier expectations, the Russians simply would not evacuate the western Vistula River area at the beginning of an armed conflict. General Schemua, for the moment still Chief of the Austro-Hungarian General Staff, began to press for the immediate transfer of nine cavalry regiments to the Galician frontier, as well as the increase to war footing of the three Galician frontier corps (I, X, XI). Also discussed was the possibility of raising seven other Austro-Hungarian corps to a war standing.[11]

By the end of November 1912, a military confrontation in Poland between Russia and Austria-Hungary appeared imminent, while the Dual Monarchy had also inaugurated — and now continued to increase — war preparations at the Serbian frontier. On 7 December 1912, Conrad, soon to be renamed chief of the Austro-Hungarian General Staff, again insisted that the last opportune moment for settling accounts with Serbia had just about passed. According to his calculations, Russia could not support Belgrade militarily because she herself was not prepared for a major war, despite her threats and corresponding military measures.[12] The nine cavalry regiments Schemua had demanded earlier were prepared for transfer to the Galician frontier, where the enemy now had six or seven cavalry divisions already on a war footing. The three Austro-Hungarian frontier corps would also be increased to full war footing strength by 30 November because of the growing concern that if the cavalry units in Galicia remained at peacetime strength and a large enemy offensive ensued, any necessary Austro-Hungarian mobilization movements could be vitally affected by disruptions in the Galician railroads, supply points, and assembly areas. Russian troop increases had meanwhile raised the Russian Army strength to 1,600,000 men, and it appeared that other interior area corps had been prepared for movement to the frontier. The mounting tension proved so great that by 18 November 1912, Austro-Hungarian representatives in St. Petersburg received instructions concerning what steps to take if war did break out.[13]

With the threat of an Austro-Hungarian-Russian armed conflict looming, General Schemua traveled to Berlin to review cooperative military arrangements against Russia. Kaiser Wilhelm assured Schemua that Vienna could rely on German support under all circumstances. But Archduke Franz Ferdinand's attempts to convince Berlin of the necessity of "War Case B," because of the Serbian Adriatic harbor issue, failed.

In Russia, meanwhile, at a council meeting held on 23 November, the proposal to initiate further advanced military measures would not be approved because of the lack of support for these measures from Russia's French and British allies. Sazonov then proceeded to sound out Vienna about the possibility of a common Austro-Hungarian-Russian reduction of troop numbers.[14] But the continued extensions of the service time of Russian troops proved to be a very serious obstacle to improved Austro-

Hungarian-Russian relations. Thus both Vienna and St. Petersburg repeatedly justified their military activities as being initiated in response to those
begun across the frontier.

Meanwhile, Sazonov, in the heat of a serious situation, resorted to
giving his solemn vow to Vienna that no Russian military personnel or
units had been transferred from one military district to another. His statement contradicted the contents of the steady stream of Austro-Hungarian
intelligence reports.[15] Russia obviously did not want to appear to be
"stepping down" as she had been forced to, because of military unpreparedness, in the Bosnian Crisis. Tragically, this series of events would
recur in 1914.

On the other hand, Russian statesmen claimed that the so-called "mobilization" measures of Vienna proved so threatening to them that they
might be forced to instigate new measures themselves. Berchtold and his
government, however, disclaimed any Austro-Hungarian intention to mobilize their armed forces, suggesting rather that certain security measures
had been undertaken because of the threat raised by the extended duty
tours ordered for Russian military personnel due for discharge.[16] Actually,
the Dual Monarchy could not be charged with the introduction of any
provocative military steps until November 1912. Even then, the measures
that were instituted paled in comparison to those of the Russians. Neither
Berchtold nor Archduke Franz Ferdinand desired an Austro-Hungarian-
Russian confrontation, but Berchtold would not accept Sazonov's peaceful
approach unless Serbia moved to withdraw her soldiers from Albania,
where they had been moved. Berchtold would thereby prevent the Balkan
states from increasing their political demands. Eventually, however, reassuring news regarding Russia's lessening "war fever" was received from
St. Petersburg on 22 November 1912.[17]

At the same time, in Germany, the question of a new army law came
to the forefront of military affairs. Moltke's arguments favoring such a
numerical increase in the German army included Italy's stated inability to
transport her Third Army to the Rhine frontier in the event of war; the
obvious difficulties involving a possible Austro-Hungarian-Romanian war
in the Balkans if a concurrent Austro-Hungarian conflict with Russia
occurred; and the disquieting effect of Turkey's unexpected disastrous
defeat by the Balkan states. Moltke's case did not persuade the allied
military leadership.

In the opening days of December 1912, the Austro-Hungarian-Russian
crisis did not abate because of continuing reports of the Russian military

activities which were transpiring in Poland. Reputedly, large cavalry concentrations had been formed along the eastern Galician frontier. In the following days, in spite of a quieter political situation, intelligence reports continued to detail further Russian military measures.[18] These measures were taking place even after an armistice had already been signed between Bulgaria, Serbia, Montenegro, and Turkey on 3 December 1912, and after the London Peace Conference had opened. In military circles, it was decided in Berlin and Vienna that if an armed conflict developed, the Russians would attempt to postpone its outbreak until early 1913. In the interim, Russia's armed forces maintained a higher combat readiness than usual, so Austro-Hungarian forces also had to be maintained at a war stance. The Russian ambassador in Berlin, meanwhile, excused St. Petersburg's military measures by stating that they had become necessary to anticipate a speedier German mobilization, an argument that would be repeated tragically in July 1914.[19]

Conrad himself opposed any reduction in the raised Austro-Hungarian troop levels while the Balkan situation remained fluid. In fact, he pressed for permanent retention of the troops called up in both Galicia and Bosnia-Herzegovina.[20] Conrad's mission to Bucharest in December 1912 had served as a background to his reappointment as Chief of the General Staff on 1 December 1912, and his return to his former position during the crisis period of December 1912 caused further alarm, particularly in the capitals of Italy, Russia, and Serbia.

In Austro-Hungarian General Staff studies which had been prepared for the event of the eruption of a "War Case R," three eventualities were anticipated: a Russian invasion of East Prussia; a simultaneous offensive into Austria-Hungary (and possibly Romania); and an offensive against Turkey. It could be anticipated that to counter Germany the Russians would deploy their Vilna and Warsaw Armies consisting of nine corps, ten cavalry and two reserve divisions. Both armies would presumably launch an early cavalry invasion into East Prussia to disrupt the Prussian railroad network, spread panic, and, if possible, disturb the German mobilization. The Bessarabian Army (military district Odessa) undoubtedly would be fielded against Romania. The Kiev Army, composed of five corps, five cavalry, and seven reserve divisions, would counter Austria-Hungary. The St. Petersburg and Central Armies (Moscow and Kazan), consisting of nine corps, three cavalry and eighteen reserve divisions, would serve as reserve forces to be divided up and inserted against Vienna and Berlin.[21]

The mortal enemy, Serbia, also received special attention. If war was to erupt with this troublesome neighbor, the Austro-Hungarian Operations Bureau would field one cavalry and eighteen infantry divisions to parry her,[22] a significant increase in troop numbers compared to earlier "War Case B" plans. Vienna's major question became what position Italy and Russia would assume in the event of an Austro-Hungarian-Serbian war. If a full "War Case B" resulted, Austria-Hungary would retain thirty infantry and ten cavalry divisions to counter any major powers, particularly Russia. The possibility of an Italian invasion of the Dual Monarchy could be discounted at this time because eighteen Italian divisions were still tied down in Tripoli.

If Russia should intervene in an Austro-Hungarian-Serbian war, Conrad's military planners would hope to achieve a decision over Serbia in the fourth week of operations. A victory over Serbia would release ten divisions for utilization in Galicia. The Austro-Hungarian General Staff planners reached the conclusion that as long as Italy and Russia did not ally, a two-front "War Case R+B" could be risked with a favorable chance of success. Naturally, the longer Russian interference could be forestalled while Austro-Hungarian forces battled Serbia, the more advantageous the situation would be for Vienna.

Conrad continued to press for a "War Case B." He foresaw that time worked against Vienna. In the First Balkan War, Serbia had already enlarged herself both militarily and territorially. She also continued to encourage South Slav agitation in the Dual Monarchy. In addition, Serbian leaders knew that St. Petersburg's armed forces had been significantly improved, and their size and effectiveness expanded. Meanwhile, Romania grew more unreliable as an ally for Vienna. Considering these factors and aware that a rapid Austro-Hungarian victory over Serbia would preclude Russian intervention, Conrad insisted in December 1912 on an immediate attack against Serbia. Otherwise, Conrad emphasized, Belgrade could increasingly rely on Russian aid in a future Austro-Hungarian-Serbian war. For Conrad, a war in 1913 seemed an absolute necessity for the continued existence of the Dual Monarchy as a great power.[23]

While Conrad pressed for "his" Balkan war, a so-called war council convened in Germany. In this 8 December 1912 meeting, Kaiser Wilhelm called for an immediate war against Russia and France on the grounds that if Vienna launched a war with Serbia, and Russia supported Belgrade by advancing into Galicia, war would be unavoidable for Germany. At the same meeting, Moltke agreed that war was inevitable. To him, the moment to attack Serbia could never be more favorable, and he further asserted that a war against France would now be successful.[24] The decision of the war council, however, went against launching a war at this time, as is evident by its failure to inaugurate any mobilization measures.

Central Power diplomatic unity, in the meanwhile, appeared to have been restored when, in a Reichstag speech on 3 December 1912, Bethmann Hollweg proclaimed that if the Austro-Hungarian ally became threatened, Germany would feel compelled to fulfill its alliance pledge.[25] The specter originally raised by the 1909 Bosnian Crisis had reappeared.

Russian military activities continued along the Austro-Hungarian-Russian frontier well into January 1913; for example, month-long maneuvers commenced in Volhynia and Podolia. The seriousness of the situation prompted Wilhelm II to contact the Tsar to express concern about these measures.[26]

Conrad, meanwhile, remained bellicose. On 2 January 1913, he declared that the Dual Monarchy's situation had progressively worsened because of Greater Serbian and Greater Romanian agitation and propaganda.[27] War seemed to him to be the only immediate solution to the Monarchy's pressing problems.

Conrad reopened written communication with Moltke in a letter dated 10 January 1913. In the letter, he voiced serious concern about Italy's announcement that she could no longer transport her Third Army to the Rhine as had been agreed upon in 1888. Conrad was particularly concerned that Germany would reduce her troop commitment in the east because of the Italian renege. He concluded the letter by reviewing possible "War Case R + B" combinations. Moltke, in his reply, assured Conrad that Italy's action would not provoke a reduction of German soldiers destined for the eastern front.[28] In 1914, however, this would no longer be true. In 1913-1914, the question of Italian loyalty was fundamental; in the July 1914 crisis, it would be crucial.

Conrad's bellicose attitude throughout the Balkan Wars can best be understood by examining his 20 January 1913 memorandum to Franz Joseph. The salient point of the memo proved to be Conrad's view that the evolution of a Greater Serbia presented an imminent threat to Austria, particularly because of the danger of losing many of the Monarchy's most important territories, i.e., South Slavic coastal possessions. He emphasized that as a result of the Balkan Wars, Serbia had developed into a significant military opponent requiring further attention, and also that Serbia's Balkan War victory had produced a moral advantage for her in the future — which in turn would lead to a decline in the morale of the Monarchy's armies. Conrad concluded the memorandum by insisting that political preparations should be initiated for a war against Serbia.

Should St. Petersburg choose to intervene in such an Austro-Hungarian-Serbian war, Conrad promised that the mass of the Austro-Hungarian armies would be shifted to Galicia. An Austro-Hungarian military victory over Russia, according to the Chief of the General Staff, would help solve Vienna's Southern Slav problem, which also would benefit allied Germany.[29] Conrad supplied his view that Romanian and Bulgarian friendship should be attained in order to free Romanian armed forces for use against Russia which otherwise would be utilized to counter Bulgaria in armed conflict. Conrad argued that for an Austro-Hungarian-Serbian war to be successful, the neutrality of Bulgaria would have to be secured to reduce Romanian fears, and, in addition, that Albania would have to be armed as a counterweight against Serbia.

In the meantime, Berchtold's failure to adhere to firm diplomatic guidelines raised serious questions in Berlin concerning Vienna's position in relation to the Balkans. Although Archduke Franz Ferdinand and Berchtold led the peace party, Conrad's constant pressure for a "War Case B" created a bad impression. Bethmann Hollweg warned Berchtold that this time Russia would probably not sit back if Vienna attacked Serbia, thereby insisting that Berchtold keep him informed of Vienna's plans before taking any action.[30] General Moltke also pushed Conrad towards a more peaceful stand, in the process stating to Jagow, the German Undersecretary of State, that:

> For us, it is unquestionably extremely inconvenient to have fallen into a certain dependence on Vienna through our treaties and from the necessity of preserving Austria. Your Excellency's chief task is, as far as possible, to prevent Austro-Hungarian follies, no pleasant or easy task.[31]

Moltke later proclaimed that indeed allied loyalty would result if Austria-Hungary's existence was actually threatened by a Russian attack, but that such loyalty would be difficult to achieve if Austria-Hungary provoked such a war.[32]

At the same time, intelligence reports listing Russian military preparations continued to arrive into February 1913. On 11 February, for example, further troop transfers from Russia's interior to the Galician frontier were confirmed, and reports of continued military unit movements persisted throughout the month.[33]

Russia's continuing military measures, which could easily be construed as mobilization preparations, began to irritate members of the German General Staff. Therefore, Moltke prepared a memorandum on 18 February 1913 which emphasized that Germany could not allow Russia to initiate yet another trial mobilization without calling up her own reserves. Both Moltke and the Prussian War Minister, Falkenhayn, felt that any future Russian mobilization must result in the outbreak of war.

Toward the end of January 1913, however, less vociferous exchanges began between Vienna and St. Petersburg. On 23 January, Sazonov suggested that if the question of disarmament could be discussed, Austro-Hungarian-Russian relations would most certainly improve. His initiative resulted in the dispatch of Prince Gottfried zu Hohenlohe-Schillingfürst from Vienna on a goodwill mission to St. Petersburg, a mission which Sazonov welcomed as a means for easing tensions. Prince Hohenlohe, the ex-ambassador to St. Petersburg for years, carried a personal letter from Franz Joseph to the Tsar. Consequent diplomatic reports received from St. Petersburg emphasized that the Russian government sought to avoid a war and, further, that the slightest Austro-Hungarian move towards disarmament would be beneficial in preventing one.[34]

In February 1913, an apparent *quid pro quo* provided that the Dual Monarchy reduce her military force in Galicia, and Russia then reciprocate the movement. However, Vienna quickly announced that she would not reduce her troop standings to the pre-crisis level.

Following a month of difficult deliberations, Hohenlohe's peace mission to Russia finally seemed to be close to becoming successful. By 11 March, a mutual agreement had almost been attained. By its terms, certain defensive military measures would be withdrawn, and Austria-Hungary would reduce her troop stand in Galicia to a level commensurate with those of Germany and Russia at their own frontiers. The crisis finally appeared to have dissipated when Sazonov received confirmation of the Austro-Hungarian order to reduce the troop numbers called up in Galicia.[35]

Yet the danger of conflict remained. In April 1913, the possibility of an Austro-Hungarian advance against Serbia over the Albanian question caused a new strain in Austro-Hungarian-Russian relations. Russia threatened to prohibit unilateral Austro-Hungarian action against Serbia, which had, in the interim, marched troops into Albania. War clouds again appeared because of the Balkan situation.

In March, the Serbian seizure of the port of Scutari in Albania raised a new question of prestige for Vienna — this time accompanied by obvious German and Austro-Hungarian disagreements over the correct allied policy to follow. Wilhelm II openly supported the creation of a Greek-Romanian bloc associated with the Triple Alliance, but his suggestion that the Serbs also be included in the package made this idea abhorrent to Vienna. Berchtold countered Wilhelm's proposal with his own, for a Romanian-Bulgarian-Turkish connection to the Triple Alliance system which, he argued in its defense, would prevent westward Russian advances into the Balkans. The lack of allied cooperation resulting from this disagreement crippled Vienna's diplomatic maneuvering during the remainder of the Balkan Crisis.

In an effort to alleviate the evident allied friction, Wilhelm journeyed to Vienna, where he again voiced his position that the best Austro-Hungarian-German Balkan policy would be his Romanian, Serbian, and Greek combination. Berchtold, like other prominent Austro-Hungarian leaders, fearing the results of a "Greater Serbia" movement, vehemently argued against the feasibility of such a league. He naturally was in favor of seeking a rapprochement between Sofia and Bucharest in order to provide a counterweight to both Russian and Serbian Balkan machinations.

In strategic planning considerations, it became obvious that Conrad now believed that the military odds were increasingly turning against Austria-Hungary. On 25 March 1913, he informed the Kaiser of his worries while stressing the absolute necessity of keeping Romania attached to the Triple Alliance in an effort to counter his disheartening numerical calculations comparing Triple Alliance to Triple Entente troop stands. He cited discouraging new intelligence reports indicating Russia's possession of one hundred field divisions. Serbia, for her part, could deploy sixteen and one-half operative divisions (this figure would later reach twenty-one after absorption of her recently conquered territories) and Montenegro five or six more. If Romania's present sixteen and one-half divisions (later to increase to twenty) should be added to the potential opposing military bloc, the resulting power constellation would possess an overwhelming numerical superiority to Austria-Hungary's forty-eight operational divisions. Germany, by earlier agreement, would deploy only thirteen or fourteen divisions in the Russian war theater, so that the Central Powers would be at a severe numerical disadvantage overall in the event of an eastern conflict. Conrad proposed a partial solution to the pressing situation — the creation of a reserve army of twenty divisions to be operational by the early 1920s.[36] Austria-Hungary had no actual reserve forces at her disposal, whereas the other Great Powers did.

Conrad also intimated in the spring of 1913 that Russia planned to increase the size of her army by adding at least three new army corps. Of these, two would probably be garrisoned in European Russia. One could be anticipated at the East Prussian frontier area, and the other in the Kiev-Odessa region east of the Dnieper River. He suggested that such an increase of Russian troop strength would serve to neutralize the numerical gains to be achieved by the new 1913 German army law.[37]

To help offset the expected Russian troop increases, Vienna pressed Bucharest to renew her ties to the Triple Alliance. Conrad's December journey to Bucharest, mentioned previously, had produced a written military agreement, but the value of such a treaty, of which only a handful of people in the Romanian government were aware, remained questionable. Growing Romanian public hostility to Hungarian domestic policies in Transylvania which were aimed at the Romanian minority added to the uncertainty.

Franz Joseph had initiated serious efforts to renew Romanian adherence to the alliance in a letter sent to King Carol on 20 December 1912. On 12 January 1913, King Carol expressed his satisfaction with Franz Joseph's proposal. When ratified, the treaty served to maintain Romania's secret adherence to the alliance, but did not assure her reliability in the future. Berlin, not to be outdone, attempted to coerce King Carol into renewing the alliance treaty by promising that if Romania should be threatened by war, she could count on active German assistance. King Carol's pro-Hohenzollern proclivities had certainly not waned, but he now feared that the Liberal Party in his country could take the reins of government and then alter the present Triple Alliance orientation towards the Triple Entente.[38]

Following the unsuccessful London Peace Conference in March 1913, the St. Petersburg Conference convened in an attempt to end the Balkan conflict. One problem that immediately came to the forefront was Romania's demand for territorial compensation resulting from the fluctuation in the Balkan balance of power as a result of the Balkan wars. Instead of supporting his ally's attempts wholeheartedly, Berchtold insisted that Bulgaria also obtain territory as compensation for her losses. His proposal merely served to create additional friction between Bucharest and Vienna, while enhancing St. Petersburg's position in Romania.

Despite renewal of the Romanian Triple Alliance Treaty in March 1913, disturbing news began to arrive from Bucharest. Count Ottokar Czernin, dispatched as an envoy to Bucharest, informed Berchtold on 2 April that Romania, in the event of an Austro-Hungarian-Russian war, instead of actively participating with Austro-Hungarian forces, would await decisive military results and then join the apparent victor to deliver the *coup de grace* with "her million soldiers." The Romanian prize for her assistance would have to be either the province of Bessarabia from Russia, or Transylvania from Austria-Hungary. Three weeks later, Czernin reported to Vienna that King Carol would under no circumstances march against Austria, but that should he die, this purely personal Romanian Triple Alliance connection might well lapse.[39]

Certainly, to the Austro-Hungarian military leadership the Romanian alliance was critical, but Berchtold continued to press for an understanding between Romania and Bulgaria, Romania's traditional enemy. His strategy also involved presenting Adrianople to Bulgaria as compensation for her losses in the Balkan War, and as a means of attracting her into the Triple Alliance and, thus, utilizing her as a counterweight to Serbia. Germany, however, consistently supported Romania's demands, while counseling Vienna to follow the same strategy. Berlin's position, simply stated, was that she feared the loss of one ally, Romania, for the sake of a far less dependable one, Bulgaria.

If any facet of Berlin's Balkan policy was consistent, it had to be the desire to retain Romania in the Triple Alliance. What Berlin's statesmen did not understand was that Vienna not only had the same goal, but perhaps had evaluated the Balkan situation more accurately. Wilhelm and the German government steadfastly opposed the adhesion of Bulgaria to the Triple Alliance because they felt that collusion with Bulgaria would drive Romania into the arms of Serbia and Russia. Indications that Vienna's Bulgarian policy had this greatly undesired effect indeed soon appeared. Persistent diplomatic rumors also indicated that a Serbo-Romanian agreement now existed. The Bulgarian-Romanian question became even more critical in the months ahead.

Berchtold, however, had continued to press (1 May 1913) for Bulgarian adherence to the Triple Alliance, while Berlin, on 26 June 1913, insisted, to the contrary, on maintaining a healthy alliance grouping with Romania as one of the main aims of German foreign policy in the Balkans. In this

Austro-Hungarian-German divergence of position, Vienna sought Bulgaria to serve as a military counterweight to the hated Serbia. Bulgaria had, before the Balkan Wars, been considered the strongest military element in the Balkans, and, in addition, Sofia and Vienna had no serious conflict of interests. Indeed, they had parallel aims, and if Bulgaria joined the Triple Alliance, the charge that the Triple Alliance was anti-Slavic would collapse, while Serbia's growth might powerfully be checked.

Berlin's counter-arguments continued to emphasize that Vienna's diplomatic approaches to Bulgaria led to a weakening of Triple Alliance ties to Romania; that, in attempting to gain Bulgaria as an ally, an insecure adherent would cause the loss of a certain one; and, furthermore, that Vienna's machinations simply aided Russian diplomats who were attempting to draw Romania away from the Triple Alliance.[40]

With these problems serving as a background, the specter of a European conflagration reappeared in April 1913. Conrad would again press for armed action against Serbia on the familiar grounds that if Vienna backed down now, she would only imperil her Great Power status in Balkan affairs, while also preparing the circumstances which would lead to the loss of her Southern Slav territories and the Adriatic coastline. To Conrad, only three possible variants existed. First, if Russia guaranteed her neutrality in the case of an Austro-Hungarian-Serbian war, then he would demand an immediate full mobilization "B." Secondly, if St. Petersburg intended to intervene in such a conflict, Germany and Romania would be invited to cooperate militarily with Vienna on the grounds that Austria-Hungary had been indirectly attacked. Thirdly, if St. Petersburg did not move, then mobilization against Serbia and Montenegro would immediately commence, and if Russian military intervention occurred later, it would then lead to an Austro-Hungarian counter-mobilization against her. The third possibility, according to Conrad, would result in the full brunt of the Monarchy's forces being turned against Russia between the fifth and sixteenth "Balkan" mobilization days.[41]

If St. Petersburg did enter an Austro-Hungarian-Serbian fray at this time, Conrad calculated that chances would be much better for an Austro-Hungarian victory, since Serbia and Bulgaria would militarily neutralize each other. Undoubtedly, as Conrad would summarize the situation, a "War Case B" would be more advantageous now than in a few years.[42] Conrad thus continued throughout the spring of 1913 to urge an armed settlement with Serbia.

By now, however, German military circles also began to regard war as inevitable. Accordingly, the German military attaché in Vienna informed Conrad on 27 April 1913 that German military circles now favored a war with Russia. He also informed Conrad that Germany stood by her ally Austria-Hungary and would favor a definitive settlement of the conflict.[43] Through diplomatic channels, even France was warned of a possibly dire situation developing. It appears that Germany would not, at this time, have stood aside if Austria-Hungary became involved in armed conflict with Russia.

Bulgaria, in the meantime, had extended diplomatic feelers to Vienna towards her own adherence to the Triple Alliance, but on 16 May 1913, Vienna advised Sofia to address her approaches to Bucharest first. Then, on the night of 29-30 June 1913, King Ferdinand of Bulgaria, without informing his ministers, ordered an attack on Serbian and Greek forces, thereby initiating the Third Balkan War. Berchtold had already decided that Bulgaria must not be allowed to be defeated badly if Serbia gained the upper hand in an armed conflict. On 21 June, he informed Conrad that Austria-Hungary must intervene if a battle began to favor Serbia.

Romania opposed Vienna's new position, causing Berchtold to request that Berlin intercede on his behalf in Bucharest. Berlin, however, flatly refused.[44] Meanwhile, the Bulgarian attacks on Serbian and Greek positions resulted in a Romanian general mobilization on 3 July 1913. Romanian troops then proceeded to open a new front, and troops entered Bulgarian territory on 11 July. Two days later, Turkey, defeated in the first two Balkan Wars, also entered the fray. On 15 July, King Ferdinand, with his back against the wall, personally appealed to Franz Joseph for diplomatic assistance. Berchtold immediately assured Sofia of Viennese diplomatic support if she would first reach an agreement with Bucharest.[45]

When Berlin learned on 4 July 1913 that Vienna was contemplating active intervention in the new Balkan War, she attempted to soothe Berchtold and counter his ardor, while recommending that no Austro-Hungarian action be initiated without Berlin's approval, in the case of which she would give her absolute support to Vienna.[46]

The threat of a possible Austro-Hungarian military intervention in the Balkans caused great excitement in Rome. The relations between Italy and Austria-Hungary, usually quite strained, fluctuated violently during the crisis years of 1912-1913. The friendliest diplomatic contact between Rome and Vienna grew out of the creation of Albania, which effectively prevented the appearance of any new competition, i.e., Serbia, as an

Adriatic Power. The nadir in Austro-Hungarian-Italian relations occurred over the interpretation of Article VII of the Triple Alliance treaty regarding both the balance of power and compensation for any territorial change in the status quo in the Balkans. Article VII stipulated significantly that if one of the signatory Powers, Austria-Hungary or Italy, should gain territory in the Balkans, the other should receive some form of territorial compensation. Vienna, however, argued that Article VII applied merely to former Turkish territory; Italy's interpretation would be very different during the July 1914 crisis.

The question of Vienna's actively intervening against Serbia in the ensuing Scutari crisis raised further difficulties between Rome and Vienna later in 1913. The main friction between the two allies during the Balkan War period, however, evolved from the creation of an independent Albanian state, something that, interestingly, both supported. Austro-Hungarian attempts to ensure a viable barrier to Serbia's drive to the Adriatic Sea, nevertheless, also raised the unwelcome thorny question of the perceived Austro-Hungarian-Italian balance of power in the Balkans, as well as the compensation questions. From the moment in early 1913 that Vienna attempted to obtain the important Montenegrin mountain of Lovcen by an exchange with Montenegro, trouble quickly developed between Rome and Vienna. The antagonism would become so serious that, in April 1913, Italy's membership in the Triple Alliance became openly questionable.

Late in the Scutari crisis, and partially posed as a possible solution to the allied problem, the question arose of the possibility of a combined Austro-Hungarian-Italian armed advance in the Balkans. The two governments accordingly had to tread very lightly concerning the question of a joint military action, yet Vienna put pressure on Rome by threatening to act unilaterally. Italian statesmen resisted this extreme Austro-Hungarian position. The Austro-Hungarian-Italian debate over Triple Alliance terms proved to be most significant for the outbreak of the First World War. The Italian government, in the heat of the Balkan conflicts, argued that any Austro-Hungarian military action against Serbia-Montenegro had to be termed an aggressive act rather than a defensive one, and for this reason Italy could not consider Austro-Hungarian action as creating, for her, the *casus foederis* according to the terms of the Triple Alliance. The Italian argument continued that the threat of Russian intervention in an Austro-Hungarian-Serbian armed conflict could lead to a general European war, and thus Rome could not tolerate an aggressive interpretation of the Triple

Alliance.[47] This controversy transpired after the aforementioned Austro-Hungarian-Italian Naval convention had been signed on 23 June 1913.

At the same time, Conrad, true to character, relentlessly pressed for war against Serbia. In a letter to Berchtold on 12 July 1913, he inquired as to whether he must count on a "War Case R" in 1913 and, if so, upon which allies he could rely. Conrad emphasized that Romania's stance would be decisive in an eastern conflict. Conrad also desired that Bulgaria's military machine tie down Serbian troops, instead of allied Romania, which, according to military agreement, was supposed to cement the extreme Austro-Hungarian right flank against Russia. If, somehow, Bulgaria and Romania ended up opposing each other on the battlefield, Serbia would be free to fight the Dual Monarchy alone. Romania, on the other hand, according to Conrad's scenario, could tie down significant Russian armed forces. But if she remained neutral in an eastern war, loss to the monarchy would be fifteen divisions, or 400,000 men. On the other hand, a Romania that actively sided with Russia would align against Austria-Hungary an equivalent force of thirty field divisions, or 800,000 men — certainly not an insignificant number.[48]

At the height of the new Balkan crisis in 1913, Berchtold forwarded an interesting Austro-Hungarian position paper to Berlin on 1 August. This document encapsulates Austria-Hungary's Balkan policy during the 1912-1913 crisis and also contains one of the main arguments on which Vienna's position would be based in the July 1914 crisis. Berchtold's position paper encouraged the formation of a Bulgarian-Romanian understanding, so as to establish, in Austro-Hungarian fashion, the foundation of a solid right-flank position against Russia. Bucharest's and Sofia's affinity for remaining at odds with each other would only serve, in the long run, to neutralize Romania as an ally, thus precluding fulfillment of her assigned military task against Russia. Berchtold pleaded that Bulgaria, though not formally accepted into the Triple Alliance, should receive such consideration once Bucharest and Sofia had arrived at some form of diplomatic agreement. He also emphasized in the document that an Austro-Hungarian-Serbian armed conflict was inevitable. When such a conflict broke out, according to Berchtold, Vienna would be in the position of the attacked, no matter who had initiated the military decision.[49]

A second document assailing Berlin's Balkan policies accompanied this position paper, but complete harmony of Austro-Hungarian-German Balkan policy would not actually occur until July 1914. Meanwhile, by 8 August 1913, the European situation had become so strained that Berchtold wrote to the Austro-Hungarian ambassador in Berlin lamenting the lack of allied diplomatic coordination, which he felt could seriously jeopardize the foundations of the Triple Alliance.[50]

Some of this allied discord was a result of the signing of the 10 August 1913 Treaty of Bucharest, which terminated the conflict between Bulgaria and her opponents — Serbia, Romania, Greece and Turkey — in the so-called Third Balkan War. Austria-Hungary immediately sought to have the treaty revised in favor of Bulgaria, while her allies Germany and Italy opposed any such move. By 14 August, anyway, the idea of a possibility of revision of the treaty had become a dead issue, resulting in the temporary diplomatic isolation of Vienna.

Austro-German mistrust merely intensified when Kaiser Wilhelm and King Carol exchanged congratulatory telegrams over Romania's "victory" over Bulgaria. The public airing of these telegraphic exchanges incensed Vienna's statesmen, since it spotlighted the lack of a common Berlin-Vienna Balkan policy. The breach between the allies worsened even further on 5 August, when Vienna once again attempted to convert Berlin to its Balkan viewpoint. The German reply from the Kaiser went so far as to suggest that Berchtold be relieved of his position. Berlin still favored a Greek-Romanian-Serbian Alliance adherence, whereas Berchtold steadfastly maintained that Vienna's Balkan policy had to be based on a Bulgarian and Romanian tie.[51] In September 1913, Conrad continued to press for armed action against Serbia, while Bulgaria renewed her efforts to join the Triple Alliance. In the process, Berchtold's policy involved playing for time.[52]

As a result, in September 1913, Bulgaria initiated diplomatic feelers towards Turkey, arguing that establishment of a Bulgarian-Turkish understanding could result in the maintenance of Austro-Hungarian influence in the Balkans. Turkey indeed reciprocated the contacts from Sofia, but for the Central Powers, the tragedy in 1914 would be that neither Bulgaria nor Turkey would enter the war as an ally in August or September. In October 1913, with continuing reports of Serbian advances into Albania, Berchtold had finally reached the end of his patience. Therefore, he notified Germany, Italy, and Romania that he desired their allied support because Austria-Hungary could not accept any further diplomatic or military encroachments from Serbia. When Germany responded by assuring Berchtold of Berlin's support, Berchtold decided that he must finally force Serbia to yield. An ultimatum to Serbia, dispatched on 18 October 1913, demanded that Serbia's troops be withdrawn from Albania.

On the same day, Wilhelm assured Vienna of Germany's "full moral support" in the matter. He agreed that Austro-Hungarian prestige had sunk so low that Vienna had to resist further Serbian penetration into Albania.[53] But on 25 October, Vienna received formal notification that Serbian troops had been withdrawn from the disputed area. Conrad and Berchtold had both reached the conclusion that if the Serbian troops had not been withdrawn, the situation would have called for a Balkan mobilization, in spite of the opposition of both Franz Joseph and Franz Ferdinand to such a war.[54]

On close scrutiny, the sequence of events in October 1913 resembled those fatal ones of July 1914. First came a diplomatic warning from Vienna to Serbia concerning her Balkan machinations, which was followed by Vienna's appeal to her allies for support. Germany indeed promised support, encouraging Berchtold to dispatch an ultimatum to Serbia. Notification of Vienna's other Triple Alliance allies came only after the ultimatum had been dispatched to Belgrade while, as in July 1914, the Italian Foreign Minister was not in Rome. In the meantime, Conrad urged Franz Joseph to approve an attack on the erstwhile Balkan enemy, claiming that only a military success over Serbia could conclusively settle the Balkan problem. He further argued that Serbia should be issued an ultimatum with a very short time limit. If Belgrade ignored it, a "War Case B" mobilization should immediately follow.

On 21 October, Conrad again urged the Kaiser to seize the particularly opportune moment by not delaying the launching of a war with Serbia. Conrad also asserted that if his demands for the development of Austria's army were not met, the Army would fall behind other Great Power armies, rendering it worthless as a German ally.[55]

Then, on 26 October 1913, Kaiser Wilhelm visited Vienna, where any lingering doubts he had about the seemingly disparate diplomatic positions of Berlin and Vienna disappeared. In particular, concerning Serbia, Wilhelm declared, "of this you can be certain, that I stand behind you ready to draw the sword whenever your action makes it necessary."[56] For the first time since the Balkan troubles began, the two allies truly came together.

Vienna now decided that it was necessary to test the sincerity of Romania's oath of loyalty to her by dispatching Count Ottakar Czernin to Bucharest to push for a clarification of the treaty terms. After evaluating the situation in Bucharest, Czernin informed Vienna that the idea of pressing Romania to publish her treaty agreements would be a mistake.

Czernin recommended that that job should go to Berlin, because of her obviously better standing in Bucharest.

Meanwhile, Romanian public opinion continued to veer against Austria-Hungary because of the feeling that Viennese diplomatic policy favored Bulgaria over Romania. The Romanian officer corps, in particular, became increasingly anti-Austro-Hungarian. This now raised serious doubts about the Romanian army's willingness to fight, according to treaty, against Russia. Two other issues further strained relations: the Romanian nationality question flaring in parts of the Empire, most significantly in Transylvania and Bukovina; and the issue of whether Romania's secret adherence to the Triple Alliance should be made public, an obvious Austro-Hungarian attempt to force Bucharest to show her true position. Reports from Bucharest to Vienna became progressively more pessimistic. In November 1913, for example, one report related that Romania would, at best, remain neutral at the outbreak of a European war. If, however, the Triple Alliance did not achieve an immediate military victory, the real danger existed that Bucharest might join the Entente. Thus, on 6 November, pressure was again brought to bear on Bucharest to force her to publish the secret Triple Alliance connection. If the Romanian government refused to publish the treaty, so the argument went, at least Vienna would be apprised of where matters in Bucharest really stood. Even King Carol, a Hohenzollern himself and always a firm adherent to the Triple Alliance, indicated to the Austro-Hungarian statesmen that his people opposed Vienna's Balkan policies and that his army's active participation in an allied war could not be assured.[57]

The Balkan Wars and their aftermath also had a significant effect on Central Power military plans. The wars themselves and the concomitant creation of Russian reserve formations, the rapid improvements in Russian military proficiency, and significantly improved strategic railroads resulted in a serious revision of Austro-Hungarian "War Case R" and "War Case B" deployment plans for 1914-1915. For example, Conrad's III and XIV Corps, originally assigned to guard the Italian frontier in the event of an eastern war, would now be deployed in Galicia to help counter Russian gains achieved through her war-preparation measures. This change resulted partly from the foresight that St. Petersburg could use a period of diplomatic tension in the Balkans to initiate a secret partial mobilization and to assure assembly of cavalry and support troops at the frontier in order to disrupt any necessary Austro-Hungarian mobilization measures.[58]

Conrad continued to insist on military grounds that Romania had to be associated with the Triple Alliance, because the Romanian infantry corps could, in his opinion, enable the Triple Alliance to gain a victory in an eastern war. While articulating such views to Franz Ferdinand on 3 November 1913, Conrad informed him that Moltke had promised fourteen, or possibly more, German infantry divisions to be fielded against Russia in the event of a war.[59] Since Romania now appeared definitely lost to the Triple Alliance, it became necessary at the end of November to order that contingency plans for a war against Romania be drawn up. But if Austria-Hungary had to wage war against Russia, Serbia, and Romania, Conrad felt that Austria-Hungary would lose,[60] because the Monarchy simply did not possess the requisite military means.

Further controversy continued over the correct diplomatic course to be followed in regard to Romania and Bulgaria. Bucharest's alliance with Vienna certainly did not fit Bucharest's newly consummated understanding with Serbia. Austro-Hungarian diplomats had earlier ignored warnings that Romania was slipping away from Vienna's grasp, but Berchtold, regardless, refused to relinquish a possible tie to Bulgaria. With the known existence of a Serbo-Greek alliance, coupled with Serbian intransigence in regard to Austria-Hungary and Bucharest's wavering, he considered it unwise to reject completely Bulgarian alliance approaches. Berchtold also stressed that he felt that Germany should use her powerful influence in Bucharest to prevent Serbo-Romanian relations from becoming too intimate.[61]

Greater difficulties became apparent when it became known in Austro-Hungarian military circles that Romania had dispatched intelligence agents into Austria-Hungary. On 28 November 1913, the Austro-Hungarian General Staff decided it must now definitely prepare more than just contingency plans for a "War Case Ru" (Romania).[62] But contrary to Conrad's position, Moltke still hoped to regain Romania for the Triple Alliance.

By December 1913, however, Austro-Hungarian-Romanian relations had reached a crucial stage. Count Czernin reported from Bucharest that King Carol had declared his inability to enforce his country to honor the secret Austro-Hungarian-Romanian Treaty if an eastern war erupted. To counter King Carol's decision, Czernin frantically pleaded for some last-minute Hungarian reforms in Transylvania, and he insisted that the treaty binding the two countries be published "through an indiscretion." The German Foreign Minister, however, opposed the idea.[63]

The further bad news followed that General Alexander Averescu, loyal to the Austro-Hungarian tie, had been ousted as Chief of the Romanian General Staff on 10 December 1913. On 12 December, Conrad therefore ordered a study to be prepared concerning a "War Case Ru." Conrad also received further confirmation that, under present conditions, King Carol had stated that he could not fulfill his secret treaty obligations.[64]

This news was not welcome in Berlin. Kaiser Wilhelm declared that although Germany supported Vienna in the Balkans, "we can in no case be indifferent as to whether twenty divisions of your army are tied up for an offensive operation against the South Slavs or not."[65] German concern could only increase relative to Conrad's war plans, particularly the numerical ratios involved in his more and more likely mutual "War Case R+B."

By December, both Conrad and Franz Joseph learned that even Berlin now considered Romania to be in the enemy camp. In addition, Russia had begun organizing three new army corps in Europe to support her goals, while simultaneously attempting to win Bucharest to her side. The Russians continued frantically to attempt to shorten their mobilization timetables, and Conrad calculated that three to four new Russian divisions would exist already by 1914. While French loans to pressure the Russian regime to develop strategic railroads had made Moscow more dependent on France, they had also significantly increased the capabilities of the Russian railroad to carry troops to the Galician and Prussian frontiers.[66]

One can easily comprehend the far-reaching effects of the Balkan Wars on the power relations in Europe. First, the Balkan Wars influenced the Great Powers to revise their concrete war preparations. Russia, meanwhile, steadily improved her armed forces both quantitatively and qualitatively, while at the same time improving her war preparations through trial mobilizations. Also, in the future she could now count on a larger and numerically stronger Serbia-Montenegro — the major victor in the Balkans conflict — while, on the other hand, Bulgaria and Turkey had been so weakened by their military defeats that they could no longer serve as effective military counterweights for Berlin and Vienna against Serbia. In addition to this total realignment of the military balance of power in the Balkan peninsula, Romania could no longer be trusted to protect the badly exposed Austro-Hungarian right-flank positions against Russia. Austria-Hungary now even began to prepare war plans for a possible "War Case Ru," while the concept of a strategic rearward deployment (*Rückverlegung*) which could occur in the event of Russian mobilization after the initiation of a "War Case B," and first discussed in 1912, became a real possibility for the Vienna General Staff.

At the same time, Great Power armaments increased, and the military establishments of France, Germany, and Russia passed new army laws. Coinciding with these changes, as in the Bosnian Crisis, alliance systems drew together and tightened. A new, tenuous balance of power had been created following the destruction of the old, and for both Vienna and Berlin the result did not bode well.

For 1914, two problems would be crucial for the Allies: Russo-German rivalry at Constantinople, and the Austro-Hungarian-Serbian conflict in the western Balkans. The second problem led to a diplomatic struggle between both alliance groupings for the allegiance of Romania and Bulgaria.

Franco-German relations also were affected. The German Army Bill of 1913, an answer to the negative swing of the Balkan balance of power, led to uneasiness in France, which began seriously to consider the inauguration of three-year army service for her armed forces.

For Germany, the new European situation led to a momentous decision. Because France and Russia would now undoubtedly cooperate in a major war, and because of Russia's improved military prowess and future potential to maintain it, Moltke decided that the yearly Great Eastern Deployment plan should no longer be prepared.[67] The Schlieffen Plan remained as the sole mobilization and deployment plan for Germany. Conrad had to face the loss of Romania as an ally, his ever-increasing enemy numerical disadvantage, and a much more dangerous opponent in the Serbian army. This explains his demand for the creation of an Austro-Hungarian reserve army at a time when Germany already possessed twenty-eight and Russia thirty-eight reserve divisions.[68]

German-Russian relations would be negatively affected by the dispatch of the Liman von Sanders mission to Turkey in December 1913 to reform the badly defeated army. The strained relations would lead to a diplomatic crisis in early 1914.

In toto, the effect of the 1912-1913 events on Vienna can best be summarized by statements from Conrad and Franz Joseph. Conrad, in a 27 December memorandum to his Operations Bureau Chief, stated: "The Balkan War had drawn a line, we must start back at 'A' in order to produce a new situation;" while Franz Joseph expressed his fear that the Treaty of Bucharest was untenable for the future and signified the threat of a new

war: "God grant that it may be confined to the Balkans." The prospects
for the Triple Alliance were not bright for 1914.

CHAPTER VI

The July 1914 Crisis

The repercussions of the Balkan Wars reverberated through Europe until the outbreak of the war of 1914. The newly-created balance of power in the Balkans produced many strange interactions. In early 1914, the climax of the last serious diplomatic crisis before July occurred. The Liman von Sanders' military mission to Turkey to reorganize the shattered Turkish armies resulted in a near German-Russian clash.

Hungarian intransigence in the nationalities question continued to poison relations between Bucharest and Vienna. Periodic anti-Austro-Hungarian demonstrations in Romania incensed public opinion over the Transylvanian problem. France and Russia appeared to be gaining adherents in Bucharest in direct proportion to the decline of Austro-Hungarian supporters.

Conrad became progressively concerned with Romania's diplomatic and military stance, because Romania's obtained promise to cover Austria's extreme right flank in the event of a war with Russia remained a key factor in his Operation Bureau's war planning. However, contrary intelligence reports from Romania indicated that she was moving away from her role as an Austro-Hungarian ally.[1]

When Romania's position became increasingly doubtful, Conrad suggested as a counter move to build strategic rail networks into Transylvania, and to commence the construction of forts on the Austro-Hungarian-Romanian frontier.[2] The turning point in the precarious relations between Bucharest and Vienna occurred with the visit of Tsar Nicholas II to the Romanian port of Constanza in June 1914. As Romania continued to drift away from the Triple Alliance, Berchtold increased his efforts to garner German approval for Bulgaria to join the Triple Alliance as a substitute for Romania, and to serve the role as a counter to Romania and Serbia. Austro-Hungarian-German dueling over this problem pervaded the 1914 communications.

In April and May 1914, Italy renewed her 1888 military pledge (which had elapsed in December 1912) to transport three army corps and two cavalry divisions to fight with German forces against France in the event of war. Even the possibility of Italy sending troops to serve against Serbia or Russia was discussed among Viennese military authorities.[3]

Conrad had earlier written to Moltke on 14 February 1914 asking that he pressure Italy with regard to the dispatching of the three Italian army corps promised for use at the Rhine River. Conrad also used his letter to complain about the effect French money had upon improving Russia's military capability as well as to Romania's growing disaffection towards Austria-Hungary. Conrad expressed the hope that German pressure could win the errant ally back.[4]

Moltke's reply assured Conrad that the promised Italian forces would be sent to the German front by the twenty-second mobilization day with the significant proviso if the *casus foederis* arose. Since Moltke anticipated a German victory within that time span, Germany would commence the war as if the aid from Rome were not to be dispatched. If, however, they did arrive at the German theater, he stated that he would transport more German army corps to the eastern front. Moltke also took the occasion to acknowledge the effect French money had upon present Russian military preparations and indicated that he did not favor a doubtful Bulgarian alliance over a Romanian tie. He concluded the correspondence by writing that the Balkan Wars had demonstrated Turkey's negligible value as a military ally.[5]

In May 1914 the two Chiefs of the General Staffs met for the last time before the outbreak of the World War. Conrad took the opportunity to again pressure Moltke to dispatch more troops to the eastern front in the event of war. Moltke replied vaguely that he would deploy twelve infantry divisions and perhaps "a few more" east of the Lower Vistula River area, and stated cogently, "I will do what I can; we are not superior to the French."[6]

In answer to a Conrad question, Moltke replied that German main forces would move east approximately seven weeks after the start of operations against France. To Moltke, variably a constant theme, the present moment appeared favorable for the Central Powers in the case of a war; perhaps later it would not. Conrad, for his part, confirmed that Austria-Hungary had accepted the mission to protect Germany's rear flank against Russia for those seven weeks of the French campaign.[7] This certainly would not be an easy task.

A significant factor in Central Power military calculations in 1914, albeit difficult to understand, was the opinion that Russia would not participate in a European war, since the crash Russian military improvement program was thought to be aimed at a completion date of 1916 or 1917. It also was felt that the numerous civil problems in the summer of 1914 would prevent Russian intervention.[8]

Other military leaders, however, were convinced that Russia would indeed fight if sufficiently provoked. In fact, Russian diplomats had warned that an Austro-Hungarian move against Serbia would elicit a Russian reaction. Serbia, in turn, had been assured by St. Petersburg that she would not again be let down.[9] Because the Russians had backed down due to German pressure in both the Bosnian Crisis and during the Balkan Wars, they felt that they could not possibly do so again without losing face with the Slavic peoples in the Balkan peninsula.

Meanwhile, Kaiser Wilhelm and Archduke Franz Ferdinand met on 12-13 June 1914, at the Archduke's estate at Konopischt, to reaffirm Germany's unconditional support of Austria-Hungary. However, the assassination of Franz Ferdinand a few weeks later overshadowed these important discussions, leading to the virulent anti-Serbian elements in the Austro-Hungarian leadership to demand a final settling of accounts with the troublesome neighbor. In fact, already on 29 June, a day after Sarajevo, Conrad demanded an Austro-Hungarian mobilization as an answer to the Archduke's murder. However, final action would be dependent on Germany's stance. But the Viennese General Staff presently considered Russia to be militarily unprepared for a war in support of Serbia. Conrad himself felt, therefore, that this would be the last favorable opportunity for Vienna to upset Serbian designs and to prevent disintegration of the Dual Monarchy before the tide had turned completely to the Entente's favor.[10]

On 1 July, Berlin informed the Viennese government that she could maintain her great power position only if she took advantage of the present situation to annihilate Serbia. To cloud the situation, on 2 July, King Carol informed Vienna that Romania could not fulfill her treaty obligations. The importance of Romania to Conrad's strategic planning has been noted, but according to the Austro-Hungarian General Staff, Romanian neutrality would mean the loss of the equivalent of twenty divisions or 400,000 soldiers. A hostile Romania would increase the numerical deficit to the loss of approximately forty divisions, or 800,000 men. Italy, still weakened by the military occupation of Libya since the Tripoli War, could not be

expected to offset such a significant loss of manpower. Thus, according
to Conrad, a war that pitted Austria-Hungary against Russia, and Germany
against France would be feasible only if Romania were an ally drawing
Russian troops from the Austro-Hungarian front. A neutral Romania, on
the other hand, would free at least three Russian corps for action against
Austria-Hungary. If Romania and Serbia both countered Vienna, it would
obviously seriously endanger Austria's chances for a victory over Russia.
Conrad concluded that as a preliminary measure permanent forts must be
constructed to prevent a Romanian invasion of Transylvania in a wartime
situation.[11]

Diplomatic events began to accelerate on 2 July with the dispatch of
a delegation to Germany headed by the Austro-Hungarian Secretary of
Balkan Affairs and Chief of Berchtold's Cabinet, Count Alexander Hoyos,
with a personal letter from Franz Joseph to Wilhelm in which Franz Joseph
lamented the fact that Romania could not fulfill her alliance obligations.
The aged Kaiser informed Berlin that Vienna's basic policy was that
Serbia must be isolated, reduced in size, and removed as a power factor
in the Balkans. In the process, Bulgaria would assume more importance
in Vienna's eyes.

An overall review of the Balkan situation in summary form revealed
that: Turkey could no longer be considered a military counterweight in
that region; Serbia had become more powerful; Bulgaria, seeking closer
ties to the Triple Alliance, had been weakened; and Romania had become
very friendly to Serbia. Even the possibility of Bucharest's merely issuing
a proclamation of neutrality rested solely upon King Carol's promise.
Franz Joseph concluded the letter by stating that the Balkan situation could
be rectified only "if Serbia, which at present forms the pivot of Pan-Slav
policy, is eliminated as a political power factor in the Balkans."[12]

Also, on 5 July, the German ambassador to the Austro-Hungarian
court, Heinrich von Tschirschky, informed Franz Joseph that he could rely
on Germany's solid support if Vienna were forced to defend her vital
Balkan interests. Vienna was urged to formulate a concrete plan of action
that Berlin could wholeheartedly support. As early as 2 July, with the
presentation of the Franz Joseph letter and accompanying document, the
German Foreign Office foresaw, and accepted the possibility of, war with
Russia.

Conrad, in an audience with Franz Joseph on 5 July, asked his Kaiser,
"If the answer runs that Germany will take her stand at our side, do we
then make war on Serbia?" Franz Joseph replied, "In that case, yes."[13]

On 5 July, the so-called "Potsdam War Council" convened in Germany. Although no actual war council ever really met, Wilhelm and his chancellor had decided to grant Vienna a "blank check" earlier the same day. During the reputed "War Council" later in the day, General Falkenhayn, the Prussian War Minister, when questioned as to "whether the army was ready for all eventualities," answered affirmatively.[14] The High Command was then sent on vacation to camouflage the gravity of the unfolding situation.

In Vienna, on 6 July, a telegram arrived from Berlin that has become an important document in the post bellum "war-guilt" issue. In replying to Franz Joseph's letter of 2 July, Wilhelm was reported to have stated that since he expected that immediate Austro-Hungarian measures against Serbia be initiated, Vienna could count on Germany's full support and, further, since Russia was not prepared for war at this time there should be no delay in undertaking such measures.[15] The Kaiser further relayed his position that he would no longer oppose a Bulgarian affiliation with the Triple Alliance as long as he was assured that no aggressive intent was manifested towards Romania. The Austro-Hungarian diplomats departing from Berlin on 6 July were convinced that the German government supported an immediate offensive action against Serbia, fully realizing that it could inevitably lead to a clash of the alliances. With Wilhelm's affirmation that Berlin would be "standing faithfully at your side," Franz Joseph stated that Wilhelm "was of our opinion that it was necessary . . . . to put an end to the intolerable conditions in connection with Serbia."[16]

On the following day, 7 July, largely due to Germany's manifestations of support, an Austro-Hungarian Council of Ministers meeting decided to issue an ultimatum to Serbia, and Conrad, in an afternoon session, stated that he would commence preparations for a military conflict with Serbia. He added that it was imperative to know whether to anticipate Russian hostility which, if it did occur, would certainly need to be countered. This information, according to Conrad, had to be ascertained by the fifth day of a Balkan mobilization to preserve valuable time and, most significantly, to avoid disturbing fixed railroad deployment timetables. Opinion was fractious at the meeting. Count István Tisza, Premier of Hungary, emphasized that a war with Serbia would definitely result in Russian intervention and that Romanian, Russian and Serbian armies all battling Austria-Hungary would surely prove to be disastrous.

By 8 July, German leaders began to become restless, fearing that Vienna, although seriously considering military action against Serbia, would not act aggressively. As Count Laszlo Szögyény, the Austro-Hungarian ambassador to Berlin, reported to Berchtold, German leaders were "emphatically encouraging us not to miss the present opportunity."[17] While maintaining this diplomatic pressure, German military leaders also began to become concerned that the possibility existed that major Austro-Hungarian forces might not be deployed against Russia if St. Petersburg became involved in the Serbian issue. The concern arose as to Conrad's intentions to possibly deploy an excessive number of troops to ensure that Serbia be crushed on the battlefield.

Meanwhile, the German Foreign Office's frustration with Vienna's stance increased. This became evident when, on 14 July, Berchtold announced that he desired to postpone presentation of the ultimatum to Serbia until 23 July. On 16 July, Berchtold further stated that the delay in taking action resulted from the visit of French President Raymond Poincaré and his Foreign Minister, René Viviani, to St. Petersburg. The time limit for an answer to the ultimatum was set for 25 July with Austro-Hungarian mobilization slated to commence forty-eight hours later. On 28 July, Austria-Hungary would declare war on Serbia.

As the Austro-Hungarian-Serbian crisis began to boil behind the scenes, Berlin also began to exert pressure upon Vienna to reach an understanding with Italy regarding her interpretation of Article VII of the Triple Alliance Treaty. Thus, Vienna should negotiate territorial adjustments if necessary. Similar pressure came from the German General Staff to Conrad. Although diplomatic reports from Rome did not bode well for allied cohesion, Berlin continued to consider Italy indispensable for the maintenance of an alliance stance. Germany, therefore, accepted Rome's interpretation of the critical Article VII that any alteration in the Balkan balance of power would require compensation to Italy. Vienna, on the other hand, argued that the clause only pertained to Turkish, not Serbian, territories, therefore she had no obligation to negotiate with Rome.

The Italian Foreign Minister repeatedly stated that Rome's position was dictated by the fact that she had not been notified of Austro-Hungarian intentions regarding Serbia as had been called for in the treaty, and that, furthermore, the Austro-Hungarian ultimatum to Serbia represented an aggressive act, whereas the Triple Alliance was a purely defensive grouping of powers. If Russia intervened in an Austro-Hungarian-Serbian conflict, therefore, Italy would not accept that the *casus foederis* had arisen and thus would await events. The question of Italy's stance now became increasingly crucial and the profusion of German suggestions that Vienna provide satisfactory compensation to bring Rome into an active participation in the Alliance became a key issue for weeks.

Adding to the Austro-Hungarian-Italian friction, claiming the necessity to keep the advantage of secrecy, Berchtold steadfastly refused to inform Rome of his diplomatic maneuvers. Berlin and Vienna would haggle over the question of the value of forewarning Italy about Vienna's intentions, but Berchtold appeared determined, regardless of circumstances, to present Italy with a diplomatic *fait accompli* while at the same time declaring that Italy had no right to compensation in the form of Balkan territory in the case of the outbreak of an Austro-Hungarian-Serbian war. Berlin, however, insisted that Italy should receive compensation to neutralize her resistance to an Austro-Hungarian attack on Serbia, and to attempt to maintain her adherence to the Triple Alliance. On 23 July, Conrad cryptically remarked regarding the situation, "If Italy became an enemy, then we do not mobilize."[18] Conrad understood that a war on three fronts provided no chance of success for Austro-Hungarian arms.

Meanwhile, Russia's Foreign Minister, Serge Dmitrievich Sazonov, announced that Russia would not allow any form of Austro-Hungarian infringement of Serbian independence. Bethmann Hollweg had meanwhile wired his ambassadors in the Entente capitals to express that they should take the position that Germany desired a localization of an Austro-Hungarian-Serbian conflict, because otherwise Great Power intervention could be catastrophic, leading to either a continental or world war.

On 19 July at another Council of Ministers meeting in Vienna, Conrad announced that for military reasons he favored a speedy commencement of the impending action against Serbia. When queried by the other attendees whether it would be possible to begin a mobilization first against Serbia and then, if it became necessary, also against Russia, his answer was "yes" concerning Serbia, and a qualified "yes" concerning the beginning of a Russian intervention. If mobilization had to be ordered against Russia and if it occurred within five days after the commencement of a "War Case B" mobilization, Conrad foresaw no difficulties in its execution and even stated that he considered chances for military success at the moment to be favorable.[19]

At 6:00 p.m. on 23 July, the Austro-Hungarian ambassador to Serbia delivered the Austro-Hungarian ultimatum as instructed so that news of its delivery could not reach St. Petersburg until after the French President and his Foreign Minister had departed from their state visit. When the ultimatum did become known to the Russian Foreign Minister, Sazonov, he became highly indignant exclaiming passionately that "that means war... If Austria-Hungary swallows Serbia, we shall make war on her."[20]

On 24 July, the earlier dispatch of the Austro-Hungarian ultimatum led to the calling of a special meeting of the Russian Council of Ministers. Two fateful decisions resulted from this gathering: four military districts bordering on Austria-Hungary would be mobilized signifying a partial Russian mobilization, and stock-piling of war materials would be accelerated. This decision raised the crucial question of whether Russia could actually initiate only a partial mobilization, as favored by Sazonov, without disturbing overall Russian strategic plans. Certain generals argued vehemently against its potentially disastrous effects. For one thing, if the Warsaw Military District would be mobilized, because it bordered on Berlin, Germany might consider it to be an aggressive Russian act. The partial mobilization was aimed solely at Austria-Hungary yet, despite the fact that the entire Warsaw military district would not be mobilized because it was not one of the four Russian military districts cited, the partial mobilization of four reserve divisions that were bivouacked in the Warsaw district that were needed for the Austro-Hungarian front could still be claimed by Germany to be a provocative step against her. The Russian military leaders further argued that a partial military call-up would make no sense since a Russian move intended solely against Vienna would naturally cause an allied German intervention. Also, a general mobilization proclaimed after a partial one had been instituted would serve only to create utter confusion. For some unexplained reason, the new Chief of the Russian General Staff in 1914 did not make clear to Sazonov what a terrible military mistake a partial mobilization would be. Meanwhile, the French ambassador to St. Petersburg, Maurice Paléologue, without the knowledge of his government, on 27 and 28 July pledged his country's unconditional solidarity with Russia.

Reports of Serbian mobilization measures meanwhile began to pour in to Vienna on 24 and 25 July. The command for Vienna's own "War Case B" mobilization came at 9:23 p.m. on 25 July, when Franz Joseph ordered Austro-Hungarian partial mobilization.[21] This signified the call-up of the Minimal Group Balkan and the B-Group (the Second Army). The first mobilization day would be proclaimed for 28 July, with 27 July being designated the first "Alarm Day." So as not to provoke Russia in any way, no military activity would be initiated in Galicia. All troops not mobilized for "War Case B," however, were ordered back to their garrisons.[22] Conrad's basic plan for his Balkan war consisted of the concept of a rapid, decisive defeat of Serbia before any Russian intervention could occur. If this proved successful, it would, according to Conrad, certainly draw Italy, Bulgaria, Romania, and Turkey towards Vienna. Just in case Russia did threaten a Balkan mobilization, the "Alarm" preparatory orders for "War Case R" were forwarded to the commanders of the I, X and XI frontier Corps in Galicia.[23]

On 24 July, Berlin again began to exert diplomatic pressure on Vienna for immediate action to be launched against Serbia to preclude the possibility of other powers intervening. But when Berchtold pressured Conrad as to why an immediate declaration of war shouldn't be proclaimed, Conrad replied that his armies could only commence operations on approximately 12 August.[24] Berchtold warned the Chief of the General Staff that the present diplomatic constellation would not hold for that long. Austro-Hungarian military problems, however, simply could not be overcome. For example, demands for the construction of additional strategic railroad trackage had been ignored for years. In July 1914, only one rail line led to a crucial part of the Serbian frontier, where the terrain was unsuitable for military use anyway.

On 25 July, the Russian Council of Ministers reconvened, whereupon it again approved the decision to initiate a partial mobilization affecting the four military districts of Kazan, Kiev, Odessa, and Moscow, thus calling up 1,100,000 men. This partial mobilization was actually preparation for a general mobilization and was termed a "Period Preparatory to War." Other action at the Council included the decision to commence further military measures.[25] These particular measures were to be kept strictly secret while Sazonov diplomatically attempted to prevent the impending Austro-Hungarian attack against Serbia.

Some Russian generals, as early as 24 July, had demanded the proclamation of a general mobilization. In particular, the Grand Duke Nikolai Nikolaevich and the Russian War Minister, General Vladimir Sukhomlinov, insisted that a partial mobilization would be disastrous for subsequent military measures on both technical and political grounds. This pressure group developed a very negative influence over the Tsar. In particular, they felt certain that if Austria-Hungary attacked Serbia a Russian-German military confrontation would have to follow. Since Germany could mobilize so much more quickly than Russia, they argued that a full mobilization should be inaugurated.

Despite the secrecy of the 25 July meeting of the Russian Council of Ministers, reports quickly reached the Central Powers that an order for

Russian partial mobilization along the Austro-Hungarian border had been issued. Almost immediately Russian troop movements, some of them occurring on the German frontier as well, also were detected.[26] On 26 July, the German military attaché in St. Petersburg reported to Berlin that the four military districts along the Austro-Hungarian frontier had been mobilized. This report was quickly confirmed by dispatches from other sources as well.

The real danger to world peace, however, would occur when those decreed Russian military measures aimed solely against Austria-Hungary in turn provoked a German counter-mobilization. A German mobilization unquestionably signified a European war. Germany was the only continental power with just one mobilization plan — the Schlieffen Plan — which called for a victory of annihilation against France in the opening weeks of war, whether France instigated the conflict or not. Moreover, the timely activation of the Schlieffen Plan was considered essential to preserve the significant German advantage of rapid mobilization, especially if Russia were given too much time to make her own preparations.

Meanwhile, more warnings that Russia would not stand quietly aside while Austria-Hungary devoured Serbia proliferated. Basically, Russia could not allow Austria-Hungary to become the predominant power in the Balkans. Berlin, however, rejected such warnings and attempted to soothe Russian suspicions with the argument that Vienna did not intend to seize Serbian territory.

Then Sazonov, on 26 July, informed the German ambassador to St. Petersburg that the "rumors" circulating of Russian military measures being initiated were incorrect, indeed neither one horse nor one reservist had been called up. The War Minister, Sukhomlinov, on the same day gave the German military attaché his word of honor that no mobilization order had been issued. He repeated Sazonov's assurances, but he further warned that if Austro-Hungarian troops crossed the Serbian frontier, the four military districts bordering Austro-Hungarian territories would be immediately mobilized. Under no circumstances, however, he assured, would military measures be initiated at the German frontier. The German military attaché telegraphed Berlin that in actuality Russian military measures to date had become quite extensive; Russia's strategy obviously was to gain time for new negotiations and at the same time to insure continuation of her advancing military measures.[27] The veiled half-truths spoken by Russian leaders would only exacerbate the situation.

Bethmann Hollweg, on being informed of the Russian military measures, dispatched an urgent telegram (7:15 p.m., 26 July) to inform Sazonov that the alleged Russian preparatory military measures begun against Germany would result in German counter-measures (i.e., an order for mobilization). For Germany, it was emphasized, this would signify war. Bethmann Hollweg thus resorted to the tactic of threatening Russia in an attempt to force a localization of the forthcoming Austro-Hungarian-Serbian conflict.

In the meantime, Sazonov admitted that his government had initiated certain military measures so as not to be caught by surprise by Berlin and Vienna. He further stated that the balance of power in the Balkans was of vital concern to Russia. This warning does not appear to have been taken seriously by the Central Powers; in fact, it had no real effect on their actions.

On 26 July, the German ambassador to Great Britain, Karl Lichnowsky, in a telegram, relayed to Berlin an ". . . urgent warning no longer to believe in the possibility of localization of an Austro-Hungarian-Serbian War," intimating that the English would come to the aid of France if she were attacked.[28] But the German Foreign Office, following Bethmann Hollweg's policy line, continued to be convinced that Great Britain would remain neutral if a European war erupted.

In the meantime, rumors of Russian mobilization measures began to increase in intensity. Both the German ambassador and military attaché in St. Petersburg revealed to the Austro-Hungarian ambassador the content of their conversations with Sazonov on 26 July. He, in turn, wired Berchtold reports of the conversations. Berchtold then informed Conrad, who proceeded to insist that Germany now threaten Russia with the beginning of her own mobilization. On the evening of 27 July, Conrad repeated his demand that Russia should be warned that because of her military measures corresponding measures would be taken by Berlin.[29]

In response to the ever-increasing German pressure for Vienna to act, Berchtold telegraphed Berlin that he would "issue the official declaration of war tomorrow (28 July), or the day after at the latest, principally to forestall any attempt at mediation." The German diplomats and military leadership had not been pleased with the news that no serious military movements against Serbia could commence before 12 August.

To add confusion to the situation, the German Foreign Secretary now reversed himself and stated categorically that if Russia indeed mobilized, Germany would also be obligated to mobilize at once; and, further, that if Russia attacked Austria-Hungary, Germany would not stand aside. Thus, on 27 July, the German Ambassador to Russia relayed to Sazonov the German position that any Russian military measures aimed at Germany would force Berlin to take counter-measures which signified that she would commence her mobilization. That, in turn, meant war. Sazonov did not realize the significance of the warning; therefore, it had to be repeated to him again on 29 July.[30]

On that day alone, 27 July, thirteen different reports of Russian mobilization measures, of which seven listed activity on the German frontier, were received. The only German military activity to date, on the other hand, consisted merely of strengthening railroad protection squads.[31] The European situation now became progressively more strained.

On the same day, 27 July, Wilhelm and some of the German military leaders returned to Berlin from their ordered vacations. Wilhelm, Bethmann Hollweg, Moltke, and Jagow met in Potsdam at 3:10 p.m. The German War Minister later announced that he learned that Germany "would fight the business out."[32]

Bethmann Hollweg now sought as a basis for his diplomacy to place the responsibility for a general mobilization and war, if it occurred, squarely on St. Petersburg. As part of this strategy, the chancellor convinced the Kaiser to send a telegram to the Tsar worded in such a way that if a war erupted it would help cast Russia in the role of the aggressor.

The Austro-Hungarian declaration of war against Serbia and the first Austro-Hungarian mobilization day for "War Case B" ensued on 28 July. Belgrade was bombarded by artillery on the same day from across the frontier. Also, early in the morning of 28 July, the Central Powers' ambassadors in St. Petersburg both reported the mobilization of the military districts of Kiev, Warsaw, Odessa, and Moscow. This Russian military call-up encompassed fifty-five infantry and eight and one-half cavalry divisions. (The entire Austro-Hungarian army, it should be recalled, consisted of forty-eight divisions.) Austria-Hungary had announced that she would mobilize eight of her sixteen corps — those in the closest proximity of Serbia — totaling twenty-six divisions. The Russian military reaction to the threat to Serbia which was ostensibly designed to preclude a rapid Austro-Hungarian overrunning of Serbia, also seriously endangered the tense European diplomatic situation.

Sazonov meanwhile justified his government's military action by citing the Austro-Hungarian mobilization order and concomitant declaration of war which "must be regarded as directed partly against Russia."[33] Previously, he had only warned that Russia would act if Austro-Hungarian troops actually crossed the Serbian frontier. Now, a large portion of the Russian army had been mobilized before the actual invasion occurred. Sazonov reiterated that these Russian military measures implied no aggressive intent towards Germany, but that an Austro-Hungarian crossing of the Serbian frontier would mean war against her. The Russian military leadership now began to gain control of affairs and to exercise their weight in diplomatic decisions. With war growing ever more probable, if not inevitable, the Russian General Staff wanted to lose no more valuable time and thus pressed for general mobilization.

Sazonov was finally convinced that it would be impossible to shift from a partial to a general mobilization without causing a logistical catastrophe. The Tsar, however, opposed issuing the order for the Russian general mobilization to the very end.

Commencing on 28 July, military circles in Berlin and Vienna also began to increase their pressure on the civilian leadership. Accordingly, Moltke prepared a memorandum to Bethmann Hollweg in which he argued that Austria-Hungary could not possible launch a "War Case B" without Russia intervening. Further, he argued that the Russian partial mobilization would result in Vienna being forced to mobilize her remaining armed forces which, in turn, would make an Austro-Hungarian-Russian war inevitable. This state of affairs would create the *casus foederis* for Germany. Russia could then claim that she had been attacked by the Central Powers, and France could claim provocation and enter the fray via terms of the Triple Entente.

Since, as Moltke argued, an Austro-Hungarian-Russian war was now inevitable, Germany must prepare for the resultant two-front war. Austria-Hungary, for her part, should mobilize in advance of Russia to secure the Galician front while she dealt with Serbia. Moltke emphasized that under no circumstance should France and Russia be allowed to gain time that could be used to their military advantage because this could work to the detriment of the Schlieffen Plan. His memorandum served as the first serious military incursion into the political realm. Moltke also prepared a note to be delivered to the Belgian government (4:40 p.m., 28 July).[34]

Turning to the frantic afternoon activity in Vienna on 28 July, Conrad began to pressure Berchtold, saying he must know by 1 August if Russia would intervene in "War Case B." If not, he would deploy all his forces for the Balkan campaign, meaning the twelve-division B-Group would supplement the Minimal Group Balkan's effort to seek to achieve a thoroughgoing "chastisement" of Serbia. If Russia did mobilize, Conrad acknowledged that he would redirect the preponderant bulk of his forces against Russia, signifying a reversal of direction of the B-Group back to Galicia in conjunction with the A-Group.

Conrad was justified in his pressuring Berchtold since information about a possible Russian mobilization was absolutely essential in attempting to also pursue a war against Serbia. At Conrad's insistence and to reinforce his own demands, Berchtold urged Berlin to threaten Russia with a German mobilization. But Bethmann Hollweg felt that the time was premature for such a drastic step. But renewed reports of Russian military measures caused the German ambassador in St. Petersburg to warn the Russian government that continuation of such measures could result in war.

On 28 July, France also began to actively enter the diplomatic and military picture. The French Chief of the General Staff, perhaps anticipating political decisions, assured the Russian military attaché of France's "full and active readiness faithfully to execute her responsibilities as an ally."[35] At this particular moment, French diplomacy was partially paralyzed because the French President and his Foreign Minister were still returning from their cruise to St. Petersburg.

Meanwhile, on 29 July, in reply to direct questioning, the Chief of the Russian General Staff, General Nikolai Ianuskevich, reaffirmed his word of honor that he had earlier given that the 26 July mobilization had not been ordered in Russia. But reports of Russian military measures multiplied early on 29 July indicating the possibility of an initiation of a full mobilization, although no formal announcement had been issued.[36] The extensive military measures alluded to did present the advantage for Russia — and disadvantage for the Central Powers — of reducing by days the time necessary for a general mobilization. This could conceivably negate one of the crucial advantages of the Schlieffen Plan — the anticipated much speedier allied mobilization and deployment.

When on 29 July the Russian ambassador in Vienna finally announced the Russian partial mobilization, Conrad proposed a new double course of action: St. Petersburg should be questioned as to "what this step signified" and at the same time be informed that Vienna would not be deterred from action against Serbia; and Berlin should inform both France and Russia that a Russian mobilization against the Dual Monarchy would result in a German counter-mobilization.

Moltke renewed and intensified his pressure upon Bethmann Hollweg on 29 July. As the Bavarian military attaché stated, "Moltke is exerting all his influence in favor of taking advantage of the exceptionally favorable opportunity for striking a decisive blow."[37] Moltke himself asserted that he must know "whether Russia and France intend to let it come to a war with Germany." He and the German War Minister then pressured for proclamation of the "imminent danger of war" by necessity. But for the time being, Bethmann Hollweg successfully resisted such pressure from the military hierarchy.

Kaiser Wilhelm, when he learned of the Russian partial mobilization, exclaimed, "That means that I've got to mobilize as well." The news of Russian mobilization resulted in a threat from Berlin to also mobilize, which actually meant war if it occurred.[38]

Berlin initiated her own first serious military measures on 29 July. Falkenhayn, the German War Minister, sought more extensive measures, but Bethmann Hollweg continued to reject the proclamation of "imminent danger of war" partly because Moltke, apparently seconding the Kaiser's feelings, did not push for extreme military measures. Bethmann Hollweg's policy was to attempt to bait Russia into commencing the first general mobilization, thus being able to brand her as the aggressive party. He hoped such a success would have its effect on Britain.

On the evening of 29 July, a meeting took place in which the implications of the Russian partial mobilization were discussed. The most important question to be decided was whether the Russian partial mobilization should lead to a German counter-mobilization.[39] In the 1909 Conrad-Moltke correspondence, Moltke had written that "as soon as Russia mobilizes, Germany will mobilize her entire army." According to the assembled German leaders, Russia had two choices: either submit to pressure from Berlin, thus presenting Germany with a great diplomatic triumph as in 1909, or accept the terrible onus of starting a continental or world war.

Bethmann Hollweg also continued unsuccessfully to delude himself of British neutrality in the event of a European war.

Wilhelm telegraphed Tsar Nicholas during the night of 29-30 July as part of the Willy-Nicky exchanges, warning him that the Russian mobilization threatened to result in the outbreak of a war. The Tsar, upon receipt of this telegram, countermanded his just-given order for a general mobilization. However, a telegram received from the Tsar on 30 July greatly disturbed Wilhelm and the German General Staff. The key sentence creating the shock was "the military measures which have now come into force were decided five days ago." The news of the Austro-Hungarian artillery bombardment of Belgrade on 29 July had meanwhile caused the Chief of the Russian General Staff to argue the indispensability of preparing for war by initiating a general mobilization in place of the partial one.[40]

At 7:00 p.m. on 30 July, the Russian government announced the decision to initiate a full mobilization for the next day. Two factors seem to have convinced Sazonov of the necessity for this extreme step urged by the military: Gottlieb von Jagow's (German Secretary for Foreign Affairs) reversal of his previous position of 27 July, that a Russian partial mobilization commenced against Austria-Hungary would not lead to a similar German reaction; and Tschirschky's (the German ambassador to Vienna) statement that pressure on Vienna for conciliation would be useless. Pressure from the Russian General Staff also had its effect on Sazonov. Among other arguments, the General Staff insisted that a general mobilization was a necessity on the technical grounds that allied France would balk if it appeared that St. Petersburg would once again yield to German diplomatic pressure.[41]

Before official announcement of the Russian mobilization became known, Falkenhayn and Moltke continued to press for a proclamation of the "imminent danger of war." Bethmann Hollweg, however, wished to await a negative reply to his demand wired to St. Petersburg that Russia stop her anti-Austrian military activities. Thus, he was able again to temporarily resist the pressure from the generals, but promised that a final decision would be made on the following day.

Commencing on the morning of 30 July, Moltke began to direct a steady stream of pressure upon his opposite Conrad to assume a strong stance against Russia. At about noon on that day, Moltke did an about-face in attitude when he learned that Russia admitted to have been carrying on military activities for five days. He now began to push incessantly for mobilization and war.[42] Moltke now felt that the military situation had become disadvantageous to Berlin and Vienna. He therefore proceeded to urge Conrad to demand an Austro-Hungarian general mobilization since Germany could only act in the event of an Austro-Hungarian-Russian conflict. The significant proviso was, however, that Russia must declare war; Vienna must not.

Moltke also encouraged Vienna to bring about an honorable arrangement with Italy by assurances of compensation through Article VII of the Triple Alliance treaty to keep Italy on the side of the Triple Alliance; also he urged Conrad to be sure to leave no troops stationed at the Italian frontier; and he urged his colleague to realize that the last means possible of preserving Austria-Hungary was to fight out a European war. For that, "Germany is with you unconditionally," Moltke assured.

On the same evening, when Moltke wired Conrad personally to that effect, it raised the serious question as to whether he had usurped the powers of the Chancellor by such a message to his counterpart.

But on 30 July, Moltke also notified Conrad:

> Russia's partial mobilization is not yet a reason for [German] mobilization. Not until a state of war exists between the Monarchy and Russia. In contrast to the mobilizations and demobilizations which have been customary in Russia, Germany's mobilization would unconditionally lead to war. Do not declare war on Russia, but await her [Russia's] attack.[43]

Conrad replied to Moltke's message that "We will not declare war on Russia and not begin a war,"[44] but he seems to have misread the intent of Moltke's telegram. He believed that his counterpart had declared that a Russian mobilization did not provide a basis for Austro-Hungarian mobilization. In actuality, Moltke had predicated a German mobilization on an immediate Viennese general mobilization.

Moltke prepared a further telegram on 30 July to Conrad (sent on the following morning):

> Stand firm against Russian mobilization. Austria-Hungary must be preserved. Mobilize at once against Russia. Germany will mobilize. Bring Italy, by compensation, to her alliance obligations.[45]

By this telegram, Moltke had definitely exceeded his lines of authority by transmitting political advice to Conrad without the approval of Bethmann Hollweg. At the same time, however, Moltke insisted upon receiving a third confirmation of the actual Russian general mobilization before himself ordering a full German mobilization.

On 30 July, Conrad met with Franz Joseph and explained to him that a Russian attack on Austria-Hungary would cause Germany to make a counter move, resulting in a Russian announcement of their own general mobilization. Further, he stated that before any decisive action was begun in Galicia, a victory over Serbia could, and should, be obtained. Russian mobilization would not be carried out rapidly, an old theme for Conrad, and that breathing space before Russia could mount a serious threat to the

Austro-Hungarian position could be utilized for the thorough chastisement
of Serbia. This would prove to be a serious miscalculation on Conrad's
part, for Russian mobilization had already been confirmed by the three
Galician army corps commanders. If the Russian mobilization were not
instantly countermanded, when it did become a known fact, the Austro-
Hungarian General Staff felt a general mobilization must be ordered.

On the same day, Tsar Nicholas wired Wilhelm that "Russia stands
behind Serbia." While again the German ambassador in London, Lichnowsky, warned his government that the appearance of Austro-Hungarian
troops on Serbian territory would provide the *casus belli* for Russia.
Regarding diplomacy, Conrad stated:

> Berchtold can open discussions preliminary to negotiations as much
> as he wants, but operations against Serbia must not be held up by
> them. Any delay can only worsen the military position of Austria-
> Hungary.[46]

The Austro-Hungarian military authorities had by now resolved to
crush Serbia regardless of the consequences, or what Russia did in opposition.

A crucial step toward the outbreak of the war occurred when Berlin
dispatched two ultimatums on 31 July. The first, forwarded to St. Petersburg, demanded that the Russian mobilization be immediately terminated.
A twelve-hour time limit for a reply was demanded because of the extent
of Russian military measures. Paris received the second ultimatum. This
one demanded French neutrality in the event of a Russo-German war and
an answer within eighteen hours; if France actually accepted the position
of neutrality, the Germans would then send a follow-up telegram demanding the surrender of Metz and Toul, two of France's most vital fortresses
on the German frontier — a move designated to provoke France into war.
While these two telegrams sped to their destinations, the German Foreign
Office prepared the actual declarations of war.

Telegrams from Wilhelm and Nicholas crossed each other on this
fateful day. The one from the Tsar stated that:

> It is impossible to halt our military preparations because of Aus-
> tria's mobilization. As long as the negotiations with Austria-Hun-
> gary in regard to Serbia continue, my troops shall not initiate any
> provocative action."[47]

Wilhelm's telegram read: "Responsibility for the safety of my Empire forces upon me preventive defensive measures."[48]

At 7:00 a.m., Moltke called his corps commander at the Polish frontier to confirm the Russian mobilization; otherwise Germany could not mobilize. Before Moltke could receive such notification, a telegram arrived from St. Petersburg stating: "General Mobilization army and navy ordered. First day of mobilization 31 July."[49] The telegram arrived as Bethmann Hollweg conferred with Moltke and Falkenhayn about the situation. The decision to proclaim "imminent danger of war" was the immediate result of reading the telegram. This action was to be followed within twenty-four to forty-eight hours by a German mobilization.

At 1:00 p.m., the state of "imminent danger of war" was proclaimed in Germany. During the night of 31 July, irrefutable reports arrived of Russian mobilization measures being performed at the German frontier. For Moltke, the fact of Russian mobilization left him no time to lose. According to the Schlieffen Plan's strategy, no potential enemy should even minutely compromise the German war timetables. Moltke, however, took the time to meet with the German Chancellor twice before final action was taken.

Bethmann Hollweg then wired the German ambassador in Vienna, Tschirschky, stating that the Russian general mobilization would force Germany's proclamation of "imminent danger of war," which would presumably be followed by mobilization. Further, he stated that "This inevitably means war. We expect from Austria-Hungary immediate active participation in the war against Russia."[50] During the afternoon and evening, Moltke telegraphed Conrad, while Wilhelm wired to Franz Joseph the same message.

When Conrad read Moltke's telegrams to Berchtold, he responded, "Who runs the government, Moltke or Bethmann Hollweg?" Berchtold's subsequent action appears to have answered his question. He accepted Moltke's position as preeminent to that of the political leadership. The most immediate result of the Berchtold-Conrad meeting was the decision to request Franz Joseph's signature on an Austro-Hungarian general mobilization order,[51] which was duly signed at 12:23 p.m. on 31 July.

Conrad, in a subsequent audience with the Kaiser, suggested that the following telegram be transmitted to Berlin:

. . . war against Serbia shall be waged . . . mobilize remainder of army and concentrate it in Galicia. General Mobilization will be

ordered on 1 August, with 4 August as the first day of mobilization.
Request notification of your first day of mobilization. . . .[52]

Conrad prepared the telegram at 7:30 p.m. on 30 July, but did not send
the message until 8:00 a.m. 31 July, suggesting that either he was not
anxious that Moltke learn of the extent of the continued military efforts
against Serbia or that he awaited Franz Joseph's approval for dispatching
it.

This message could not have been welcome to Moltke, who wanted
Austria's main forces to counter Russia, the much more serious military
opponent, thus making Serbia a purely secondary effort. Franz Joseph then
himself cabled Wilhelm: "The action of my army against Serbia now
proceeding can suffer no interruption from the threatening and challenging
attitude of Russia."[53] While Conrad continued to claim that the Russian
mobilization was perhaps a bluff and that, in any case, there would be
sufficient time to complete a military campaign against Serbia before
Russia could present a serious challenge, Berchtold had also made clear
to his German colleagues that "War Case B" could not be retarded or
halted regardless of any actions begun by St. Petersburg.[54]

Kaiser Wilhelm then telegraphed Franz Joseph at 4:05 p.m., 31 July:

In this difficult struggle it is of the greatest importance that Austria-Hungary employ her main forces against Russia and not divide
it by a [simultaneous] offensive against Serbia. This is even more
important because a large portion of my army will be bound by
France. In the gigantic struggle . . . Serbia plays a secondary role,
requiring only the most necessary defensive measures. Success in
the war . . . can only be expected if we meet the powerful enemy
with our total forces.[55]

He appended to this telegram the hope that Vienna would make contact
with Italy to gain her as an active ally. The substance of the above telegram
is quite explicit. To Germany, Russia was to be Austria-Hungary's major
opponent. Berlin thus desired that every possible Austro-Hungarian soldier
be pressed into an offensive into Poland to tie down the Russian armies
covering Germany's eastern flank, while the vast majority of German
forces smashed into France in Schlieffen style. At 4:15 p.m., a follow-up
telegram was dispatched from Conrad to Moltke.

The Austro-Hungarian mobilization against Russia is provoked only by the Russian mobilization. It has only the purpose to guard against a Russian attack without the intention to declare war.[56]

Moltke telegraphed to Conrad at 7:00 p.m.:

Chief of the General Staff has received a message from Conrad that Austria-Hungary does not intend to wage war against Russia. Germany will proclaim mobilization of entire military forces probably 2 August and open hostilities against Russia and France. Will Austria-Hungary leave her in the lurch?[57]

Moltke's main fear now became obvious: if Vienna delayed the mobilization against Russia, the weak German forces to be deployed in East Prussia would be overwhelmed by the enormous onslaught of Russian troops. Conrad then wired the following reply to the above telegram to Berlin:

Today the information arrived only about the German intention to immediately begin the war against France and Russia. Request return statement whether this is the correct interpretation of German intent, so our action is coordinated accordingly.[58]

The Austro-Hungarian military attaché in Berlin telegraphed 31 July (3:00 p.m.) to Vienna that Germany would mobilize her entire army very shortly, which really meant war against Russia and France would be fought. The telegram concluded that "Germany stands solidly with Austria." Moltke again pressed and demanded that all available Austro-Hungarian forces be fielded against Russia and that the offensive against Serbia should be deemphasized.

Austro-Hungarian general mobilization being proclaimed on 31 July, but not until 4 August the first "R" mobilization day resulted from the confused railroad situation created by the deployment already under way against Serbia and the upcoming "War Case R" mobilization encompassing the B-Group already mobilized for "War Case B." 4 August would prove to be too late to effect a viable Austro-Hungarian deployment. While the Austro-Hungarian general mobilization proclamation occurred eighteen hours after the Russian one, four additional precious days would be lost to ensure a smooth-flowing railroad deployment.

In the meantime, the Central Powers began to exert pressure on both potential allies as well as upon each other to attract allies to their side.

For example, Wilhelm telegraphed King Carol of Romania, appealing to him as a fellow Hohenzollern to honor his country's treaty with the Central Powers. According to Wilhelm, he "counted unconditionally on active Romanian support."[59]

Italy occupied a very significant position in the Berlin-Vienna calculations during July and August 1914, but the Italian Council of Ministers, meeting on 31 July, decided that Vienna's ultimatum to Serbia was, in actuality, an unannounced aggressive act, and, furthermore, that assurances of compensation to Italy, according to Article VII of the treaty of alliance, had not been forthcoming. Therefore, Rome announced its intention to remain neutral.

Conrad, meanwhile, somehow retained the illusion that it might be possible to induce Italy to fulfill her military obligations against France and codeterminously to place some fighting forces in Galicia to aid Austria-Hungary in her eastern struggle. Moltke, in turn, had previously pressured Conrad to pressure his diplomatic corps to ensure Italy of compensation so as to guarantee Rome's participation in the war. For Germany, Italy was an indispensable ally.

To make matters worse for Austria-Hungary and Germany, Lichnowsky, the German ambassador in London, telegraphed Bethmann Hollweg that Britain could not remain neutral on Berlin's terms. Bethmann Hollweg's entire diplomatic structure had collapsed!

When St. Petersburg failed to reply to the German ultimatum by noon on 1 August, the declaration of war was dispatched at 12:52 p.m., to be presented at 6:00 p.m. Russian time. The peace of Europe would now be shattered by a series of declarations of war and deployments of armies, formally launching the first total war.

CHAPTER VII

Mobilization

European military doctrine before 1914 called for the most rapid possible mobilization, a railroad deployment planned to the exact minute and hour, and the earliest possible launching of an opening offensive. Conventional thinking in nineteenth-century Europe held that these factors would be decisive in the opening battle of a war, and if past examples — e.g., the Franco-Prussian War — sufficed in the entire campaign as well. Thus, European military planners anticipated a war of short duration, an expectation today termed the "short war illusion."[1]

This theory proved inconsistent with the realities of both the American Civil War (1861-1865), and with the 1904-1905 Russo-Japanese War. In these wars, the experience of heavy casualties sustained in week- and month-long battles, involving maneuvers and skirmishes that would appear to gain victory, would ultimately result in defeat. These lessons were largely unheeded in 1914 European military planning, particularly in Vienna.

The advent of the railroad had become decisive for effective war planning, as the Elder Moltke and Schlieffen in Germany recognized; and strategic plans, including attempts to shorten the rail deployment time of troops, received yearly review by the various General Staffs.

Rail deployment planning proved to be particularly troublesome in Austria-Hungary because of insufficient rail lines for the deployment of large armies either rapidly or strategically, especially for "War Cases R" (Russia) and "B" (Balkan) or, in particular, in a combined "War Case R+B." The Austro-Hungarian military planners also had to face the most difficult geographical conditions in Europe for warfare, e.g., many mountain areas, including the Carpathian range.

The Dual Monarchy's unique difficulties in planning and then implementing a successful war can be partly ascribed to the long common frontier with Russia, Serbia-Montenegro, and Romania, which totaled over 2,000 kilometers in length. The campaign planners also had to consider

159

and prepare for the possibility of a three-front war, while other European powers only had to contend with a two-front or even a one-front struggle.

Meanwhile, only seven Austro-Hungarian deployment railroad lines with a total capacity of 153 trains daily led to the Russian frontier and only four rail lines with a capacity of 112 trains daily could transport troops to the Serbian front. A potential eighth deployment line to Russia would not be brought into service due to a gap in the line, which would necessitate a four-day march for the troops.

Four of the seven Austro-Hungarian military rail lines to the Russian frontier extended through the Carpathian Mountains to eastern Galicia, a route which presented difficult conditions both for the building and the operation of such lines, depending particularly on the time of year and the weather conditions.

Austro-Hungarian military planners had for years based their planning on the assumption that a Russian mobilization and deployment would be an extremely slow maneuver because of the vast distances to be traversed by troop trains. Russian slowness, according to captured plans in 1908, would allow the Viennese General Staff a two-week time advantage for mobilizing, deploying, and then striking the Russian forces before either their overwhelming numerical superiority could be brought to bear, or the armies could meet on a common battlefield.

This plan, however, assumed that the Austro-Hungarian mobilization and deployment movements would occur either before or — at worst — at the same time as the Russian maneuvers. This synchrony was not achieved in July and August 1914. What went wrong?

For Austria-Hungary, an "official" version of what transpired during the 1914 mobilization period is found in the memoirs of Conrad von Hötzendorf, as reflected later by the Austro-Hungarian official history, *Österreich-Ungarns letzter Krieg*. Memoirs of the leading military figures of 1914-1918 and numerous periodical articles written after the war served to perpetuate the "official" version — a kind of "Austro-Hungarian Command Conspiracy" of the events of July and August 1914.

In particular, Major Emil Ratzenhofer, leader of the R (Russian) Group of the Railroad Bureau and fourth in the command structure, wrote numerous articles and private manuscripts which served as apologies for the problems of the Railroad Bureau during the dual deployments against Russia and Serbia-Montenegro. These problems led to a misguided deployment at both the Russian and Serbian fronts.

Ratzenhofer's postwar editorship of the *Militärwissenschaftliche und technische Mitteilungen*, the foremost military periodical in Austria, would be used in the interwar years to perpetuate the "Austro-Hungarian Command Conspiracy." His writing would serve to counter any critical literature dealing with the Austro-Hungarian mobilization and deployment, particularly that which focused on the fatal decision on 31 July to continue the "War Case B" (Balkan) Group deployment, even after it had become obvious that Russia would not stand aside and allow Vienna to invade Serbia. Most significantly, Ratzenhofer's scholarship concentrated on the July 1914 exchanges between leaders of the Railroad Bureau and Conrad on whether the "B" deployment movement could be halted at the end of July once Russian had seriously threatened intervention, and thus whether the twelve division swing force B-Group could be shifted to "War Case R." One of the individuals most directly involved, if not the most significant participant, in this critical decision on 31 July would be the same Major Ratzenhofer.

It is necessary to examine in detail the circumstances surrounding the momentous decision, reached the night of 31 July and confirmed on the morning of 1 August, to continue the "B" deployment rail transport and simultaneously initiate "War Case R," rail activity. The ultimate fate of both military campaigns can be traced to these dates. The decision entailed whether or not the Railroad Bureau could alter the overall Balkan deployment, encompassing approximately one-half of Vienna's military forces (twenty-three divisions), being transported to the Serbian frontier at a time when Russia had first proclaimed her partial mobilization, then expanded it by announcing proclamation of a general mobilization.

In the full "War Case R," according to the Conrad-Moltke pre-war agreements, forty Austro-Hungarian divisions would be hurled against the numerically superior Russian forces in Galicia. This situation would leave only an eight-division defensive force to counter Serbia's larger battle-proven eleven-division army. These eight divisions, comprising the Minimal Group Balkan, had already been mobilized with the B-Group swing force on 28 July when full "War Case B" had been proclaimed in Vienna.

But in a "War Case R," as seen in pre-war operational planning, the forty designated divisions included both the A- and B-Groups. General Staff planning specified that only if Russia did not intervene in an Austro-Hungarian-Serbian war ("War Case B") would the B-Group's twelve divisions be deployed with the Minimal Group Balkan in order to provide an armed force strong enough to crush the Serbian armies.

As we have seen, St. Petersburg refrained from initiating a full mobilization during the Bosnian Crisis and Balkan Wars, but in 1914 the gigantic strides achieved in her military and railroad rebuilding program, particularly from her Great Program, would suggest that Sazonov meant what he said when he announced, in conjunction with the partial Russian mobilization of fifty-five divisions on 25 July, that Russia would not countenance an Austro-Hungarian invasion and concomitant crushing of Serbia. While Austria-Hungary possessed only forty-eight divisions in her entire army; St. Petersburg, in her partial mobilization, called up 1.1 million men.

It must be emphasized that the Viennese military authorities had early and clear indications that Russia would actually intervene in an Austro-Hungarian-Serbian War, although the opposite scenario would be argued after the war. Regardless, it is significant that the Viennese military and diplomatic leaders' desire to punish Serbia overcame any overriding fears of a Russian military intervention in July 1914. Conrad, knowing that, contrary to the prevalent interpretation, Russia would indeed intervene in a Serbian conflict, gambled everything on a "lightning stroke" attack against Serbia — the success of which he hoped would preclude a simultaneous Russian war against the Monarchy.

In late June 1914, Conrad claimed that Vienna had the military advantage of a two-week interlude, which would separate Austro-Hungarian military action against Serbia from any serious Russian military countermoves,[2] and thus allow ample time for thorough chastisement of Serbia. On 28 and 29 June, he pressed for war against Serbia, and he would increase such pressure throughout the July 1914 crisis.[3]

On 30 June, Count Tisza, the Hungarian Prime Minister, met with Foreign Minister Berchtold, who had begun to advocate the complete crushing of Serbia. Franz Joseph himself would soon urge the same course of action.[4] By 3 July, many senior policy makers, except for Tisza, had come to the same conclusion.

A relevant question in evaluating the diplomatic and military decisions arrived at in Berlin and Vienna in early July 1914 involved the extent and continuing progress of Russian military preparations. Both allied General Staffs feared that the great Russian military rebuilding program would be completed in 1916-1917. By 1917, Russia would have a million more operations-ready men to transport on newly completed railroads than they did in 1914.[5] Thus the allied military staffs considered the present moment in July 1914 more advantageous than a later date for settling accounts with Serbia, regardless of Russia's announced position,[6] particularly since Berchtold and Conrad both hoped at this stage that if Germany countered Russia diplomatically, an Austro-Hungarian-Serbian war could be localized. Berlin also calculated that St. Petersburg was not yet prepared to become involved in a war.

The irrevocable tendency before 1914 to settle accounts with Serbia (i.e., Conrad's call for a preventive war in 1907, 1908-1909, and 1912-1913) had been countered by a simultaneous intense dread of fighting a two-front war with Russia. In 1914, however, Berlin and Vienna believed that their failure to act energetically would be perceived in Europe's capitals as an indication of Austro-Hungarian weakness. This perception, according to the leading figures, would result, in turn, in further undermining the South Slav loyalty to the Monarchy relative to increasing Serbian irredentism. In effect, the assassination of Archduke Franz Ferdinand had both brought forth the pretext for a final solution to the Dual Monarchy's South Slav problem and had provided an excuse to halt, at least temporarily, the perceived decline in prestige and power of the Dual Monarchy.

On 1 July, Germany's military leaders had already expressed concern about the progress of Russian armaments and their preparations for a new trial mobilization scheduled for implementation in the winter. Berlin thus immediately encouraged rapid Austro-Hungarian military action against Serbia.[7] On the same day, 1 July, Conrad ordered the review of the earlier plans for a *Rückverlegung*, or a rearward deployment, of the detraining areas troops designated for a "War Case R."[8]

On the next day, 2 July, Romania announced that she would assume a neutral stance in the event of an Austro-Hungarian-Serbian war. Romania's decision, as suggested, signified to Conrad the loss of 400,000 Romanian soldiers to counter Russia's numerical advantage, and the simultaneous release of the three Russian corps no longer necessary to counter a Romanian front. Also on this date, a personal letter and new position paper relative to the Balkans, stating that the time for action against Serbia had arrived, were dispatched from Franz Joseph to Kaiser Wilhelm and Berlin. Vienna, feeling incapable of acting alone, requested that Berlin affirm support of an Austro-Hungarian action to punish Serbia.

On 5 July, Ambassador Tschirschky assured Franz Joseph of German support of an Austro-Hungarian military action against Serbia. On the same day, Franz Joseph revealed to Conrad that if Germany supported Vienna, war would be launched.[9] This turn of events was the result of the infamous German "blank check" to Vienna. Meanwhile, the German High Command was speedily sent on vacation in order to camouflage the potential seriousness of the situation.

With the promise of firm German support, a Common Council of Ministers Meeting was convened on 7 July to decide when war should commence against Serbia. Berchtold categorically stated to the assembled that both he and Franz Joseph regarded immediate action against Belgrade as necessary, and the present moment favorable for this action. In an afternoon session, Conrad agreed that war should be launched immediately to exploit the chance of crossing the Balkan river barriers before Serbia could initiate countermeasures (the common frontier encompassed the course of the Save, Danube and Drina Rivers). The debate centered on whether Vienna should mobilize and attack Serbia without warning or initially place certain demands in the form of an ultimatum on Belgrade. Conrad questioned as to whether a mobilization against Serbia would enable another to be initiated against a possible Russian mobilization, replied that if St. Petersburg did respond militarily, Austria-Hungary must also mobilize, and that in the event of an actual Russian intervention, Russia would become the main enemy.

In the case of a Russian intervention, only subordinate Austro-Hungarian military units would be left to face Serbia and Montenegro. Conrad thus emphasized to the assembled Council of Ministers that it would be possible to mobilize first against Serbia and then, if necessary, also against Russia as well, with no time loss for either, if the Russian intervention occurred by the fifth "War Case B" mobilization day. After that fifth mobilization day against Serbia, simultaneous mobilizations against both opponents would become more difficult to achieve without a disadvantage to one mobilization scenario.[10]

His reply to direct questioning demonstrates that Conrad anticipated at least the possibility of Russian intervention against an Austro-Hungarian attack on Serbia. But Conrad, Berchtold, and other Austro-Hungarian leaders, in their insatiable desire for war to punish Serbia and protect the declining prestige of their Monarchy, disregarded any information that would negatively affect their decision to chastise Serbia.

In military terms, if "War Case B" was fought alone, the B-Group (twelve divisions), and Minimal Group Balkan (eight divisions) had the mission of invading Serbia in order to overwhelm quickly the eleven-division Serbian army. If Russia chose to intervene during this maneuver, the swing B-Group would have to be redirected immediately to the

Galician frontier in order to counter Russia in conjunction with the defensive A-Group (twenty-eight and one-half infantry divisions and ten cavalry divisions). The two forces, the A- and B-Groups, formed the forty-division offensive force which Conrad and Moltke had agreed before the war would be necessary to invade Russian Poland and draw Russian forces away from the Prussian frontier.

The fifth "B" mobilization day, alluded to earlier, was crucial to General Staff arguments. It was important in that B-Group units if already in rail transport south would face extremely difficult problems if they had to be redirected to the northern Russian theater. This concern was partly because only four major rail lines led towards the Balkan theater or Serbian frontier, and seven led to the Galician deployment area. On 31 July, the leaders of the Austro-Hungarian Railroad Bureau would claim that reversing rail transport of the destination of the B-Group from the south to the north on the fourth Balkan mobilization day would create chaos on the rail lines. The sudden decision of the Railroad Bureau that the B-Group could not be redirected to Galicia in timely fashion in order to counter the Russian menace would produce fatal results on both the Serbian and Russian fronts.

Meanwhile, by 8 July, German Foreign Ministry leaders felt compelled to pressure Vienna to initiate rapid military action against her Balkan neighbor. Such pressure would steadily increase, particularly as the German General Staff began to intervene while also seeking a clarification of the exact Austro-Hungarian deployment numbers to be fielded against Russia if she should intervene in an Austro-Hungarian-Serbian war that had already commenced.

But the diplomatic documents of July reveal that very little information on deployment would be transmitted from Vienna to Berlin after 7 July. The German "blank check" of 5 July provided Vienna with the military and diplomatic cover it felt necessary to enable the leadership to continue their plans for crushing Serbia; they acted accordingly, and at their own speed.

Franz Joseph himself would call for rapid decisive action against Serbia in early July, and on 14 July he approved the taking of military measures against her.[11] However, there would be no rapid campaign against Serbia, as originally anticipated and called for. Instead, an ultimatum would finally be dispatched to Belgrade sixteen days later, to be followed on 28 July by an Austro-Hungarian declaration of war and mobilization for "War Case Balkan."

This inexplicable three-week interlude before any decisive action was taken ran counter both to Conrad's earlier demands for a rapid armed stroke against Serbia[12] and to the similar diplomatic and military pressure from Berlin to take immediate action. Serbia was thus able to gain a significant military time advantage, and the delays resulted in the inability of the Austro-Hungarians to launch surprise strikes across the frontier river barriers to seize Belgrade, which lay at the common frontier.

On 13 July, Conrad, citing the progress of Russian military preparations and the unreliability of Romania as an ally to anchor his extreme right flank as had been agreed upon, ordered the planning for the anticipated *Rückverlegung* of the Austro-Hungarian deployment if "War Case R" actually erupted.[13] This new rearward deployment called for the Austro-Hungarian forces now to be fielded back at the San-Dniester River line, not forward at the frontier boundaries as he had originally planned for a war against Russia in 1914-1915. According to the original 1914 strategy, if Russia intervened in an Austro-Serbian conflict, the left-flank northern First Austro-Hungarian Army would be buttressed by the IX Corps, the Fourth Army by the VIII Corps, and the Second Army by the VII Corps. A fourth corps, the IV Corps, would serve as a High Command reserve. Meanwhile, these four corps, all of which belonged to the B-Group, had already been mobilized on 28 July to march against Serbia, because "War Case B" remained in force as the Russians began to start significant military measures of their own.

The railroad portion of the *Rückverlegung*, according to the Railroad Bureau planners, would produce no serious difficulties with mobilization and deployment in the Russian theater. To the Bureau, this strategy merely signified that troops would be detrained further rearward and earlier than by the earlier designated plans. For example, the First Army would now be deployed south of the San River between the area at the mouth of the Vistula River and the area west of Jaroslau. The Fourth Army, to its right, would now be grouped on both sides of the major San River fortress of Przemyśl. On its right flank, the Third Army would be fielded on both sides of Sambor, with a group pushed forward to Lemberg.

The available Second Army units on the extreme right flank, designated the Group Kövess, would be transported by rail to south of the Dniester River into Styrj and Stanislau. Another smaller group would be deployed at Zaleszczyki and Czernovitz, and a further infantry division would be deployed at Brzezany. The cavalry divisions on the other hand would advance to the Polish frontiers.[14]

Conrad's decision to instigate this rearward deployment of Austro-Hungarian forces proved to be a serious mistake. Planning difficulties immediately arose because the new deployment scenario required the utilization of railroad stations not earmarked in earlier Railroad Bureau planning. Trivial details that had been neither reviewed nor contemplated further hindered the rail movements when they began.[15]

Having dispatched the order for the preparation of the rearward redeployment of his northern armies, Conrad departed with great fanfare for vacation on 7 July after the Council of Ministers meeting, although both the Kaiser and his Chancellery questioned his timing.[16] Conrad returned to Vienna for one day to attend the 19 July Council of Ministers meeting before his final return to duty on 22 July.

Colonel Straub, commander of the Railroad Bureau, also departed Vienna for vacation. Because other senior officers had also begun their vacations during these critical July days, the fourth-ranking officer in the section, Major Emil Ratzenhofer, would make crucial decisions concerning what would become the dual deployment against Russia and Serbia. Other vital military functionaries, including the War Minister,[17] were also on vacation, because the officer corps' leaves were not countermanded.

In Germany, by careful decision-making, on 28 June the Kaiser departed for his customary summer cruise and Moltke fortuitously had begun his annual excursion to Karlsbad. The German Intelligence Bureau, meanwhile, had sensed no dangerous Russian military activity being conducted, and the Berlin "R" Group did not interrupt its vacation schedules, fearing that such a disturbance would cause public concern. In fact, as described earlier, the German Chancellor, Bethmann Hollweg, purposely encouraged these departures from official duty as a "smoke screen" to cover the plans of the erstwhile Austro-Hungarian ally.

In the meantime, German diplomatic pressure on Vienna increased when Berlin learned that the final dispatch of the Austro-Hungarian ultimatum to Serbia would be postponed until 25 July in order to preclude French-Russian collusion as a result of President Raymond Poincaré's and Foreign Minister René Viviani's visit to St. Petersburg. Berchtold responded to his allies that although the time limit for an answer to the Serbian ultimatum would expire on 25 July, on 23 July the ultimatum would be forwarded. Mobilization would then commence on 28 July.

One reason for the German pressure on Vienna was earlier intelligence reports that the English and the Russians had attempted secret negotiations for the creation of a joint marine convention. This convention, if concluded, would provide for English ships to transport Russian troops for a landing in Pomerania, a maneuver which would, in effect, open a third front for Germany in the event of an eastern war.[18]

Meanwhile, on 19 July, at the second Joint Council of Ministers meeting, Conrad declared that he personally favored a rapid military stroke against Serbia. In response to questioning, Conrad replied that it would be feasible to mobilize first against Serbia, but he gave only a qualified positive reply concerning Russia. If a mobilization against Russia occurred within five days after a mobilization for "War Case B," Conrad foresaw no major problems and so considered chances for military success good.[19]

Conrad, however, was less than candid about the potential Austro-Hungarian military situation. He should have informed the assembled leaders that Germany and Austria-Hungary could not definitely overpower Russia when Germany had first to crush France in the agreed-upon Schlieffen fashion. Vienna also would have to neutralize Serbia while being threatened by a much more dangerous foe, Russia. The Council of Ministers agreed to prepare the final touches on a note which was to be delivered to Belgrade on 23 July, its delayed delivery to assure that President Poincaré's visit to Russia had ended and the feared allied collusion avoided.

Events began to take place rapidly. On 20 July, for instance, the Hungarian Ministerial Council raised the question of whether to call up reserve troops, and decided to recall vacationing members of the Railroad Bureau.[20] Conrad himself returned from his vacation on 22 July, while other key military functionaries still on vacation received telegrams ordering them to return to active duty. The basic result of their vacations was four weeks of serious military inactivity after the assassination of Franz Ferdinand. In the interim, the preparation and movement of provisions and ammunition, as well as other important pre-mobilization concerns, had been ignored.

On 22 July, Conrad conferred with Colonel Straub, his Railroad Bureau leader, informing him that an ultimatum to Serbia would be issued on the next day and, therefore, that all railroad line commanders and transportation officials should be summoned back to duty. Simultaneously, the "War Case B" march plans were readied for dispatch and the decision reached to declare the first "Alarm" day for "War Case B" to fall on 27 July.[21]

Thus after weeks of delay, Vienna finally dispatched the ultimatum, with a forty-eight hour deadline, to Serbia. All major decisions relative to the creation and forwarding of the ultimatum were made in Vienna, not

Berlin, although Berlin certainly was notified of significant sections of the document.

Conrad, in his memoirs written after the war, would blame the Austro-Hungarian diplomats for the creation of the unfavorable situation that first led to a war in the Balkans and resulted in Russian military intervention. Conrad further claimed in his memoirs that St. Petersburg might have been bluffing during the July crisis, and would have backed down once Germany openly supported Vienna.[22] Conrad's assertions were lame excuses for inaction, faulty judgment, and command failure in Vienna during the July crisis.

On 24 July, Serbia began mobilization measures and Russia warned Vienna against an Austro-Hungarian armed move on Serbia,[23] while at the same time initiating a secret partial mobilization of her own and stockpiling of war materials. Berlin, caught in this threatening situation, once again pressured Vienna to begin immediate action, and Berchtold warned Conrad that the diplomatic situation could not hold until 12 August. To Berchtold's surprise, Conrad claimed that his troops would be unable to move against Serbia for a sixteen-day period.

Reports of Serbian mobilization measures, in the meantime, had begun to proliferate, leading to the Austro-Hungarian Command order to institute security measures for the designated Balkan deployment rail lines. At the same time, couriers began to dispatch the "War Case B" plans to the relevant corps commanders.[24]

The alarm instructions for "War Case B," basically preparation measures to mobilize, quickly arrived at the II, IV, VII, XII, and XIII Corps Headquarters. The War Minister also ordered that activated railroad security measures be taken in the II, IV, V, VI, VIII, XIII, XV, and XVI Corps areas. While as yet the official mobilization had not been proclaimed, the Railroad Bureau nonetheless had already received instructions to prepare for the Alarm transport on 27 July.[25]

During the morning of 25 July, Conrad discussed the impending situation with the Heads of the Austro-Hungarian Operations and Railroad Bureaus. The possibility that a "War Case R" deployment and Alarm transport would have to be conducted in conjunction with the simultaneous "War Case B" deployment was also discussed, but Colonel Straub argued against any further work being performed on such matters, claiming that it would be a non-productive utilization of his personnel.[26]

In his memoirs, Conrad, in attempting to explain the ensuing Austro-Hungarian military debacle, related that with a "War Case B" deployment already in progress, no time would be lost if a deployment against Russia began; but he magnanimously stated that "disturbances and friction" could occur if the Balkan rail movement actually became enmeshed with a Russian one.[27] This is quite an understatement!

On 25 July at 9:23 p.m., Austria-Hungary's partial mobilization for a "War Case B" was officially announced. Berchtold at that time dispatched a circular to Austro-Hungarian diplomats in the various European capitals informing them that the impending military advance against Serbia could result in Russian interference.[28] Although the Austro-Hungarian partial mobilization had been declared on 25 July, the first "Alarm" day of preparation for such an event would not become official for two more days or on 27 July, while the first mobilization day would not be proclaimed until 28 July. Conrad also dispatched new instructions for the III Corps (Graz) now to be mobilized for "War Case B." Conrad reputedly issued the unexpected order because the III corps troops contingent might become necessary to fill in gaps in the ranks of "Czech" corps if trouble occurred in the mobilization process in Bohemia, as had occurred in both the 1908 and 1912 crises. Also, Conrad would argue that the III corps could serve as flank protection against the erstwhile ally Italy if necessary, or even be utilized as reinforcements in the upcoming Balkan campaign. "Alarm" orders and the order for all non-mobilized troops to return immediately to their garrisons were also forwarded on this day to the I, X, and XI Corps at the Russian frontier, as well.[29]

Reports of serious Russian troop movements began to appear in Austro-Hungarian and German diplomatic and military documents.[30] Contrary to the post-war revelations of Conrad's reputed fantasies that Russia would not intervene in an Austro-Serbian war, such reports signified that Russia might indeed actively intervene in 1914, contrary to the experiences of the 1908-1909 Bosnian Crisis and the 1912-1913 Balkan Wars Crisis.

Russia's preparatory military activities, in fact, had reportedly become so extensive that the Railroad Bureau began preparing for the deployment of "War Case R" alarm troops, which consisted mainly of cavalry units — while non-modified full "War Case B" mobilization plans continued to be in official effect.[31]

On 26 July, additional reports of Russian military measures surfaced,[32] but once again these reports had no affect on the "War Case B" mobilization plans, which still targeted 28 July for the first military activity in order to provide extra time to assure a smooth railroad deployment for the Balkan theater.[33] It was also announced that Archduke Friedrich would be the nominal Commander-in-Chief of the forces designated to fight against Serbia, and Conrad would serve as his Chief of the General Staff. Conrad now briefed the Commanders of the Fifth and Second Armies on the expected deployment situation and their particular missions in the unfolding Balkan war. The III Corps also received orders to activate their frontier protective measures.[34]

Conrad turned his attention to the northern theater when he ordered the three Galician frontier Corps (I, X, and XI) both to concentrate their attention for a possible Russian military threat, and to take other measures, such as preparing explosives to blow up key targets. In addition, he warned that the fortresses at Cracow and Przemyśl should be prepared to resist a Russian surprise attack, while measures should be instituted to prepare the fortification works of Lemberg and the San-Dniester River line for an eventual war.[35]

Berchtold and Tschirschky pressured Conrad to commence war against Serbia immediately in order to preclude any Russian intervention in the ensuing conflict, but Conrad remained adamant. Conrad was, however, aware that he had failed to inform both the 7 and 19 July Council of Ministers' meetings that he could not mobilize and deploy the Austro-Hungarian troops in Serbia for sixteen days after the official announcement of a Balkan mobilization, or not before 12 August. Berchtold urged him to seize the initiative, while Conrad countered by merely suggesting that it would be crucial for him, Berchtold, to clarify St. Petersburg's military intentions by 5 August at the very latest.[36] If Russia were to intervene in Vienna's Balkan adventure, the Monarchy's initial military weakness would become strongly evident in the northern theater against her.

On 27 July, as new reports of Russian military activities in the four Russian military districts bordering the Dual Monarchy poured in,[37] the first "War Case B" Alarm rail transport trains began to roll. Activities on this first Alarm Day for "War Case B" included the marshaling of troops to secure the frontier against Serbia and the initiation of active intelligence services. The remaining "War Case B" troops prepared for combat footing and transport and began the formation of supply trains in their respective mobilization stations.

In anticipation of an invasion, preparation of the necessary bridge and river crossing materials for the Save and Danube Rivers was also ordered. Relative to the increasingly threatening conduct of Russia, the 19. Infantry Division destined for deployment in Dalmatia in "War Case B" now received orders to remain in its mobilization stations until further orders.[38]

The declaration of war against Serbia finally occurred on 28 July, despite the changes that had taken place on the European diplomatic horizon during weeks of Austro-Hungarian foot-dragging and inaction. The only military action that occurred on this date was the commencement of an artillery bombardment of Belgrade.

The Austro-Hungarian declaration of war should have come as no surprise to anyone, since the events that unfolded during the Bosnian Crisis and Balkan Wars had produced a growing sense of pessimism and desperation in Austro-Hungarian diplomatic, political, and military circles. On three occasions during the Balkan Wars, Austro-Hungarian leaders had resolved to take military action if such action became necessary in order to protect Vienna's basic Balkan position. In all three resultant crises, Vienna, threatened by internal disruption, initiated aggressive diplomatic initiatives. Much to the Viennese diplomats' surprise, this type of diplomacy proved successful for them — a lesson that would prove to be a primary factor in understanding the motives of leaders during the 1914 crisis in Austria-Hungary.

As early as 7 July at the Council of Ministers meeting, if not before, Conrad had argued that Austria-Hungary must attack Serbia immediately; but the final decision leading to the war declaration date of 28 July created a significant time advantage gain for Belgrade to utilize, since Serbia's mobilization had already begun as early as 24 July.[39]

Throughout the July crisis, Conrad continued to pressure Berchtold to ascertain what position St. Petersburg would take. Conrad wanted to deploy all his mobilized troops against Serbia, which besides the Minimal Group Balkan consisted of the swing force B-Group. But if Russia did decide to mobilize, the B-Group might have to be redirected north to face the new and greater military threat.

The first "War Case Balkan" mobilization day should actually have been proclaimed on 26 July. The two precious days lost, added to the earlier Serbian mobilization date, allowed Belgrade to initiate preparatory defensive measures that would not otherwise have been possible. Russia, meanwhile, had also continued to intensify her military activities,[40] already decided upon at a Council of Ministers' meeting on 24 July.

Postwar "official" Austro-Hungarian arguments explained the delay in the date of declaring war on Serbia as a result of time spent procuring some insurance that the Balkan railroad mobilization as planned would run smoothly, and of successfully implementing various operative considerations.[41] As an example of the explanations made for the late date of the beginning of military measures, Emil Ratzenhofer would claim after the war that among the major considerations in the choice of 28 July as the date for the declaration of war was that 25 July fell on a Saturday. Ratzenhofer argued that few telegraph dispatchers worked on Saturday nights and even fewer on Sundays,[42] and that a mobilization order declared on 25 July would have been transmitted after 8:15 p.m. Thus the mobilization date had to be moved back. This argument, however, serves as but another subterfuge to conceal Railroad Bureau planning mistakes and lack of initiative in the July crisis.

Germany also introduced her first serious military measures on 28 July. Bethmann Hollweg, however, succeeded in rejecting repeated requests from Moltke that the "imminent danger of war" be declared in Berlin. This "imminent danger of war" was similar to the Austria-Hungary Alarm Day, in that it encompassed measures to be initiated as pre-mobilization steps.

On 28 July, Kaiser Wilhelm also insisted that Austria-Hungary immediately occupy Belgrade in order to satisfy the Austro-Hungarian army, which, after all, had been forced to mobilize on two previous occasions during the Bosnian Crisis of 1908-1909 and the 1912-1913 Balkan Wars.[43] This maneuver, Wilhelm's famous "Halt in Belgrade" position, would supposedly serve to placate Viennese political and military leaders without having to embark on a full-scale war against the hated Balkan neighbor.

In any event, it proved to be both a terrible and inexcusable blunder for Vienna to declare war on Serbia on 28 July, when the Austro-Hungarian army was incapable of launching any serious military action. The declaration of war came two weeks before Austria-Hungary's forces could even assemble at the Serbian frontier before becoming operationally ready. Vienna should have issued her ultimatum to Belgrade only when prepared to take immediate military action to follow it up.

Reports of Russian mobilization measures along the frontiers and inland meanwhile continued to proliferate, while the Austro-Hungarian artillery bombardment of Belgrade on 29 July produced further military pressure on the Tsar from the Russian General Staff to proclaim a general mobilization.

Austria-Hungary's declaration of war also had the effect of terminating Austro-Hungarian-Russian talks concerning calming the crisis, and Berlin now threatened St. Petersburg that a German mobilization could result from continuation of the Russian military measures in motion, which were supposedly aimed at Vienna.

On 29 July, the Habsburg railroad system began to carry military traffic exclusively. At 11:00 a.m. on that day, the decision was made to order the III Corps, originally designated for the Russian front but mobilized in the Balkan Group, to be shipped to the Serbian theater. It was also decided that the 1. Cavalry Division should continue rail travel to the Balkan front but the 11. Cavalry Division halt its movement southward on 3 August.[44]

Concern about Russia's military intentions increased on 29 July as new reports confirmed that St. Petersburg had now begun to mobilize all her forces, reputedly because her honor as a Great Power required her to take action against Austria-Hungary's war on her protege Serbia.[45] Russia took the position that the mobilization of eight Austro-Hungarian Corps, or half the army, was excessive for use against her Balkan neighbor and that the large mobilization must therefore be regarded as a provocation against St. Peterburg as well.[46] By evening, a veiled threat had been transmitted to Vienna that a Russian general mobilization would commence if Austro-Hungarian troops crossed the Serbian frontier.

At stake for Vienna in this mounting crisis lay the destruction of one of the basic tenets of Austro-German military strategy — the more rapid mobilization of the Central Powers *vis-á-vis* Russia. Considering the circumstances of July, even if the Russian mobilization was not countermanded, her time advantage alone would necessitate the proclamation of an Austro-Hungarian general mobilization.[47] Moltke, because of the increasing pressure being put on the Schlieffen Plan timetables, had also begun to push his government to initiate more extreme military measures.

Conrad conferred on 30 July with various of his military representatives, raising with his Railroad Bureau leader the critical question of when a first mobilization day against Russia could be proclaimed — with the serious proviso that it would occur while the "B" movement continued in force. Colonel Straub immediately requested twenty-four hours in order both to consider the question and examine the details involved in such a maneuver. When he returned with an answer, he replied that the first "War Case R Alarm" day could not be proclaimed before 2 August; the first actual mobilization day against Russia not before 4 August.[48] As to the issue of redirecting the B-Group from the Balkan to the Russian theater, Straub asserted that on railroad technical grounds, attempting such an impossible maneuver could only result in chaos. He would repeat the same argument — namely that the swing force B-Group could not be reversed and retransported to the Polish theater — on 31 July.[49] Meanwhile, each hour's delay in not proclaiming a general mobilization seriously damaged

Vienna's military position against both Serbia and Russia. A Russian threat as received would not halt the decision to continue deployment against Serbia, but did introduce for the first time the serious possibility that "War Cases R" and "B" might have to run concurrently. The tragedy for Austria-Hungary was that preparations had not been made for this most likely scenario.

Additional intelligence and diplomatic reports about the Russian partial mobilization measures being initiated poured in on 30 July, the third Balkan mobilization day.[50] Then, at 12:45 p.m., the stinging news arrived in Vienna: Russia had announced a general mobilization.[51] Germany now began to insist that the greater portion of the Austro-Hungarian forces must be deployed against Russia, not Serbia, as the major opponent, if Russia indeed became bellicose. In the meantime, the Balkan deployment rail transport commenced as scheduled, with, according to Ratzenhofer's accounts, thirty percent of the designated movement on the railroads occurring.[52] In truth, and contrary to the above, only pre-transport rail traffic had begun, resulting in only very minimal rail utilization.[53] The significance of the low levels of rail transport was seen.

On the same day, 30 July, two diplomatic notes arrived from Rome. The first informed Vienna that Italy did not consider herself obligated to go to war because the Triple Alliance was a defensive agreement and the action against Serbia was an aggressive act. The second Italian note addressed Article VII of the agreement which dealt with the issue of territorial compensation for Italy in the Balkans if the balance of power should be disturbed. Romania's position in the upcoming conflict remained uncertain, and Bulgaria and Turkey had not announced their intentions either.[54]

In a meeting he held with Berchtold, Conrad requested that Franz Joseph be persuaded to order a general mobilization. Raising the issue of the effect of inaction on the Monarchy's prestige and the army's honor as major factors in a war with Serbia, Conrad insisted that "War Case B" could neither be halted nor altered. He emphasized that it would not be advantageous for the Monarchy to postpone further reckoning with Serbia.[55] It must be recalled that earlier Conrad had assured Franz Joseph that in the event of a two-front war, a decisive military victory could be obtained over Serbia before any serious military action could occur in Galicia against Russia. A major factor in his planning was his incorrect expectation that a Russian mobilization would take so long to be com-

pleted that Serbia could be eliminated as a military foe before a serious
Russian attack could be launched against the Monarchy.

On the German side, Moltke, from noon on 30 July, when he himself
learned that Russian military measures had been progressing for five days,
lobbied his counterpart for an immediate Austro-Hungarian general mobilization.[56] Moltke judged that the allied military situation would become
increasingly critical if no general mobilization occurred. When Vienna
finally ordered her full mobilization, Germany would follow suit.

Kaiser Wilhelm, for his part, when he learned through a telegram sent
by Tsar Nicholas that Russia had initiated military measures five days
earlier, demanded immediate German military action since Russia now
had a week's head start on Berlin in military preparations for war.[57] On
the following day, 31 July, Franz Joseph cabled Wilhelm that he had
indeed "ordered the mobilization of all my armed forces. The action of
my army against Serbia now proceeding can suffer no interruption from
the threatening and challenging attitude of Russia."[58] Franz Joseph's commitment could not please German leaders, who expected Austria-Hungary
particularly to counter Russia, and who considered Serbia the secondary
opponent in a Austro-Hungarian two-front war.

Vienna had ordered her general mobilization on 31 July, but 4 August
would be proclaimed as the first actual mobilization day against Russia.
2 August would be the first "Alarm" day. The delay of several days in the
actual commencement of mobilization measures against Russia resulted
from the confused railroad situation created by the deployment in progress
against Serbia. The Austro-Hungarian general mobilization thus had occurred eighteen hours after the Russian announcement of their general
mobilization, but actual military measures would be delayed further for
several days.

At 12:30 p.m., 31 July, the Austro-Hungarian deployment rail line
commanders had already received notification of the Austro-Hungarian
general mobilization that had been proclaimed at 12:23 p.m. They were
also told that the "War Case B" deployment measures remained in force,
and that "War Case R" rail traffic would run simultaneously with it in
order to avoid the Railroad Bureau's predicted chaos if "War Case B" rail
movement had to be reversed in order to reroute the B-Group to the
northern theater of battle.[59]

Deployment "R" packets were put into order to be dispatched to the
designated commanders. Yet no one could be found in the War Ministry
except a section chief, and where were Conrad and his Operations Bureau

chief during this confused time?[60] Key personnel were unavailable at crucial times during these crisis days.

Conrad, meanwhile, further changing his military plans, decided to revert to his earlier agreement with Moltke to launch an offensive against Russia in the event of a two-front struggle. His new position differed radically from his plan of early July to deploy against Russia not at the Galician frontier but rearward at the San-Dniester line while Serbia was being militarily crushed. This *Rückverlegung* or rearward deployment was designed to gain time to assure that Serbia could be firmly dealt with, while attempting to gain time before facing the deploying Russian army.

Conrad's change of plans occurred, however, when the troops' train unloading points in Galicia could no longer be altered. Thus, to launch an attack now, Conrad's armies would have to march almost 100 miles from their rearward deployment detraining areas to the original jump-off points for the Austro-Hungarian offensive. Not only were the troops exhausted by the time they reached the reestablished earlier deployment locations, they had presented their enemy with further valuable time advantage. But the tragedy is that the Austro-Hungarian railroads could actually have transported the troops forward to the reestablished deployment points both to save time and to conserve troop energy, precluding the long, tiring marches that became necessary in August 1914.

On 31 July, Conrad also found himself occupied with probably the most critical problem he would face during this crisis — the thought of redirecting a significant portion of the troops already bound for or destined for the Serbian theater, instead to the Russian front. The troops in question entailed the B-Group, but Conrad's increasing uncertainty as to the need to reverse his priority from "War Case B" to the "War Case R" led him to include units of the Minimal Group Balkan also. Specifically, the units he considered for railroad transfer from the Balkan to the northern theater included the IV, VII, and IX Corps from the B-Group, and the VIII Corps, the 40. and 20. Infantry Divisions and the 36. *Landsturm* Infantry Brigade from the Minimal Group Balkan.[61] These vacillations illustrate Conrad's confused decision-making process in the ensuing critical crisis hours.

At 9:15 p.m. on 31 July, Conrad conferred with Colonel Straub, the commander of the General Staff Railroad Bureau, and specifically asked Straub whether the full "War Case B" mobilization could now be halted and the B-Group's twelve divisions retransported immediately to the northern theater. Kaiser Wilhelm's letter to Franz Joseph calling for Austro-Hungarian troops against Russia, which Conrad read to Straub at the meeting, led to Conrad's request to transfer the B-Group to Galicia so that the agreed upon forty divisions could be fielded against Russia.[62] On the same evening, Berchtold wired to Berlin that war would indeed be fought against Serbia, and that the first "War Case R" mobilization day would be on 4 August. Conrad's perception that a full "War Case B" mobilization could be reversed to a "War Case R" mobilization if the decision to do so fell on or before the fifth "B" mobilization day influenced his question for Straub of whether the "War Case B" B-Group movement could now be halted. Straub, however, informed Conrad that attempting now to reverse the B-Group rail transport to the north would result in chaos; it was literally impossible to do.[63]

Straub had given his negative reply to Conrad on 31 July, the fourth "B" mobilization day, not on 1 August, which would have been the assumed fifth day of the Balkan mobilization. Conrad had informed both the 7 and 19 July Council of Ministers meetings that the fifth mobilization day would be the final day that would allow enough time for the B-Group to be both safely redirected and transferred to the Russian front if St. Petersburg actively intervened during a Austro-Hungarian Balkan mobilization movement. To back up his negative reply, at 11:30 p.m. Straub reported to General Conrad[64] that portions of five different corps had already begun rail transport southward to the Balkans. These units included the vanguard of the 9. Infantry Division of the VIII Corps, 29. of the IX, 31. and 32. of the IV, and one-third of the 17. and 34. divisions of the VII, as well as parts of the 1. Cavalry Division and one-half of the 10. Cavalry Division. Straub also reported that the 42. Infantry Division and 13. Infantry Brigade of the XIII Corps must also continue rail movement to the south as already planned. On the other hand, Straub revealed that the 20. Infantry Division and 36., 104., and 107. *Landsturm* Brigades could safely be shifted to the northern theater, while the III Corps and 1. and 11. *Honvéd* Cavalry Divisions could be reversed to the Galician theater. Straub stated emphatically to Conrad that to halt the "War Case B" deployment at this time would unconditionally result in disaster — for which he, as leader of the Railroad Bureau, would under no circumstance accept responsibility. Thereupon, Conrad claimed that he was fully convinced that the "War Case B" deployment rail movement could indeed not now be altered, and that was that![65] This decision would result in far-reaching disaster on both battlefields, but for now it enabled Conrad to continue his cherished "War Case B" deployment. However, at least the

III Corps and 1. and 11. *Honvéd* Cavalry Divisions were being transferred north to meet an increasing Russian threat.[66]

Political considerations also strongly supported Conrad's command decisions relating to the dispersement of his forces for a two-front war. Accordingly, to be defeated militarily by tiny Serbia would be more devastating to Austria-Hungary's prestige than would be a setback in the north against Russia. A military defeat on the Balkan front would also adversely affect potential Balkan allies, such as Romania and Bulgaria.[67]

Emil Ratzenhofer, leader of the Railroad Bureau "R" group, meanwhile had prepared the relevant calculations and a written proposal in order to ensure a successful continuation of the Balkan deployment which supposedly would not interfere with the mobilization and deployment against Russia. Ratzenhofer thus emphasized that the "B" rail deployment, including the transport of the B-Group, would be completed by 10 August, at which time the relevant troops could be consolidated at the Balkan front for further disposition. In the meantime, the A-Group could safely be transported to the northern front where the left-flank First and Fourth Armies set for the initial offensive action could arrive in Galicia by 20 August, the right-flank protective Third and Second Armies in eastern Galicia on 23 August.[68]

Ratzenhofer was able to convince both Straub and Conrad not to interrupt the Balkan rail deployment thus to allow the IV, VII, VIII, and IX Corps to continue rolling to the Serbian front, where they could detrain and then reload for transport to the Russian front. According to Ratzenhofer's various calculations, these four corps of the B-Group would arrive in Galicia at precisely the same time as they would have in the original "War Case R" planning, because original plans would have required the B-Group to wait several days until the necessary railroads would be free for their transport north. Meanwhile, the A-Group would have successfully been deployed anyway.[69] Ratzenhofer further calculated that in seven to eight days the VII, VIII, and IX Corps would be reloaded and redirected, utilizing the designated "R" railroad lines number III, IV, V, VIII.[70]

The continuing historical debate regarding the reasons for the failure of the 1914 Austro-Hungarian deployment to field sufficient troops according to pre-war planning centers on the decision of 31 July/1 August to continue the full "War Case B" Balkan rail movements, although Russian general mobilization was a real concern by 31 July. The decision signified that the "War Case B" transport received top priority in the upcoming two-front war scenario.[71] The catastrophic military defeats in both Galicia and Serbia in August and September 1914 can be traced back to this ill-fated decision demanded by the Railroad Bureau leadership and accepted by Conrad. Continuing the rail movement of the B-Group to Serbia then to detrain the troops, then to reload them and send them north, became the unsatisfactory and fatal solution to Vienna's critical strategic problems in 1914.

In examining this fateful situation, it is obvious to the outside observer that when Russia proclaimed her general mobilization she posed by far the most serious military threat to Vienna. In these circumstances, even pre-war planning demanded that as many combat troops as possible should have been immediately deployed against Russia. The 31 July Railroad Bureau decision on the fourth "B" mobilization day, however, meant that the B-Group transport could not be immediately reversed.

We must now examine the background to Conrad's repeated reference in his memoirs to his belief that the B-Group rail movement could be reversed to the north by a fifth Balkan mobilization day, if necessary, in order to parry a Russian threat that had arisen. Where had Conrad developed the notion that he had this safety valve of five days to reverse priorities in a two-front conflagration?

On 1 April 1913, the then section leader of the Railroad Bureau, Colonel Rziha, had informed Conrad that in the event of an Austro-Hungarian mobilization initiated only against Serbia which then resulted in a Russian threat of intervention, the B-Group, if it had begun rail movement, could be safely reversed from its course to the Serbian frontier and re-routed to Galicia. This maneuver, according to Colonel Rziha, could most easily be implemented until the fifth "B" mobilization day. Although the transfer could be accomplished until the sixteenth Balkan mobilization day, it would obviously become more difficult to achieve once military operations had commenced against Serbia.[72]

On 11 November 1913, following the Balkan Wars crisis, Conrad ordered preparations be made for the now-likely eventuality that Russia would intervene in a war initiated against Serbia.[73] The existence of a specific order to this effect contradicts one of Ratzenhofer's later post-war key allegations that, before the war, the Railroad Bureau had never been given explicit instructions to prepare concrete war plans for a "War Case R" occurring after a "War Case B" had begun. There is, however, no satisfactory explanation of why the Railroad Bureau ignored Conrad's order and its inherent request to prepare a "War Case R+B" plan. After the war, Ratzenhofer falsely asserted both that everything commanded of the Railroad Bureau had been successfully completed, and that Conrad never accused Straub or the Bureau of any misdoings.

Ratzenhofer would become the main apologist in the post-war attempt to excuse both the failure to prepare a viable "War Case R+B" rail plan, and in the case of the July crisis on the fourth "B" mobilization day, even to attempt to redirect the B-Group to the northern theater, where a military threat obviously far more serious than in the Balkans existed.

Several possible solutions to the Railroad Bureau's dilemma of a sudden mutual "War Case R+B" did exist. These included: upon a Russian mobilization, the immediate redirection of the B-Group units in rail transit to the Balkan front back to their original mobilization stations; the redirection of these B-Group divisions to Galicia on the main northern deployment lines before the A-Group could be transported; or a combination of these two possible solutions, which would utilize rail lines not included in the then existing deployment plans.

Both Straub and Ratzenhofer of the Railroad Bureau would argue that because of the Monarchy's existing nationality problems, returning the B-Group which was already moving southward back to their original mobilization stations would not be a desirable solution. In particular, they emphasized that in both the 1908-1909 and 1912-1913 crises, portions of the VIII and IX Bohemian Corps, now reputedly already in rail movement to the Serbian front, had caused difficulties when called up earlier.[74] Further, they argued that railroad technical difficulties would make the immediate reassignment of the troop transports of the B-Group to Galicia impossible. This particular argument would be emphasized in post-war polemics. Another Straub-Ratzenhofer claim was that stopping to unload transports on the various Balkan railroad stretches would destroy operational unity, hindering further utilization of the railroad lines.[75] Another argument to justify their 1914 decision was that the reversal of the B-Group train movement would cause overburdening of the Hungarian railroad stretches needed for mobilization transport to both war theaters. They espoused the idea that it would be impossible to change transport plans because of the low capacity of the single-track rail lines crossing the Carpathian Mountains, and that the general difficulties that would arise associated with such a large reversal of troop movements would prove to be insurmountable.[76]

These excuses were based on excessive exaggerations; indeed, no such chaos occurred once the "War Case R+B" movements went into effect.[77] But the accumulated arguments of these two Railroad Bureau leaders resulted in the sending of the B-Group to the Serbian theater, then it being redirected north to Galicia because the Railroad Bureau could not find a suitable solution to the newly emerged tactical situation.

After the war, Ratzenhofer would also make the interesting claim that the German Military attaché in Vienna had pressured Conrad to take advantage of the mobilization of the B-Group for "War Case B" and for the benefit of redeployment in Galicia according to "War Case R." Couldn't the next week, the argument ran, be used to retransport the B-Group to the Russian front, since it had already been mobilized? Ratzenhofer's claim was but a further attempt to camouflage his overall responsibility for the accepted plan to continue the prevailing rail deployment as it began on 27-28 July.

But since it would not be until 4 August that the first "War Case R" mobilization day would take effect; and since rail traffic north would not actually commence until 6 August; and, further, because the A-Group units would not then be ready to march, the interim period could have been effectively used for rail transport of "B" Group units — such as the IV, VII and IX Corps — to the northern theater before the A-Group could even begin its rail movement.

On the other hand, another feasible solution to the imbroglio involved the two mobilized Bohemian Corps (VIII and IX) which could have been transported by rail laterally across Galicia, while the movement of the two Hungarian Corps (IV and VII) could have been reversed from the area of Budapest and Temesvár and redirected north over Carpathian rail lines not being utilized in the deployment movements.[78] Thus the two Bohemian Corps designated in a "War Case R" for the main offensive northward between the Bug and Vistula Rivers could have been transported across western Galician rail lines not planned for utilization in any A-Group movements. Another possibility was that the "War Case B" trains already carrying the VIII and IX Corps from Bohemia to Syrmia could have been halted and unloaded, then reloaded and retrained to their original mobilization stations after the military formations reassembled. Although this scenario would present an enormous planning problem, it could have been achieved, but, according to Ratzenhofer, these possible solutions to the quandry of transportation problems were unrealistic in 1914 due to the negative effect they would have on the morale, discipline, and political feelings of the Austro-Hungarian soldiers. Ratzenhofer also added for good measure that to reverse the rail movement running southward would result in a loss of confidence in the General Staff's first war-planning measures.[79]

This confusing and tragic Railroad Bureau planning in 1914 was because for some time "War Case R" and "War Case B" operational work had been prepared separately each year. Surprisingly, no detailed plans existed in 1914 for the most likely possibility — that of a deployment begun against Serbia and followed by a redeployment against Russia to counter her; nor had a mutual "War Case R+B" deployment plan ever been prepared.[80]

It rapidly became evident at the end of July that neither did the Railroad Bureau's deployment variants fit the 1914 deployment situation that arose nor, even more seriously, did Conrad's strategic planning meet the actual military scenario that had arisen. Colonel Straub could weakly claim that the problem of a double deployment involved a serious matter of written planning technicalities, but as he himself stated, he could not give Conrad his unconditional guarantee of success.[81]

Ratzenhofer, in numerous articles and manuscripts produced between the World Wars, would defend the Railroad Bureau against attacks on its proficiency and planning in the 1914 mobilization and deployment period. As a contributor and editor of the *Militärwissentschaftliche und technische Mitteilungen* and author of numerous articles in other journals, he produced numerous graphs, travel plans, overviews of troop dispositions, etc., to justify his argument that was accepted by Conrad in July 1914: that the B-Group could not have been shifted from their movement to the Balkan theater to the Russian front without producing a technical disaster for the railroads.

Ratzenhofer, a prolific writer, ensured that in the Austro-Hungarian official history, *Österreich-Ungarns letzter Krieg*, the railroad mobilization mistakes for which he was largely responsible received a whitewash, in which his depiction (he wrote that particular section) of the events does not fit the facts. Indeed, the first volume of the series, dealing with the 1914 war year, which was printed in 1929, had to be recalled and partially rewritten because of the public outcry against it. This first volume was then rereleased in 1931. Ratzenhofer had written the scanty, insufficient, and faulty portion of this work concerning the Railroad Bureau's role in the mobilization period. In general, Austria-Hungary's official history bypassed any critique of the military leadership or its responsibility for the outcome of particular battles or campaigns. Thus, it could be argued that the serious tactical and strategic mistakes of July and August 1914 would be concealed largely because of the sincere efforts to protect the honor and prestige of the Royal and Imperial Army.

Ratzenhofer would also claim after Conrad's death that two weeks before the Serbian mobilization he had forwarded to Conrad for review an operational study which questioned him as to what would occur if Russia chose to intervene in a Balkan deployment which had already begun. Conrad, according to Ratzenhofer, replied that he would have fourteen days to make any relevant decisions concerning railroad matters because the Russian army would not have obtained operational readiness that rapidly. Conrad's reputed two weeks' leeway in making strategic decisions never came to be because Russia mobilized much more rapidly than anticipated;[82] Conrad's time safety valve, as mentioned earlier, was based on captured Russian war plans from 1908!

Ratzenhofer, whose writings or apologia on the 1914 mobilization and deployment would be self-modified over the years, would also continue to make arguments that the limited capacity of the single-track rail lines traversing the Carpathian Mountains and the overburdening of the overall Hungarian railroad system in August were mitigating factors in making the decision that it would be impossible to change the B-Group rail movements.[83] If the two Bohemian Corps, the VIII and IX, had been transported across the western Galician rail network for "War Case R" (as originally planned for 1914-1915), rather than accompanying the B-Group to the Serbian front in "War Case B," these arguments would have been groundless. In summary, the VIII and IX Corps could easily have been transported to join the main attacking A-Group armies as intended, rather than being sent to the Balkan theater first. The transport of these two corps to the Balkans resulted in a deficiency of five infantry divisions which should have been available for the major northern offensive. Only twenty-one divisions would be available in August to launch the initial attack on the left flank between the Bug and Vistula Rivers. The failure to provide twenty-six divisions drastically affected the outcome of the initial campaign between the two rivers.

Ratzenhofer also later contended that a dearth of locomotives and operational personnel for "War Case R," resulting from the simultaneous "War Case B" deployment, caused the delay of the original "R" mobilization until 4 August.[84] He failed to mention that both locomotive and railroad personnel had become available from the evacuated eastern Galician rail lines as a result of the *Rückverlegung*, or strategic rearward redeployment, of July 1914. The rearward deployment freed quantities of both locomotives and personnel to be utilized elsewhere. Also, the men and equipment assigned prior to 1914 to transport the three Italian corps to the German front, according to the Triple Alliance Treaty agreement, would have more than replenished any deficiencies in locomotives and personnel caused by the "War Case B" mobilization's preceding the "War Case R".

Another relevant factor in the 1914 Railroad Bureau travesty was Ratzenhofer's and Straub's apparent failure to consult other members of the Railroad Bureau about their momentous decision to continue the southern movement of all the "War Case B" deployment trains.[85] Ratzenhofer would also add to his list of excuses the most serious exaggeration that a 100,000-man working force had been enlisted in the "War Case B" deployment,[86] resulting in a depletion of manpower for the "R" section when that became necessary.

The Railroad Bureau obviously played a crucial role in the outcome of the July crisis, but a realistic appraisal of the overall Austro-Hungarian railroad system reveals that the rail situation was not favorable for conducting a two-front war. The Bureau made a bad situation worse. The seven Galician rail lines leading to the deployment areas proved insufficient, as only 141 trains daily could carry troops on these lines. On the other hand, the Russians could run at least 260 trains daily on their improving strategic rail lines leading to the Monarchy's frontier.

Much criticism can therefore justifiably be leveled at the Railroad Bureau planners, who should have better utilized the Monarchy's existent rail lines for deployment purposes. For example, the Railroad planners allowed the train troop transports to move too slowly to be effective, and at the same time emphasized security to the detriment of speed. More trains could also have operated on the existing lines than were foreseen; the two Bohemian corps should have been better handled, as we have seen; and the overall railroad transport planning was based on the outdated experiences of the wars of 1866 and 1870-1871 and ignored significant advancements in rail transportation technology, such as more powerful locomotives and improved signal apparatus.

Reviewing these factors, the first criticism — that the Monarchy's track system should have been better utilized — refers to the under-utilization of trains, particularly on the existing two-track line systems.[87] Specifically, two major lines, the North and the Karl Ludwig, could handle a much higher train capacity than Railroad Bureau planners assigned to these key stretches. In fact, pre-war commercial use of the lines was almost twice as extensive.

According to Railroad Bureau orders for the overall deployment movement, the speed on the slowest rail stretch, or the speed of the slowest locomotives, became the measure by which all travel on that particular line was calculated. This procedure would reputedly provide both security and uniformity of movement. Thus while German military transports would roll at up to thirty kilometers per hour, in Austria-Hungary a train running on one track traveled at eleven kilometers per hour, or eighteen kilometers per hour when moving on a double-track section.[88] Some of these individual trains could actually travel up to forty kilometers per hour, but regardless of speed every train paused six hours a day for meals, coaling and watering. The meal stops occurred even though the various units had their cooking stoves on board, and often, after the train had stopped, two meals would be cooked and served late in the evening!

A few examples of the Railroad Bureau transport time tables illustrate the incredibly lethargic train movement: for a train traveling from Prague to Przeymsl, the trip required two days and three hours travel; from Budapest to Lemberg, rail movement took one day and 20 hours; from Kolozsvár to Stanislau, one day and 18 hours were needed; from Prague to Semlin, two days and 20 hours; and, finally, from Budapest to Semlin, a full day. Further examples of ridiculously slow train movement in the deployment phase garnered from Army log books and commanders' memoirs include the Fourth Army commander's forty-hour journey from Vienna to the San River deployment area, a trip that consumed *three times* the usual peacetime travel time![89] The Third Army Commander, for example, would leave Pozsony (Pressburg, Bratislava) at 6:00 a.m. on 5 August only to arrive at his final destination of Zsombor at 6:00 a.m. on 10 August.[90] One could almost have *walked* that distance in five days![91]

Mobilization trains were further slowed down, in many cases, because the railroad planners also limited deployment traffic to fifty-car, 100-axle trains, a strategy which ignored the regular peacetime traffic on several track sections of 150- to 200-axle trains. Use of 100-axle train units suited military planning, for it made convenient the transport of an infantry battalion, an artillery battery, or a cavalry squadron.[92] This concession to convenience is but another example of how Railroad Bureau planning proved insufficient for a war in 1914, although military plans were revised annually in an effort to gain every second of any possible time advantage in an actual deployment situation. This strategy followed the nineteenth-century military axiom that a first and decisive victory in modern battle went to the army able most quickly to mobilize and launch an offensive. The nineteenth-century experience, excepting of course the significant American Civil War and Russo-Japanese War, had borne out this theory.

This line of thinking involving the need for a rapid mobilization and deployment was especially significant for the Austro-Hungarian military planners because they recognized that the Russians would have an overwhelming numerical advantage in the event of an eastern war. The anticipated earlier operational readiness of the Austro-Hungarians, according to the Operations Bureau, would give the outnumbered Austro-Hungarian forces the advantage of having to battle decisively only one segment of the deploying enemy forces before they had completed their total concentration of forces.

Both Austro-Hungarian and German rail deployment planning in 1914 were based on the experiences of the Austro-Prussian War of 1866 and the Franco-Prussian War of 1870. But at those earlier dates, weaker and less extensive railroad nets had existed, locomotives were less powerful, no telephone network had existed, and only poor signal apparatus had been available. In other words, Austro-Hungarian railroad military planning proved obsolete for the realities of the 1914 era. The Railroad Bureau's conservative plans for track usage relative to speed of movement, supposedly in order to gain better security, did not prevent severe congestion and disruptions on the individual lines. Many of the unforeseen crises created by a wartime situation had also been underestimated. Apparently, only very specific deployment movements and some supplemental traffic had been foreseen in the pre-war planning. No detailed provisions had been made for other rail necessities, such as the combined "War Cases R+B." Evidently the unforeseen contingencies which would result in the necessity to revise planned procedures, familiar considerations at the beginning of any war, had not been considered,[93] nor had room been left for any compromises or changes.

Other factors precipitating the disaster of 1914 included the pre-war transfer of some trained railroad officers to other military branches, such as infantry and artillery. Also, no pre-war cooperative efforts had been established between Railroad Bureau and other military functionaries. Also a source of trouble in 1914 was that military officers were better at theoretical railroad planning, while the civilian railroad personnel were more proficient in practical planning and carrying on the day-to-day activities of railroad usage. General Staff officers proved to be intransigent in planning, railroad workers more flexible in their carrying out of their duties.

With respect to the matter of materiel and supply planning, the irregular stream of empty train cars and refugee trains that began traveling in the reverse direction of the deployment trains quickly plugged up numerous railroad stations. As a result, further deployment transport movements were hindered,[94] the troops had to undertake further tiring footmarches.

The Austro-Hungarian mobilization thus proved to be a disaster, resulting from poor planning, lack of flexibility, and a general unpreparedness for war in 1914.

CHAPTER VIII

The Historiography of Mobilization, the Railroad Bureau, the Creation of a Habsburg Command Conspiracy and its Critics

The "official" history of 1914 mobilization and deployment events was written between the World Wars based on Conrad's five-volume memoirs, Ratzenhofer's numerous articles and manuscripts, and the official Austrian history of the war, *Österreich-Ungarns letzter Krieg*, as well as on numerous memoirs and articles written by leading Austro-Hungarian military leaders of the war. Only a few exceptions refuted this "official" version.[1]

Immediately after the war, some former officers of the Imperial Army began to write private manuscripts for deposit in the Vienna War Archives. These manuscripts present an interpretation of how the events of 1914 unraveled very differently from that presented in the "official sources." Examining the general political and social atmosphere in Austria, but especially in Vienna, after World War I is crucial to understanding how a "Habsburg command conspiracy" evolved in the first place. Particularly for the former Austro-Hungarian Officer Corps, this milieu would have a profound effect on the method and content of the historical descriptions of World War I's outbreak and course. It must be emphasized that the world of the Imperial officer corps collapsed along with the 1918 military defeat and disintegration of the old monarchy. The Austro-Hungarian Army had fought far better than anyone could have imagined before the war, considering its extreme backward condition upon entering the conflict, particularly relative to the sparcity of modern equipment.

The Austrian newspapers castigated the former officers corps in 1918 and 1919 and, in addition, the Law of Exclusion of 19 December 1918 would be largely aimed at those officers who formerly held the rank of major or above, excluding them from any rights of the new republic. The Austro-Hungarian officer corps was thereby not unjustifiably accused of remaining monarchist at heart after hostilities terminated and after the core of the Imperial Monarchy had become the truncated Republic of Austria. These various assaults against the former officer corps and their bitterness at accepting military defeat galvanized the old officer corps as a separate entity and intensified the inbred respect for their fellow officers and compatriots — a situation which resulted in the phenomenon that they basically agreed that they would utter no public criticism against the last Austro-Hungarian Chief of the General Staff's military actions or military planning in general.[2]

To this end, the vast majority of interwar military literature would serve to create and simultaneously glorify the mystique that Conrad had been the greatest Austro-Hungarian army commander since Prince Eugen. Praising Conrad and his actions would also serve to maintain the honor and glory of the old Imperial Army. Therefore, any criticism of Conrad or his strategical decisions would be confined to private manuscripts, writings, and self-published books that would be deposited in the Vienna War Archives, precluding negative publicity to the outside public, for circulation only among the former officer corps.

The first assaults on the previously printed glorified version of events and the Conrad mythos begun in 1914 would appear immediately after the war in 1919, but these assaults were especially prevalent as rebuttals after the appearance of the first volume of Conrad's memoirs in 1921. Conrad's five-volume work, appearing between 1921 and 1925, is an amalgam of his memories and some of the most important official documents of the time, as well as many misleading assertions that gradually became enmeshed in an unofficial publication of the War Archives. Conrad, it seems, researched, prepared, and wrote his memoirs in the Vienna War Archives with a great deal of assistance from fellow former officers Rudolf Kiszling and Glaise Horstenau, among others. It should also be considered that Conrad was already very ill at this time.

Conrad, in the important fourth volume of his memoirs *Aus meiner Dienstzeit*, blamed the Austro-Hungarian diplomats' uncertainty regarding the possibility of Russian intervention in the event of an Austro-Hungarian-Serbian war, and the German allies' failure to announce their intentions in time, for the disaster that resulted from the 1914 mobilization situation — particularly his 31 July/1 August decision to continue the rail transport of the B-Group to the Balkans even though he knew that St. Petersburg had proclaimed her general mobilization.

According to Conrad, the diplomats deserved criticism for the fateful results that transpired in 1914, because had they confirmed Russia's true intentions just two days earlier than they did, a successful full "War Case R" could have been implemented,[3] and, in fact, the B-Group could have been successfully rerouted to the north in a timely fashion. His argument, however, does not match the facts. The delay of the "War Case R" mobilization until as late as 4 August was due to the decisions he accepted on the night of 31 July to have the B-Group continue its rail transport to the Balkans and to the failure of the 1914 Railroad Bureau leadership to develop any form of flexible contingency planning. In addition, the Evidenz (Intelligence) Bureau of the General Staff had early and clear indications — well before 31 July — that Russia would simply not stand aside and let Serbia be humiliated again, as she had in both the 1908-1909 Bosnian Crisis and the 1912-1913 Balkan Wars. Similarly, one must also consider that no Railroad Bureau plans existed for a simultaneous "War Case R+B" mobilization, and that Conrad mistakenly believed that a shift to a "War Case R+B" mobilization and deployment could be accomplished if the decision to do so transpired within five mobilization days of the commencement of a full Balkan mobilization.

Reading between the lines of Conrad's memoirs, and after a thorough examination of the diplomatic and military documents of July 1914, one comes to the conclusion that Straub and Ratzenhofer's negative replies on 31 July/1 August relative to the possibilities concerning the B-Group merely served to reinforce Conrad's objective of sending too many troops to Serbia in his insatiable desire to crush her.[4] Most leading figures in the Dual Monarchy concurred with his desire to annihilate the hated Southern Slav neighbor. So once Serbia had been thoroughly defeated, Conrad argued, the way would be paved either to regain any lost territory from the Russians or to defend Galicia, Bukovina, or northern Hungary if Russia had invaded their territory in the meantime.

In his memoirs, Conrad's second major argument relative to the July crisis, that no one could discern whether Russia was merely bluffing or would indeed actually intervene in an Austro-Hungarian-Serbian war, is simply untrue. It had become obvious already by 24 July with the decision for a partial Russian mobilization, if it had not been clear since 20 July that Russia would not stand aside this time and allow Serbia to be crushed militarily. From 24 July, many diplomatic communiqués citing Russian warnings about an Austrian-Hungarian invasion of her Slavic neighbor and the initiation of significant military measures proliferated. In addition, the General Staff Operations Bureau leaders had anticipated a Russian intervention in a war against Serbia since the 1908-1909 Bosnian Crisis, and particularly since the 1912-1913 Balkan Wars.

Conrad's other post-war assertion, namely that Berlin had not made its position clear in time to allow him to commence a timely Austro-Hungarian mobilization against both Russia and Serbia, is also false. The decision to wage war against Serbia had been made as early as 5-7 July and, as mentioned, documents reveal that a clear threat of Russian intervention existed as early as 20 July.[5] After the war, Conrad also strongly criticized Germany for not sending the promised military support for their mutual eastern conflict against Russia;[6] but in fairness to Moltke, Italy's defection from the Triple Alliance, which signified that Rome would not send her Third Army to the Rhine as agreed upon before the war, caused Moltke to withhold the five reserve divisions promised for the Prussian theater. He did, however, inform Conrad of his intention well before the opening battles began.

Following the publication of Conrad's memoirs between 1921-1925, former Army Commanders and field officers immediately began criticizing its contents, particularly those concerning military and technical questions, and rebutting attacks by the author on their leadership successes. Several of these rebuttals would be published by the authors themselves, rather than by publishing firms,[7] because Conrad, as the last Chief of the Austro-Hungarian General Staff, had become literally sacrosanct after the war. In other words, no criticism could be published against Conrad's military planning, leadership style, or successes. For seventy years after the fall of the Habsburg monarchy, almost all literature focusing on World War I has portrayed him idealistically. For example, both the last Conrad biography, published in 1938, and a huge book published in 1955 lavished undeserved praise on him, making an accurate assessment of Conrad or his military leadership in the war difficult.

August Urbanski authored the 1938 biography of Conrad.[8] The book, entitled *Conrad von Hötzendorf*, epitomized the then prevailing "hero cult" or glorification of Conrad. Such revealing statements as "the boldness of his decisions and his tenacity in execution enabled him to also handle the most critical situations. Conrad lacked only one thing — luck," clearly indicate the prevailing tone and viewpoint of the book. Urbanski himself had worked closely with Conrad in the war and had become related to him by marriage in 1915. Urbanski obviously was a member of that group of former Imperial officers who exalted Conrad as a great military commander.

The actual roots of the forthcoming "official" history and hero cult of Conrad emerged already during the war and are demonstrated by the appearance of a book published in 1916 entitled *Conrad von Hötzendorf.* Contributing to their growth would be a book that appeared in 1919, authored by a Karl Nowak, that heaped outlandish praise upon Conrad.[9] Other later Conrad biographies included a short 1942 monograph by Ferdinand Stoller, which was preceded by a short article-length work on him of 1934 entitled *"Conrad von Hötzendorf, Eine Studie über seine Persönlichkeit."*[10]

The Conrad interpretation of the 1914 mobilization and deployment events, as found in his memoirs, would be championed after his death in revised form by Emil Ratzenhofer. But this was the same Emil Ratzenhofer, then a major in the R-Group of the Railroad Bureau, who had declared that the B-Group transport could not be reversed to the north on 31 July and 1 August, and who had convinced everyone, including Conrad, that the B-Group, if allowed to travel to the Balkan front, unload, reload, and travel northward, would arrive at exactly the same time in Galicia as if it continued to the Serbian frontier. Ratzenhofer wrote prolifically after the War to convince people that the decision of 31 July/1 August to continue transport of the B-Group to Serbia could not have been worked out otherwise. His various articles and private manuscripts, which served as the most notable apologia for the 1914 actions of the Railroad Bureau, would be accepted as authoritative, even in Norman Stone's book, *The Eastern Front.*

Ratzenhofer also contributed to the Austrian "official history," *Österreich-Ungarns letzter Krieg.* Volume one of the series was published in 1929 and would be recalled, rewritten, and re-released in modified form in 1931, because of the major outcry against its lack of factual accuracy. Ratzenhofer himself penned the parts of both versions which described the railroad mobilization and deployment of 1914. Then, as an editor of the most prominent Austrian military periodical during the interwar years, *Militärwissentschlaftliche und technische Mitteilungen*, he helped perpetuate the "official" version both of the events leading to the outbreak of the war and of the military's role, particularly that of the Railroad Bureau. *Österreich-Ungarns letzter Krieg*, was researched and written only by "officers of the late Imperial Royal Army."[11] A total of seventeen such officers participated in the project. Twelve had served as active officers. These former officers have been described as the *"Österreich-Ungarns letzter Krieg* group" in a recent article authored by, Peter Broucek, the former head of the World War I section of the Vienna War Archives, which supports this official version of the events of the war. These officers purposely presented no judgments relative to the leadership or conduct of the actual battles and operations.[12] The author of the article stated that the few judgments made were "very lenient" on the commanders, still he claims that the official history "is a pragmatic description of Austria-Hungary in World War I."[13] This claim is debatable, but it should be noted that, of the major participants of World War I, only in Austria would actual military participants from the officer corps be the sole authors of the history of the war.

The "official" history version of the events of 1914-1918 had its antecedent in the fifth volume of Max Schwarte's series which contained articles describing the many campaigns on the Austro-Hungarian front. The various authors were former Austro-Hungarian General Staff and Army field officers. These articles, which are not particularly revealing about the campaigns, serve rather as a series of justifications for the leadership of, and of the events themselves, that occurred.[14]

Vienna War Archives agreements with the German *Reichsarchiv* led to the publication of a series of books related to individual major Austro-Hungarian battles or campaigns that occurred on the Russian front. Several of these books would be written by the same former imperial officer, Rudolf Kiszling, who would become one of the major "conspirators" to white-wash the blunders of the Austro-Hungarian Command. He perpetuated these interpretations as Chief Administrator of the Vienna War Archives from 1939-1945. In numerous personal interviews, the last survivor of the original officer group insisted emphatically that all relevant facts concerning the July crisis and the August mobilization could be found in his many writings. Kiszling's numerous articles focusing on the outbreak of World War I, the writing of which commenced in 1922, would establish the exact same themes and explanations of events which he would maintain until his last publication in 1984. This book, appearing 62 years after his first article, finally admitted to "some errors" in leadership on Conrad's part during the War,[15] but elsewhere in his vast collection of writings relative to the war, Kiszling never deviated from the official interpretation.[16] He wrote numerous articles for the German periodical, *Berliner Monatshefte*, after 1926. His topic usually concerned war preparations and the outbreak of the war from Vienna's perspective. Much of this early Kiszling material would be incorporated in the Austro-Hungarian official history of the war, and his interpretation of the events of 1914 would be accepted by authors of later general histories and biographies.[17]

The main purpose or mission of the "official" Habsburg historians was to protect the honor of the old imperial army and its officer corps. A secondary goal was to camouflage the mistakes perpetrated in the original mobilization, deployment and opening campaigns of the war, as well as those in all later campaigns.

On the other hand, several private manuscripts deposited in the War Archives by former officers, the first ones written immediately after the war, began an assault on Conrad's wartime decision-making and his leadership in general. One of the most significant allegations raised relative to the mobilization period was that the Russians had simply mobilized and deployed much more rapidly than Conrad had anticipated, regardless of Conrad's many excuses for the disaster in 1914.[18]

As early as 1919, General Maximilian Csicerics, a former officer admired by many of his peers, wrote a "character picture" of Conrad that offered a far different portrayal of him than did the general post-war literature which strove to idealize him as the last "great" Austro-Hungarian military commander and to paint the Imperial army in the best possible light.

General Csicerics vigorously attacked the "hero cult" worship of Conrad of the time, emphasizing that Conrad's strategic ideas and plans seldom, if ever, corresponded to the material and manpower of the Monarchy's army. This tragedy, according to the author, resulted in a great deal of blood unnecessarily being shed on many battlefields.[19]

Csicerics further argued that Conrad consistently failed to consider the key factors of terrain and movement routes in his planning, and did not consider carefully enough such vital factors as the movement of supplies, particularly that of ammunition of all forms. Neither would Conrad consider weather factors nor the time of year in his planning, as per the Carpathian disaster in 1915. Csicerics also portrays Conrad as being overly pessimistic, which is a factor cited by his later critics. His personal conduct, according to the author, coupled with the many errors made by the High Command, resulted in the loss of trust, respect, and confidence of many in the army ranks. Former commanders such as Generals Erich von Falkenhayn further, Rudolf R. Brudermann, Alfred Krauss and Arthur Arz are also among the former Imperial officers who questioned Conrad's many assertions and claims of effectiveness.

Csicerics asserted that after the major defeats in the two battles of
Lemberg, and the campaigns in Serbia, Conrad complained that many of
the Generals were "incapable" of commanding effectively and that the
troops failed to achieve their missions. This claim resulted in Conrad
taking the opportunity to remove higher commanders whom he feared
might eventually replace him as Chief of the General Staff. Further,
Csicerics alleged, a feeling rapidly pervaded the army ranks after the
terrible losses suffered in the two battles of Lemberg, that the initial
Austro-Hungarian offensives amounted to nothing more than useless
bloodshed. Other critics of Conrad and of his leadership period would
later repeat these views in private. The accusation was also leveled that
Conrad was always too "removed" from his army, that he very rarely
considered the conditions and needs of his own troops, and that he did
not make the effort to travel to the front lines to investigate first-hand the
situation in the trenches. He also was accused of expecting and demanding
far too much from both his officers and troops.[20] These charges are echoed
in various diaries and private manuscripts deposited in the *Nachlässe*
collection in the War Archives in Vienna. Other former officer corps
members would also prepare unpublished manuscripts for the Vienna War
Archives that were written specifically to counter the Conrad-Ratzenhofer-
Kiszling interpretation of events. These works were purposely not publi-
cized, hence they were never brought to the attention of the general public.
General Alfred Krauss, a distinguished Austro-Hungarian General, a
former commander of the Austro-Hungarian War College and a successful
commander in the opening Balkan campaigns, and a man considered a
leading theoretician and historian, would become one of the very few
significant former field commanders to attack openly the "official" interpretation of the opening campaigns presented in Volume I of *Österreich-
Ungarns letzter Krieg*. Krauss wrote extremely critical letters to the Vienna War Archives in 1930 after the publication of the first volume of the
official history[21]. In particular, Krauss attacked the "official" interpretation
of the first three Balkan campaigns as an attempt by the editors and writers
to place General Oskar Potiorek, commander of the Balkan forces and
thus Krauss's own commander, in a more favorable light than he deserved.
Krauss chastised Potiorek for launching his initial operations against Serbia in a direction most unfavorable for attack, thereby totally ignoring the
centuries-long historically successful invasion route that led through Belgrade into the Balkans. Potiorek would also be accused of pushing his
troops too harshly while demonstrating no real consideration for their

heavy battle losses, and for not carefully preparing for his operations. Krauss further leveled the serious charge that pre-war preparations against Serbia had been faulty, i.e. that there existed no evidence of serious reconnaissance undertakings to scout for potential favorable river crossing areas, defiles, etc.

Also, Krauss made the accusation that both the Fifth Army's advance into northwest Serbia, and the Sixth Army's advance much further to the south, southwest, and into the Lim area did not demonstrate a uniformity of purpose for the entire campaign, nor did the initial assembling of troops at the Balkan front transpire with any semblance of conformity to each other. Little chance of success or victory would be the obvious result of these failures in planning. Krauss emphasized that, almost immediately in the campaign, shortages occurred, resulting from the extreme confusion in the chain-of-command and general command relations, the difficult terrain to be traversed, and total lack of a sufficient and smooth-flowing supply movement. Water shortages also became apparent while troops were ordered to march incessantly, and often unnecessarily, in the heat.[22] These numerous criticisms of the first Balkan campaign are also confirmed in diaries, manuscripts, and reports from that particular theater. General Krauss's most famous post-war books include *Die Ursachen unserer Niederlage* (1923) and *Theorie und Praxis in der Kriegskunst* (1936), in which we see one of the very few public attacks on the General Staff and High Command functionaries.

Another critic of Conrad, his leadership and command methods, and the Austrian official history was Maximilian Pitreich, who wrote the significant monographs *Lemberg 1914* in 1929 and *1914, Die militäris-chen Probleme unseres Kriegsbeginnes, Ideen, Gründe und Zusammen-hänge* in 1934, as well as several private manuscripts attacking the "Habsburg command conspiracy." As was the case with other military detectives of historical truth, Pitreich did not intend to blemish the honor of the old Imperial Army. Thus, he would expose the "errors" in the Austrian official history, Conrad's memoirs, and the many Ratzenhofer articles and manuscripts, but would do so most effectively in the excellent private manuscripts which he deposited in the Vienna War Archives and which are cited in this study.[23]

Pitreich's two published works produced a controversy about the veracity of the facts surrounding the immediate background of the war as related in his book *1914*, and about the "official" military versions of the opening battles in both *Lemberg* and *1914*. But, again, to preserve the

honor of the former Imperial Army, Pitreich carried on his one-man cru-
sade to bring the historical truth to light mostly within the old military
officer circles, preferring to avoid a public airing.

Pitreich's basic and most significant arguments can be summarized as
follows: not for one moment in July 1914 could there be any thought of
a "War Case B" mobilization's being implemented without the expectation
of a swift Russian intervention, a claim which certainly contradicts one
of Conrad's basic arguments. He also emphasized that the Railroad Bureau
leadership failed to support Conrad in his belated attempts to rectify the
horrendous situation that had developed at the end of July. In addition
Pitreich states that the Railroad Bureau displayed a total lack of initiative
to attempt to adjust the faulty 1914 railroad deployment plans when it
became absolutely imperative to do so; further, that no "War Case R + B"
plan had been even remotely prepared for the eventuality of a simultaneous
mobilization and deployment against both Serbia and Russia; that the
situation that appeared on the evening of 31 July to 1 August without
question demanded the command for a general mobilization and pre-"War
Case R" — there should have been not a second's delay; further, that the
31 July decision to allow the B-Group to continue to roll by rail to the
Serbian frontier became the major factor leading to the defeats on both
the Serbian and Galician battlefields; and, in addition, that this same
decision resulted in the absence in the opening offensive in Galicia of five
divisions that were crucial to the hope for a success of the left-flank
offensive of the First and Fourth Armies. Also, he claimed that the Railroad Bureau did not accurately brief Conrad on the true railroad situation
relative to the "War Case B" deployment and, in 1913, had also failed to
carry out his orders to prepare a combined "War Case R + B" plan for a
simultaneous mobilization, for the scenario now most likely in the outbreak of a conflict.

Pitreich insisted, contrary to all arguments presented by Ratzenhofer,
Straub and the Railroad Bureau, that the Balkan deployment could have
indeed been halted as late as 31 July. He also explained the inaccuracy of
the numerous graphs, lexicons, and charts which Ratzenhofer had produced in various articles to prove his contention that substantial B-Group
units had already begun their railroad transport to the Balkans by 31 July.
To the contrary, very few of the designated top units had actually begun
rail transport by this date. Later writers, as we shall see, would carry
Pitreich's arguments even further in their own private manuscripts, adding
even more substantiation to the validity of his assertions and countering

the Ratzenhofer claims that to have halted the B-Group railroad movement would have resulted in a chaotic situation.

Pitreich also became one of the first Austrian writers to maintain that the declaration of war against Serbia should have been proclaimed on 26 July, not 28 July. As he convincingly argued, at least two valuable days were lost for what would be claimed as Railroad Bureau matters, to the detriment of commencing deployment against Serbia. The later war declaration was supposedly made in an effort to ensure that the railroad part of the mobilization plan ran smoothly. This, when Conrad had insisted on numerous occasions that not one hour should be lost to Belgrade's military advantage! Serbia thus became the big winner in the time factor equation of armed preparations.

"War Case R," Pitreich maintained, should have been proclaimed earlier than it was on 4 August. An additional four days' valuable time were given to Russia, whose military measures had begun, at the latest, on 25 July. Pitreich insisted that the "War Case R" mobilization could have been announced on 2 August, if not 1 August.[24] In both cases of the Russian and Serbian mobilizations, the time delay accepted in order that the Railroad Bureau would assure a smooth railroad deployment, would produce significant time advantage for the enemy.

Relative to the charge that the Railroad Bureau had not prepared a simultaneous "R+B" mobilization and deployment plan although ordered to do so, Pitreich presents irrefutable documentary evidence that a year earlier, on 29 November 1913, Conrad had ordered that an *Instradierungs Elaborat* be prepared for a mutual "War Case R+B." The then chief of the Railroad Bureau, Colonel Rziha, informed Conrad that a front change from "War Case B" to "R" could indeed be accomplished. It would have been easiest to accomplish if ordered by the fifth mobilization day of a "War Case B" deployment, but could also have been achieved up to the sixteenth mobilization day or before actual military operations commenced. Conrad, it should be mentioned, related these same facts in his memoirs.[25] Earlier in March 1913, Conrad had assured Kaiser Franz Joseph that if "War Case B" occurred and Russia then chose to intervene, an immediate transfer of the B-Group to the northern theater would be possible.[26]

But on 30 and 31 July 1914, Straub and Ratzenhofer could neither attempt nor accomplish the shift from a "War Case B" to a "War Case R" mobilization — on only the third and fourth mobilization days.

Pitreich also disagreed with Ratzenhofer's argument that the B-Group forces had attained march readiness by 1 August. As he pointed out, totally contrary to Ratzenhofer's position, march readiness for these particular troops could only be attained between the fifth and tenth mobilization days. Thus, on 1 August it was possible that early vanguard rail transports could have begun the B-Group movement, but total transport readiness could not have been attained by that date. As evidence to substantiate his points, Pitreich utilized Ratzenhofer's own graphs and charts to demonstrate that on 30 July only thirty-one, and on 31 July only forty-two trains had begun to roll toward the Serbian frontier.[27] Thus, Pitreich insisted that "War Case B" could have easily and successfully been switched to a "War Case R" railroad mobilization plan because the overwhelming number of "War Case B" transports had not even begun to roll.

Pitreich would thus become the foremost critic of the "Habsburg command conspiracy" historians. In his detailed private manuscripts, he exposed the inaccurate and insufficient presentation in the "official" Austrian history series regarding the railroad deployment. Significantly, he also demonstrated that in neither war theater did the railroad deployment plan result in a unified strong military force being deployed, as was demanded in Conrad's strategic plans. Further, he charged that the Railroad Bureau leadership demonstrated incompetence in claiming that Conrad had never issued the command for the preparation of a comprehensive mobilization and deployment plan for the most likely scenario of a Balkan war eruption which would lead to a Russian intervention. The Railroad Bureau also obviously failed to produce an alternative plan for carrying out the full "War Case B" instead of switching to a full "War Case R" when St. Petersburg proclaimed its general mobilization. The Railroad Bureau, which had very little contact with Conrad, is also accused of possessing seriously deficient knowledge of the major operational ideas being developed by the General Staff.

Pitreich, in his self-published book *1914*, also openly questioned and then corrected the "official" interpretation of why the *Rückverlegung*, or rearward strategic redeployment, occurred in 1914. This rearward deployment order, presented in 1914 and forwarded to the troop commanders, is basically explained in that the order for the redeployment was a result of the Austro-Hungarian military hierarchy's overwhelming desire to crush Serbia before having to reverse themselves and send significant troop numbers to counter Russia. Instructions forwarded to the various corps commanders emphasized the uncertainty as to the moment at which Russia might intervene in a "War Case B." As a "smokescreen," however, the order for the strategic rearward deployment cited Romania's declaration of neutrality leading to the exposure of the extreme right flank in eastern Galicia as an important factor in the issuing of the order.

But, if Romania had truly been a factor in the order for the *Rückverlegung*, the railroad deployment should have been advanced forward toward the Romanian frontier to provide such flank protection, rather than rearward to the San-Dniester River line. This inconsistency, according to Pitriech, signified that primacy in war planning evolved during the July crisis to the operations matters of the Railroad Bureau, rather than to the key factor of rapidity of deployment.[28]

Pitreich also reexplained Conrad's basic strategic concept in his war planning against Russia as a major left-flank offensive northward between the Bug and Vistula Rivers and simultaneous defensive stance on the right flank at the San-Dniester River line. This deployment would result in a half-moon configuration in front of the rivers. To Conrad, it was essential that the right-flank forces should be as far forward of the rivers as possible. Thus, the "official" argument that the *Rückverlegung* resulted from Romania's neutral stance does not fit the facts. In any case, by 1913, Conrad had already discounted Romania's actively siding with Austria-Hungary in an eastern war, and thus had no compulsion whatsoever to place his right-flank position forward to the Romanian frontier.[29] In fact, at their Karlsbad meeting in early 1914, Conrad had informed Moltke that even Bucharest could be in the enemy camp.

In the "War Case R" railroad deployment that actually occurred, the deployment of troops varied significantly from that in Conrad's original strategic plan. As a result of the railroad deployment plan, only seventeen divisions would be transported to the designated left-flank positions at the San River. This plan meant that the Austro-Hungarian armies would be merely of equal strength to the opposing Russian armies when they launched their offensive, but Conrad had always intended that the left-flank attacking force must outnumber the enemy in order to ensure victory. The numerical configuration for "War Case R," as planned by Conrad, called for thirty divisions to be deployed on the left flank for the offensive northward while ten divisions on the right flank would maintain a defensive posture. The weaker than anticipated offensive force which the actual deployment plan would deliver obviously should have raised the critical question of whether a left-flank offensive could lead to a success, because simultaneously with this offensive the entire military operation in Galicia would be jeopardized.

On 13 July 1914, specific units of the B-Group had been designated to be deployed against Russia if she intervened in a Balkan war. Thus, the IX Corps would join the left-flank First Army, the VII Corps the Fourth Army, which would complete the designated composition of the main offensive strike to be hurled against Russia. At the same time, the B-Group VII Corps would be inserted on the right defensive flank in a position between the III and XII Corps. The IV Corps would serve as a High Command reserve force and would be sent to Chyrov. As a result of this plan, four infantry divisions, the IX and VIII Corps, would be deployed at the upper San River line in eastern Galicia, and three further divisions of the VII Corps would be deployed at the Dniester River. The two reserve divisions of the IV Corps would be approximately in the middle of the line. The August 1914 deployment fielded only twenty-one divisions instead of the thirty called for to complete the left-flank offensive force. Nor were the sixteen divisions designated for the Dniester River eastern defensive force line placed in position.

Pitreich pointed out that the catastrophic 1914 railroad deployment could easily have been performed in such a way that favored Austro-Hungarian purposes. Simply put, Pitreich demonstrated that a total of 100 deployment trains could have run daily to the area of Rzeszov-Jaroslau-Przemyśl, while forty-five trains could have been sent to the Dniester front, resulting in a much more favorable two-to-one ratio of troop numbers.

Further, Pitreich, as others would later, asked why the VIII and IX Corps, originating in Bohemia, couldn't have been moved by railroad across western Galicia to the San River line. This would have alleviated or prevented the stoppage of deployment transports of the B-Group, particularly in the bottleneck area of Budapest. Budapest served as the central rail foci for almost the entire B-group being deployed in "War Case B." It also served as a central crossing point for rail movement to the Carpathian Mountain rail lines, and deployment areas in eastern Galicia and at the Dniester River line for "War Case R."[30]

Pitreich's private studies and manuscripts were overshadowed for decades by Ratzenhofer's published articles. Pitreich died in the 1940's. His cause would be similarly championed privately in the War Archives manuscript collections by Gustav Hubka. Hubka's essays were written during the 1950's, followed by other writers in the 1960's and 1970's who would pursue Pitreich's arguments.[31] Hubka was the Austro-Hungarian military attaché to Montenegro during the Balkan Wars and in 1914 served proudly as an officer in the Imperial Army.

In the late 1940's and 1950's, Hubka would author some penetrating private essays that demonstrated his solid ties to the old Army, but also presented a struggle to reveal the factual events of World War I to the post-World War II Austrian generation. In particular, Hubka drew attention to some negative Conrad attributes. Hubka is an invaluable source of historical information through his private manuscripts, because during the Balkan upheavals, he came into contact with the most important figures to participate in the 1914 drama. He knew Conrad and, at critical times, had audiences with Kaiser Franz Joseph and Berchtold, as well as General Arthur Bolfras, General Adjutant to the Emperor.[32]

Immediately after the war ended, Hubka interviewed leading figures such as Giesl and Conrad, and utilized their memoirs and published documents to prepare his manuscripts. Hubka would emphasize that by the July crisis, contrary to Conrad's memoirs and the Austrian official history, Austro-Hungarian military dogma held that a war against Serbia also meant one against Russia.[33]

Also contrary to the "official version," Conrad and his General Staff possessed accurate information about pertinent Russian military advancements, although their own strategic planning would be based upon obsolete calculations and vague, unexplainable hopes that Russia would not intervene in the event of an Austro-Hungarian-Serbian war.

Hubka would also provide initial insight into the effect of Conrad's private life in the 1914 drama, earlier a forbidden subject. For example, in 1907, Conrad became enamored over a twenty-seven years younger married woman with five children. Over the years, Conrad became obsessed with his "Gina."

Hubka writes that his obsession robbed Conrad of both spiritual and mental balance during the critical days of 1914.[34] Conrad labored in the July crisis with his heart in Tirol. Hubka revealed that in mid-August, when the High Command departed for Galicia, his compatriots noticed a new gruffness in the Commander. It is evident that Conrad hoped to have enough time to defeat Serbia and, if Russia would intervene, then realign his troops against the northern threat.

Concerning the Austro-Hungarian B-Group's (Second Army) travail, Hubka described how the army would be hauled to the Balkan theater, then reversed to Galicia because the original deployment plans had been altered. In the process, numerous contradictory orders and directives were dispatched to various railroad stations, adding to the overall confusion. This had its psychological effect upon the troops.

According to Hubka, Conrad's removal of army, corps, and division commanders, after the first battles, did little to provide loyalty and trust in his leadership. While these changes may have effected battle results, the Russian's overwhelming superiority in numbers certainly had its effect. By December 1914, Conrad had removed four of six army commanders and eight of the seventeen corps commanders.

Hubka emphasized in his various manuscripts that his purpose in writing was to seek historical truth about the Austro-Hungarian military planning before and during 1914. He further wrote that "a picture without its dark side did no justice to the form, where a light shines, it must also throw a shadow," reflecting on the hero cult of Conrad.

Hubka delved into the most interesting facet of the July crisis, a vacation by Conrad, and its effect on military affairs. Conrad requested a vacation at his 5 July audience with Franz Joseph. After the audience, Franz Joseph's General Adjutant suggested that Conrad reconsider his request. But Conrad left for Innichen in Tirol where he would remain until 22 July except for a one-day break to return to Vienna to attend the 19 July Ministerial Council meeting.[35]

Hubka also reveals that in July in both the General Staff and War Ministry many officers were on vacation. Important war preparations would thus not be completed, especially by the Railroad Bureau. The Chief of the Railroad Bureau vacationed in Dalmatia, and during the period prior to 31 July, Major Emil Ratzenhofer, fourth in rank in the Bureau, would be in charge of affairs. He later became a leader of the "official" interpretation of events.

In 1955, Oskar Regele authored a massive work about Conrad.[36] This is the only major work relating to Conrad written between 1945 and the present. It is far from objective, passing over the July crisis with some generalized statements. Regele ignored such critical factors as Conrad's vacation time during the simmering July crisis, the effect on his actions of his relationship to Gina, and mood shifts throughout July and mobilization days of August.

In particular, Regele does not examine the controversy surrounding the decisions of 31 July/1 August relative to rail movement of the B-Group.

The book, a long, detailed glorification of Conrad, skips over key topics, by not critiquing Conrad's strategic planning, but merely quoting leaders relative to Conrad's "great" leadership traits. Regele, director of the Vienna War Archives from 1945 until 1955, would find his book attacked because of his "uncritical attitude."[37]

An interesting 1972 publication from the Austrian *Bundesministerium für Landesverteidigung* appeared commemorating the 120th anniversary of Conrad's birth.[38] The publication continued the "official" version of the 1914 events, that because of railroad technical difficulties and to avoid chaos, the B-Group had to continue transport southward, and suggested that no other alternatives existed for moving the B-Group to the Russian front once it had begun its movement to the Serbian frontier. The fact is that almost sixty years later, the "command conspiracy" still held the forefront in Austrian historiography.

More recently, a former Railroad official, who had served during World War II on the same rail network that was utilized in July and August 1914, reacted to the various arguments of Ratzenhofer and Pitreich, particularly to two recent articles relative to the mobilization of 1914. Utilizing his "theoretical and practical experiences to examine in detail whether the railroad deployment in July-August 1914 could have been performed otherwise," this excellent study, a private manuscript, provides in exacting detail an alternative to the disastrous rail decisions in 1914. The study destroys, point by point, Ratzenhofer's contentions presented over the years. Pitreich's original arguments are repeated, but examined in much more depth.

The manuscript, submitted to the Vienna War Archives[39], contends that the activities of the Railroad Bureau in 1914 were inexcusable; the railroad planning was replete with serious omissions. No plans had been produced, although ordered by Conrad, for a simultaneous deployment "War Case R+B." Rail information imparted to Conrad derived from superficial, non-verified information; that, as a result of the railroad deployment plan, at no front would there be Austro-Hungarian superiority in numbers; the continued rail movement of the B-Group would result in too many troops being fielded for the Balkan campaign, and insufficient numbers versus Russia; that some divisions earmarked for "War Case R" would not arrive there until 1915; and the rearward deployment movement (*Rückverlegung*) so changed the railroad system that much of the planning became little more than improvisation, which would result in time-killing and tiring foot marches for the troops. Most of these points are found in Pitreich's earlier writings.

Further, the author demonstrates in minute detail that: contrary to Ratzenhofer's calculations to justify the 1914 railway planning, no major troop movements had occurred by the critical evening of 31 July; the planning for the return of empty rail cars and other matters hindered deployment movement and blocked rail stations; the planning for the mobilization and deployment of 1914 ignored post-1870 railroad technical developments; and that when retreat movements became necessary in August, rail evacuation had not been foreseen nor prepared for, resulting in panic retreats. These retreats produced astronomical losses in men and material, crippling further efforts of the Imperial Army to launch offensive operations.

The argument against the "unpardonable" behavior of the Railroad Bureau leaders is attributed to the fact that Straub did not possess the strength of character to assume the responsibility his predecessors could. In other words, he would not assume the responsibility for any changes in the railroad deployment plans in 1914, so that Conrad, anticipating that he had five days to shift his deployment, learned that his Railroad Bureau had no plans for a simultaneous "R + B" war, and that no detailed plans had been prepared for a war breaking out against Serbia, with Russian intervention forcing the B-Group to be transported north to Galicia.[40] This was a catastrophic omission as Pitreich and Hubka had earlier argued.

Kálmán Kéri, author of the manuscript, like Pitreich, and Hubka, argued convincingly that Conrad had indeed ordered simultaneous "War Case R + B" planning in 1913, and that, actually, only a change in some details would have been necessary to have altered the plans, not a major shift in the deployment.

The 1914 railroad planning, or lack of it, also resulted in the Austro-Hungarian military deployments possessing no numerical superiority, particularly on the crucial left flank offensive position. Instead of twenty-six divisions launching the offensive, only twenty-one would. The other five divisions (VIII and IX Bohemian Corps) had been sent southward with the fatal decision of the night of 31 July.

Also, the Austro-Hungarian extreme right flank positions in eastern Galicia would be lacking the IV and VII Hungarian Corps at critical moments, because of delayed rail transport from the Balkan front and the insertion of the IV Corps into the fighting at Sabac. Both corps would arrive too late to affect the 1914 battle, and would then neither be positioned advantageously nor utilized in a unified manner because of railroad planning necessities.

It also is demonstrated that the fateful decision of 31 July resulted from superficial graphics, tables, and charts, and Ratzenhofer's argument that a significant number of troops had already begun transport was simply untrue. The "railroad technical difficulties" had been severely exaggerated.[41] Ratzenhofer had simply overwhelmed people in his post-war writings with unreadable details hiding the reality that extremely few units had actually begun rail movement. This also follows the Pitreich argument.

Regarding the next assertion that Conrad planned for forty divisions to be mobilized in Galicia on 22 August, in actuality, resulting from "railroad technical grounds," between 28 and 30 August, units would arrive at their designated areas, a full twelve divisions short.[42] Too many troops had been deployed south to perform the originally designated defensive mission, but not enough to overwhelm Serbian forces. Meanwhile, the severely weakened forces opposing Russia soon found themselves overwhelmed and forced to retreat, almost catastrophically, on 11 September 1914.

The rearward deployment behind the San-Dniester river line signified that the Russians would be much stronger when the opposing armies met, because it provided the enemy time to consolidate and deploy its forces.

The rearward deployment's newly-designed unloading stations had to be improvised, which, in part, didn't correspond to directives. Transport could no longer be prepared in detail, particularly the cohesive flow of empty cars. In effect, again according to Kéri, the deployment area had been designated by Conrad with the thought that the rearward deployment unloading would occur ten hours earlier than by the original planning.

In the meantime, the irregular stream of empty rail cars and refugee trains often clogged the train stations, preventing further movement of deployment transports. Another effect, the railroad technical evacuation of personnel and rolling material to the designated areas resulted in tiring foot marches for the troops.

It also is emphasized that the allied Chiefs of the Railroad Bureaus met only twice before the outbreak of the war, once at a German maneuver, and at the meeting at Karlsbad in early 1914. No agreements or planning could have been possible.

Perhaps most significantly in the manuscript, line by rail line, unit by unit, an alternative plan for a successful double "War Case R + B" deployment is presented. It involved utilizing the partially double-track lines such as on "War Case R" deployment line II, and by putting into service the numerous trains reserved for "unforeseen" purposes by the Railroad Bureau. This was possible because the planned number of trains on a particular line fell well below peacetime traffic.

It also is argued that "War Case R" line I, the most significant one, required no additional railway personnel, nor locomotives as Ratzenhofer claimed. Railroad lines not mentioned in Railroad Bureau planning are also listed as having not been utilized. War traffic commenced on 6 August, but much of it was designated as optional traffic. On 31 July, little rail traffic moved.

On 1 August, Ratzenhofer's calculations led to the proposal that the Balkan deployment continue to be completed on 10 August. In waiting for the A-Group to be transported to Galicia, the four B-Group Corps could be directed to the Serbian front, unloaded, reloaded, and moved to Galicia without losing any time from the original plan (again, a Pitreich argument).

At a meeting of Conrad and the leaders of the "War Case B" and "R" groups, it is stated that Straub presented his gloomy prediction that to halt the "B" deployment would lead to disaster, and he would not accept that responsibility.

In actuality, "War Cases R, I and B" were planned independently of each other. Besides having no planning for a combined "War Case R+B", the "War Case B" and "War Case I" were only conceptionalized in general, and for "War Case B" followed by "War Case R" rudimentary plans only extended through the fifth mobilization day.

Relative to the Bohemian Corps (VIII and IX), ordered with the B-Group to the Balkan front, Kéri's study emphasizes that German railroad lines, which could have been used for the transport of these two corps, were not fully utilized in southeastern Germany for her mobilization, and that, in fact, the German deployment had been completed by 14 August. These German rail lines could have been utilized to transfer the two Bohemian Corps to Cracow without disturbing either the Austro-Hungarian or German rail movement. Accordingly, by Kéri's calculations, the 26., 19., and 21. Divisions could have been transported on 19 August to the area of Jaroslau-Przemyśl, thereby increasing the left-flank offensive force with three of the missing five divisions.

One cannot mention the "Command Conspiracy" without emphasizing that only in Austria would serious military histories be authored exclusively by the former participating General Staff officers and Generals themselves. This phenomenon did not occur in Germany, Russia, France or Great Britain. It must also again be stressed that the actual mobilization events and the initial military campaigns of 1914 have been distorted by these Austrian "official" military historians from as early as the interwar period to as late as the 1980s and 1990s.

It must also be noted that the most reputable post-war diplomatic and military history sources have assumed the accuracy of such sources as Conrad's five-volume memoirs and the Austrian official military history. In particular, some of the most admired diplomatic works on the outbreak of World War I emphasize Conrad's memoirs.[43] Even one of the better military histories in English, Winston Churchill's *The Unknown War: The Eastern Front*, is based upon such "Command Conspiracy" sources.[44]

CHAPTER IX

The War: Failure of the Schlieffen Plan

In August, the mobilization of the Great Powers proceeded towards the inevitable military clashes. Meanwhile, attempts were made to improve the chances of victory as rapidly as possible by gaining allies.

If Austro-Hungarian-German calculations had been sound, the overall situation would have unfolded as Bulgaria would have immediately mobilized and launched a coordinated offensive with Conrad's Balkan forces into Serbia, thus releasing Austro-Hungarian troops for use in Galicia; Romania would have mobilized and attacked into Bessarabia in conjunction with Austro-Hungarian forces, thereby cementing the Habsburg right flank; and Italy would have followed suit by transporting troops to — and even joining the campaign in — Alsace-Lorraine, thus releasing German troops for deployment in East Prussia against Russia.[1] The aid of these three allies would have maximized the possibility of a German and Austro-Hungarian victory over France and Russia.

Unfortunately, however, only one Balkan country appeared ready to side with the Central Powers from the beginning. On 2 August, Turkey signed a treaty with Germany in which she agreed to attack Russia in the event of a war. Germany desired, but did not obtain, an immediate Turkish declaration of war on Russia; instead, Turkey mobilized and proclaimed armed neutrality on 3 August.[2]

As for Bulgaria, Vienna hoped that she would also enter the fray alongside the Central Powers, in return for which Austria-Hungary would accept Bulgaria's conditions for entrance into the Triple Alliance. But Russia also approached Sofia, offering her all of Macedonia to prevent her from siding with the Central Powers. Bulgaria, fearing Greece, Romania, and Turkey, did not move.[3]

The role of Italy was paramount in Berlin-Vienna military planning throughout August and September 1914. At stake for the Central Powers were: the exposed Austro-Hungarian rear flank; the Franco-German frontier, where Italy had agreed to send three corps and two reserve divisions;

and the German advance through Belgium, since Italian pressure in the Alps would keep French troops tied down there. General Conrad wrote the Chief of the Italian General Staff, General Pollio, reminding him of the agreement with the German General Staff, and asked him whether Italian troops could also be assembled to aid Austria-Hungary. Conrad also requested that the Italian commander send a military delegation to Vienna promptly. Furthermore, he pressured Berlin to influence Rome, reminding General Moltke that as many Austro-Hungarian troops as possible were needed in Galicia to cover Germany's rear flank.[4]

But to the Central Powers' chagrin, on 31 July and 3 August Italy declared her neutrality on the grounds that the Central Powers' action was aggressive, and contrary to the defense posture of the Triple Alliance.[5] The Italians also were sensitive to testy public opinion, among other internal pressures.

When Kaiser Wilhelm wrote King Victor Emmanuel on 31 July in an effort to influence him to join the Triple Alliance war effort, Victor Emmanuel replied on 3 August that, for the present, Italy would remain neutral because the *casus foederis* had not arisen. On 1 August, Franz Joseph also wrote his fellow sovereign in Rome, but the 2 August reply was similar to that to Kaiser Wilhelm. Kaiser Wilhelm then notified Franz Joseph on 3 August that Victor Emmanuel "is not with us." The allies agreed, however, that everything had to be tried to ensure that Italy remained neutral.[6]

To General Moltke, this development signified that not only would Italy not dispatch the promised troops to Alsace-Lorraine, but also that the five German reserve divisions promised to General Conrad for use in East Prussia would have to be deployed in the west. Moltke's "excuse" would irritate Austro-Hungarian-German military relations when Conrad learned of it on 21 August.[7]

The German General Staff pressured their Viennese counterparts to provide compensation to Italy to enlist her active support in the war, but Conrad replied that no one in Austria-Hungary would accept the cession of Austro-Hungarian territory to Italy. General Moltke had stated, "It is not important that Italy should carry out her full agreement to dispatch bodies of troops to Germany. If Italy sends only one cavalry division, it is enough."[8]

Negotiations over territorial compensation continued without results into 1915. For Conrad, Romania remained central in his strategic considerations *vis-á-vis* Russia. Thus:

It is for us of the most imminent importance to bring Romania actively to our side, that means that she mobilizes and mutually advances with us. Say to Romania: 1) Bulgaria will not attack her; 2) Austria-Hungary and Germany will not conclude peace until Romania gets Bessarabia; and 3) that she will receive the Njegotian area.[9]

On 1 August, a Romanian Crown council declared Bucharest's neutrality on the grounds that since Vienna had provoked the Serbian war, the *casus foederis* did not apply. Kaiser Wilhelm, meanwhile, wired King Carol, appealing to him as a fellow Hohenzollern, and Franz Joseph wired asking him to honor his country's treaty obligations and to accept Bessarabia as compensation.[10]

On 2 August, Berlin tried to persuade Bucharest that Russia had forced the war upon Germany and that therefore Germany had to mobilize on 1 August. Berlin now expected an immediate Romanian mobilization and deployment against Russia, and Bessarabia was again promised as compensation. However, Russia was pressuring Bucharest by offering her Transylvania and was also contacting Italy, promising Rome Valona and a free hand in Albania.[11] On 4 August, another Romanian Crown council reaffirmed the neutrality proclaimed on 1 August. On 8 August, Bucharest stepped up her position to that of armed neutrality, and King Carol asked the Austro-Hungarian military attaché to divulge the location in Galicia where the Austro-Hungarian right flank would advance. Conrad immediately replied to Bucharest that a Romanian General Staff officer should be dispatched to Vienna for orientation. On 9 August, the Romanian Chief of Staff asked the Austro-Hungarian military attaché whether his troops should deploy with their left flank at Botosani and the right at Jassy. The military attaché reported that Romania awaited an Austro-Hungarian victory before any final decision to actively participate in the war.[12]

King Carol's explanation for his government's declaration of neutrality included the factors that the Romanian army was not ready for a war; that hundreds of kilometers separated the Austro-Hungarian and Romanian armies, thus Romania could easily be invaded, while her Black Sea coast was undefended; and that a Russian invasion could result in a revolution in Romania. Ottokar Czernin, the Austro-Hungarian special envoy in Bucharest, was reassured that Romania would maintain her neutrality, and if possible, field two corps if Russia invaded her territory.[13]

The threat to the Austro-Hungarian right flank in Galicia can be understood because Romanian fighting forces were to have tied down the entire Russian Fifth Army. The Fifth and Kiev Armies — fifteen firstline, ten reserve and two cavalry divisions — could be hurled at the Monarchy's exposed eastern Galician frontier. The extremely poor Austro-Hungarian railway networks there assured the Russians of overwhelming numerical superiority. General Conrad, in that case, would have to attempt to guard this flank in the line Lemberg-Halicz-Stanislau until a military decision could be obtained by his offensive between the Bug and Vistula Rivers.[14]

Already on 3 August, intelligence reports indicated that the Russian VII and VIII Corps (what was believed to be the Fifth Army) had moved from the Romanian frontier to the north and northwest, which, if the report were true, would seriously worsen the Austro-Hungarian situation vis-á-vis Russia. General Conrad, on the same day, wired General Moltke to influence active Romanian cooperation with Austria-Hungary.[15]

Then, when the necessary decisive victory in the Balkans did not materialize by 21 August (following the Austro-Hungarian offensive of 12 August) the Habsburg diplomats came to the conclusion that under the circumstances the Balkan states would not commit themselves for the moment to the Central Powers. They therefore demanded an immediate decisive victory over Serbia to impress the smaller states.[16] But this demand created an insoluble dilemma for Conrad and the military. Russian forces quickly began to overpower the outnumbered and outgunned Austro-Hungarian forces in Galicia, so that the B-Group (Second Army), originally designated for deployment in Galicia in a "War Case R" but instead transported to the Serbian theater in early August, had to be recalled to the north. Thus, sufficient troops were not available for the desperately needed victory over Serbia. Leading Austro-Hungarian governmental officials pressured for a military decision against Serbia, while Conrad reversed his earlier position and insisted that the main enemy, Russia, had to be defeated first. It was thought that after Russia had been halted, a campaign against Serbia would be a mere sideshow. Almost immediately (20-21 August), however, the Austro-Hungarian armies had to retreat behind the Save and Drina Rivers. The retreat occurred as the Austro-Hungarian VII Corps was being transferred to Galicia, the IX Corps being prepared for transfer, and the IV Corps being held back in the Balkans.

It became obvious that the Balkan countries did not want to hurry into the Balkan conflict. Bulgaria, Turkey, Romania, and Italy awaited a first success on the battlefield before committing themselves. But Vienna's dilemma was that she had to achieve a rapid victory in the Balkan theater in order to release troops for the north. Conrad maintained steady pressure to gain active military support from Bulgaria, Romania, and Turkey,[17] but they continued to wait until that decisive military victory, which never came.

Before the Austro-Hungarian mobilization and Russian campaign are analyzed, the situation on the German eastern front must be examined. On 1 August, Germany had proclaimed general mobilization and then declared war on Russia. For a brief period confusion reigned as Kaiser Wilhelm, under the influence of inaccurate information regarding Great Britain's position, pressured General Moltke abruptly to reverse the Schlieffen strategy and wheel the massed German armies against Russia, not France. Besides badly shaking General Moltke, this strategy led Admiral Alfred von Tirpitz to conclude that German political leadership had lost control of the situation and caused Moltke to state that he must take the political leadership in hand.[18]

The main strategic principles for Berlin in the first period of war involved gaining time until an overwhelming victory of annihilation could be obtained in the west, freeing troops for operations in the east. If no Russian offensive ensued, the anticipated result was to be an advance in support of the planned Habsburg attack; and, at the minimum, the Vistula River line had to be held as a base for future operations. Accordingly, a National Guard Corps would advance from Silesia and Posen to link up with and support the Austro-Hungarian left flank advance, thus preventing Russian northern armies from intervening in the Habsburg offensive. German troops, it was hoped, also would stall a Russian offensive against East Prussia. If the Russians did not advance against East Prussia, the German Eighth Army would launch an offensive to tie down as many enemy forces as possible to prevent them from countering the Austro-Hungarian advance.

German maneuvers would result in charges and countercharges, because General Conrad understood, or claimed to understand, that General Moltke had promised to launch an offensive by his German East Army towards Siedlce in Poland.

In the pre-war agreements, the Austro-Hungarian General Staff had assumed the responsibility of tying down the Russian armies, while Germany crushed France according to the Schlieffen plan. General Moltke, at his last meeting with General Conrad at Karlsbad on 12 May, had promised to field twelve to fourteen divisions in East Prussia. Due to Italy's defection and failure to send troops to Alsace-Lorraine, Moltke would not deploy the promised five reserve divisions in the east. In Moltke's defense, an all-out battle against France would not allow for reinforcements in East Prussia.

The German strategy to counter the first Russian forces to enter East Prussia led to further allied misunderstandings. Geography favored German chances of countering Russian armies piecemeal, because the Masurian Lakes would force a division of forces directed towards Prussia. If the Russian Niemen (northern) Army advanced initially, the advance would threaten German rearward connections to Königsberg, the key German bastion in the east. The Warsaw or Narev (southern) Army advancing westward would threaten Austria-Hungary's left-flank offensive, so it was not to Vienna's advantage that the northern Russian army be the first to draw the German Eighth Army against it.

The battles in the north became the basis for Austro-Hungarian recriminations about being "left in the lurch" by the Germans. The allied "pre-war agreement" called for a German military thrust across the Narev River to prevent as many Russian forces as possible from intervening in General Conrad's offensive between the Bug and Vistula rivers. Although this German offensive would be launched with only the forces of the German Eighth Army, General Moltke had promised that seven weeks after operations against France commenced, the battle of annihilation there would have been concluded, and that the transfer of the victorious German armies would then commence.[19] Conrad, realizing that his forces alone could not successfully invade Russia, had accepted that he would have to hold the Russian armies until Germany had defeated France. Conrad had also accepted that the Germans would deploy only twelve to fourteen divisions in East Prussia and a militia corps in the Silesia-Posen area.[20] Conrad based his war planning on these facts. Impelling St. Petersburg to launch an offensive into East Prussia in August and September 1914, France pressured for the small German contingent in the east to be at least tied down, if not defeated. This plan would draw German troops from the western front. The overall Russian strategy was to encircle both flanks of the German Eighth Army and crush it. In the meantime, the Russians hoped to win a victory over the Austro-Hungarian armies, so that combined Russian forces could overwhelm Germany. For this purpose, two additional armies had been created in August. French money had helped to enable such Russian military capabilities,[21] which naturally gave Paris grounds to pressure St. Petersburg for an early offensive.

The first Russian troops actually crossed the eastern Prussian frontier on 17 August to begin the planned encirclement of German forces. The first Russian Army (Niemen) advanced north of the Masurian Lakes on a forty-mile front, drawing German troops eastward towards it. The mission of this Russian army was to deflect the German left flank and isolate the fortress of Königsberg. The Russian Second Army (Narev) advanced northwestward, crossing the southern frontier of East Prussia to strike the right flank and rear of the German Eighth Army on a thirty-mile front.

The battles at Tannenberg between 26 and 30 August and at the Masurian Lakes, 3-14 September, have become two of the most famous encounters of the World War.[22] The events surrounding those battles need not be surveyed in detail, whereas the events at the Austro-Hungarian front, which are far less well-known or understood today, shall be analyzed.

Austro-Hungarian plans prepared in the winter of 1913-1914 for war in 1914-1915 were based upon the assumption of a "War Case R" without any preceding mobilization against Serbia. These plans ignored the most likely occurrence. In a "War Case B," the plan had been to send a large number of troops against Serbia without disturbing the overall deployment planning, in case the Austro-Hungarian A-Group had to be sent from the Carpathian Mountains against Russia while the B-Group Second Army was in transit to the Balkans.[23] The failure to correct the faulty assumption through the summer of 1914 resulted in disaster.

The eastern frontier of the Central Powers extended nine hundred kilometers from the Baltic Sea at Memel to the northern Romanian frontier, or over four times the length of the frontier with France extending from Luxembourg to Switzerland (220 kilometers). The Russians guarded the middle Vistula River area with their fortresses at Ivangorod, Warsaw, and Novogeorgiesk. The Russians could outflank any German deployment in East Prussia or Austro-Hungarian deployment in Galicia. But Russia first had to assemble her forces. Until then, due to their more rapid operations readiness, the Central Powers could smash the assembling enemy armies in the center of Poland by advancing from East Prussia and Galicia. This concept, as already seen, was the basis for Conrad's strategic planning.

On the basis of this plan, the Austro-Hungarian General Staff would launch an offensive at the beginning of a war. The decision is understandable, contrary to the arguments of many critics, because a defensive posture on the part of the Austro-Hungarians (as well as the Germans) in the immense eastern flatland areas would be impossible with the enormous Russian numerical superiority. Defensively deployed armies could be outflanked, giving the Russians complete freedom of action to assemble their massive armies undisturbed. Also, if the Russians had a free hand in Prussia, their presence could seriously affect the outcome of the western campaign in France by forcing German troops to the eastern front.

Thus, the main principle of Austro-Hungarian strategic war planning against Russia was the operational readiness of the left flank (First and Fourth Armies) on the seventeenth mobilization day in preparation for either an offensive northward between the Bug and Vistula Rivers towards the enemy bastion at Lublin, or to the northeast toward Vladimir-Volynski.[24]

Conrad's central idea was to launch an offensive northward to clear his left flank position and to crush the Russian armies as they assembled in central Poland. These goals would be accomplished with the aid of the "promised" German offensive over the lower Narev River in the direction of Siedlce, or so Conrad would say after the war. Both advances would create "air space" for future maneuvering. After smashing the separately assembling enemy forces, Conrad would wheel his two attacking armies eastward in the direction of Kiev. While this main Austro-Hungarian offensive unfolded, the eastern armies would ward off any threats on the right flank in East Galicia. The Second Army had the task of countering enemy advances over the Zbrucz River, while the Third Army would counter any thrusts from the fortress triangle area of Rovno-Dubno-Luck.[25] If the Russians launched their main offensive from the east, Conrad would swing his left flank immediately eastward.

The Austro-Hungarian deployment, as restudied in the winter of 1913-1914 for use in 1914-1915, called for the assembly of the First Army with its vanguard in the line San River mouth — Sieniava-Lubazov-Niemirov; the Fourth Army at Lemberg with an infantry vanguard forward in the line Kunin-Zolkiev-Kamionka-Strumilova-Busk; and the Third Army south of the railway line Lemberg-Brody on the line Zloczóv-Borov-Kozova to advance towards Tarnopol, where a threat to its right flank existed. The available portion of the Second Army would be along the Strypa River between Visnivczyk and Buczacz, with a flank group at Zaleszczyki-Sniatyn to prepare to launch an offensive over the Sereth River. Cavalry divisions and alarm troops would be deployed about a day's march from the frontier.[26] The most serious danger was a Russian encirclement of the Second and Third Armies in East Galicia.

The launching of an offensive northward between the Bug and Vistula Rivers was to counter the Russian armies expected to assemble in the region of Lublin and Cholm. If these enemy forces were allowed to assemble undisturbed, they might attack and cut off Austro-Hungarian forces from their connections and supply lines to central Austria-Hungary. Also, if the Austro-Hungarian armies could be thrust aside by a Russian flank attack from the north, the maneuver could force open the Carpathian mountain passes for an invasion of Hungary. The Russians had, after all, a vast numerical superiority.

A large number of Russian troops in the regions north of western Galicia could disturb an Austro-Hungarian assembly close to the frontiers of eastern Galicia or even in the area of the bastion of Lemberg. Thus, in Spring 1914, the decision was made to assemble the Austro-Hungarian armies behind the San-Dniester line, the earlier mentioned strategic rearward deployment.[27]

Thus, the Austro-Hungarian plan in August 1914 consisted of a strategic re-deployment (*Rückverlegung*), or shifting of the left flank approximately forty kilometers to the west, and a contraction of the First and Fourth Army front from one hundred and seventy kilometers to one hundred. The Second and Third Austro-Hungarian Armies were drawn back to a distance of a three- to four-day march. This change was executed to deploy safely all immediately available forces for an offensive against Russia while "War Case B" was being executed against Serbia.[28]

This decision to change the Habsburg deployment resulted from several interlocking circumstances, but not, as claimed by the "official version," by the defection of Romania, which exposed the Austro-Hungarian right flank. In August 1914, several other factors helped to explain why Conrad ordered the strategic re-deployment behind the San-Dniester River line. These factors included the necessity of obtaining greater security by shortening the A-Group front; avoiding the threat from the much greater capacity of Russian military railroad lines, which could jeopardize Austria-Hungary's reputed advantage of a more rapid operations readiness (Russia 260 trains daily, Austria-Hungary 153) while creating the danger of large enemy cavalry groups disturbing the Austro-Hungarian deployment and railroad networks.[29] Additionally, the likely threat of Russia launching an attack only after Habsburg forces advanced against Serbia would require the rapid transfer of the Austro-Hungarian Second Army

B-Group from the Serbian theater to Galicia.[30] The underestimation of Russian fighting forces was finally rectified by 1914. The Redl espionage case also brought responses. The deployment plan changed, but its basics remained,[31] although now a long march would be necessary to reach the planned attack positions.

In the original planning for a "War Case B" for 1914-1915, twenty infantry and three cavalry divisions, plus replacement and reserve formations — or more than one-third of the Monarchy's military resources — would be fielded in the Balkans. If Russia entered such a conflict, troop levels in the Balkans would be reduced to eight infantry divisions, while forty and one-half infantry and eleven cavalry divisions would be deployed against Russia.[32] The original plans were not carried out in 1914. Instead, a total of twenty-six and one-half infantry divisions were originally designated to be deployed to the Balkans.

Despite the planning for a strategic re-deployment in Galicia, Conrad, until the end, did not want to believe that Russia would intervene should war break out between Austria-Hungary and Serbia. He held to this belief even though indications to the contrary abounded in St. Petersburg and even when he learned of the German ultimatum to St. Petersburg on 1 August. It is very possible that Conrad's desire to crush Serbia led him to hope that Russia would repeat the stance she took in the Bosnian Crisis and the Balkan Wars. Conrad's optimism led him to order an extra six and one-half divisions to the Balkan front and to confirm and reconfirm these orders even after the German ultimatum to St. Petersburg.[33]

The dispatch of an enlarged Second Army to the Balkan front was one of the most tragic decisions the Austro-Hungarians made during the early stages of the First World War. The Second Army would detrain in the south in early August and deploy north of Serbia. After some two weeks, portions of the Army would be re-embarked and dispatched piecemeal to the Galician front. These troops left the Serbian theater too early to gain the decision there, but they arrived at the exposed right flank in Galicia too late to prevent a ruinous defeat for the main Austro-Hungarian forces at the two battles of Lemberg.

On 1 August, Conrad learned from General Moltke of Germany's demand that Russia immediately rescind her military measures lest Germany declare war immediately. Russia's decision was due on 1 August.

On the same day, Moltke dispatched a telegram to Conrad stating that Kaiser Wilhelm had ordered full mobilization against Russia with 2 August as the first official mobilization day for both his army and his navy.

Then he sent a second telegram stating that the deployment would follow smoothly and, as agreed upon, against both France and Russia. His statement answered a Conrad telegram (10:00 p.m.) inquiring whether the German mobilization was directed against Russia only or also against France. The German declaration of war was delivered by the German Ambassador in St. Petersburg at 7:00 p.m. after an emotional scene in which, according to the ambassador's account, he pleaded with Sazonov to stop Russian mobilization.[34] Not receiving a positive reply, he handed to the Russian minister the note containing his government's declaration of war.

Conrad then wrote the following letter to General Moltke. Dated 1 August, it was forwarded on 2 August:

We hoped to wage this as a localized war without further complications. . . . It is natural that we should assemble for this [localized] war sufficient forces to hold out a prospect of success by weight of numbers. When Russia, by mobilizing her southern military districts, showed herself hostile to the Monarchy, we turned to Germany with the request that she would declare that this step taken against us would also be unacceptable to Germany. At the same time, mobilization of the remainder of the army was ordered, for their assembly in Galicia was envisaged. . .

It was hoped that these measures, in conjunction with the energetic diplomatic pressure of the other Powers, more especially Germany, would restrain Russia from hostile action against the Monarchy, and would also afford to the latter the possibility of carrying through her action against Serbia.

Such being the case, we could, and must, hold fast to the idea of the offensive against Serbia, the more so since we had to bear in mind that Russia might merely intend to restrain us from action against Serbia by a threat, without proceeding to war against us ....

It was not until July 31 that there came suddenly the declaration of Germany that she was now willing to carry through the Great War against France and Russia. This produced an entirely new situation. It was immediately reckoned here that we must assemble the preponderant mass of our forces in the North, and I beg Your Excellency to accept the assurance that, in spite of the great complications caused by our transport of troops to the South which has already been completed, this will be carried through.[35]

Conrad's letter thus indicates that to the last moment of the crisis he experienced cognitive dissonance, a blind faith in an outcome which was contrary to all evidence. He believed that Serbia could be crushed before Russia intervened.

The General Staff estimated that even with the necessity of re-deployment from the Serbian frontier, the Second Army would arrive at their originally designated Galician assembly areas at the same time as they would have had they followed the original plans for a "War Case R." The calculations that followed this conclusion led to the decision to continue the movement of the Second Army to the Balkans. In fact, the General Staff and the Railroad Bureau argued on technical grounds whether the Second Army could be re-routed before they had actually arrived in the south. To effect a reversal while the troops were in transit, according to the commander of the Railroad Bureau, would lead to "chaos." The result was that this army, which was sorely needed to counter the massing Russian forces, did not receive the order to return to the north until 6 August, while it was traveling south, and while the Balkan Commander had already begun his offensive deployment.

A further reason for continuing the movement of the Second Army south was the influence the Army might have on other Balkan states. If Serbia could be brought down, perhaps Bulgaria, Turkey, and even Romania would align with the Central Powers. The new alliances, in turn, would enable the Habsburg General Staff to release troops for the crucial struggle against Russia.

Because German pressure had necessitated the above message from Conrad to Moltke, Conrad stated with seeming irony, "the main forces in Galicia serve above all to cover Germany's rear-flank." While this letter was in transit to Moltke, a 2 August reply to Conrad's letter stated:

The one goal, the overthrow of Austria-Hungary's mortal enemy Russia, will be kept in view in all measures taken. The hour demands that all available forces shall be used for this objective. Serbia can be held in check with limited forces.[36]

Germany now began increasingly to pressure Vienna to declare war on Russia.

At 5:45 a.m. (2 August) Franz Joseph's telegram in response to Kaiser Wilhelm arrived. In summary, it said:

> As soon as my General Staff learned that you had determined to immediately commence war against Russia and carry it out with all power, the decision was here arrived at to assemble our main forces against Russia. You may rest assured that the utmost will be done to bring the great struggle to a successful conclusion by my army.[37]

Franz Joseph further stated that he desired that German pressure be placed on Italy, and that Austria-Hungary would accept the Italian interpretation of Article VII if she fulfilled her treaty obligations.

General Moltke, in a 2 August reply to Conrad's letter of 1 August, concerning particularly the "delay" in a German declaration of war against Russia, stated:

> I fully appreciate Your Excellency's difficulties in these last days. But in spite of all endeavors, I was not able to speed up the tasks of the diplomatists and give Your Excellency enlightenment earlier about our mobilization. Now things have gotten underway. We march against France and Russia and operations begin at once. I know that Your Excellency's purposeful energy will at this moment once again meet with success in overcoming all difficulties. The one goal, the defeat of Austria-Hungary's mortal enemy, Russia, will be kept in view in all measures taken. The hour demands that all available forces shall be used for this objective. Serbia can be kept in check with limited forces.[38]

Berlin persistently demanded that Austria-Hungary share her estimation of Russia. Vienna should consider Serbia a secondary campaign theater and field her preponderant forces against Russia, drawing away major Russian forces to protect the weak German Eighth Army.

In particular, Moltke promised:

> Should the Russians undertake a premature offensive against East Prussia with forces greatly superior to the [German] Army of the East, an Austro-Hungarian victory will thereby be facilitated, and the more so, the earlier the A-H. army enters upon its advance towards Russia. Should no such . . . offensive against Germany north of the Vistula take place, the Army of the East will advance in the direction which brings greatest relief to the A-H Army. In

addition a German National Guard corps . . . would invade Russia on the twelfth day of mobilization . . . . The Austro-Hungarian Army can consequently count with certainty upon a tactical support of its offensive against Russia by the whole of the German forces assembling in the east. The earlier and more continuous the advance towards Russia, the greater will be the combined success.[39]

On the same day, Conrad informed Moltke that by the end of August he would have deployed a combined force in Galicia of thirty-eight and one-half infantry divisions, two replacement and eight reserve brigades, and ten cavalry divisions. The figure would total thirty and one-half infantry divisions in early August.[40]

But General Conrad and Count Berchtold delayed the presentation of the Austro-Hungarian declaration of war against Russia. Conrad, although proclaiming that Austria-Hungary would go through "thick and thin" with Germany, also explained that as of 2 August, no military grounds existed for declaring war on Russia. Bethmann Hollweg wired his ambassador in Vienna that Austria-Hungary was expected to fulfill her alliance duty by immediately intervening against Russia. Berchtold seconded Conrad's desire that the Austro-Hungarian mobilization and deployment be allowed to commence without creating a situation (war) in which Russia could disturb them.[41] Intelligence reports which noted the assembly of significant enemy units at the Galician frontier, seemed to add strength to this argument. St. Petersburg was not deceived; Vienna's failure officially to declare war was attributed to her desire to complete her military preparations.

On 3 August, Conrad sent a very interesting letter, written 2 August, to his German counterpart. He began the letter by assuring Moltke that the sole reason for the delay in the declaration of war was to complete the Austro-Hungarian mobilization without enemy interference. Such intervention during a Balkan deployment would seriously delay deployment in Galicia.[42] A very serious admission by Conrad! The Second Army, assigned to Galicia in a "War Case R" with the all-important task of protecting the extreme right flank of the Austro-Hungarian deployment, had been ordered to the Serbian theater, primarily because Conrad believed that Russia would not intervene in a war against Serbia, and because he felt that he would have ample time to chastise Serbia before the lumbering Russian masses could be assembled.

Conrad went on to reassure Moltke that the Austro-Hungarian main battle would be conducted in Galicia. He hinted that the mistake in sending extra troops to the Serbian frontier presented the "advantage" that these troops could be utilized to "threaten" Serbia, while they were still capable of reassembling in Galicia with no delay of any consequence. Conrad's inability to fulfill this last prediction led ultimately to chaos, defeat, and the destruction of Austro-Hungarian war plans.

Conrad telegraphed Moltke on 3 August, requesting that German eastern forces advance quickly towards the objective of Siedlce.[43]

On 5 August, before Vienna declared war, Moltke telegraphed Conrad:

Assemble your entire forces against Russia. Even Italy cannot be so unfaithful as to fall upon your rear. Unleash Bulgaria against Serbia and let them tear each other to pieces. There must be only one objective — Russia. Thrust the whip-carriers into the Pripet marshes to drown.[44]

On 6 August, Austria-Hungary officially declared war on Russia. One day later, troops began to move in numbers by rail to Galicia. Also on 6 August, an army order called for the retransport of the B-Group Second Army to the northern theater about 18 August, because of the impending hostilities against Russia.[45]

On 9 August, Germany announced that she would not be able to launch an offensive towards Siedlce. The Russian First Army maneuvers made the promised German offensive across the Narev River impossible, but once this enemy force had been successfully dealt with, the advance over the Narev River would become feasible. On the same day, Moltke pressured Conrad to support the granting of territorial concessions to Italy and Romania to gain their active participation in the war. Conrad refused on 13 August.[46]

On 11 August, the Austro-Hungarian Army High Command released the goals for their cavalry reconnaissance missions for 15 August. In particular, the enemy flank positions between the Bug and Vistula Rivers and at the eastern Galicia frontier were to be ascertained, because this information would be crucial for setting the direction of the northern offensive. Because of faulty preparation and the successful resistance of the numerically superior Russian cavalry supported by infantry units, the Austro-Hungarians could not pinpoint the main Russian assembly areas or extreme flank positions. At the same time, the Russian cavalry invasion they expected to counter never materialized.[47] These failures will be documented as the deployment and battles in Galicia are described.

On 12 August, meanwhile, the First Army received the command to be prepared to advance either in a northerly or northeasterly direction, and the Fourth Army was given information regarding its designated reconnaissance areas.[48]

On 13 August, Conrad informed Moltke that a strong enemy army, one which should have been neutralized by a Romanian offensive, presumably would be fielded east of the Zbrucz River in Podolia. Another army assembled around Dubno, an even stronger one massed between the Bug and Vistula Rivers, and an additional strong group gathered at Brest-Litovsk. Conrad then indicated that if he launched his major offensive east of the Vistula River, it would be crucial that the Germans advance towards Siedlce with the strongest possible forces. He believed that the launching of a coordinated attack between the Bug and Vistula Rivers could guarantee success for their cooperative action against Russia. Conrad stated again that the purpose of his offensive was to cover Germany's rear flank.[49]

On 14 August, General Conrad telegraphed basically the same message to General Maximillian Prittwitz (commander of the German Eighth Army), reporting that the Austro-Hungarian left-flank offensive would be launched on 22 August in the direction of Lublin and Cholm. He emphasized that the total situation called for a German offensive in the direction of Siedlce. Conrad's military representative in East Prussia, however, telegraphed that for the moment a German offensive in the direction of Siedlce should not be anticipated because the northern invading Russian forces had to be countered; only then could operations be initiated towards Siedlce. Even though it was not advancing into the designated area (Narev River), the German Eighth Army would draw numerous enemy forces towards it, which would facilitate the upcoming Austro-Hungarian offensive as promised.[50]

On 15 August, Conrad again pressed to launch an offensive towards Siedlce, citing suspected Russian troop dispositions. In particular, he emphasized the threat of Russian troops being able to outflank the deploying Austro-Hungarian forces in Galicia from the direction of Lemberg and Stanislau. Conrad explained that the success of his attacking northern armies would create breathing space in the north so that he could then strike the Russian flank in eastern Galicia. If, however, he had to parry the threat from eastern Galicia, the German attack towards Siedlce would relieve the threat to his left flank forces. He wrote ". . . only by cooperation can success against Russia be achieved."

In addition, he relayed that the defense of East Prussia could be handled by reserve and national guard units linked to the fortress system while a main advance aimed for Siedlce. However, he had learned that Prittwitz was now striking against the invader, necessarily delaying the operations against Siedlce.[51]

Conrad suggested that at least two or three divisions advance a hundred miles into hostile territory crowded with Russian troops of unknown strength, but the Germans, expecting to be attacked from two directions by nearly two and a half times their numbers, had neither the inclination nor the means for such adventures.

On 17 August, after receiving numerous reports of strong Russian forces assembling in the areas of Warsaw, Siedlce, Lukov, and Ivangorod, Conrad renewed pressure on both Moltke and Prittwitz. He again insisted upon an immediate German offensive towards Siedlce to coincide with the Habsburg offensive designed to parry an eventual thrust at Berlin.[52]

But reports from Germany's Eastern Headquarters stated that "events here are moving towards a rapid decision" with strong Russian forces advancing.[53] This declaration meant, of course, that the "promised" German stroke towards Siedlce, much to Conrad's chagrin, could not be executed.

General Prittwitz replied to Conrad's 15 August letter stating that he sought to cooperate as soon as possible with his Austro-Hungarian allies, but that the advance of major Russian forces against East Prussia temporarily prevented this. He further argued that with only four and one-half corps at his disposal, the enemy threat made an attack across the Narev River an impossibility. In addition, he lacked the originally designated five reserve divisions. As soon as conditions warranted it, however, he planned to launch an offensive.

On 19 August, Conrad received word that five and one-half Russian corps had crossed the East Prussian frontier on a front extending from Stallupönen-Goldapp-Lyck, while at the same time, a group of one and one-half corps advanced northwest of Lomscha-Ostrolenka. Then, on 20 August, he was notified that the Germans were not attacking along the line Gumbinnen-Lötzen and south against the Russian invading forces. The German forces' failure in this regard led to the first serious Russo-German military encounter of the war, the battle of Gumbinnen.[54]

In the meantime, as early as 5 August, the first intelligence reports of enemy dispositions on the Habsburg right flank misled the Austro-Hungarian General Staff. According to these sources, significant enemy forces apparently had been transferred northward from east of the Zbrucz River. The Austro-Hungarians therefore assumed that the Russians awaited events in the east from a defensive posture. Information on the following day, 6 August, indicated that there were only weak Russian forces, particularly cavalry, between the Dniester and Pruth Rivers, and that Russian troops had been withdrawn from the Romanian frontier, although further unit transports were also reported. The reports on 8 August confirmed the notion that enemy units apparently had been removed from the area east of the Zbrucz River and between the Dniester and Pruth Rivers, but reports concerning the Russian VII and VIII Corps were confused. The first suggestion of a strong Russian deployment against Lemberg came only on 11 August, at the same time reports indicated an evacuation of the area from Proskurov south to Kamieniec-Podolsk. To the General Staff, the assembly of the enemy's main forces remained an enigma. On 12 August, indications of definite enemy activities appeared in the entire frontier area east of the Zbrucz River. By 14 August, strong enemy forces were reported in the Proskurov area, as well as along the line Zmerinka-Proskurov-Rovno-Dubno-Voloczyska.[55]

But on 17 August, Austro-Hungarian air reconnaissance reported no valuable information on the Galician eastern flank, while the cavalry had been repulsed by enemy units of superior strength. On 18 August, the enemy's main force was pinpointed in the area of Brest, Ivangorod, and Cholm, with only one army facing eastern Galicia and the Bukovina.[56] There were no definite indications of strong enemy forces at the eastern Galician frontier.

Meanwhile, the Austro-Hungarian deployment continued; on 19 August, the Third Austro-Hungarian Army received orders to advance from their rearward deployment positions to assemble forward of the bastion of Lemberg, as indications multiplied that strong enemy formations were assembling to the north in the Vladimir-Volynski area. Such enemy units could create havoc with the exposed Austro-Hungarian right flank, but, as late as 20 August, Conrad did not anticipate a strong enemy offensive into eastern Galicia against Lemberg. Aerial reconnaissance at the eastern frontier failed to spot Russian troop locations because of bad weather and primitive airplanes,[57] yet reports mounted that Russian forces were moving into the Ravaruska region.

Definite indications of Russian strength approaching eastern Galicia increased. The new reports contradicted earlier intelligence reports and ran counter to Conrad's notions. Strong enemy cavalry forces advanced into the area of Ravaruska, and their move forward continued on 17-18 August, while the Third Army Commander reported a "strong" enemy force advancing from the north towards Brody and strong Russian forces being located at Vladimir-Volynski.[58]

Conflicting intelligence reports still confused the situation at the Monarchy's right flank on 21 August. The overall impression remained — as Conrad had hoped it would — that the enemy did not intend any major undertakings south of the rail line Proskurov-Smerinka. Although air reconnaissance could locate no strong enemy forces between the Dniester River and main routes to Proskurov-Tarnopol, Army Group Kövess (the part of the Second Army deployed in eastern Galicia), protecting the right-flank positions originally designated for the entire Austro-Hungarian Second Army to cover in a "War Case R," parried numerous enemy thrusts. The most pressing question, however, remained unresolved — how large would the enemy deployment be on the eastern flank, between the Vieprz River and Vladimir-Volynski?[59] Two Russian armies were marching by night and camouflaging themselves in the wooded terrain during the day.

At the same time, 21 August, Conrad received a disappointing dispatch from German Headquarters. His attaché reported that only a few German tactical forces had been deployed in East Prussia, and that the German command did not intend to launch an offensive over the Narev River because of the fear of invading Russian cavalry masses. For Germany, all was staked on the great invasion of France. The Germans never intended more than the defense of East Prussia.

Also on 21 August, Conrad learned definitively that the five promised German reserve divisions from the east had been withdrawn. Moltke explained that they had been re-allocated to the French theater largely because Italy's stance forced such a move. On the same day, unknown to Conrad, Moltke decided to send two army corps (originally announced as seven) to the east.[60]

The transfer resulted from the increasingly unfavorable military situation in East Prussia. After some initial successes, the news arrived that three to four Russian corps had begun advancing along the line Novogeorgiesk-Pultusk from the Warsaw region and across the Narev River. Some Russian troops had already crossed the frontier. This advance created a serious threat to the German flank; indeed, to the entire German operation against the Russian invaders. Since these Russian forces could not be defeated, the Eighth Army began a rapid retreat so that it might encircle the attacking enemy force in the south. This maneuver suited Conrad's concept of a thrust towards the Narev River to better the chances for the Austro-Hungarian northern offensive.

Conrad's own summary of the events of 21 August reveal how bad the situation had become for the Central Powers before the commencement of the Austro-Hungarian offensive: the Austro-Hungarian offensive against Serbia of 12 August had failed; the German Eighth Army was in "retreat"; there would be no German offensive in the direction of Siedlce as "agreed" upon; Romania had proclaimed her neutrality, exposing the Austro-Hungarian right flank; Bulgaria and Turkey remained aloof, so too many Austro-Hungarian troops had to be retained in the Balkans although they were sorely needed for the struggle against Russia; Italy might turn against Austria-Hungary; and the Balkan Command had been removed from Conrad's jurisdiction.[61] General Potiorek, upon the Kaiser's request, now commanded the forces versus Serbia.

Disregarding these factors, Conrad stuck tenaciously to his idea of an offensive in western Galicia. On 21 August, the order was issued for a general offensive of the First, Fourth, and Third Armies, and portions of the Second Army. Large parts of the Third and Second Armies, however, were still in transit to their deployment areas, and the Third Army in particular was delayed two days because fleeing civilians were clogging the roads.[62] The offensive was, therefore, in trouble even before it began. Partly because the main portion of the Second Army B-Group had not been retransported from the Balkan theater, the Second and Third Armies were detrained further forward than earlier planned.

The offensive would hurl the First Army towards the Russian fortress of Lublin, and the Fourth Army in a north or northeasterly direction to ward off any enemy thrusts from the direction of Zamosc, or the Bug River stretch Grubieszov-Krylov. In the process, if the right flank of the First Army were attacked, the Fourth Army's left flank would launch an offensive towards Krasnostav. The major northern thrust, however, could not be attempted before the Third Army defending the east flank had assembled. While this right-flank army assembled, it had the mission of delaying or halting enemy assaults from the direction of Sokol-Radziechóv and Brody. Second Army contingents (Group Kövess) must halt or delay any enemy thrust from the area south of Tarnopol (the southernmost eastern flank) towards Lemberg.[63] An enemy advance from this direction was the prospect most dangerous to the overall Habsburg strategy. The Austro-Hungarian High Command still continued to believe, or, worse, hope, that no large Russian troop concentrations existed on the eastern Galician flank.

The failure of intelligence and reconnaissance to detect massive Russian forces in eastern Galicia was bad enough, but the forces designated to hold this area, the entire Second Army, had not even arrived in any degree of strength. Group Kövess (XII Corps), a small contingent of the Second Army, was completely inadequate for defending eastern Galicia.

After the Second Army had disembarked at the Serbian frontier in early August it became tragically involved in the war on that front. The commander of the Balkan forces, General Potiorek, demanded that the troops participate in his Serbian offensive, but Conrad countered that these forces must travel to Galicia, and that under no circumstances must they cross the Save-Danube River line into Serbia.[64] Potiorek and others pressured Conrad, which led him "with heavy heart" to allow the Second Army to participate in the Serbian theater to the extent of "demonstrating" at the Save-Danube River line to aid the Austro-Hungarian Fifth and Sixth Armies, which were to invade Serbia from Bosnia on 12 August. Conrad affirmed, however, that the Second Army was to retrain and proceed to Galicia (along the line Dniester River-Mikolajov-Halicz), where it was most needed to protect the offensive into Poland.[65]

The minimal mission of the Balkan forces was to protect Bosnia, particularly Sarajevo. Thus Potiorek's task was a defensive one. He had the choice of launching an offensive because an initial success gained would be highly significant. He also knew that he should count only on a Second Army participation in a demonstration until 18 August when the Army would be retransported to Galicia.

On 12 August, the offensive began against Serbia. The Second Army would secure the left flank from 12 to 18 August; and on 12 August it began its "demonstration," but, perhaps inevitably, its units were drawn into the fighting.

The offensive ran into severe difficulties from its onset. Bridge crossing materials, grossly insufficient for the river crossing, precluded a broad area crossing. This shortage restricted what was a difficult maneuver in any case.

The psychological effect of fighting an enemy concealed by the terrain produced a demoralizing effect upon the troops. Where there were no railroad lines, nor "modern" roadways, formidable supply difficulties appeared immediately, and shifting troops was a problem. The movement of ammunition also proved extremely difficult. Even the artillery could not keep pace with the advancing infantry. This time lag, another manifestation of the difficult terrain, resulted in infantry attacks with no, or insufficient, artillery preparation.

This first Balkan campaign in August resulted in severe losses (600 officers and 230,000 men). Some of the casualties resulted from inadequate peacetime training, organization and leadership. The troops, particularly those from Bohemia, had not been prepared for the rough Serbian terrain.

Potiorek's offensive disregarded the age-old invasion route through Belgrade. Instead, two armies would advance, a week apart, over one hundred kilometers from each other. The Second Army, ordered to the north, had orders not to cross the Save and Danube Rivers. The Fifth Army attacked before being operationally prepared, against the advice of its commander.

The Serbian Commander quickly perceived the Austro-Hungarian war plan and launched a counterattack to foil it. Thus as the Austro-Hungarian Fifth Army pressed slowly towards its main objective, General Radomir Putnik, the Serbian Commander, ordered a counter thrust at Sabac which placed the Fifth Army in an extremely difficult situation. Against this background the Second Army became involved in the battle at Sabac.

Meanwhile, the travail faced by the Fifth Army at Jadar between 16 and 19 August forced its retreat. By 24 August, the Second Army positions at Sabac also had to be abandoned. The Sixth Army had advanced on 19 August much too far south. The Army, despite successes, ended by joining the general retreat on 24 August.

While Potiorek has received much criticism for his initial war plan, his disregard for his men's welfare, and preparation for the offensive, it must be stated that Conrad did not sufficiently orient him during the July crisis, and did not inform him in a timely fashion that the B-Group would be retransported to the northern theater (until 6 August).

In addition, in 1906, when Conrad became Chief of the General Staff, Potiorek had been the leading candidate for this position because he had served as Beck's Operations Bureau Leader. Bad feelings naturally resulted. Any Potiorek-Conrad contact would be tainted by irreconcilable personal differences. The untenable situation ultimately led to Potiorek's 21 August appointment, owing to his relationship with the Kaiser and his adjutant, as a separate commander of the Balkan fighting forces. Even after the defeat in August and later in September, Potiorek retained Franz Joseph's confidence until a third catastrophic defeat in December 1914 led to his ultimate downfall.

The Balkan campaign, in hindsight, faced disaster from the moment the Russian general mobilization was acknowledged.

The B-Group had begun rail movement southward for a full "War Case B." It would continue south on "railroad technical grounds." With the departure of this Army from the Balkans, the northern Serbian front became denuded, increasing the ability of the Serbians to outflank the isolated Fifth and Sixth Armies, which already fought in terrain unsuitable for a major victory for them.

The Austro-Hungarian offensive into Serbia from Bosnia was repulsed, producing panic at the command level in Galicia, and on 15 August, the order for Second Army troops to depart for the Russian front was reaffirmed. Potiorek, however, continued to insist that the Second Army be utilized against Serbia to counter a pending disastrous defeat. While some units of the Second Army began to re-embark for Galicia, on 19 August Conrad conceded allowing some units to continue to "demonstrate" until they were transported north.[66]

As the hour for the northern offensive approached, while the Second Army was beginning to retrain, Conrad telegraphed General Prittwitz that the Austro-Hungarian general offensive would commence at the latest in a week's time.

As the Habsburg armies neared their strategic deployment positions between 22 and 25 August, reports of enemy thrusts into eastern Galicia began to increase. This was a threat to the exposed Austro-Hungarian right flank, where the Second Army had yet to be assembled. The Third and Second Austro-Hungarian Armies could not move to meet this threat without endangering the Fourth Army's flanks while it advanced north. The Austro-Hungarian Fourth Army could not advance until the Third Army had completed its assembly. Thus, any Third Army military setback, however insignificant, could weaken the Fourth Army's maneuverability, also ultimately leading to a retreat of Austro-Hungarian forces behind the San-Dniester line.[67]

Air reconnaissance tended to reconfirm Conrad's plans for his northern stroke by pinpointing strong enemy forces in the Lublin and Krasnostav region, but none between the Dniester River and along the roads connecting Proskurov and Tarnopol. Nevertheless, out of nowhere a powerful enemy offensive commenced across the Zbrucz River on 22 August and advanced towards Tarnopol-Trembovla and Czortkov. The Austro-Hungarians did not believe this was a major thrust.

With the threat to his flank positions increasing, Conrad, at 8:15 p.m., 23 August, telegraphed General Prittwitz, inquiring where the German Eighth Army had been deployed and what was its mission. It is quite clear that Conrad still sought a German thrust towards Siedlce. This is confirmed by a telegram to General Moltke on the same day. He also again pressed for the committal of the promised five German reserve divisions and further troops to secure the success of the anticipated Austro-Hungarian stroke against advancing Russian troops. Conrad also said that his left-flank offensive had begun, although the right flank could not begin serious movement until 27 August.[68] Conrad was trying to indicate to the Germans that he, at least, was fulfilling his obligations.

The Russian High Command anticipated the main Austro-Hungarian deployment and attack in Galicia. The Russian offensive, like the Austro-Hungarian, was divided into two groups of two armies. At the northern front of Galicia, the Fourth and Fifth Russian Armies had moved into the vicinity of Lublin and into lines around Cholm and Kovel, respectively, by 23 August. At the eastern front of Galicia, the Third and Eighth Russian Armies had assembled on both sides of Dubno and around Proskurov southward to Dunajevsky by August 19. The Russian strategy was to encircle both Austro-Hungarian flanks and cut off the Austro-Hungarian line of retreat to the south behind the Dniester River and west to Cracow.[69] The eastern Russian armies, totaling twenty-one divisions, smashed across the eastern Galician frontier on 22 August. The northern Russian Fourth and Fifth Armies advanced southward into western Galicia, where they unexpectedly ran into the advancing Austro-Hungarian First Army.

On 23 August, a captured Russian officer revealed that the entire Russian Eighth Army had already been deployed in the area of Proskurov and had begun their offensive.[70] But Conrad still refused to believe that this was a major offensive because most reconnaissance sources continued to locate only scattered enemy formations. The enemy forces advancing from the southern Sereth River area appeared to be large cavalry and small infantry detachments.[71] But, in fact, by 23 August the twenty-one Russian divisions had deployed inside the Galician border in the line Radziechov-Tarnopol and south. On 24 August, they advanced towards the Austro-Hungarian bastion at Lemberg with the unknown advantage that the Austro-Hungarian High Command remained unaware of their presence until contact was finally made near Radziechov. No reports of enemy activity emanated from the even more important area between Brody and Tarnopol, but enemy troops reached the upper Bug River and the Zlota Lipa line by 25 August.

General Conrad, still unaware of the magnitude of the eastern Russian offensive, continued to worry about the northern front. He felt that the Germans here had undertaken operations contrary to agreement which placed his armies in a most difficult situation. With the news of the imminent arrival of the Russian Siberian Corps, Conrad pressured the Habsburg political leadership to secure Romania's active military intervention to relieve the increasing enemy pressure on his right flank. The ever-present danger was that if the northern offensive was defeated, his forces in eastern Galicia would be cut off from the heart of the Empire; and if the eastern Galician troops failed to hold, the northern offensive could be cut off from the rear. He also wanted Bulgaria to be encouraged to declare war on Serbia, which would free troops for Galicia.[72]

Thus, as the left flank advanced northward on 23 August, concern shifted to the threatened Third and Second Armies on the right flank. Increasing pressure was brought to bear upon Franz Joseph to obtain the more rapid retransport of Second Army troops that had become embroiled in the Serbian campaign. The General Staff arguments in favor of the retransport were sound and would prove to be prophetic. The General Staff emphasized that the main decision in the war would be attained in the northern theater against the main enemy, Russia. Overpowering enemy forces battled the northern armies; the Germans, contrary to agreement, had fielded only nine divisions in the east because of Italian neutrality; reports of the approach of additional Russian troops (the Siberian Corps) threatened to aggravate the situation, and Romania's declaration of neutrality had freed Russian forces for use against Austria-Hungary. Most significant, however, the overwhelming invasion of Russian forces in eastern Galicia necessitated the strengthening of Conrad's forces southeast of Lemberg.[73]

Reacting to these arguments, Franz Joseph accepted the transfer of the IV Corps to Galicia on the stipulation that the Save-Danube River line be adequately protected.[74] The VII Corps, which had re-embarked on trains on 22 August, did not begin to arrive at terminals in Galicia until 31 August. The IV Corps reloaded on 30-31 August, not reaching the terminals in Galicia until 8 September.

The Austro-Hungarian situation had indeed deteriorated badly. Bulgaria, anticipated as a military counter to Serbia, did not enter the war and tie down Serbian forces, its reluctance partially due to Russian intimidation. After pressure had been put on Bucharest, a Crown Council reaffirmed Romanian neutrality. With the failure of the initial Austro-Hungarian offensive into Serbia on 12 August, all energetic approaches to both Bucharest and Sofia failed to sway them. Count Berchtold, supporting the arguments of General Potiorek, the Balkan commander, argued that if troops were transferred to Galicia, no effective offensive could be launched against Serbia for some time, while the danger of a Serbian thrust against Bosnia and Hungary increased. This maneuver would produce serious political consequences which could also lead to military catastrophe. If no military victory could be garnered against Serbia, Bulgaria and Romania would never support the Central Powers in the field. But, was it not Count Berchtold's pre-war diplomacy that had created this situation?

CHAPTER X

Epilogue: The Battles of Lemberg

Between 23 and 25 August, the Austro-Hungarian First Army defeated the Russian Fourth Army at Krasnik after encircling it from the left flank and forcing a Russian retreat. The First Army then advanced towards Lublin. Strategically, the battle of Krasnik gave Conrad the initiative in the most important region for his major offensive while, at the same time, it encouraged the expected German offensive from the north. Conrad's victory also protected the exposed Silesian area. Now, as a next step, Conrad approved pushing the enemy toward the east. Also, the Russian High Command diverted the new Ninth Army, which had been designated to face Germany, towards its now precarious position between the Bug and Vistula Rivers. This retreat also caused the Russians temporarily to order the transfer of forces from the Austro-Hungarian right flank to the north, although this order was soon rescinded. On 24 August, dispositions for the general offensive were forwarded, in accordance with the dogma of the offensive.

While the Fourth Austro-Hungarian Army launched its own attack against "weak enemy forces" in the general direction of Cholm, the ever-increasing enemy threats to the eastern Galician flank offset the favorable reports in the north. The report that four enemy divisions were approaching the Fourth Army led to a countering attack order.[1]

Thus, the original attack plan, which had depended on the First Army to be the heavyweight of the northern offensive (left flank) along the Vistula River, had shifted. Now the major effort would engage the Fourth Army. In the process of changing position, the Fourth Army outer flanks advanced, creating both the gap between the Fourth and First Armies and another in the area towards the Third Army.

The available Second Army units, Group Kövess received orders to unify forces as rapidly as possible at the right flank and rear of the attacking Austro-Hungarian armies to guard against the enemy advances over the Zbrucz River.[2] The Third Army was ordered to defuse the enemy

attacks from Brody and Tarnopol (XII and XI Corps and 11. Infantry
Division) by attacking in the general line from Lemberg to Zloczóv. This
order was intended to stop the enemy incursions against the lower Zlota
Lipa and Dniester River lines and to protect Lemberg.[3]

Pushing relentlessly westward, on 25 August Russian forces approached the Austro-Hungarian defensive line Kamionka Strumilova-
Busk-Zlota Lipa. Further major enemy forces advanced from Zaleszcyki.[4]

As he became aware of the Russian threat, Conrad telegraphed the
German Command that a total success for Berlin and Vienna in the east
depended upon German troops being transferred from the French front to
East Prussia. He failed, however, to tell the Germans that his own Second
Army was not in on the fight, and would not be for some time. On the
same day, Conrad learned that two additional German army corps would
indeed be transferred to the eastern theater, but news from Prussia recon-
firmed that there was no hope of a German offensive in the direction of
Siedlce.[5] Seven to ten Russian corps had been confirmed opposing the
German Eighth Army. The mass of the German Eighth Army, four regular
and one mixed corps, desperately maneuvered to encircle the invading
Russian Second Army (five corps) while one German corps and one
cavalry division, as well as the main reserve of the fortress of Königsberg,
covered the movement of the Russian First Army (five corps). Conrad
thought that after the German forces defeated the Russian Second Army,
they would immediately wheel against the Russian First Army, fulfilling
the German pledge to launch a thrust towards the lower Narev River area.[6]
But, obviously, no immediate relief could be expected for Conrad's sorely
pressed and outnumbered forces while the German Eighth Army battled
the enemy forces invading Prussia.

In eastern Galicia, meanwhile, as the Second Army continued assembly
of numerically inferior fighting forces for its offensive, the overall situation grew more critical. While the left-flank First and Fourth Armies
successfully advanced northward towards Lublin and Cholm, the Austro-
Hungarian right-flank armies faced an enemy that continued to roll its
defensive positions back to the Zlota Lipa River line. Additional enemy
forces advanced from Brzezany over Podhajce and Monasterzyska. In
addition to this disheartening news, Conrad received the shocking report
that his Third Army had not yet been deployed on its assigned high ground.
He immediately wired the Third Army commander that the success of the
attack towards Zloczóv was crucial to the overall decision in the eastern
theater, that in order to achieve this success, the Third Army had to be on

the high ground as he had ordered. The army must at all costs halt enemy forces advancing towards Lemberg. The available portions of the Second Army, although still assembling, received the order to launch an offensive across the Dniester River. Victory, however, depended upon the Third Army's struggles around Lemberg.[7]

On 25 August, the Russians hurled three to four divisions into the growing gap on the left flank between the First and Fourth Armies. As the Fourth Army advanced north and, thus, away from the First, Conrad ordered the First Army now to fulfill two missions — its original advance towards Lublin and now also support for the Fourth Army. The First Army's adherence to these orders would lead to a weakening of its right flank.

As the Fourth Army battle of Komarov developed, the Army consisted of seven infantry and two cavalry divisions facing approximately six to seven enemy infantry and two to three cavalry divisions. The Army group Joseph Ferdinand, three infantry and one cavalry division, would join the right flank, and this change would weaken the Third Army, which had original authority over the forces. Thirty kilometers behind the Fourth Army, the two divisions of the newly created XVII Corps advanced. Army supply trains could not maintain the pace of the troops, and the Army attacked before completing its deployment.

On the far right flank, the Russians approached the Zlota Lipa River line. Conrad gave his Third Army a free hand to attack these formations. According to intelligence reports, five to six enemy divisions were advancing from the area Brody-Tarnopol, and others from the Sereth River area. The Third Army was assigned to deflect them from the Fourth Army flank, but Conrad gave no indication of enemy strength where General Rudolf Brudermann was to advance towards Zloczóv. Consequently, the Third Army Commander anticipated three separate opposing Russian groups.

Conrad's orders — to halt the enemy advance towards Lemberg at any cost — produced colossal losses in the first days of battle, resulting partly from the well-positioned, deadly accurate, and numerically superior Russian artillery fire.

On 26 August, the Third Army advanced with uncoordinated assaults and no artillery support into enemy attack formations. Meanwhile, it became more likely that the enemy might encircle the Army's right flank, because the Second Army had not been deployed in sufficient strength.

Conrad ordered the five infantry and two cavalry division strong Second Army to strike north toward the Third Army, where a gap of sixty to seventy kilometers existed between the two armies (a one-hundred-kilometer gap between the Third and Fourth Armies). Russian units poured into these gaps.

Disaster appeared imminent on 27 August. Overwhelming Russian forces struck the Third Army as it began to attack. The onslaught of an enemy vastly superior in numbers and artillery made retreat unavoidable; five enemy corps and six cavalry divisions attacked along the front Kamionka Strumilova-Tarnopol, and additional strong forces advanced in the area of Wyszgorodok and Wisznievczyk. Thus, while the Austro-Hungarian left-flank armies successfully continued their battle towards Lublin and Cholm, the right-flank forces were paired off against vastly superior advancing Russian forces in eastern Galicia, northeast of Lemberg and at the Gnila Lipa River line. Yet, Conrad ordered offensives on all four fronts. He reasoned that while the First and Fourth Armies advanced "victoriously" northward, the entire campaign depended upon the outcome of the battle raging around Lemberg. Although his Second Army was supposed to be halting the enemy offensive south of Brzezany in this struggle while preventing Russian assault against the southern flank of the Third Army at Lemberg, its IV Corps designated for this area had yet to board the trains in the south.

The crisis on the eastern flank caused the General Staff to prepare the Fourth Army to move from its area (Zamosc-Laszczov-Tomaszov) in either an easterly or southeasterly direction to support the sorely pressed Third Army.[8] A very threatening gap had meanwhile opened between the northern First and Fourth Armies, while a one-hundred-kilometer break occurred between the Third and Fourth Armies. The cavalry attempting to fill the gaps between armies raced the Russian cavalry attempting to penetrate them. Fierce fighting raged through 27 August.

As the situation deteriorated, Conrad expressed his disgust with the German military "successes" earned at the expense of Austria-Hungary. He argued that of one hundred operational German divisions, only nine regular and three national guard divisions had been deployed in the east, so that the Austro-Hungarian forces had borne the overpowering brunt of the Russian onslaught. Italy and Romania's failure to honor treaty obligations made matters worse for Vienna, i.e., Italy's defection robbed her of five promised German divisions in East Prussia, although two German corps would be transferred to the eastern front, with the vanguard arriving in the east on 1 September.[9]

On 28 August, when disaster was obviously imminent on the eastern flank, Conrad continued to complain of Germany's failure to fulfill her pre-war "agreements."[10] In a letter to Bolfras of the Austro-Hungarian Military Chancery, Conrad rehashed Germany's promise to deploy at least twelve divisions east of the lower Vistula River, assembling them north of Thorn with additional units to advance in the direction of Siedlce, while the main forces advanced toward Lublin. He pointed out that although Vienna had fulfilled her side of the agreements, Germany had assembled only nine divisions northeast of Thorn. In addition, the numerically deficient German units were not advancing to the southeast as had been promised but rather to the northeast, toward Gumbinnen. Conrad concluded that his armies now faced the overwhelming weight of the Russian armies, which had penetrated Galicia as far as Lemberg. He did not admit to Bolfras, however, that he, too, had made a mistake by sending the Second Army to the Balkan theater.

German intelligence reports concerning these matters, had estimated eight definite and one possible Russian corps opposing the Austro-Hungarians, but it had been determined in battle that ten to eleven corps opposed Germany. Five additional Russian corps which could be directed against either Austria-Hungary or Germany had been pinpointed in the area of Ivangorod, Warsaw, and Siedlce. Seven to eight Russian reserve divisions countered Germany, and nine to ten opposed Austria-Hungary.[11] Conrad also wired Moltke that it was urgent that German troops be directed towards Siedlce both to help preserve the momentum of the Monarchy's success at Lublin and to support the sorely pressed forces east of Lemberg.[12]

Meanwhile, the Russian Third and Eighth Armies on the eastern flank shifted northward toward Lemberg, which led to the Third Army's retreat, through devastating Russian artillery fire that helped turn both its flanks. Conrad decided to attempt a new defensive at the Gnila Lipa River line, the next readily defendable position. But the Third Army was too weak and the position too wide to ensure an effective defense.

As the battles on the eastern flank raged relentlessly, the overwhelming superiority of Russian numbers and artillery exacted a heavy toll.[13] On the evening of 28 August, the Monarchy's Third Army received the order to "unconditionally hold their positions," and the Fourth Army, although some of its units had been transferred to the endangered Third Army, had been instructed to defend against incursions by strong enemy cavalry forces from the area Mosty Wilky towards Zolkiev. The Second Army, still lacking its IV and VII Corps, received the order to attack northward from the Dniester River against the enemy's southern flank, which was now advancing against the hard-pressed Third Army.[14]

On 28 August, however, the enemy hurled back the left flank of the Third Army as it approached the Gnila Lipa line, creating the gap between the Third and Fourth Armies. It simultaneously appeared that strong enemy cavalry units were beginning successfully to penetrate into the gap between the Third and Fourth Armies, which had been caused by the shifting of Fourth Army troops northward. The hard-pressed Third Army began to withdraw from the Gnila Lipa line, where it met strong enemy pressure. The Third Army had suffered staggering casualties, its supply lines had become intertwined, and its troops were shaken and unnerved from continuous marching, battle, artillery fire and confusion. Second Army assistance was crucial.[15]

On 29 August, Conrad declared that the German victory at Tannenberg (26-29 August) had been achieved with Austro-Hungarian blood, because his fighting forces had been forced to take the brunt of the Russian onslaught. He explained that the two German corps being transported east would arrive too late to help the situation in Galicia,[16] and he concluded that the German High Command was only concerned with Prussian territory.

On 29 August, when the stunning German three-day victory over the Russian Second Army at Tannenberg was announced, Conrad was informed that the German Eighth Army would now advance between the Masurian Lakes and the Narev River to strike at the Russian First Army. Further, that immediate efforts to undertake "Operations over the Narev River toward Ostrov-Siedlce was not definitely promised." In a congratulatory telegram, Conrad stressed his confident expectation of a German advance toward Siedlce.[17] But he was informed that the German Eighth Army now had to defend against the advancing Russian First Army.[18] The thrust toward Siedlce would have to be delayed as long as General Pavel K. Rennenkampf's army threatened the German rear. Due to this change of plans, the Austro-Hungarian military leadership would later charge that it had been left in the lurch.

Heavy fighting continued around Lemberg, where the entire Third Army front reeled from enemy attacks. The Second Army received instructions to attack the enemy forces advancing toward the Gnila Lipa line, although several of its divisions remained in the Balkans. Aerial reconnaissance reports confirmed that additional enemy columns were advancing westward.[19]

The attacks of the First and Fourth Armies continued in the north, but the First Army's advance was halted. The Fourth Army continued to seek its battle of encirclement around Komarov, but it was first necessary that the Third Army maintain its positions. At the battle of Przemyślany, however, the Third Army's front disintegrated, and its flanks were turned.

To the south, the Russians marched through the area between assembling Second Army units.

At dawn on 30 August, the Russian armies continued their drive westward. General Conrad sought to relieve some of the pressure of their advance by ordering the available forces of the Second Army (five infantry and two cavalry divisions) to attack the enemy from the south towards Rohatan at the Gnila Lipa. When he realized that such meager forces would not be able to accomplish this task, he ordered the Second Army to retreat behind the Dniester River to await the IV Corps, scheduled to arrive from the Serbian frontier on 1 September (actually to arrive on 8 September).[20]

The failure of the Second Army to assist the Third Army led to the collapse of the Third Army's right flank, which, in turn, caused the entire Third Army to retreat from the line Gliniany-Gnila Lipa to Lemberg. The retreat, in turn, seriously endangered the Fourth Army position and encouraged the suggestion that the attempted encirclement of the Russian Fifth Army at Komarov be stopped.

As the Austro-Hungarian right-flank defensive position was rolled back, Conrad continued to press the offensives of his First and Fourth Armies, which he thought would aid the Third and Second Armies. In the process of rolling back, the Second, Third and Fourth Armies would meet, creating one front, and thereby closing the dangerous gaps between the Armies. To hold the line in the interim, a strong cavalry corps of four divisions was inserted into the gap between the Third and Fourth Armies.[21]

Conrad focused his attention on the Fourth Army's attempt to encircle the enemy's Fifth Army. By 30 August, however, he had changed his mind about this maneuver. Reports of the arrival of new Russian units — particularly the Siberian Corps — led him to believe that a victory short of the extensive encirclement plan would have to be sufficient.

The Third Army orders for 31 August were to defend Lemberg at all costs, as well as to prevent the enemy from reaching the Fourth Army's flank. But Conrad, for some reason, considered the situation not to be as serious as it had been on 30 August.[22] He ordered the right flank armies to hold the line Lemberg-Mikolajov, and only in the "most serious" circumstances to retreat behind the Vereszyca River line. At the same time, he ordered the Third Army to form a group to prevent an enemy advance from Zolkiev and Magierov. At this stage, intelligence sources claimed that Conrad's fighting forces countered four enemy armies composed of fifteen to sixteen corps and other assorted forces, totaling forty to forty-three divisions.[23] The Russian Eighth and Third Armies opposing the Austro-Hungarian Third and Second Armies numbered seven corps, four to six cavalry, and three reserve divisions. The Russian Fifth Army (four infantry corps and two cavalry divisions) countered the Austro-Hungarian Fourth Army. The Russian Fourth Army (four infantry corps and two reserve divisions) opposed the First Army south of Lublin.

As the Fourth Army attempted to encircle the retreating Russian Fifth Army around Komarov, the General Staff concluded that in lieu of a victory, it should withdraw its eastern flank to Ravaruska. At the same time, the Third Army had to defend the heights west of Kulikov and Lemberg (Third Army left flank).[24] The defense would allow the Fourth Army to join battle with the Third and Second Armies against the Russian onslaught around Lemberg.

But overwhelming enemy pressure on 31 August forced the Third Army again to withdraw westward towards Lemberg where, on 1 September, it was ordered to hold a defensive line from Lemberg to Mikolajov. This new development endangered the Fourth Army's southeast flank as it strode toward its anticipated victory. The Army's northern flank also seemed threatened. That there were no Austro-Hungarians reserves, while the Russians continued to receive fresh reinforcements, compounded the critical situation. The battle was going so poorly that Conrad's Headquarters notified German Headquarters that the Second and Third Armies would soon be forced to retreat.

On 1 September, there was some good news for the Austro-Hungarian command. The Fourth Army's seven-day battle near Komarov had ended with the enemy in full retreat,[25] although not encircled or annihilated as had been anticipated because the Austro-Hungarians possessed neither the time nor sufficient forces on the northern flank. Conrad now ordered the main body of the Fourth Army to prepare to extricate the imperiled Third Army by marching towards Lemberg. In the meantime, the Second Army continued to retreat in the face of strong enemy thrusts from the area of Halicz.[26]

The Third Army's situation was desperate. Eighteen to twenty Russian divisions were attacking both flanks, and discipline within the army had collapsed as some troops broke rank and fled. On 2 September, this army yielded Lemberg without battle and retreated twenty miles to the rear, ending the first battle of Lemberg. The Russians occupied the city on 3 September. The Third Army had to be regrouped and its morale rehabilitated, an impossible chore in the Lemberg area. The necessity of regrouping forced Conrad to terminate forward movement of his First and Fourth Armies because of the danger of encirclement in the Lemberg region.[27]

The situation became so critical that Conrad wrote Moltke requesting that at least two German corps be sent in the direction of the fortress of Przemyśl. Conrad also had the nominal commander of the Austro-Hungarian forces, Archduke Friedrich, write Kaiser Wilhelm that:

> We attacked between the Bug and Vistula Rivers as agreed upon and at the expense of our right-flank group, which has faced superior enemy forces and lost East Galicia. The Germans did not attack over the lower Narev River in the direction of Siedlce as agreed upon. Now, it is decisive for the crushing of Russia that an energetic attack be launched in the direction of Siedlce.[28]

Friedrich's letter led Wilhelm to inform Conrad's military representative in supreme headquarters:

> Our small army in East Prussia had drawn twelve enemy corps against it and destroyed one-half and battled one-half, thus facilitating the Austro-Hungarian offensive entirely in keeping with the agreements. More than this one could not demand of them.[29]

Austro-Hungarian battle orders for 3 September called for the assembly of the Third Army on the Vereszyca River line, with a strong battle-ready group at the northern flank. The Fourth Army, after reversing its front 180 degrees from north to south, would attack the northern flank of the enemy advancing against the Third Army force while maintaining its line of communications to the San River. The Third Army had to hold its positions until the Fourth Army arrived, and the Third Army's situation obliged the First and Fourth Armies to maintain their positions.[30]

The Second Army, on the southern flank, was to strike northward towards Lemberg to relieve the pressure on the Third Army. The two armies would initially make contact at the Dniester River. The main priority was to prevent the enemy from crossing the Vereszyca River. But the Russians suddenly began to maneuver to the north and northwest against the flank and rear of the Fourth Army while still surrounding Lemberg.[31]

On 4 September, the Russians also renewed their broad westward advance on a wide front from Zolkiev, Lemberg, Mikolajov and south of the Dniester River towards the Stryj area. But the Austro-Hungarians did not know where the enemy was — for the second time, their reconnaissance had failed them.[32] In the meantime, it became obvious that the Austro-Hungarian Third Army needed to pause for a few days at its ordered positions on the Vereszyca River. Since new reports showed Russian troops shifting in a northerly direction, however, its northern flank appeared endangered. The troops at the north flank appeared incapable of offering any effective resistance, and intelligence sources suggested that the main enemy attack would be against this flank.

Also on 4 September, the Russians launched an assault against the previously victorious First Army, which now found its flanks threatened. The First Army's mission then became to prevent an enemy attack on its right flank against the rear of the Fourth Army while holding its left flank at strongly defended positions south of Lublin. But on 5 September, the First Army's right flank was hurled back by enemy assaults. General Dankl, estimating that thirteen Russian divisions opposed him, informed Conrad that he could hold his positions, but had to await reinforcements.[33]

At this crucial stage, Moltke informed Conrad that as soon as his German forces defeated General Rennenkampf's invading forces, the Germans would advance an army of four to five army corps towards Siedlce. Moltke further explained that "in the east Siedlce was the goal from the beginning," but that at the moment, his forces could not simultaneously bind the invading Russian Army and attack towards Siedlce.[34] Undoubtedly Moltke must have known that Conrad was in a very desperate situation, but he could not leave an enemy force of eleven and one-half infantry and five and one-half cavalry divisions at this flank and attack in another direction. He also learned that the Russian Niemen Army would soon be reinforced, so that it would be composed of twenty infantry divisions.

On 5 September, in desperation, Conrad gambled on a bold offensive thrust: His Third Army would launch an attack as soon as the Fourth Army had connected with its left flank. The Fourth Army would then strike into

the area of Zolkiev and Lemberg. The exposed Fourth Army rear area —
its front had reversed itself on the assumption that the enemy Fifth Army
had been defeated — would be protected by a small force of three infantry
and one cavalry division situated between the Bug and Vieprz Rivers. On
7 September, the Second Army would advance south of Lemberg, leaving
a group of two corps to prevent an enemy advance south of the Dniester
River.[35]

In the interim, the newly formed Russian Ninth and supposedly defeated Fifth Armies advanced into the sixty-kilometer-wide gap between
the First and Fourth Armies. Two enemy corps advanced toward the First
Army eastern (right) flank and two against the Fourth Army's exposed
rear area. This maneuver, which threatened the First Army with encirclement and the Fourth with annihilation from the rear while engaged fron-
tally near Lemberg, was one of the reasons for the defeat around Lemberg.

Despite these perilous conditions, on 6 September Conrad planned a
double battle of encirclement against the enemy troops advancing westward from Lemberg. Even while his battle-weary and hard-pressed armies
retreated, Conrad retained his tenacity. Unfortunately, his troops were
simply not prepared successfully to carry out such a wide-scale counterattack. Conrad's plan was based on his assumption that his Third and
Second Armies had been rehabilitated from the earlier debacle. They had
not been.

Meanwhile, Moltke responded to charges by Conrad in a letter he wrote
on 4 September and which was delivered on 6 September. Moltke described the serious situation in the French theater, recalling that he and
Conrad had "agreed" that France must be initially disposed of before they
could make a coordinated advance in the east. Moltke wrote that only dire
necessity had led him to transfer two German corps to the east, and he
reassured Conrad that the Germans had intended to launch an offensive
in the direction of Siedlce, but that only circumstance — the invasion of
twenty-four Russian infantry and ten to eleven cavalry divisions — had
altered the plan. The German forces had annihilated Samsonov's Second
Army, but then had to counter Rennenkampf's First Army, which had also
invaded East Prussia. As long as an enemy army remained in Prussia, there
could be no German thrust into Poland. Once Rennenkampf's army had
been defeated, then nine divisions, to be designated the German Ninth
Army, could advance into Poland toward Siedlce.[36] Conrad knew that the
General Staff could not count on immediate direct German support. His
representative in German Eastern Headquarters confirmed this deduction

in a letter stating that since the First Russian Army was now northwest of the Masurian Lakes, the Germans would not be able to move towards the Bug and Vistula Rivers. The representative also suggested that the Germans were more interested in clearing East Prussia of the enemy than cooperating in the allied struggle against Russia.[37]

Meanwhile, the Russian menace had become so great that Conrad now had to plan on defending the passes through the Carpathian Mountains into Hungary against Russian cavalry and infantry forays. The Second Army was assigned to establish this defense while the Russian onslaught continued.

Conrad began to remove commanders from their posts, citing as grounds for their dismissals their lack of energy and inability to discipline their troops, their loss of nerve in battle, and their inclination to abandon their battling troops in moments of danger.

The situation on 7 September remained critical. The First Army, suffering staggering losses, was fighting a defensive battle against strongly reinforced Russian units to the northwest of Lemberg. The Fourth Army, having lost fifty percent of its officer corps and twenty-five percent of its manpower, had retired from Zolkiev. The Third Army reported no battle on its front, but it prepared for new action. The Second Army, still awaiting the IV Corps, prepared to attack east of the Vereszyca River in conjunction with the Third and Fourth Armies' proposed offensive against Lemberg, where, obviously, Russian artillery was still active and where the Russians' main thrust was expected to originate.[38]

On 8 September, Count Berchtold contacted Conrad regarding his complaints about lack of German cooperation in the eastern campaign. Conrad replied that Moltke had promised him both orally and in writing that the Germans would cooperate with him in his offensive operation towards Lublin, which depended upon a German attack in the direction of Siedlce. Because the Germans did not fulfill these obligations and were selfishly making their primary goal the clearing of the enemy from East Prussia, it followed that Austria-Hungary had to carry the main burden of the battle against Russia, which had resulted in the forced evacuation of East Galicia, the Bukovina and Lemberg. Whatever successes had been won on the left flank were lost as the First and Fourth Armies were forced to retreat.[39]

Count Tisza, perceiving a threat to Hungary, demanded that Berchtold intervene in Berlin. Because of Entente claims of victory and the retreat of Austro-Hungarian forces from Lemberg, he could foresee disastrous repercussions in the Balkans if there were further enemy successes. In European capitals, many believed that Russia would soon achieve complete victory, and Tisza feared that Romania would now intervene against Austria.[40]

Exchanges about "their agreements" continued between the allied leadership while Conrad maintained steady pressure on Berchtold. On 9 September, Conrad repeated his arguments that the German decision to clear East Prussia of Russian troops rather than cooperate with his thrust towards Lublin had jeopardized the overall success in the Polish theater. Austria-Hungary thus had to absorb the main force of the Russian onslaught and evacuate the Bukovina, eastern Galicia and Lemberg. Conrad added that if Russian armies paralyzed a portion of Austria-Hungary during their further advances, it would become extraordinarily difficult for him to continue the campaign.

Conrad, who now admitted that Austria-Hungary had promised to assume the heaviest weight of the Russian onslaught while Germany fought in the west, now predicted disaster if German aid should arrive too late. Piqued by what he felt was Germany's failure to fulfill her obligations and by the consequent loss of eastern Galicia, he wired the Foreign Office that Berlin should be notified that Austria-Hungary would now have to negotiate a separate peace with Russia. "Why," he said, "should Austria-Hungary bleed needlessly?"[41] In a letter to Moltke, Conrad blamed his calamity (First Army having to retire to the lower San River area) on German failure to attack towards Siedlce.[42] Although a German thrust towards Siedlce was at best improbable by this time, Conrad continued to harangue the Germans about Siedlce.[43]

On 8 September, Berchtold also inquired in Berlin whether the Germans intended to supply sufficient troops to relieve the overpowering pressure in Galicia. A diplomatic reply of 9 September from Undersecretary of State Zimmermann emphasized that Germany's first task was to crush France, and that only then would sufficient German forces be available to be sent to the eastern front. The six Russian corps advancing into East Prussia had to be defeated. In the process of that battle, as in the battle at Tannenberg, Germany's tying down large numbers of Russian troops in the north would indirectly benefit Austria.[44] Undersecretary Zimmermann countered Conrad's argument that Germany had not upheld her military agreements by stating that he, Zimmermann, could not believe that the German General Staff would not fulfill its obligations.

Bethmann Hollweg also replied to the accusations by stating that the German armies in the west were fighting an enemy numerically superior by 300,000 troops, while, in the east, German troops had pulled at least twelve Russian corps from Galicia. Germany, he said, would be more than pleased to send the desired aid, but because of the military situation on both fronts it was presently impossible. Bethmann Hollweg added that aid would be sent as soon as the German troops repulsed the invading Russian forces.

The Chancellor further advised Vienna to win Romania back to her side and added that Romania's Austrophobia had originated with the Dual Monarchy, not with Germany. Romanian aid would help bring the war to a successful conclusion. For these reasons, Vienna was advised to cede territory to Romania, if necessary, to gain her support.[45] The allied General Staffs continued to feel, unjustifiably, that Romanian aid would enable them to obtain a victory over Russia. This stubbornness established a pattern for future exchanges between Vienna and Berlin. Whenever Conrad said "Siedlce," the Germans responded "Romania."

Vienna replied that Romania would not join Austria-Hungary if Russian power was not broken, that the cession of Austro-Hungarian territory would be construed in Bucharest as a sign of weakness or defeat. Romania had not fulfilled her pre-war agreements and could not be expected to do so in the future. Also, if Austria-Hungary ceded territories to Romania, Italy would seek her pound of flesh too, which might affect the stance of Bulgaria and Turkey as allies. The Monarchy would also be demoralized if Austria-Hungary should cede territory, it was argued.[46]

By 8 September, the Fourth, Third and Second Armies had finally formed a single line of resistance to the enemy onslaught on the battlefield, but now 50,000 enemy soldiers threatened the rear of the Fourth Army in the gap between the First and Fourth Armies.[47] General Conrad's tenacity in the face of disaster is admirable. If his battle-weary, overpowered, and defeated troops could have made the effort he asked, it is possible that the situation might have been saved.

The supposedly defeated Russian Fifth Army (battle of Komarov) reappeared unexpectedly on 9 September when it smashed into the Fourth Army's II Corps and further reduced the stand of that corps from 50,000 to 10,000 men. As the enemy forces advanced, they severed Austro-Hungarian supply lines and retreat routes and began to encircle the Fourth Army's flank. The Army Commander learned of this mortal danger in a captured Russian radio broadcast. Enemy pressure also mounted in the

Carpathian Mountains, and Conrad was seriously concerned that his three eastern armies might be forced into the mountains.

By the evening of 9 September, however, the Second and Third Armies and a large portion of the Fourth Army continued a slow, but successful, advance towards Lemberg. The advance opened the possibility of a decisive second battle of Lemberg, somewhere west of the city. Conrad's daring and aggressive planned offensive was to attack in the direction of Lemberg. From the south, he would surprise the enemy forces advancing from the Zbrucz River. The Austro-Hungarian offensive advanced to within twelve kilometers south and west of Lemberg, but the retreat of the First Army put all of Conrad's forces in a critical situation.[48] The First Army, besides preventing its own encirclement, had to again prevent additional Russian forces from intervening in the impending battle near Lemberg.[49]

The situation at the right flank remained tenuous. The order demanding an energetic advance by the Second Army shows the desperation of the Austro-Hungarian struggle. The order concluded with the appeal that the Second Army could not fail the Third and Fourth Armies, who fought heroically against an overpowering enemy and that the victory and destiny of the Fatherland depended upon the unceasing advance of the Second Army.[50] There had been, however, no liaison in the various attacks, particularly the IV and VII Corps (Second Army) ventures, which contributed to the military problems.

By 10 September, Conrad sensed that his right-flank offensive against Lemberg had failed, while the left-flank First Army was mortally threatened with encirclement by overwhelming numbers of enemy troops. The enemy could conceivably cut off the main retreat to Cracow. The First Army had to be withdrawn to the Tarnov-Annopol line, which decided the second battle of Lemberg (the first was the Russian capture of that city). The enemy thrust between the First and Fourth Armies (northern flank) could force the First Army to retreat to the San River line. The threat to both armies led to a general retreat, but the Fourth Army, victors at Komarov, had the unenviable task of having to fight its way back to the San River with enemy troops threatening both flanks because of the gaps between it and the First Army to the right and the Third Army to the left.[51] A deciphered enemy radio transmission also revealed that two enemy corps (V and XVII) had commenced movement southwestward, threatening the Fourth Army's rear positions and retreat routes.

Frontal attacks by the Third Army resulted in serious losses. The advances had not been coordinated and were easily repulsed in piecemeal fashion. The infantry had no artillery support and no heavy artillery concentration before the attacks.

After the decisive seventeen-day battle in Galicia, the Austro-Hungarian armed forces now began a long, demoralizing retreat to regroup for a planned new offensive, scheduled to commence after a rehabilitation period. The further west they retreated, the more significant became active German cooperation.[52]

But on 11 September, as the retreat began, the defeat at the battle of the Marne on the French front ended any hopes for a quick German victory in the west. The battle dashed any serious hope that substantial German aid to the eastern theater would be forthcoming.

Unaware of this new development, Conrad notified German authorities that he had been forced to withdraw his troops to the San River because of the serious threat to his northern flank and interior supply lines. He noted that his request for two German corps to be transported to the fortress at Przemyśl had not been implemented. He now requested that at least three German corps be sent to the fortress of Cracow. Conrad added that if the Germans had indeed deployed the promised divisions at the lower Vistula River and had attacked towards Siedlce, a military victory would have been possible. After the battle of Tannenberg, because the Eighth Army had turned against General Rennenkampf, the Russians deployed additional forces against the Monarchy, precipitating the retreat to the San River.[53] Ironically, on the same day, Conrad believed that the German Eighth Army's near-encirclement of the Russian First Army at the Masurian Lakes signaled that the long-awaited German support would finally arrive.

When Conrad ordered his retreat, he dispatched a telegram to Berchtold informing him that the blame for the defeat of the Austro-Hungarian First and Fourth Armies that had been initially so successful could not be put entirely on the Austro-Hungarians, and raised the question of Germany's failed agreements and her plans to send German troops to Galicia.[54] Count Tisza, the Hungarian Prime Minister, informed Berchtold that his approaches to Berlin were unfortunately occurring at a time when Germany was locked in decisive combat on all fronts.

In response to Berchtold's subsequent inquiries, the German Ambassador explained that Germany and Austria-Hungary had agreed that France should be defeated first; a battle which pitted Germany against an enemy in the west with a superiority of fifteen infantry and three cavalry divisions. Simultaneously, twenty-four Russian divisions invaded East Prussia, of which one-half had been destroyed. Once the other half had been defeated, the Germans would send aid to Galicia.[55]

On the following day, 14 September, the German Ambassador repeated this message. The difficulty of his position reminded Conrad of Romania's unfortunate neutrality, but Conrad thought that only a decisive Austro-Hungarian victory over Russia would engender Romanian cooperation. In the meantime, continued Russian successes encouraged Bucharest to intervene against Austria-Hungary. By mid-September, as the Austro-Hungarian armies retreated towards the San River and news spread of the German defeat at the battle of the Marne, Conrad found it necessary to clarify the situation with Romania.[56] An Austro-Hungarian offer of territorial compensation (the Suczava area) did not impress Bucharest.

Since serious German aid for common operations in the east was now almost impossible because of the German defeat at the Marne, Conrad would continue to bear the brunt of the Russian onslaught. Austria-Hungary had already suffered enormous unsalvageable losses in manpower and, in fact, did not even possess a reserve army. On the other hand, Russia's reservoir of manpower was almost endless. Conrad continued to pressure the diplomats to gain Romanian assistance.[57]

The German victory over the Russian Second Army at the Masurian Lakes on 15 September enhanced the possibility of German troops being sent to Galicia. German diplomats argued that Romania's adherence to the Central Powers would produce a victory over Russia. Vienna, therefore, had to be willing to make the sacrifices necessary to obtain a victory in the joint Austro-Hungarian-German war effort.[58]

On 16 September, Kaiser Wilhelm wired Franz Joseph that in sending troops to Silesia to aid his allies, he might weaken East Prussia and expose it to Russian invasion. In a few days it would be clearer whether more troop units could be transferred. Kaiser Wilhelm then stated that the key to victory lay in Bucharest. He hoped that Vienna would attempt to win back this former ally, and he informed Franz Joseph that German troops would now be transferred to Galicia; perhaps this might induce Romania to act.[59]

By 15 September, however, Count Czernin reported from Bucharest that continued Russian military successes in Galicia had diminished prospects for Romanian participation. The public, he said, now clamored for war against the Dual Monarchy. Czernin advised that only the cession of a portion of the Bukovina and immediate but far-reaching concessions in the Transylvanian question could bring Romania actively to join the Central Powers. If these conditions were not met, the Romanian position could grow hostile. On the same day, the military attaché reported that the offer of territorial concessions to Romania would be construed as a symptom of weakness. Yet, Germany continued to pressure Vienna to satisfy Bucharest.

With Romania and Italy unlikely to join the Central Powers, attention focused on Bulgaria. Sofia presented three conditions for active participation in the war. First, Romania would have to side with Austria-Hungary to free Bulgaria's border with Romania. Second, the question of Turkish troop passage through Bulgaria had to be settled; and, third, the Bulgarian situation relative to Serbia had to be resolved.[60] Actually, Romania's stance would ultimately determine Bulgarian participation.

The battles of the Marne, Tannenberg, Masurian Lakes and the two battles of Lemberg concluded the first phase of World War I. The Marne debacle ended hopes of a rapid Schlieffen-type battle of annihilation against France and the "promised" transport of major German forces to the east as "agreed upon" before the war. The battles of Lemberg resulted in the retreat of the Austro-Hungarian armies behind the San River, the loss of most of Galicia, and the decimation of a large part of the professional officer and non-commissioned officer corps, not to mention the huge losses of regulars.

The orders for the Austro-Hungarian armies after their retreat towards the San River (12 September) were that the Third Army would parry enemy advances from the stretch Przemyśl-Jaroslau; the First and Fourth Armies would defend themselves by moving forward from the western side of the San River (the First Army would defend the San line); and the Second Army would primarily prevent enemy pressure against the fortress Przemyśl and southward.

As the German Eighth Army began to sweep the area after its victory at the Masurian Lakes, Moltke notified Conrad (12 September) that "we will be in the situation very soon to send troops in the direction of Cracow."[61] On 13 September, Conrad learned that plans had been prepared for nine German divisions (the Ninth Army) to be sent southward. The Germans now feared that Austro-Hungarian losses threatened their province of Silesia.

Now, the major tactical question for the Austro-Hungarian General Staff was whether the Russian forces, apparently in the area between

Lemberg and the Vistula River, would cross the San River or attempt to crush the rear of their retreating armies. On 14 September, Russian troops crossed the lower San River, a move which led to more battle between the advance Russian units and Conrad's forces. The Austro-Hungarian First Army was threatened with encirclement because of the length of the San River stretch it had to defend.

In the meantime, Kaiser Wilhelm was notified that further operations of the allied armies depended upon the area and time of arrival of German forces; it was crucial that German troops be transported east of Cracow. General Falkenhayn notified Conrad that four corps and one cavalry division would be operational in one week in that region.

Conrad would avoid decisive battle until German assistance arrived in the region of Cracow. The Austro-Hungarian armies began to withdraw to the proximity of the arriving Germans. This movement drew only slight interference from the Russians, but raised the specter of a Russian advance over the Carpathian Mountains into Hungary. This threat fully awakened Berlin to the Romanian situation.[62] Germany proposed that her ally cede the region of Suczava to obtain active Romanian cooperation. As General Moltke's replacement, General Falkenhayn, stated:

> the direct cooperation of Germany in the Austro-Hungarian-Russian war is now in force. The intervention of German forces could ensue after a decision in the west is gained. It is most significant, however, to gain a great decision as soon as possible to preserve Hungary and Transylvania before a Russian invasion. To achieve this before winter requires active Romanian cooperation. Thence all must be attempted to achieve this. One way is to fulfill Romanian wishes within the Monarchy, the other through the eventual ceding of the Suczava region.[63]

Conrad knew that because so many of his forces were allocated to other defensive assignments enemy forces could easily invade Transylvania without serious resistance. He realized that Bulgaria and Turkey also might not actively assist Vienna because of the Russian victories.

These developments led to the first high-level meeting between Austro-Hungarian and German military commanders since the war began. On 18 September, Conrad and General Ludendorff, Hindenburg's Chief of Staff, decided to launch an offensive of the allied armies at the end of September. Conrad, in his memoirs, claimed that he lectured Ludendorff about the failure of Germany to fulfill pre-war "agreements." Conrad bemoaned that this had resulted in the Austro-Hungarian armies being driven behind the San River and had led to the present enemy attack on the fortress of Przemyśl.

Ludendorff countered these charges, claiming that the German Eighth Army could not have attacked towards Siedlce while threatened by two Russian armies — twenty-nine divisions — on its flanks. He concurred that Moltke had promised to deploy twelve regular divisions and an additional five reserve divisions in East Prussia, but the additional divisions could not have been deployed in the east because Italy never fulfilled her treaty obligations.[64]

Ludendorff considered the northern flank of the proposed offensive to be most decisive in the forthcoming action. Conrad, on the other hand, felt his Second Army's right flank, which was now pushed into the Carpathian Mountains, was most important.[65] Ludendorff proposed an allied advance into the Vistula River area, where, he suggested, the Russians might now be weak. Conrad added his proposal, that if the Russians advanced further into western Galicia the newly created German Ninth Army — the aforementioned nine divisions — would swoop down from the Vistula River area, while his Second Army would strike northward from its position in the Carpathian Mountains, a maneuver which would result in the encirclement of the advancing enemy. If the Russians, on the other hand, did not continue to advance, the allied forces must under all circumstances seize the initiative from them.

On 18 September, an Austro-Hungarian-German diplomatic exchange led to a review of the overall allied military situation. The Austro-Hungarian position was simply that their troops had been forced onto the defensive in the Carpathian Mountains and that if the Russians' advance continued westward, the Monarchy could not hold out much longer. The transfer of the promised nine German divisions would add sufficient strength to provide a solid defense in the east until Germany had defeated France. Further troops could then be transported from the west to participate in a new offensive. In the meantime, the Austro-Hungarian armies were in dire straits defending alone against Russia. Thus, the German reinforcements were essential immediately; Austria-Hungary was incapable of launching any offensive.

The German position, put forward by Undersecretary of State Arthur Zimmermann, was: that it was understandable that Austria-Hungary alone could not halt Russian military advances before German reinforcements had arrived in Galicia; that the newly created German Ninth Army would indeed be assembled for deployment in Galicia; that a major effort in the east would still have to await a decision over France; that Berlin deplored Vienna's failure to come to terms with Romania's prerequisites for her participation; and it was hoped that the new German Ambassador in Bucharest would succeed where the Austro-Hungarian had failed.[66] On 19 September, Kaiser Wilhelm informed the Austro-Hungarian Ambassador in Berlin that the overall situation was most critical. Wilhelm pressured for Austro-Hungarian action towards Romania through territorial concessions. He indicated that if, in fact, Romania should invade Transylvania, Vienna should not declare war but rather announce that Romania was defending the province from Russia! Wilhelm repeated the old theme that France must initially be defeated and that no separate peace should be considered.[67]

Strategic discussions were continued on 19 and 20 September with General Paul von Hindenburg, the commander of the newly created German Ninth Army. Hindenburg displayed his battle plans and troop-arrival schedules, and requested that as many Austro-Hungarian cavalry units as possible be deployed on the north Vistula River bank, particularly in the area that would enable them both to probe the area south of Ivangorod and to provide protection for the transport of German forces.[68] He also announced that the new German Ninth Army would deploy by 30 September. On 20 September, Conrad notified the German High Command that he accepted the proposed Austro-Hungarian-German plans for the utilization of the German Ninth Army, but he requested additional German troops even if they had to be composed of second- or third-line forces.[69]

As the Austro-Hungarian-German allies prepared the groundwork for the second phase of the war in the east, the Austro-Hungarian armies continued their retreat before fifty-seven to fifty-eight reinforced enemy divisions. But inexplicably to Conrad, the Russian advance westward was not rigorously pursued. Thus no serious attack had been launched against the key fortress of Przemyśl, even though the Russian Fifth Army had already crossed the San River and the Russian Eighth Army had reached the area just south of Przemyśl.[70]

General Conrad meanwhile continued to harangue his allies. On 20 September, he informed his staff that Austria-Hungary had had to assume the entire brunt of the Russian assaults, because the Germans had let them down for a second time.[71] However, already on 18 September the German Foreign Secretary, Jagow, was refuting some of Conrad's charges. Jagow claimed that the Austro-Hungarian-German pre-war agreements had been based upon the understanding that France, as the most dangerous opponent, must initially be crushed by the main weight of the German armies. The German deployment plans had also been based upon the assumption that German forces would not be tied down by Russian forces in northern Prussia. Jagow explained that in the eastern struggle the German troops had already destroyed at least seven of the twelve Russian corps opposing them, while in the western theater German troops faced an enemy force superior numerically by fifteen infantry and three cavalry divisions. If significant German troops had been quickly removed from the French theater to be thrown into battle in the east, the switch would have threatened the chances for the ultimate decision in the western campaign. In the east, however, once the northern flank had been cleared of the enemy, a German-Austro-Hungarian offensive could ensue.[72]

On 22 September, as plans continued for the joint operation, Hindenburg asked Conrad whether an Austro-Hungarian army, which he considered absolutely necessary for success, could be shifted northward to the upper Vistula River area. He deemed critical such deployment of Austro-Hungarian forces between the Vistula River and the southern flank of the German Ninth Army. Hindenburg made his request after army intelligence reports indicated that a new Russian Army (the Ninth) had been created in the Ivangorod region and that the Russian Eighth Army had probably been transferred from the Bukovina area to north of the Upper Vistula River, exactly where the German High Command wanted the Austrians to deploy an Army.[73]

Hindenburg also suggested to Conrad that in the event that the bulk of Russian forces did not pursue the now retreating Austro-Hungarian armies, some of his forces could be transferred north of the Vistula River to participate in the actual German offensive. He further hinted that the other allied armies could be deployed in echelon formation south of the Vistula River at the German right flank. Conrad immediately realized that the request camouflaged Hindenburg's desire to protect Silesia. But Conrad feared that any new Russian military initiative would be south of the Vistula River, a location which would produce severe difficulties for his forces. Therefore, he proposed that the Allies await developments before he made a final decision on their offensive. Then, if facts warranted it, Conrad would not oppose transferring his First Army to the region north of the Vistula River. Meanwhile, Conrad continued to complain to anyone who would listen to him about German "duplicity" and, as an excuse for the defeats at the battles of Lemberg, explained that his four hundred and eighty battalions countered nine hundred and twenty-six enemy battalions.[74]

By 24 September, major battle finally ensued around Przemyśl, which, as a result, became militarily isolated. On 23 September Russian forces had reached the environs of Przemyśl, but the Russian High Command had also learned about the assembly of the German Ninth Army and that it could be prepared to advance much more rapidly than expected. By 26 September, most details had been prepared for the upcoming German offensive. Conrad, although pessimistic about the state of the rehabilitation of his armies, grouped his forces for the coordinated offensive to be launched on the last day of September.[75]

As the day approached for the launching of the major Austro-Hungarian-German advance, intelligence reports indicated that Russian fighting forces had begun to retreat to behind the San River line in anticipation of a massive German assault. This information again raised the question of how to pressure Romania to join in the allied struggle against Russia before the impending "great" victory.[76]

On 23 September, Hindenburg indicated that the German Ninth Army would attempt to outflank the Russian forces, who were themselves attempting to outflank the retreating Austro-Hungarian armies. Perhaps the often mentioned battle of encirclement against the main Russian forces would finally succeed. To achieve this victory, the German Ninth Army would advance along the northern bank of the Vistula River, while the Austrians followed suit along the southern bank. Speed of action would be the greatest necessity for success.

The Austro-Hungarian-German offensive was launched at the end of September. But because of a lack of sufficient manpower — Germany was still committed to total victory in the west and still sought a breakthrough there — this offensive failed in early October. It would not be until May 1915 that a combined Austro-Hungarian-German offensive, based upon Conrad's original plans for an allied military undertaking, against the Russians succeeded at Gorlice-Tarnow. By the fall of 1915, Russia had lost all the gains of 1914 and more. Nevertheless, this small victory did not compensate for the defeat of the Schlieffen plan at the battles at the Marne and at Lemberg and the defeat of hopes for both a brief war and a rapid victory over Russia and Serbia.

Conclusion

Since the ultimate limits to the effectiveness of diplomacy are frequently determined by military capabilities and the readiness to activate them, the central position of Germany in European diplomatic circles after 1871 was at least in part due to Germany's proven abilities on the battlefield. But the quick, successful wars of the unification period (1864-1871) were not fought on two fronts, and Bismarck had carefully worked to avoid such an eventuality. The Dual Alliance with Austria-Hungary in 1879 was an attempt to protect Germany's eastern frontier and thereby preserve her predominance.

This study has examined the ways in which Germany and Austria-Hungary tried to coordinate their military strategy to prepare for the possibility of a two-front war and has focused particularly on the often neglected role of Austria-Hungary. Unquestionably, Germany took the lead in overall strategy, but relations between the two powers in military planning were not always close, and, in fact, there was little coordination on the details of fighting side-by-side.

During the tenures of first the Elder Moltke and Beck, and then Waldersee and Beck, the two General Staffs engaged in close relations, but they reached no formal strategic or tactical understandings. When Schlieffen became Chief of the German General Staff, this rapport deteriorated badly partly because of Schlieffen's preoccupation with Germany's own military problems and partly because he considered Austria-Hungary's military capabilities so low that she would assume a purely defensive posture should war with Russia break out. As he saw it, Germany was on her own and should keep her plans secret. Between 1896 and 1909, only Christmas greetings were exchanged between the two General Staffs.

In 1905, however, Schlieffen developed a plan whereby Germany could deal with the problem of a two-front war. This plan fit the situation of 1905 very well. Since Russia had been badly weakened by her defeat in the Russo-Japanese war, Germany would field the greatest part of her

forces against France and crush her in four weeks; then troops would be
transported across Germany to the east to a weak and sluggishly mobilizing Russia. This country, temporarily being held off by a relatively small
contingent of German troops, would be defeated. The strategy became
dogma in German military circles and was not altered by the summer of
1914 even though circumstances (particularly relative to Russia) had
changed considerably.

Only when the Bosnian Crisis led to a reopening of the old Austrian-
Hungarian-Russian conflict in the Balkans did the Austro-Hungarian and
German military leaders come into close contact again. To Austria-Hungary, the Dual Alliance appeared to be paying off when German saber-
rattling caused Russia to back down. At this point, in 1909, Conrad and
the Younger Moltke began an exchange of letters that some historians
have mistakenly construed to be a formal military pact between the two
powers. At most, however, they can be seen as general strategic understandings which originated during the emergency of the Bosnian Crisis
and from which, in 1914, both sides felt free to deviate. From the correspondence between Conrad and Moltke in the years 1909-1914 two general
points of agreement emerged: Austria-Hungary was to launch an offensive
northward between the Bug and Vistula Rivers with forty divisions to tie
down Russian forces and thereby protect Silesia and Prussia until Germany
could defeat France; and Germany would field twelve to fourteen first-line
and five reserve divisions in East Prussia and attack into Russian Poland
in the direction of Siedlce while her main forces were directed against
France. That is the full extent of the "agreements" between the two General
Staffs.

The loose nature of these agreements was dictated in part to the fact
that both Germany and Austria-Hungary had enemies other than Russia
with which they had to deal — German planning demanded that the
Russian front be secondary to the western front, and Austro-Hungarian
planning included Serbia, and possibly others. Perhaps it would be fair to
say that Conrad and Moltke did not want to tie their hands to some binding
strategy that might not allow them to determine their individual responses
to enemies they did not have in common. In any case, in 1914 both leaders
expected more from each other than they got and gave less than they had
"promised."

Whatever the nature of the agreements, neither Austria-Hungary nor
Germany committed the resources necessary to match the growing strength
of the Entente. Because of her humiliation in the Bosnian Crisis, Russia

entered upon an ambitious program to improve the effectiveness of her military machine. French money poured in, and the Russian railroads leading to the Austro-Hungarian and German frontiers were greatly improved; by 1914, Russia's railroads easily surpassed Austria-Hungary's. The Russian General Staff also engaged in a series of trial mobilizations which considerably reduced the time necessary to deploy troops for battle. Although Russia did not feel strong enough during the Balkan Wars of 1912-1913 to avoid backing down to another Austro-Hungarian-German threat, by 1914 she was no longer the same weak power upon which Schlieffen had based his strategy in 1905.

Not only did the Central Powers fail to keep pace in military expenditures, but they also failed to make the best use of the forces they had by winning some important allies to their side. This was an Austro-Hungarian problem in particular, since her entire southern frontier was exposed. Italy had joined the Dual Alliance in 1882 and promised to send troops to Alsace-Lorraine and to tie down French forces in the Alps to further aid Germany; for Austria-Hungary, the Italian connection meant that Austro-Hungarian units on the Italian frontier could be sent elsewhere. But Beck and Conrad felt that in a crisis Italy would not be reliable, and they were proven right in 1914.

After 1903, Serbia was clearly in the enemy camp. Austria-Hungary looked to Romania and even Bulgaria as allies. Romania was especially important because of her geographical position at Austria-Hungary's extreme right flank on Russia's border; it was hoped that she would field troops against Russia and thereby protect eastern Galicia. But Romanian support for the Dual Alliance was very shallow, and limited to King Carol and a few others. Most of the Romanians, like the Italians, harbored strong anti-Habsburg feelings. By 1914 Romania had not actively joined the Central Powers, and Bulgaria and Turkey were also reluctant. The Balkan Wars did not produce the ultimate test between the Entente and the Central Powers, but they did have some unfortunate effects: German and Austro-Hungarian diplomats disagreed over whether Bulgaria should be tied to the Dual Alliance, Romania became a very questionable ally, Serbia was aggrandized, and Bulgaria and Turkey were weakened.

In the summer of 1914, another confrontation between the Dual Alliance and Russia took place over Vienna's ultimatum to Serbia. This time Russia decided not to back down and instead ordered a partial mobilization in July. This maneuver, if allowed to proceed very far, would negate one of the crucial aspects of the Schlieffen plan — the more rapid mobilization of the Central Powers *vis-á-vis* Russia. The situation become so serious, and the diplomats understood it so poorly, that in Austria-Hungary and Germany the military leaders took over the leadership of the government on 30-31 July. Moltke saw that he must force Russia to stop mobilizing immediately or enter upon a war at once while there might still be a chance for the Schlieffen plan to succeed. An unsatisfactory Russian response to a German demand to demobilize led to war on 1 August and the other Great Powers followed Germany's lead. In the meantime, in early July, without consulting Germany, Conrad had ordered a rearward deployment plan for Galicia and had sent his Second Army, augmented by six and one-half infantry divisions, to the Serbian frontier to settle accounts in the area.

Even while the First World War was beginning there was no close military contact between Austria-Hungary and Germany and no reconfirmation between the two powers that they would fulfill the terms of their "agreements" to the full. Changes in the strategic situation in the preceding few years made the agreement imperative. Both sides seriously underestimated Russia — Conrad hoped that she would not support Serbia fully and had no real plans for a contingency in which a war with Russia would follow an outbreak of hostilities with Serbia. As it stood in August, Moltke fielded only ten divisions in East Prussia rather than the "promised" twelve to fourteen, and Conrad placed only thirty divisions in Galicia instead of the "agreed" forty. Obviously both powers regarded Russia secondarily and were straying from the pre-war "agreements".

In the fighting in the east in August and September it became apparent that both Germany and Austria-Hungary had not fulfilled the terms of their mutual understandings. In both cases, the troops designated to face Russia were insufficient and both sides initially suffered severe losses. Mutual recrimination was the result: Conrad correctly accused Moltke of not sending sufficient troops to the east as he had promised at Karlsbad in May and of not attacking in the direction of Siedlce. Moltke offered as excuses that his Eighth Army could be outflanked by Russian forces, that Italy had not fulfilled her promises, that his forces were outnumbered in the west, and that Austria-Hungary had not secured Romania as an active ally. It is very possible that he never intended to launch an attack into Poland and that he expected his allies to carry the burden in the east while he merely defended German territory from Russian invasion. To Moltke's credit it may be said that his Eighth Army, insufficient as it was, did tie down twelve Russian corps (he had agreed since 1909 to tie down only nine and one-half) and that he did win two great defensive victories at Tannenberg and the Masurian Lakes; also, to the detriment of his offensive into France, he had shifted two corps from the west to the east to fortify the Eighth Army. He had done the best he could with the forces he had committed to the area.

Compared to those of the Germans, however, the Austro-Hungarians' errors and miscalculations were even more serious, particularly relative to the front in eastern Galicia. Not only had Austria-Hungary failed to win Romania to her side, but Conrad, by ordering the rearward Galician deployment and by sending the Second Army to Serbia instead of to eastern Galicia, left the area east and southeast of Lemberg extremely vulnerable from the start to massive Russian forces that reconnaissance and intelligence missions had failed to detect. If the Schlieffen plan had any chance of success, which is doubtful, Austria-Hungary had to send almost everything she had against Russia. Conrad did not do this in the crucial early stages of fighting, and he did not inform Moltke of his intentions. More ironic was that the long-desired victory over Serbia was not gained, and that potential Balkan allies were not impressed by Austria-Hungary's performance.

As to the fighting itself, Conrad could, and did, claim that he had fulfilled at least one part of the "agreements," that is, the attack by the Austro-Hungarian First and Fourth Armies north between the Bug and Vistula Rivers into Poland. But this advance was only temporary and was thrown back by the Russians, who were launching a massive assault into poorly defended eastern Galicia toward Lemberg. The result was that by 11 September, after the second battle of Lemberg, Austria-Hungary was on the defensive and had to withdraw behind the San River line and await German aid. It was, however, not until 18-20 September that the Austro-Hungarian and German General Staffs established permanent and close relations.

By then it was too late to reverse the military situation. In the west the Germans were stopped at the battle of the Marne and in the east they had won only defensive victories within East Prussia. Historians have rightly judged these events to be crucial, but they have neglected the vital significance of the battles of Lemberg and the Austro-Hungarian role in the earliest stage of the war. The battles of Lemberg (26 August to 3 September and 7-11 September) decimated the Austro-Hungarian officer corps, led to Conrad's accusation that Germany had left Austria-Hungary in the lurch, ended all hope that Austria-Hungary could assume an offensive role in the east (precisely what Schlieffen had predicted in 1905), and forced Moltke to turn his attention, and some of his forces, to the east.

One of the great difficulties compounding the situation was the deplorable lack of communication among the military and diplomatic leaders within and between the two powers. Neither the German nor the Austro-Hungarian diplomats were fully aware of the nature of the "agreements" between Moltke and Conrad or of the strategic considerations behind the Schlieffen plan. This explains why the diplomats were pushed aside by the military in late July.

Diplomatic and military historians specializing in German or Austro-Hungarian history have also been slow to coordinate their findings or produce an accurate picture of the events and developments leading up to World War I. They have generally failed to see that, everything considered, the Central Powers entered World War I with an outmoded war strategy for which they were ill-prepared, and which, at least in the east, they implemented rather poorly.

Notes

Chapter I
Elder Moltke 1871-1888

1. Hajo Holborn, "Moltke and Schlieffen: The Prussian-German School," *Makers of Modern Strategy: Military Thought from Machiavelli to Hitler*, ed. Edward Mead Earl, (New York: Atheneum, 1967), p. 180.
2. Ferdinand von Schmerfeld, ed., *Helmuth Moltke, Die deutschen Aufmarschpläne 1871-1890* (Berlin: E.S. Mittler & Sohn, 1929), p. 1 (Moltke, *Aufmarschpläne*). See Gerhard Ritter, *The Schlieffen Plan: Critique of a Myth* (New York: Frederick A. Praeger, 1958), p. 18 (Ritter, *SP*).
3. Moltke, *Aufmarschpläne*, Nr. 1, p. 9; Gerhard Ritter, *Staatskunst und Kriegshandwerk. Das Problem des Militärismus in Deutschland*, II: *Die Hauptmächte Europas und das Wilhelmische Reich, 1890-1914* (Munich: Verlag R. Oldenbourg, 1960), p. 244 (Ritter, *SK*), and Ritter, "Der Anteil des Militärs an der Kriegskatastrophe von 1914," *Historische Zeitschrift*, (*HZ*) 193 (1961), p. 73, and Ritter, *SP*, p. 18.
4. Reichsarchiv: *Der Weltkrieg*, I, *Die militärischen Operationen zu Lande* (Berlin: E.S. Mittler & Sohn, 1925), pp. 3-4, 6 (*RAWK*); Moltke, *Aufmarschpläne*, Nr. 1, pp. 4, 9; Gerhard Ritter, *Staatskunst und Kriegshandwerk*, I, *Die Altpreussische Tradition (1740-1889)* (Munich: Verlag R. Oldenbourg, 1954), p. 230, and "Anteil," pp. 73-74; H. Von Staabs, *Aufmarsch nach zwei Fronten: Auf Grund der Operationspläne 1871-1914* (Berlin: E.S. Mittler & Sohn, 1925), p. 10; Helmut Otto, "Zum strategisch-operativen Zusammenwirken des deutschen und österreichisch-ungarischen Generalstabes bei den Vorbereitungen des Ersten Weltkrieges, "*Zeitschrift für Militärgeschichte*," II (Berlin: 1963), p. 425. The problem for Germany was the 1,000-kilometer distance between eastern and western fronts, and the eastern frontier, stretching for 900 kilometers. The vulnerability

of this area produced a situation in which the land east of the Vistula River was seriously threatened. *RAWK*, I, pp. 3-4.

5. See Map, Appendix.

6. Germany, *Die Gross Politik der Europäischen Kabinette 1871-1914 (GP)*. Edited by Johannes Lepsius, Albrecht Mendelssohn-Bartholdy and Friedrich Thimme, 40 vols. (Deutsche Verlagsgesellschaft für Politik), pp. 34-37; George H. Rupp, "The Reichstadt Agreement," *American Historical Review*, 30 (1925), pp. 503-510.

7. *GP*, II, Nrs. 265-266; W.N. Medlicott, *The Congress of Berlin and After: A Diplomatic History of the Near Eastern Settlement 1887-1880* (Edinburgh: Frank Cass & Co., Ltd., 2nd edition, 1963), p. 2; Hans Uebersberger, *Österreich zwischen Russland und Serbien: Zur südslawischen Frage und der Entstehung des Ersten Weltkrieges* (Cologne-Graz: Verlag Herman Bohlaus Nauchf, 1958), p. 6.

8. Moltke, *Aufmarschpläne*, Nr. 16, pp. 66-67; Ritter, *SP*, pp. 18-19; Staabs, *Aufmarsch nach zwei Fronten*, p. 12; *RAWK*, I, pp. 6-7.

9. Ritter, *SP*, p. 19; *SK*, II, pp. 230-231; and "Anteil," p. 73; Staabs, *Aufmarsch nach zwei Fronten*, p. 113.

10. Kriegsarchiv: Generalstab, Operations-Bureau (KAGOB), Faszikel (fasz.) 1, Aufmarschelaborat, Kriegsfall "R" (Russland), 1876, 1877, 1880, 1882-1883.

11. Moltke, *Aufmarschpläne*, Nr. 19, p. 77; Ritter, *SK*, II, pp. 244-245.

12. Moltke, *Aufmarschpläne*, Nr. 19, pp. 78, 81, 87; Eberhard Kessel, *Moltke* (Stuttgart: K.F. Koehler Verlag, 1957), p. 675.

13. Moltke, *Aufmarschpläne*, Nr. 19, p. 80; Wolfgang Foerster, *Aus der Gedankenwerkstatt des deutschen Generalstabes* (Berlin: E. S. Mittler & Sohn, 1931), p. 44; and "Politische Ziele und Operationspläne, *Deutscher Offizierbund (DOB)*, Nr. 6 (1926), p. 214.

14. Moltke, *Aufmarschpläne*, p. 77, Nrs. 19-20 (also *GP*, III, Nr. 505).

15. Ibid., Nr. 20, p. 83; Nr. 22, p. 87.

16. Ibid., Nr. 22, pp. 81, 86, 87-89, 94-95, 97; Otto, "Zusammenwirken," p. 425; Kessel, *Moltke*, p. 675; Ritter, *SP*, p. 19; Gerhard Seyfert, *Die militärischen Beziehungen und Vereinbarungen zwischen dem deutschen und dem österreichischen Generalstab vor und bei Beginn des Weltkrieges* (Inaugural-Dissertation, Leipzig: Buchdrückerei Joh. Moltzen, 1934), p. 12; *RAWK*, I, p. 7.

17. KAGOB, fasz, 2, Memoire über Kriegsfall "I+R" (Italien und Russland) Text; KAGOB, fasz. 3, Memoire über Kriegsfall "I+R" Beila-

ge; KAGOB, fasz. 6, Geschichte des Aufmarsches gegen "R" (Russland), 1880-1905.

18. KAGOB, fasz. 2, K. K. Chef Gstbs., Res. Nrs. 98, 3ll; KAGOB, fasz. 4, Aufmarschelaborat 1881-1883, K. K. Chef Gstbs., Res. Nrs. 98, 311. According to Habsburg intelligence, Russia possessed twenty-eight cavalry divisions, to Austria-Hungary's seven. KAGOB, fasz. 3, "Darstellungen des russischen Aufmarsches gegen Deutschland und Österreich-Ungarn."

19. *GP*, III, Nrs. 556-572; Alfred Francis Pribam, *The Secret Treaties of Austria-Hungary* (Cambridge: Harvard University Press, 1922), II, pp. 18, 28, 41-42; Fritz Fellner, *Der Dreibund. Europäische Diplomatie vor dem ersten Weltkrieg* (Vienna: Verlag für Geschichte und Politik, 1960), pp. 11-16, 88-90.

20. Kriegsarchiv: Nachlässe, Archiv Beck-Rzikowsky (KANB), Folio VII, 1882, Nr. 208/3; KAGOB, fasz. 4, Denkschrift über die militärischen Vorarbeiten für das Jahr 1883; fasz. 32, Kriegsfall Russland Geheimakten (1878-1902); Edmund Glaise-Horstenau, *Franz Josephs Weggefährte. Das Leben des Generalstabschefs Grafen Beck* (Vienna: Amalthea, Verlag, 1930), pp. 285-287.

21. The 12 July 1882 Beck memoranda set the foundation of Beck's discussions with the German General Staff. KANB, Folio VII, 1882, Nrs. 208/3, 212; KAGOB, fasz. 2, and fasz. 32; Glaise-Horstenau, *Weggefährte*, pp. 285, 287, 292. The idea of a large encircling movement had actually been considered during the Crimean War, 1854-1856, and remained an integral part of the strategic operative plans for an eastern campaign until 1915. Rudolf Krieger, *Die Entwicklung des Conradischen Offensivgedankens*, dissertation, Friedrick Wilhelms University (Stuttgart: W. Kohlmanner, 1934), p. 2; *RAWK*, I, p. 4.

22. KAGOB, fasz. 6; fasz. 4; Ritter, *SK*, II, p. 291; Glaise-Horstenau, *Weggefährte*, pp. 284, 286; KANB, Folio VII, Nr. 211.

23. A secondary force would deploy between Posen and Thorn to advance from the left Vistula bank towards Warsaw, Poland. KAGOB, fasz. 32; Glaise-Horstenau, *Weggefährte*, pp. 286-288; KANB, Folio VII (1882), Nrs. 207, 208/1.

24. KANB, Folio VII, Exposé . . . .

25. KAGOB, fasz. 1; fasz. 5, K. K. Chef Gstbs., Res. Nr. 682; fasz. 4, Denkschrift . . .; fasz. 6; KANB, Folio VII, Nr. 272.

26. KAGOB, fasz. 4; fasz. 5, K. K. Chef Gstbs., Res. Nr. 519.

27. KAGOB, fasz. 6; Glaise-Horstenau, *Weggefährte*, p. 283.

28. KAGOB, fasz. 7, Aufmarschelaborat 1884-1886, k.u.k. Chef Gstbs., Res. Nr. 553.

29. KAGOB, fasz. 6; fasz. 7, "Denkschrift zum Kriegsfall gegen Russland", Gstb., Res. Nr. 362, Eb.B. Nr. 863, Res. Nr. 379; Glaise-Horstenau, *Weggefährte*, p. 292.

30. KAGOB, fasz. 7.

31. Luigi Albertini, *The Origins of the War of 1914*, 3 vols. (New York: Oxford University Press, 1952), I, p. 50. For Bismarck's warnings against Habsburg Balkan adventures, *GP*, IV, p. 338; V, pp. 8, 26, 35, 136, 149.

32. Moltke, *Aufmarschpläne*, pp. 120-121, Nr. 28; Glaise-Horstenau, *Weggefährte*, pp. 294-295.

33. KAGOB, fasz. 6; fasz. 8, Aufmarschelaborat 1887-1888, K. K. Chefs Gstb., Res. Nr. 355.

34. Moltke, *Aufmarschpläne*, Nr. 33, pp. 137, 143; Alfred Graf von Waldersee, *Denkwürdigkeiten des General-Feldmarschalls Alfred von Waldersee*, edited by Heinrich Otto Meisner, I, *1832-1888* (Stuttgart & Berlin: Deutsche Verlagsanstalt, 1923), pp. 334, 339; Friedrich von Boetticher, "Der Lehrmeister des neuzeitlichen Krieges," D. von Cochenhausen, *Von Scharnhorst zu Schlieffen 1806-1906. Hundert Jahre preussisch-deutscher Generalstab* (Berlin: E.S. Mittler & Sohn, 1933), pp. 218-219.

35. *GP*, VI, Nr. 1163, p. 61; Kessel, *Moltke*, pp. 716, 723-724; Ritter, *SK*, II, p. 234.

36. Moltke, *Aufmarschpläne*, Nr. 33, pp. 137-145, 147. See Glaise-Horstenau, *Weggefährte*, pp. 301, 304, 307-310, 313, 461; Waldersee, *Denkwürdigkeiten*, I, pp. 294, 295, 302, 308, 319, 334, 337-339; Kessel, *Moltke*, pp. 721-722.

37. *GP*, VI, Nr. 1183; Moltke, *Aufmarschpläne*, Nr. 33, p. 147; Glaise-Horstenau, *Weggefährte*, pp. 304, 313, 461; Waldersee, *Denkwürdigkeiten*, I, p. 319; Kessel, *Moltke*, pp. 721-722.

38. *GP*, VI, Nr. 1236; Glaise-Horstenau, *Weggefährte*, pp. 300-301, 307-308, 312; Gerhard Ritter, "Die Zusammenarbeit der Generalstäbe Deutschlands und Österreich-Ungarns vor dem Ersten Weltkrieg," *Zur Geschichte und Problematik der Demokratie. Festgabe für Hanz Herzfeld* (Berlin: Duncker & Humbolt, 1958), p. 527.

39. KAGOB, fasz. 6; fasz. 8.

40. Moltke, *Aufmarschpläne*, pp. 149, 151.

Chapter II
Military Planning 1888-1905

1. Waldersee, *Denkwürdigkeiten*, I, pp. 342, 349, 350, 363, 394; II, pp. 16 footnote, 85; Kessel, *Moltke*, pp. 720, 721.
2. Hans Mohs (ed.), *General-Feldmarschall Alfred von Waldersee in seinem militärischen Wirken. Auf Veranlassung von Waldersee*, II (Berlin: Verlag R. Eisenschmidt, 1929), Nr. 24B, pp. 295, 296; Nr. 24D.
3. KAGOB, fasz. F89a, Conrad, Chef der Generalstäbe; Militär-politische Korrespondenz; *GP*, VI, Nr. 1307; VII, Nr. 1464; Waldersee, *Denkwürdigkeiten*, I, pp. 376, 409; II, p. 9; Horst Brettner-Messler, "Die militärischen Absprachen zwischen den Generalstäben Österreich-Ungarns und Italiens vom Dezember 1912 bis Juni 1914," *Mitteilungen des österreichischen Staatsarchivs* 33 (1970), p. 229; Mohs, *Waldersee*, II, Nrs. 31A and B, pp. 306-307; Glaise-Horstenau, *Weggefährte*, p. 318.
4. KAGOB, fasz. 8; Moltke, *Aufmarschpläne*, pp. 149, 150, 152, 154. For German intentions, Mohs, *Waldersee*, II, Anlage 1, p. 303, Anlage 2, pp. 304, 308.
5. Moltke, *Aufmarschpläne*, Nr. 34, pp. 150-156; Ritter, "Zusammenarbeit," p. 549; Mohs, *Waldersee*, II, pp. 303-308; Wilhelm Groener, *Das Testament des Grafen Schlieffen. Operative Studien über den Weltkrieg* (Berlin: E. S. Mittler & Sohn, 1927), p. 43.
6. Mohs, *Waldersee*, II, Richtlinien für 1889-1890, Nov. 1888, p. 315.
7. Mohs, *Waldersee*, Denkschrift Moltke, Auszug, Feb. 1888, p. 308.
8. KAGOB, fasz. 6; fasz. 9; Aufmarschelaborat 1889-1890, Chef des Gstb., Res. Nr. 402. This concept is similar to Conrad's in 1914.
9. KAGOB, fasz. 6; fasz. 9, Chef des Gstb., Res. Nr. 402.
10. Moltke, *Aufmarschpläne*, pp. 150, 151, 166; Mohs, *Waldersee*, Nr. 41A,B,C, pp. 328-330; Groener, *Testament*, pp. 47-48, and *Graf Schlieffen und der Weltkrieg* (Berlin: E. S. Mittler & Sohn, 1925), p. 105.
11. KAGOB, fasz. 9, K. K. Chef des Gstb., Res. Nr. 413; Gstb. Res. Nr. 1023/II.
12. Mohs, *Waldersee*, Nr. 44, pp. 336-337; Nr. 48, pp. 340-341; Moltke, *Aufmarschpläne*, p. 166.

13. *GP*, VI, Nr. 1343; Waldersee, *Denkwürdigkeiten*, I, pp. 407-410; Glaise-Horstenau, *Weggefährte*, pp. 337-338.
14. Moltke, *Aufmarschpläne*, p. 151; Seyfert, *Die militärischen Beziehungen*, p. 73.
15. *GP*, VII, Nrs. 1357, 1360-1362, 1373; Waldersee, *Denkwürdigkeiten*, II, pp. 118-119.
16. Holborn, "Moltke and Schlieffen," pp. 193-194; Ritter *SP*, p. 49.
17. Prussia, Grosser Generalstab, *Dienstschriften des Chefs des Generalstabes der Armee Generalfeldmarschall Graf von Schlieffen*; Generalstab des Heeres. Abteilung, 2 Vols. (Berlin: E. S. Mittler & Sohn, 1937); Holborn, "Moltke and Schlieffen," p. 190; Ritter, *SP*, pp. 50, 51, 67, 73.
18. Otto, "Zusammenwirken," pp. 428 footnote, 429; von Kuhl, *Der deutsche Generalstab*, p. 171.
19. Groener, *Testament*, p. 110; Foerster, *Gedankenwerkstatt*, pp. 54-55; Ritter *SP*, Appendix.
20. Ritter, *SP*, pp. 22, 24; Staabs, *Aufmarsch nach zwei Fronten*, p. 14.
21. *RAWK*, I, p. 8; Foerster, *Gedankenwerkstatt*, p. 48; Ritter *SP*, p. 25.
22. KAGOB, fasz. 32; Seyfert, *Die militärischen Beziehungen*, p. 38.
23. Ritter, *SP*, p. 22; von Kuhl, *deutsche Generalstab*, p. 164.
24. KAGOB, fasz. 32; Glaise-Horstenau, *Weggefährte*, p. 346; Ritter, "Zusammenarbeit," p. 530, and *SP*, pp. 23, 24; Rudolf Kiszling, "Generalfeldmarschall Graf Schlieffen und die Kriegsvorbereitungen Österreich-Ungarns," *MTM* (1933), p. 154.
25. General Erich von Ludendorff, *Meine Kriegserinnerungen 1914-1918* (Berlin: E. S. Mittler & Sohn, 1921) p. 46; Ritter, *SP*, pp. 24-25; *RAWK*, II, pp. 1, 8.
26. Otto, "Zusammenwirken," pp. 431, 432; *GP*, VII, Nrs. 1433, 1434; Ritter, *SP*, pp. 22, 28; "Zusammenarbeit," p. 531, and *SK*, II, p. 254; Seyfert, *Die militärischen Beziehungen*, p. 39.
27. KAGOB, fasz. 6; fasz. 10, Aufmarschelaborat 1891-1893, K. K. Chef des Gstb., Res. Nr. 203.
28. Ritter, *SP*, p. 28. See Glaise-Horstenau, *Weggefährte*, pp. 334, 346, 347-348.
29. KAGOB, fasz. 11, Behelf zum Aufmarschelaborat 1892, Gstb. Res. Nr. 323, Nr. 974/a 1893; KAGOB, fasz. 12, Behelf zum Aufmarschelaborat 1894, Studie über die Einteilung der Kavallerie; KAGOB, fasz. 13, Behelf zum Aufmarschelaborat 1895, Chef des Gstbs. Nrs. 315 Res., 233/Ev. Bur. 1894; KAGOB, fasz. 6; fasz. 14,

Aufmarschelaborat 1894-1896, Chef des Gstb., Res. Nr. 312; fasz. 15, Vergleich der Aufmärsche Österreich-Ungarn und Russland, 1894, 1896, 1897, 1898; Foerster, *Gedankenwerkstatt*, p. 51; Ritter, *SP*, p. 29.

30. Gunther Frantz, *Russlands Eintritt in den Weltkrieg: Der Ausbau der russischen Wehrmacht und ihr Einsatz bei Kriegsausbruch* (Berlin: Deutsche Verlagsgesellschaft für Politik und Geschichte, 1924), pp. 44-45, and *Russland auf dem Wege zur Katastrophe* (Berlin: Deutsche Verlagsgesellschaft für Politik und Geschichte, 1926), p. 55; Nikolai Golovin, *The Russian Campaign of 1914*, trans. A. G. S. Muntz (Fort Leavenworth, Kansas: The Command and General Staff School Press, 1931), p. 45; Turner, L.C.F., "The Russian Mobilization in 1914," *JCH*, 3 (1968), p. 66.

31. *GP*, X, Nrs. 2497, 2500; XI, pp. 114, 123; Glaise-Horstenau, *Weggefährte*, p. 380.

32. Glaise-Horstenau, *Weggefährte*, p. 351; Seyfert, *Die militärischen Beziehungen*, p. 40.

33. Glaise-Horstenau, *Weggefährte*, pp. 351-352; Ritter, "Zusammenarbeit," p. 530.

34. KAGOB, fasz. 12, Chef des Gstb., Res. Nr. 312; fasz. 6; fasz. 15, Auszug aus Res. Nr. 509; fasz. 13, Chef des Gstb., Res. Nrs. 315, 233, 540; KANB, Folio VII, Nr. 266/1.

35. KAGOB, fasz. 32, Beck to Schlieffen 30 May 1895; Glaise-Horstenau, *Weggefährte*, p. 377; Ritter, *SP*, p. 29, and "Zusammenarbeit," pp. 530, 532.

36. Ritter, *SP*, pp. 20-29, footnote 2; Glaise-Horstenau, *Weggefährte*, p. 351; Rudolf Kiszling, "Schlieffen und Kriegsvorbereitungen," p. 155.

37. KAGOB, fasz. 13, Gstb. Res. Nrs. 202, 233, 315; KAGOB, fasz. 14, Chef des Gstb., Ev. Büro Res. Nr. 540, and k.u.k. E.B.B., Res. Nr. 319/E.B.B; Glaise-Horstenau, *Weggenfährte*, pp. 353, 379.

38. KAGOB, fasz. 32, Schlieffen to Beck 12 July 1895; Glaise-Horstenau, *Weggefährte*, p. 377; Ritter, "Zusammenarbeit," p. 533.

39. KAGOB, fasz. 14; fasz. 32; Glaise-Horstenau, *Weggefährte*, p. 378; Ritter, *SP*, p. 29, and "Zusammenarbeit," pp. 531-532.

40. KAGOB, fasz. 6; Glaise-Horstenau, *Weggefährte*, pp. 377-379.

41. KAGOB, fasz. 32; Glaise-Horstenau, *Weggefährte*, pp. 377-379; Ritter, "Zusammenarbeit," pp. 534-536.

42. Ritter, *SP*, pp.30, 31; "Zusammenarbeit," pp. 531, 535; and "Anteil," p. 76; Glaise-Horstenau, *Weggefährte*, pp. 318, 346-353, 377-378.
43. Ritter, *SP*, p. 31.
44. KANB, Folio VII, Nr. 275.
45. Ritter *SP*, pp. 44, 90, 91, and *Sword and Scepter*, II, pp. 194-195, 199, 205; Foerster, *Gedankenwerkstatt*, pp. 115-117.
46. Germany, Reichstag, Untersuchungsausschuss über die Weltkriegsverantwortlichkeit, *Zur Vorgeschichte des Weltkrieges*, Heft 2: *Militärische Rüstungen und Mobilmachung* (Berlin: Verlag von Reimar Hobbing in Berlin, 1921), pp. 73-76; Ritter, *SP*, footnote 33.
47. von Kuhl, *Der deutsche Generalstab*, pp. 165-166.
48. KAGOB, fasz. 6.
49. Groener, *Testament*, p. 118; see KAGOB, fasz. 15.
50. KAGOB, fasz. 46, Chef Gstb. Nr. 1097.
51. KAGOB, fasz. 6; fasz. F89a; KANB, fasz. 242, Folio VIII, 1900-1905, Nr. 291; Glaise-Horstenau, *Weggefährte*, p. 394; Pribam, *Secret Treaties*, II, p. 116.
52. Glaise-Horstenau, *Weggefährte*, pp. 391, 395, 396; Bridge, *AHFP*, pp. 257-268.
53. KAGOB, fasz. F89a; *GP*, XVIII, 2, Nrs. 5825-5827, 5829; Albertini, *Origins*, I, p. 127.
54. *GP*, XIX, 1, Nrs. 6127, 6128; Pribam, *Secret Treaties*, I, pp. 236-239.
55. KAGOB, fasz. 6.
56. Feldmarschall Conrad (von Hötzendorf), *Aus meiner Dienstzeit*, I: *Die Zeit der Annexionskrise 1906-1909* (Vienna: Rikola Verlag, 1925), pp. 25, 57, 241.
57. Ritter, *SP*, p. 44, 46, 79, 97, 99; Foerster, *Gedankenwerkstatt*, pp. 9, 115-117.
58. *GP*, XIX, pp. 174, 175; Ritter, *SP*, Appendix, pp. 131-164.
59. Ritter, *SP*, pp. 131, 134-135, 136, 148-149, 152-153.
60. Ibid., pp. 7, 66, 143, 152.

Chapter III
The Bosnian Crisis, 1908-1909

1. Ritter, *The Sword and the Scepter*, I, p. 229.
2. Ritter, "Zusammenarbeit," pp. 537, 539.

3. Conrad, *Dienstzeit*, I, pp. 53, 54, 68-70.
4. Ottokar Czernin, *Im Weltkriege* (Vienna: Ullstein & Co., 1919), p. 9. One of Aehrenthal's main concerns was to gain greater freedom of action within the Triple Alliance. B. E. Schmitt, *The Annexation of Bosnia 1908-1909* (Cambridge: At the University Press, 1937), p. 7; Fellner, *Dreibund*, p. 68.
5. KAGOB, fasz. 6, Studie von 1907 Aufmarsch "R," Revision; fasz. 21, Aufmarschelaborat (Kriegsfall "R") 1907-1908, Res. Gstb. Nr. 2632.
6. KAGOB, fasz. 21; fasz. 6.
7. KAGOB, fasz. 21.
8. KAGOB, fasz. 6.
9. KAGOB, fasz. 21.
10. KAGOB, fasz. 6; fasz. 95, Denkschrift 1907.
11. For the groups (Staffeln) see Austria-Hungary, *Österreich-Ungarns letzter Krieg 1914-1918*, I: *Das Kriegsjahr 1914*, Herausgegeben vom Österreichischen Bundesministerium für Heereswesen und vom Kriegsarchiv (Vienna: Verlag Militärwissenschaftliche Mitteilungen, 1929), pp. 6-7, (*OSTAOULK*); Bundesministerium für Landesverteidigung, Militärwissenschaftliche Abteilung, *Der Österreichisch-Ungarische Aufmarsch im Juli-August 1914*; Rudolf Kiszling, "Österreich-Ungarns Kriegsvorbereitungen, Mobilisierung, Aufmarsch und Operationspläne im Sommer 1914," *MTM*, 7 (1922), pp. 274-275; and Norman Stone, "Moltke-Conrad: Relations Between the Austro-Hungarian and German General Staffs, 1908-1914," *The Historical Journal*, 9 (1966), pp. 205-206.
12. Conrad, *Dienstzeit*, I, pp. 231-232.
13. Ludwig Bittner and Hans Uebersberger (eds.) *Österreich-Ungarns Aussenpolitik von der Bosnischen Krise 1908 bis zum Kriegsausbruch 1914*, I: *13. März 1908 bis 26. Februar 1909*, Diplomatische Aktenstücke des österreichisch-ungarischen Ministeriums des Äusseren (Vienna & Leipzig: Österreichischer Bundesverlag für Unterricht, Wissenschaft und Kunst, 1930), Nr. 9 (*OUA*); Pribam, *Austrian Foreign Policy*, pp. 25-26.
14. Conrad, *Dienstzeit*, I, pp. 103, 106, 109; Schmitt, *Annexation*, pp. 12-13.
15. Conrad, *Dienstzeit*, I, pp. 113-116; *GP*, XXVI, *p. 247; OUA, I, Nr. 747;* Schmitt, *Annexation*, pp. 65, 146.
16. *GP*, XXVI, *Nrs. 9074, 9079,* quoted in Albertini, *Origins*, I, p. 231.

17. Conrad, *Dienstzeit*, I, varia; Stephen Verosta, *Theorie und Realität von Bundnissen: Helmreich Lammasch, Karl Renner und der Dreibund (1897-1914)* (Vienna: Europa Verlag, 1971), p. 343; Albertini, *Origins*, I, pp. 21-22, 268.

18. OUA, I, Nrs. 606, 610, 751-753; *GP*, XXVI, *Nr. 9156*, cited in Schmitt, *Annexation*, p. 95; Conrad, *Dienstzeit*, p. 132.

19. OUA, I, varia; *GP*, XXVI, *Nrs. 9127, 9145, 9156, 9157*, quoted in Albertini, *Origins*, I, p. 269; Conrad, *Dienstzeit*, I, pp. 129, 132; Schmitt, *Annexation*, p. 94.

20. KAGOB, fasz. F89a; Kriegsarchiv, Nachlass Conrad (KANC), A fasz. 6, Chef des Generalstabes 1906-1911; Conrad, *Dienstzeit*, I, pp. 631-632; Theobold Schäfer, "Deutsche Offensive aus Ostpreussen über den Narew auf Siedlce: Ergänzungsheft 1 zum Werke *Österreich-Ungarns letzter Krieg* (Vienna: Verlag der militärwissenschaftlichen Mitteilungen, 1930), p. 2.

21. Conrad, *Dienstzeit*, I, pp. 142, 634; *OUA*, I, Nrs. 751, 752, 848; *GP*, XXVI, Nr. 9145; *RAWK*, I, p. 5; *OSTAOULK*, I, p. 12; Ritter, "Zusammenarbeit," p. 538.

22. Conrad, *Dienstzeit*, I, pp. 140, 158; Otto, "Zusammenwirken," p. 434.

23. KAGOB, fasz. F89a; Conrad, *Dienstzeit*, I, pp. 380-381. Cited in Albertini, *Origins*, I, p. 270; *RAWK*, I, p. 5.

24. KAGOB, fasz. F89a; Conrad, *Dienstzeit*, I, pp. 381, 382. Cited in Albertini, *Origins*, I, p. 270; see Schäfer, "Deutsche Offensive," p. 2.

25. KAGOB, fasz. F89a; *GP*, XXVI, 2, Nr. 9393; Conrad, *Dienstzeit*, I, p. 382; Albertini, *Origins*, I, p. 270.

26. Ritter, *Sword and Scepter*, II, p. 243.

27. KAGOB, fasz. F89a; Conrad, *Dienstzeit*, I, pp. 386-387, 389, 390-393; Schäfer, "Deutsche Offensive," p. 3, 4; *RAWK*, I, pp. 6-7.

28. KAGOB, fasz. F89a; Conrad, *Dienstzeit*, I, pp. 394-396; *RAWK*, I, pp. 7-8; Schäfer, "Deutsche Offensive," p. 4; Ritter, "Zusammenarbeit," p. 540.

29. KAGOB, fasz. F89a; Conrad, *Dienstzeit*, I, p. 396, cited in Stone, "Moltke-Conrad," p. 208.

30. KAGOB, fasz. F89a; Conrad, *Dienstzeit*, I, p. 399.

31. KAGOB, fasz. F89a; Conrad, *Dienstzeit*, I, p. 401.

32. KAGOB, fasz. F89a; Conrad, *Dienstzeit*, I, p. 404; *OSTAOULK*, I, p. 13.

33. Conrad, *Dienstzeit*, I, p. 404; *RAWK*, I, p. 101; Max Freiherr von Pitreich, *1914. Die militärischen Probleme unseres Kriegsbeginnes. Ideen, Gründe und Zusamenhänge* (Vienna: Selbstverlag, 1934), p. 53.
34. KAGOB, fasz. F89a; Conrad, *Dienstzeit*, I, p. 405.
35. *GP*, XXVI, 2, Nr. 9460; Schmitt, *Annexation*, pp. 194-195; Albertini, *Origins*, I, p. 286.
36. *GP*, XXVI, Nrs. 9427, 9428; Schmitt, *Annexation*, pp. 197-199; E. C. Helmreich, *The Diplomacy of the Balkan Wars* (Cambridge: Harvard University Press, 1938), p. 25.
37. Conrad, *Dienstzeit*, I, pp. 162-163; Schmitt, *Annexation*, p. 225.
38. *OUA*, II, Nr. 1425; *GP*, XXVI, Nr. 9538; Schmitt, *Annexation*, pp. 210, 213, 216.
39. *GP*, *XXVI*, 2, Nr. 9501; Schmitt, *Annexation*, p. 245.
40. Conrad, *Dienstzeit*, I, p. 163; Schmitt, *Annexation*, p. 227.
41. Conrad, *Dienstzeit*, I, p. 161.
42. Ibid., p. 163; Ritter, *Sword and Sceptor*, II, p. 249; Otto, "Zusammenwirken," p. 434.
43. *GP*, XXVI, 2, Nr. 9563; Schmitt, *Annexation*, pp. 248-249.

Chapter IV
Strategic Planning and Military Agreements 1909-1914

1. Conrad, *Dienstzeit*, I, pp. 368, 582-584, 585-586.
2. KAGOB, fasz. F89a, Grundzüge Kriegsfall "R" 1909; Conrad, *Dienstzeit*, I, p. 373.
3. KAGOB, fasz. F89a, *Grundzüge . . .; Conrad, Dienstzeit*, I, p. 379.
4. Conrad, *Dienstzeit*, I, pp. 374, 375, 583.
5. KAGOB, fasz. 95, *Denkschrift 1909-1910; Conrad, Dienstzeit*, I, pp. 209-210, 260; II, pp. 54, 80.
6. KAGOB, fasz. 6; fasz. F89a; Conrad, *Dienstzeit*, II, pp. 54-55; KANC, B fasz. 1, Chef des Generalstabes 1907-1909.
7. KAGOB, fasz. F89a; Conrad, Dienstzeit, II, pp. 58-59; Schmitt, *Coming of the War*, I, p. 17.
8. *GP*, XXXVII, pp. 847-848; *OUA*, II, Nrs. 2312, 2554; IV, Nrs. 3663, 3991; Conrad, *Dienstzeit*, II, pp. 9-10, 80, 207, 208, 212.

9. KAGOB, fasz. 95, Denkschrift 1910, Res. Gstb. 410; Conrad, *Dienstzeit*, II, pp. 85, 444-445; pp. 53, 69 for "R-I-B"; KAGOB, fasz. 24, Aufmarschelaborate 1910-1911.

10. KA Militarkänzlei Franz Ferdinand, fasz. 202, KAMKFF Operative Studie, *RAWK*, II, pp. 16, 22, 54; Conrad, *Dienstzeit*, II, pp. 11, 57, 59, 85.

11. KAGOB, fasz. 95.

12. KAGOB, fasz. F89a, Direktiven für operative Arbeiten für 1911.

13. KAGOB, fasz. 179, "Ausbau der Eisenbahnen, Kriegsfall 'R'" Chef des Gstb., Res. Gstb. Nr. 4391.

14. KAGOB, fasz. 24, Gedankengang für die operative Verwendung; fasz. F89a.

15. Conrad, *Dienstzeit*, II, pp. 102, 103, 105, 106-109.

16. KAGOB, fasz. F89a, Geheim Nr. 13, 1912; _____, "Zur Geschichte der deutsch-österreichischen militärischen Beziehungen 1912," BM (1933), pp. 896-897.

17. KAGOB, fasz. 61, *Balkankrise 1912-1913, Unterredung mit Moltke;* E. C. Helmreich, *"An unpublished Report on Austro-German Military Conversations of November 1912," Journal of Modern History* (*JMH*), V (1933), pp. 205-207; Stone, "Moltke-Conrad," p. 212.

18. KAGOB, fasz. 25, "Aufmarsch "R" 1911-1912, Kriegsfall 'R'."

19. KAGOB, fasz. 25.

20. KAGOB, fasz. 110, Kundschaft und Rekognoszierung 1910-1914. A Russian deployment: 1910, 27 infantry and 18 cavalry; 1911, 39 infantry and 19 cavalry, fasz. 25.

21. KAGOB, fasz. 26, Aufmarschelaborat "R" 1912-1913, Chef des Gstbes., Res. Gstb. Nr. 4300.

22. KAGOB, fasz. 26.

23. KAGOB, fasz. 26; fasz. 34, "Konkrete Aufmarschbefehle Kriegsfall 'R'" and fasz. 183, Aufmarschentwurf Bergmann.

24. KAAOKETB, fasz. 1, "R+I" 1910-1912, "Verlegter Aufmarsch 1912-1913 und drohende Lage 1912-1913"; KAGOB, fasz. 26, "Massnahme bei Rückverlegung des Aufmarsches mit Res. Gstb. Nr. 4300 von 1911".

25. KAGOB, fasz. 26.

26. Ibid., E.B.B. Nr. 595 res. Rückverlegung "R" 1912-1913; fasz. 183, Referat zu den Bemerkungen des Eisenbahnbüros zum Aufmarsch gegen "R" 1913-1914; E.B.B. Studie für 1913-1914.

27. KAAOK, Allgemeine Registratur, fasz. 1, Akten Nr. 1-500, Chef des Generalstabes Besprechung 20.12.1912; KAAOK, fasz. 495, "R" Gruppe, aus Operations Nrs. 1-1117, August 1914.
28. KAGOB, fasz. 46; Conrad, *Dienstzeit*, II, pp. 354-364, 370-371, 408; *OSTAOULK*, I, p. 3.
29. GP, XXX, 2, Nrs. 11235, 11237, 11238, 11243, 11284, 11285, 11287; *GP*, XXXIV, 1, Nr. 12593; Foerster, "Die deutsch-italienische Militärkonvention," p. 400; Waldersee, "Über die Beziehungen des deutschen zum österreichisch-ungarischen Generalstabes vor dem Weltkrieg," *Berliner Monatshefte* (BM), VIII (1930), p. 123.
30. KAGOB, fasz. F89a; KANC, B fasz. 3; Conrad, *Dienstzeit*, III, pp. 85-92.
31. KAGOB, fasz. 91, *Alleruntertänigste Vorträge (Österreich-Ungarn), 1910-1911-1912-1913-1914;* KANC B fasz. 3; KAGOB, fasz. F89a; *OUA*, V, Nrs. 5696, 6366, 6832; VI, Nrs. 8244, 8384, 8833; *GP*, XXXIV, 2, Nrs. 13277, 13281, 13225; Conrad, *Dienstzeit*, III, pp. 258, 274.
32. KANC, B fasz. 3; KAMKFF, *41-25;* Conrad, *Dienstzeit*, III, pp. 38, 82, 84, 87-92; Waldersee, "Deutschlands Beziehungen zu Italien," pp. 641-643, 658-659, and "Beziehungen des deutschen zum österreichisch-ungarischen Generalstab," p. 123.
33. KAGOB, fasz. F89a, Res. Gstb. Nr. 120; KANC, B fasz. 3; Conrad, *Dienstzeit*, III, pp. 144-145; *RAWK*, II, p. 12.
34. KAGOB, fasz. F89a; KANC, B fasz. 3; Conrad, *Dienstzeit*, III, pp. 147-150.
35. Conrad, *Dienstzeit*, III, pp. 605-607.
36. KAGOB, fasz. 27, Aufmarschelaborat "R" 1913-1914.
37. Conrad, *Dienstzeit*, III, p. 608.
38. KAGOB, fasz. 183, Eisenbahnbüro, Studie für 1913-1914.
39. Georg Marcus, *Der Fall Redl*; Egon Erwin Kisch, *Der Fall des Generalstabschefes Redl* (Berlin: Verlag die Schmiede, 1924), and Robert B. Asprey, *The Panther's Feast* (London: Jonathan Cape Thirty Bedford Square, 1959).

Chapter V
The Balkan Wars, 1912-1913

1. *GP*, XXXIII, Nrs. 12087, 12127, 12135, 12162; Hugo Hantsch, *Leopold Graf Berchtold. Grandseigneur und Staatsmann* (Vienna: Verlag Styria, 1963), I, p. 298.

2. HHSTA:PA, XII, fasz. 424; KAGOB, fasz. 61, Zu Res. Gstb. Nrs. 4302, 4221; GP, XXXIII, Nrs. 12180 note, 12193, 12256; *OUA*, IV, Nrs. 3901, 3901; Frantz, *Russlands Eintritt*, pp. 20-21, 25, 61-63, 103, 104, Anlage 24, 31.

3. KA Militärkanzlei Seine Majestät (Franz Joseph), Nr. 18-2, 3-1, Chef des Gstb. Ev. Buro Nr. 2400; Conrad, *Dienstzeit*, II, pp. 174-175.

4. KAAOKETB, fasz. 1; KAGOB, fasz. 61, Res. Gstbs., Nr. 3980; HHSTA:PA, XII, fasz. Nr. 425, Liasse XLV: Balkankrieg 1912-1913, Unsere militärischen Massnahmen 1912-1913; KAGOB, fasz. 68, Kriegsfall "R," Entwicklung Galicia: Ausrüstung generell; *GP*, XXXIII, Nr. 12392; KAMKSM, Nr. 18-2, 3-1 de 1913; *OUA*, IV, Nrs. 3901, 3902; Frantz, *Russlands Entritt*, pp. 20-21, 42-43, 61-63 and Anlagen 25-26.

5. KAGOB, fasz. 61, Res. Gstb. Nr. 3980, and Op. Bureau Nr. 5917; *GP*, XXXIII, Nr. 12216; *OUA*, IV, Nrs. 4017, 4032, 4050, 4746, 5075, 6017.

6. Frantz, *Russlands Eintritt*, pp. 41, 46, 234, Anlagen 80, 81, 83, 85, 86, 87, 88; Robert Hoeniger, *Russlands Vorbereitung zum Weltkrieg auf Grund unveröffentlichter russischer Urkunden* (Berlin: E. S. Mittler und Sohn, 1919), p. 5; Suchomlinow, *Erinnerungen*, pp. 231, 233.

7. *GP*, XXXIII, Nrs. 12151, 12162, 12180 footnote, 12348, 12349, 12397, 12405; *OUA*, IV, Nrs. 3838, 3850, 3932, 4022, 4174, 4185, 4559; Albertini, *Origins*, I, pp. 388, 399; Kiszling, *Franz Ferdinand*, pp. 181-182.

8. KAGOB, fasz. 51, Ausbau der russischen Bahnen 1913; fasz. 61, Ev.Büro Nr. 2327/I; HHSTA:PA, XII, fasz. Nr. 424; GP, XXXIII, varia; KAGOB, fasz. 161, Akten aus dem Nachlass FML Schemua 1911-1912, Nr. 4685, and *KAMKFF*, fasz. 194, Balkankrisen 1912-1913, Res. Gstb. Nr. 4221; *OUA*, IV, Nrs. 3869, 3928, 4183.

9. *OUA*, V, Nrs. 4927, 4949, 5751; *GP*, XXXIII, varia.

10. KAGOB, fasz. *F89a; 61, 161;* KAMKFF, fasz. *194;* KAMKSM de 1913, *Nr. 18-2, 13-1; KAAOKETB,* fasz. *1; HHSTA:PA, XII,* fasz. *424, 440;* Türkei, Tagesberichte des Evidenzbüros des k.u.k. Generalstabes 1912X-1913II; *OUA,* IV, Nrs. 4449, 4526, 4550; *GP,* XXXIII, varia.

11. KAMKFF, fasz. 194 and fasz. 202; KAGOB, fasz. *61,* Res. Gstb. Nr. 5056; *GP,* XXXIII, varia.

12. Conrad, *Dienstziet,* II, pp. 376, 412.

13. KAMKFF, fasz. 194; KAGOB, fasz. *61,* Res. Gstbs. Nr. 5056; HHSTA:PA, XII, fasz. 425; fasz. 440, Ev.Büro Nr. 2327, Res., 3048; *GP,* XXXIII, Nr. 12405; XXXIV, 1, Nrs. 12392, 12394, 12455, 12629, 12393; *OUA,* IV, Nr. 4476, V, varia; Hantsch, *Berchtold,* II, pp. 349-350.

14. *OUA,* V, varia; *GP,* XXXIV, 1, Nrs. 12558 footnote, 12570, 12572.

15. HHSTA:PA, XII, fasz. 424, fasz. 440; KANC, B fasz. *2; GP,* XXXIII, Nr. 12489; *OUA,* V, Nrs. 5099, 5213.

16. *OUA,* V, Nrs. 5057, 5075, 5109, 5123, 5146, 5150.

17. *GP,* XXXIII, Nrs. 12415; XXXIV, 1, Nr. 12735; KAGOB, fasz. *F89a;* KANC, B fasz. *2, 3;* Conrad, *Dienstzeit,* II, pp. 387-388, 415.

18. HHSTA:PA, XII, fasz. 424, Nrs. 29550, 70B; fasz. 425, 440, Nrs. 5-7 Res.; KAGOB, fasz. *F89a;* KAMKFF, fasz *194;* KANC, B fasz. *2; GP,* XXXIV, 1, Nr. 12571; *OUA,* IV, Nr. 4689; Conrad, *Dienstzeit,* II, pp. 387-388, 415; III, pp. 69-70; Hantsch, *Berchtold,* I, pp. 341, 349, 352-353.

19. *GP,* XXXIII, Nrs. 12437, 12438; HHSTA:PA XII, fasz. 425, 440; KAMFF, fasz. 194.

20. *GP,* XXXIV, 1, Nr. 12584 and footnote; Conrad, *Dienstzeit,* III, p. 413; Theodor von Sosnosky, *Franz Ferdinand, der Erzherzog Thronfolger. Ein Lebensbild* (Munich and Berlin: Verlag von R. Oldenbourg, 1929), p. 270.

21. KAGOB, fasz. 61. See Golovin, *The Russian Army in the World War* (New Haven: Yale University Press, 1931), pp. 68-72, 97; Sushomlinow, *Erinnerungen,* varia.

22. KAMKFF, fasz. 194.

23. KAMKFF, fasz. 61, Res. Gstbs. Nrs. 5601, 5751; Conrad, *Dienstzeit,* II, pp. 12-13; Ritter, *SK,* II, pp. 251-252.

24. Fritz Fischer, *Krieg der Illusionen. Die deutsche Politik von 1911 bis 1914 (KI)* (Düsseldorf: Droste Verlag und Druckerei, 1969), pp. 233, 234-235, 241; Konrad H. Jarausch, *The Enigmatic Chancellor.*

Bethmann-Hollweg and the Hubris of Imperial Germany (New Haven: Yale University Press, 1973), pp. 134-135, contradicts Fischer's interpretation.
25. *GP*, XXXIII, Nr. 12474 and footnote; Jarausch, *Bethmann Hollweg*, pp. 133-134.
26. HHSTA:PA, XII, fasz. 424; KANC, B fasz. *3;* Conrad, *Dienstzeit*, III, pp. 69-71, 94, 121, 127, 131; Kiszling, "Russlands Kriegsvorbereitungen 1912," p. 190; *GP*, XXXIV, 1, Nr. 12619.
27. KAGOB, fasz. *90*, Conrad, Korrespondenz mit Aehrenthal 1911, Berchtold and Potiorek, 1913; KANC, B fasz. *3;* Conrad, *Dienstzeit*, III, p. 75; *GP*, XXXIV, 1, Nr. 12793.
28. KAGOB, fasz. F89a; Conrad, *Dienstzeit*, III, pp. 147-151.
29. KAGOB, fasz. *61;* fasz. *90*, Geheim Nr. 25-1913; KANC, B fasz. 3; Conrad, *Dienstzeit*, III, pp. 12-14, 128, 418; *GP*, XXXIV, 1, Nr. 12709; *OUA*, V, Nrs. 5919, 5942.
30. *GP*, XXXIV, Nrs. 12415, 12735, 12818; Albertini, *Origins*, I, pp. 434, 436.
31. *GP*, XXXIV, 1, Nrs. 12793, 12824; KANC, B fasz. 12; Conrad, *Dienstzeit*, III, pp. 145-146; Albertini, *Origins*, I, pp. 436-437.
32. KANC, B fasz. 12; *GP*, XXXIV, Nr. 12824; Conrad, *Dienstzeit*, III, pp. 144-147; Ritter, *SK*, p. 310.
33. KA Kriegsministerium Präs; Nrs. 51-2-3, 2344, 2458, 51-2-3/39; HHSTA:PA, XII, fasz. 424, Nrs. 3-4, Kriegs Nr. 1765.
34. KAGOB, fasz. *F89a;* KANC, B fasz. *3; See OUA*, V, Nr. 5751.
35. HHSTA:PA, XII, fasz. 424, Nrs. 2-5, 8, 9, 13-15; *GP*, XXXIV, 1, Nrs. 12791, 12805, 12891; Conrad, *Dienstzeit*, III, pp. 122, 127; *OUA, V,* varia; Hantsch, *Berchtold*, p. 392.
36. Conrad, *Dienstzeit*, III, pp. 187-188.
37. KANC, B fasz. 2, Referat, Evbüro, Russische Gruppe; KAKM Präs. 1914, Nrs. 56-4-1/2; KAKMSM, Jahresbericht über die russische Wehrmacht 1913, Präs. Nr. 1849 von 1914; *GP*, XXXIX, Nr. 15644; Conrad, *Dienstzeit*, III, pp. 513-515.
38. OUA, V, Nrs. 4989, 5006-5008, 5023-5025, and varia; *GP*, XXXIV, 1, Nr. 12819; *GP*, XXX, 2, Nrs. 11302, 11304.
39. *OUA*, VII, Nrs. 9548, 9604; Conrad, *Dienstzeit*, III, p. 645; Albertini, *Origins*, I, pp. 503, 504, 505.
40. GP, XXXIV, Nrs. 13475, 13483, 13486, 13490, 13505; *OUA*, VII, Nr. 8965; Fischer, *KI*, p. 593.
41. KAGOB, fasz. 61. Nr. 1506, and Ev. Nr. 3846-1913.

42. KAGOB, fasz. *90; GP,* XXXIV, 2, Nr. 13234; Conrad, *Dienstzeit,* III, p. 275.

43. *OUA,* VI, Nr. 6757; *GP,* XXXIV, 2, Nr. 13207, 13225; Conrad, *Dienstzeit,* III, pp. 272-273, 275, 294; Albertini, *Origins,* I, pp. 443, 444, 446.

44. *OUA,* VI, Nrs. 7460, 7515, 7528, 7614; *GP,* XXXV, Nrs. 13404, 13423, 13428, 13434; Albertini, *Origins,* I, p. 453.

45. *OUA,* VI, Nrs. 7814, 7934, 7964; Helmreich, *Diplomacy of the Balkan Wars,* pp. 353, 386.

46. GP, XXXV, varia; *OUA,* VI, Nrs. 7612, 7645, 7646, 7971; Hantsch, *Berchtold,* II, p. 460, 462, 465-466.

47. GP, XXXV, Nr. 13532; *OUA, VI,* Nrs. *7747, 7748;* KAGOB, fasz. F89a; KANC, B fasz. *3;* Conrad, *Dienstzeit,* III, pp. 85-92, 151; Paul G. Halpern, *The Mediterranean Naval Situation, 1908-1914* (Cambridge, Mass.: Harvard University Press, 1971), pp. 229-253.

48. KAGOB, fasz. 44, Res. Gstb, Nr. 3025; fasz. *90,* Chef Gstbs. Nr. 3512; KAKMSM, Ev.Büro Nr. 500 res. von 1914; Conrad, *Dienstzeit,* III, pp. 417-420; Oskar Regele, *Feldmarschall Conrad. Auftrag und Erfüllung, 1906-1918* (Vienna: Verlag Herold, 1955), p. 177; Ritter, *SK,* II, p. 296.

49. *OUA,* VII, Nr. 8157; Hantsch, *Berchtold,* II, pp. 467-469, 546; *GP,* XXXVI, Nrs. 13724, 13725; Albertini, *Origins,* I, pp. 463-464; Bridge, *AHFP,* p. 358.

50. *OUA,* VII, Nrs. 8197, 8198, 8279; Fellner, *Dreibund,* p. 80.

51. GP, XXXVI, 1, Nr. 13725; *OUA,* VII, Nrs. 8157, 8498; Helmreich, *Diplomacy of the Balkan Wars,* p. 398.

52. *OUA,* VII, Nrs. 8669, 8688, 8751, 8789; *GP,* XXXVI, 1, Nrs. 13823, 13836; Albertini, *Origins,* I, p. 492; Hantsch, *Berchtold,* II, pp. 481, 487.

53. GP, XXXVI, 1, Nr. 14161, 14172, 14174, 14178, 14181; *OUA,* VII, Nrs. 8697, 8960, 8965, 9009; Albertini, *Origins,* I, pp. 483, 485.

54. *OUA,* VII, varia; *GP,* XXXVI, 1, Nr. 14170; Conrad, *Dienstzeit,* III, pp. 478-479; Albertini, *Origins,* I, pp. 428-429, 485; Hantsch, *Berchtold,* II, pp. 492, 493; Helmreich, *Diplomacy of the Balkan Wars,* pp. 427, 428.

55. KAGOB, fasz. 91, Chef des Gstbs., Nr. 3921.

56. *OUA,* VII, Nr. 8934; Albertini, *Origins,* I, pp. 488-489; Hantsch, *Berchtold,* II, p. 506; R. Seton-Watson, "William II's Balkan Policy," *Slavonic Review* VII (1929), pp. 19, 20, and Appendix A, p. 27.

57. *OUA,* VII, Nrs. 9062, 9066; *GP,* XXXIX, Nrs. 15807, 15812, 15822; Uebersberger, *Österreich,* pp. 188-189.
58. KAGOB, fasz. *34;* fasz. F89a, Res. Gstb. Nr. 4851, Präs. Nrs. 15, 446; fasz. *91;* KANC, B fasz. *3;* Frantz, *Russlands Eintritt,* pp. 22, 23, 24-25, 46, Anlage 2, 30, 82; General Sergej Dobrorolskij, *Die Mobilmachung der russischen Armee 1914* (Berlin: DT Verlag für Politik, 1922), pp. 14, 16-17, 21.
59. Conrad, *Dienstzeit,* III, p. 487.
60. KAGOB, fasz. Nr. 90; KANC, B fasz. 4, Geheim Nr. 225; *OUA,* VII, varia; Conrad, *Dienstzeit,* III, pp. 482, 484; Hantsch, *Berchtold,* II, p. 510.
61. *OUA,* VII, Nr. 8990; *GP,* XXXIX, Nr. 15717; Kiszling, *Franz Ferdinand,* p. 273; Albertini, *Origins,* I, pp. 492, 494, 498.
62. KAKM Präs 40-29/1; Conrad, *Dienstzeit,* III, p. 492, see pp. 527-533, 551-555; *OSTAOULK,* I, pp. 1, 4.
63. KANC, B fasz. 4; *GP,* XXXIX, Nrs. 15805, 15807; *OUA,* VII, varia; Czernin, *Im Weltkriege,* pp. 106-107; Conrad, *Dienstzeit,* III, pp. 496, 634; Hantsch, *Berchtold,* II, p. 519.
64. KAGOB, fasz. 46; fasz. *90;* KANC, B fasz. 4; Conrad, *Dienstzeit,* III, pp. 495-496; Kiszling, *Franz Ferdinand,* p. 193.
65. OUA, VII, Nr. 9606; Seton-Watson, "William's Balkan Policy," p. 21, Appendix, II, p. 28.
66. Conrad, *Dienstzeit,* III, pp. 495, 503, 509, 513-514; *OSTAOULK,* I, pp. 4, 14; KAGOB, fasz. 61, Ev.Büro, Nr. 4949; KAMKFF, Nrs. 39-7-5/10; *OUA,* VII, Nrs. 9411, 9428; VIII Nr. 9714; Frantz, *Russland auf dem Wege,* pp. 21, 22, 23-35; Suchomlinow, *Erinnerungen,* pp. 244-246; Golovin, *Russian Campaign,* pp. 54-59.
67. *RAWK,* I, p. 17; *OSTAOULK,* I, p. 9; Ritter, *SK,* II, p. 336.
68. Conrad, *Dienstzeit,* III, p. 537.

Chapter VI
The July 1914 Crisis

1. Kriegsarchiv, Militärkänzlei Seine Majestät, Nrs. 18-1, 5-3; KAMKFF, Nr. 60-1-51; KANC, B fasz. 5; *OUA,* VII, varia; VIII, Nrs. 9627, 9817, 9837, 9918; *GP,* XXIX, Nrs. 15829, 15830, 15833;

Conrad, *Dienstzeit*, III, varia, IV, pp. 9, 28-29, 30; *RAWK*, II, pp. 17-18.

2. KAGOB, fasz. 34, Chef des Generalstabs, Res. Nr. 1645; fasz. 46; *OUA*, VII, Nrs. 9463, 9846, 9918, 9984; VII, Nr. 9627; *GP*, XXXIX, Nrs. 15823, 15827, 15830, 15837; Conrad, *Dienstzeit*, III, varia; Kiszling, *Franz Ferdinand*, p. 213.

3. KAGOB, fasz. F89a; *GP*, XXXIX, Nr. 15713 Anmerkung; *OSTA-OULK*, *I*, *p. 3;* Conrad, *Dienstzeit*, III, pp. 498, 599-600, 609-610, 627, 669, 673; Generaloberst Helmuth Graf von Moltke, *Erinnerungen, Briefe, Dokumente 1877-1916. Ein Bild vom Kriegsausbruch, erster Kriegsführung und Persönlichkeit des ersten militärischen Führers* (Stuttgart: Der Kommende Tag A. G. Verlag, 1922), pp. 8-9; KAMKFF, Mb 11-240, Nr. 100 res..

4. KAAOK, R Gruppe, fasz. 495; *OSTAOULK, I, pp. 3, 6;* KAMKFF, Nrs. 39-7-5, 42-6-2; KAKM Präs, Nr. 47-22-33; KANC, B fasz. 5; *RAWK, I, p. 11; OUA*, VII, Nr. 9411; VIII, Nr. 9659; Conrad, *Dienstzeit*, III, pp. 582, 602, 624; Moltke, *Erinnerungen*, pp. 24, 243.

5. Conrad, *Dienstzeit*, III, pp. 609-612, 672; *GP*, XXXIX, Nrs. 15840, 15854; Fischer, *KI*, pp. 576-578.

6. KANC, B fasz. 5, and fasz. 6; Conrad, *Dienstzeit*, III, p. 669; Theobald Schäfer, "Generaloberst von Moltke in den Tagen vor der Mobilmachung und seine Einwirkung auf Österreich-Ungarn," BM, IV (1926), p. 515; Ritter, *SK*, II, pp. 306-307.

7. *DD*, IV, p. 151; Conrad, *Dienstzeit*, III, pp. 582, 673; *RAWK*, II, pp. 24-25; Albertini, *Origins*, I, p. 562, II, p. 487.

8. *DD*, I, p. XIX and varia; GP, XXXIX, Nrs. 15839, 15843; *OUA*, VIII, varia; *RAWK, II, p. 25;* Hantsch, *Berchtold*, II, pp. 560, 610 footnote, 625; Conrad, *Dienstzeit*, IV, p. 266.

9. *DD*, I, Nr. 120; *OUA*, VIII, Nrs. 9894, 9899, 10007; Graf A. Pourtales, *Meine letzten Verhandlungen in St. Petersburg Ende Juli 1914: Tagesaufzeichnungen und Dokumente* (Berlin: Gesellschaft für Politik und Geschichte, 1927), Nr. 5; Fischer, *KI*, p. 705.

10. Conrad, *Dienstzeit*, IV, varia; *Ö. Rotbuch*, I, Nrs. 15, 22, 32; *DD*, I, Nr. 72; *OUA*, VIII, Nrs. 10755, 10758, 10769, 10835, 10837.

11. *OUA*, VIII, Nr. 9995; KANC, B fasz. 5; Conrad, *Dienstzeit*, III, p. 789.

12. *OUA*, VIII, Nr. 9984; *DD*, I, Nr. 13; *Ö. Rotbuch, I, Nr. 14;* Hantsch, *Berchtold*, II, pp. 568, 571, 682; Fischer, *KI*, pp. 687, 689-690.

13. Conrad, *Dienstzeit*, IV, pp. 36-37.

14. *DD*, I, Nr. 74; *Militärische Rüstungen und Mobilmachung*, Nr. 17; Albertini, *Origins*, II, p. 143 footnote; Ritter, *SK*, II, p. 282.

15. HHSTA:PA, I, fasz. 496, Präs Nr. 4529; *OUA*, VIII, Nrs. 10058, 10901; *DD*, I, Nrs. 15, 18; Hantsch, *Berchtold*, II, pp. 572-576; Bethmann-Hollweg, *Betrachtungen*, I, p. 135; *Ö. Rotbuch*, I, Nrs. 6, 7; Ropponen, *Die Kraft Russland*, pp. 263-264.

16. *DD*, I, Nr. 26; Gottlieb von Jagow, *Ursachen und Ausbruch des Weltkrieges* (Berlin: Verlag von Reimer Hobbing, 1919), pp. 98, 99, 100; Hantsch, *Berchtold*, II, p. 570; *OUA*, VIII, Nrs. 10118, 10146; Conrad, *Dienstzeit*, IV, pp. 43-49, 53-56, 132, 267.

17. *OUA*, VIII, Nr. 10125; Hantsch, *Berchtold*, II, pp. 582, 583; Fischer, *KI*, p. 696.

18. Conrad, *Dienstzeit*, IV, p. 108; Kiszling, "Mobilmachung Österreich," p. 205; Albertini, *Origins*, II, p. 377 note.

19. *OUA*,VII, Nrs. 10393-10395; Austria-Hungary, Miklós Komjáthy, ed., *Protokolle des gemeinsamen Ministerrates der Österreichisch-Ungarischen Monarchie (1914-1918)*, Budapest: Akadémiai Kiadó-Publikation des ungarischen Staatsarchives, 1966), pp. 150-154; Conrad, *Dienstzeit*, IV, pp. 54-55, 87-91.

20. Otto Hoetzsch, ed., *Die internationalen Beziehungen im Zeitalter des Imperialismus* (Berlin: Verlag von Reimar Hobbing, 1932), (*IB*), I, 4, Nr. 272; *IB*, I, 5, Nr. 25; Pourtales, *Verhandlungen*, p. 19, Nrs. 13, 19; *DD*, I, Nrs. 150, 204; *OUA*, VIII, Nr. 10618.

21. *DD*, I, Nr. 158; *OUA*, VIII, Nrs. 10633, 10701; Conrad, *Dienstzeit*, IV, pp. 109, 266-267; *Ö. Rotbuch*, II, Nr. 26.

22. KAAOKEBB, fasz. 4119, Tagebuch des (Oberst Straub), Eisenbahnbüros 20.7.-31.12.1914; KANC, B fasz. 12; *OSTAOULK, I, pp. 17, 41;* Conrad, *Dienstzeit*, IV, pp. 122, 266; Kiszling, "Die Kriegserklärung Österreich-Ungarns an Serbien," *BM*, 8 (1930), p. 1130; *RAWK*, II, p. 26.

23. KAAOK, fasz. 1, Chef des Gstbes., Nr. 2659, KM, Nr. 5-5339; res. 2740/II von 1914 and Kriegsfall R, Erläuterung zum konkreten Aufmarschbefehl; Emil Ratzenhofer, "Die österreichisch-ungarischen Aufmärsche gegen Balkan und Russland," *Österreichische Wehrzeitung (OWZ)*, 39(1927), p. 2; Conrad, *Dienstzeit*, IV, pp. 71, 110, 111, 113, 122-123, 267.

24. *OUA*, VIII, Nrs. 10580, 10656, 10772, 10792; *DD*, I, Nrs. 19, 213; Anhang IV, Nrs. 11, 12, 14; Anhang IVa, Nr. 2; Kiszling, *"Kriegs-*

erklärung an Serbien," p. 1131; *OUA,* VIII, Nr. 10792; Conrad, *Dienstzeit,* IV, pp. 131-132; Hantsch, *Berchtold,* I, p. 561.
25. IB, I, 5, Nrs. 42, 47, 79; Pourtales, *Verhandlungen,* p. 22, Nrs. 16, 39, 52; Dobrorolski, *Die Mobilmachung der russischen Armee 1914,* pp. 20, 21, 102, 114, 358; Hoeniger, *Russlands Vorbereitungen,* pp. 80-81, 100; Frantz, *Russlands Eintritt,* pp. 30, 91, 242, 243-250, 258, 259; Suchomlinow, *Erinnerungen,* p. 360.
26. KAAOK, fasz. 867, Meldungen und Nachrichten über die feindliche Lage, Evidenz Gruppe "R", Operationsabteilung 27.VII-15. VIII 1914; *OUA,* VIII, Nrs. 10687, 10717, 10724, 10755; Pourtales, *Verhandlungen,* varia; Bernhard Friedrich Eggeling, *Die russische Mobilmachung, und der Kriegsausbruch* (Berlin: E. Stalling, 1919), pp. 25-28; *DD,* I, varia.
27. KAAOK, fasz. 867, Ev.Büro Nr. 2908; *OUA,* VIII, Nrs. 10758, 10788; *DD,* I, Nrs. 230, 242, 320, II, Nr. 352, IV, Anhang IV, Nr. 11, V; Pourtales, *Verhandlungen,* p. 28, Nrs. 26, 30; Eggeling, *Die russische Mobilmachung,* p. 26.
28. *DD,* I, Nrs. 218, 236; *OUA,* VIII, Nrs. 10812, 10813; Schmitt, *Coming of the War,* I, p. 322; Albertini, *Origins,* II, p. 432.
29. *DD,* I, Nrs. 219, 281; II, p. 281; Conrad, *Dienstzeit,* IV, p. 133; Albertini, *Origins,* II, p. 472.
30. *DD,* I, Nrs. 155, 219; II, Nr. 342; Pourtales, *Verhandlungen,* p. 27, Nrs. 11, 53; Albertini, *Origins,* II, pp. 428, 475, 491, III, p. 43.
31. KAAOK, fasz. 867; *OUA,* VIII, varia; *DD,* I and II, varia; Pourtales, *Verhandlungen,* Nrs. 16, 22, 26, 30, 32, 33, 34, 39-42; Hantsch, *Berchtold,* II, pp. 627-628; *RAWK,* II, p. 32.
32. Hans von Zwehl, *Erich von Falkenhayn, General der Infantrie: Eine biographische Studie* (Berlin: E. S. Mittler & Sohn, 1926), p. 56; Moltke, *Erinnerungen,* pp. 19-23; *DD,* II, Nrs. 307, 308, 323, 335; *IB,* I, 5, Nr. 184; Conrad, *Dienstzeit,* IV, p. 148.
33. KANC, B fasz. 12; *OUA,* VIII, Nrs. 10946, 11002; *DD,* II, Nrs. 343, 385; *IB,* I, 5, Nr. 168; Pourtales, *Verhandlungen,* pp. 38, 40-41 and Nr. 54; *OSTAOULK,* I, p. 19; *RAWK,* I, p. 31.
34. *RAWK,* II, pp. 29-30, 71; *DD,* II, Nrs. 349, 352, 375, 376; Ritter *SK,* II, pp. 315-316; Schäfer, "Die deutsche Mobilmachung 1914," pp. 619, 620, 623, and "Moltke in den Tagen vor der Mobilmachung," pp. 516, 518-519.
35. *IB,* I, 5, Nr. 180.

36. *DD*, II, Nrs. 365a, 370; IV, Anhang V; Pourtales, *Verhandlungen*, Nr. 59; Eggeling, *Die russische Mobilmachung*, p. 28; KAAOK, fasz. 867; *OUA*, VIII, varia; Hoeniger, *Russlands Vorbereitung*, pp. 114-115.

37. *DD*, II, Nr. 349; IV, Anhang IV, Nr. 15; Anhang IVa, Nr. 2; Moltke, *Erinnerungen*, pp. 3-7; Ritter, *SK*, p. 345.

38. *DD*, II, Nrs. 342, 378, 399; *IB*, I, 5, Nrs. 224, 241; Ritter, *SK*, p. 318; Pourtales, *Verhandlungen*, Nrs. 53, 68.

39. Zwehl, *Falkenhayn*, p. 57.

40. *IB*, I, 5, Nr. 224; Dobrorolski, *Die Mobilmachung der russischen Armee*, p. 125; Fay, *Origins*, II, pp. 456, 465, 499.

41. *IB*, I, 5, Nrs. 243, 284; Dobrorolski, *Die Mobilmachung der russischen Armee*, p. 28; Fischer, *KI*, p. 707; Ritter, *SK*, p. 320.

42. Conrad, *Dienstzeit*, IV, p. 152; *DD*, IV, Anhang IV, Nrs. 16, 18; Ritter, "Anteil," p. 87.

43. Conrad, *Dienstzeit*, IV, pp. 151-152; Geiss, *Juli 1914*, II, p. 355, and Nr. 759; Kiszling, "Mobilmachung Sommer 1914: Österreich," pp. 209-210; Fischer, *KI*, p. 713; Schäfer, "Moltke in den Tagen vor der Mobilmachung," pp. 522-523; Ritter, *SK*, p. 319.

44. Conrad, *Dienstzeit*, IV, p. 155; Verosta, *Bündnissen*, p. 482.

45. KAAOK, R Gruppe, fasz. 495; *Ö. Rotbuch*, I, Nrs. 24, 32; Conrad, *Dienstzeit*, IV, p. 152; *OUA*, VIII, Nr. 11033; Fischer, *KI*, p. 718; *RAWK*, II, p. 28; Pitreich, *1914*, p. 139.

46. *OUA*, VIII, Nr. 10876; Conrad, *Dienstzeit*, IV, pp. 143, 147-148.

47. *OUA*, VIII, Nr. 11179; *IB*, I, 5, Nr. 338; *DD*, II, Nr. 349; III, Nrs. 487, 535, 536; IV, Anhang V; Pourtales, *Verhandlungen*, pp. 60, 62, 63, and Nrs. 88, 93, 94; Schmitt, *Coming of the War*, II, pp. 267, 310.

48. *DD*, III, Nr. 480; *IB*, I, 5, Nrs. 357, 480; Pourtales, *Verhandlungen*, p. 63, and Nr. 87; Geiss, *Juli 1914*, p. 324, and Nr. 888.

49. *DD*, II, Nr. 473; III, Nrs. 513, 515; IV, Anhang IV, Nr. 23; IV, Anhang VI (Pourtales); Pourtales, *Verhandlungen*, Nr. 323; Lamsdorff, *Militärbevollmächtigen Kaiser Wilhelms II.* Telegramm Nr. 9.

50. *DD*, II, Nr. 479; Conrad, *Dienstzeit*, IV, p. 152; *RAWK*, I, p. 33; Albertini, *Origins,*, II, p. 679; III, p. 39; Schäfer, "Moltke Tagen vor der Mobilmachung," p. 541. The telegram was sent at 1:45 p.m. and arrived at 4:10 p.m.

51. Conrad, *Dienstzeit*, IV, p. 152; Albertini, *Origins*, II, pp. 674, 675; KANC, B fasz. 12; KAAOK, fasz. 1.

52. *OUA*, VIII, Nr. 11119; *DD*, IV, Nr. 825; Conrad, *Dienstzeit*, IV, p. 151; Ö. *Rotbuch*, III, Nr. 50; Schäfer, "Moltke in den Tagen vor der Mobilmachung," pp. 536-537, 539; Verosta, *Bündnissen*, pp. 485, 500, 504. Conrad wrote the telegram at 7:30 p.m. on 30 July, but did not send the message until 8:00 a.m. 31 July, suggesting that either he was not anxious that General Moltke learn of the extent of the continued efforts against Serbia or that he awaited Franz Joseph's approval.

53. *OUA*, VIII, Nr. 11118; *DD*, II, Nr. 482; III, Nrs. 502, 503; *RAWK*, II, p. 29; Verosta, *Bündnissen*, pp. 486, 505-506; Ratzenhofer, "Aufmarsch gegen Balkan und Russland," p. 3.

54. *OUA*, VIII, Nrs. 10937, 11093; *DD*, II, Nr. 424; Conrad, *Dienstzeit*, IV, p. 147; Ritter, *SK*, II, pp. 326, 328.

55. *DD*, III, Nrs. 503, 601; *OUA*, VIII, Nr. 11125; Conrad, *Dienstzeit*, IV, pp. 156, 160-161; *RAWK*, II, p. 29.

56. KAAOK, R Gruppe, fasz. 495; Albertini, *Origins*, III, p. 47; Schäfer, "Moltke in den Tagen vor der Mobilmachung," p. 539.

57. Conrad, *Dienstzeit*, IV, p. 155; *RAWK*, I, p. 33; Ritter, *SK*, II, p. 325; Schäfer, "Moltke in den Tagen vor der Mobilmachung," p. 541.

58. KAAOK, R Gruppe, fasz. 495; Conrad, *Dienstzeit*, IV, pp. 155-156; Schäfer, "Moltke Tagen vor der Mobilmachung," p. 541.

59. HHSTA:PA, XII, fasz. 496, fasz. 516, Liasse XLVII 7) Geheime Verhandlungen mit Rumänien, Allgemeines Juli-August 1914; *OUA*, VIII, Nrs. 10952, 11131, 11133, 11134; *DD*, II, Nrs. 472, 506, 507, 582; Schmitt, *Coming of the War*, II, pp. 273-274.

Chapter VII
Mobilization

1. Farrar, L.L., Jr., *The Short-War Illusion. German Policy, Strategy and Domestic Affairs August-December 1914*, Santa Barbara, California: ABC Clio, Inc, 1973

2. KA, Ms1Wkg, Allg. Nr. 99, pp. 155-156, 174, and "Die Aufmärsche gegen B und R, Folge 40, p. 2; KA Ms1Wkg, Allg. Nr. A-65, and KA Ms1Wkg, Allg. Nr. 103, pp. 2, 28, 29, 97; KA Nachlass B/61 Nr. 11, pp. 23, 51.

3. Conrad, *Aus Meiner Dienstzeit*, Vol. IV, pp. 30-31, 33-37, 40; KA
   Ms1Wkg, Allg. Nr. 98, p. 13; Baron J. von Szillassy, *Der Untergang
   der Donau-Monarchie. Diplomatische Erinnerungen* (Berlin, 1921),
   p. 29; Imanual Geiss, *Julikrise und Kriegsausbruch 1914: Eine Do-
   kumentensammlung* (Julikrise), I, pp. 55, 56, and Nrs. 5, 16, 20, 26;
   Albertini, *Origins*, II, pp. 18, 29, 123.
4. Szilassy, *Der Untergang der Donau-Monarchie*, pp. 223, 224, 226;
   William Jannen, "The Austro-Hungarian Decision for War in 1914,"
   Essays on World War I: Origins and Prisoners of War (New York:
   Brooklyn College Press, 1983), pp. 55, 56, 59, 60, 61, 66, 69; Samuel
   Williamson, Jr., and Peter Pastor, eds., "Vienna and July 1914: The
   Origins of the Great War Once More," *Essays on World War I:
   Origins and Prisoners of War* (New York: Brooklyn College Press,
   1983), pp. 17, 18, 25; Gábor Vermes, *István Tisza* (Boulder, CO:
   East European Monographs, 1985), pp. 221-232.
5. Erwin Holzle, *Der Geheimnisverrat und der Kriegsausbruch*, Historisch-Politische Hefte der Ranke-Gesellschaft, Volume 23 (Göttingen: Musterschmidt Verlag, 1973), pp. 9, 20, 22, 30; Norman Stone,
   "Die Mobilmachung der österreichisch-ungarischen Armee 1914,"
   Militärgeschichtliche Mitteilungen, II (1974)," p. 76; Risto Rappo-
   nen, *Die Kraft Russlands. Wie beurteilte die politische und militärische Führung der europäischen Grossmächte in der Zeit von 1905
   bis 1914 die Kraft Russland* (Helsinki: Turun Sanomalehte ja Kirjapamo Osakeyhtic, 1968), p. 269.
6. KA Nachlass B/1041, Nr. 56, Österreich-Ungarns zähes Ringen mit
   seinen inneren Widerständen von 1866 bis 1918, p. 13; Ole Holsti,
   Crisis, Escalation, War (London: McGill-Queens University Press,
   1972), p. 124; Czernin, *In the World War*, p. 11; Albert Freiherr von
   Margutti, *Kaiser Franz Joseph. Persönliche Erinnerungen* (Vienna:
   Manzsche Verlags-und Universitätsbuchhandlung, 1924) (*The Emperor Franz Joseph and His Times*), pp. 401, 407; Stone, "Mobilmachung," p. 77.
7. *OUA*, VIII, Nr. 9966; *DD*, I, Nrs. 3, 72; Geiss, *Juli 1914*, I, p. 56,
   and Nr. 6.
8. Conrad, *Dienstzeit*, IV, pp. 53, 54; *Österreich-Ungarns letzter Krieg
   1914-1918 (OSTAOULK)*, I, *Kriegsjahr 1914* (Vienna, 1931), p. 14;
   KA Ms1Wkg, Allg. Nr. 103, p. 3.
9. Conrad, *Dienstzeit*, IV, pp. 36-38, 40; Albertini, *Origins*, II, pp. 135,
   462; KA Nachlass B/61, Nr. 11, pp. 28, 29, 41.

10. Conrad, *Dienstzeit*, IV, p. 53; Hantsch, *Berchtold*, II, p. 57.
11. See Margutti, *Franz Joseph*, p. 395.
12. KA MslWkg, Nr. 99, pp. 155-156, 174; Ratzenhofer, "Die Aufmärsche gegen B und R"; Folge 40, p. 2; KA MslWkg, Allg. Nr. A-65, and KA MslWkg, Allg. Nr. 103, pp. 2-28, 29, 97; KA Nachlass B/61, Nr. 11, pp. 23, 51.
13. Pitreich, *1914*, p. 124; KA MslWkg, Nr. 99, p. 185; KA MslWkg, Nr. 98, pp. 25, 30; Conrad, *Dienstzeit*, IV, p. 71.
14. KA MslWkg, Nr. 99, pp. 99, 185.
15. Enderes, "Die österreichischen Eisenbahnen," p. 60.
16. Conrad, *Dienstzeit*, IV, varia; KA Nachlass B/61, Nr. 11, pp. 29, 40; KA MslWkg, Allg. Nr. 98, p. 15.
17. KA Nachlass B/61, Nr. 11, pp. 39, 40, 41, 43, 48, 51.
18. Holze, *Der Geheimnisverrat*, pp. 2, 3, 5, 6, 7, 16-17, 18, 19, 20, 21.
19. *OUA*, VIII, Nr. 10393; Komjáthy, *Protokolle des gemeinsamen Ministerrates*, pp. 150-154; Geiss, *Juli 1914*, I, Nrs. 144, 145; Conrad, *Dienstzeit*, IV, pp. 54-55, 87-91.
20. Stone, "Mobilmachung," p. 78; Ratzenhofer, "Aufmärsche gegen B und R," Folge 39, p. 2; KA Nachlass B/61, Nr. 11, p. 41; KA MslWkg, Nr. 98 and Allg. A-65.
21. KAAOKEBB, fasz. 4119, 22 Juli; KA MslWkg, Allg. Nr. 103, p. 3; Conrad, *Dienstzeit*, IV, p. 87; Ratzenhofer, "Aufmärsche gegen B und R," Folge 39, p. 2.
22. Ritter, *SK*, II, p. 328.
23. *OSTAOULK*, I, p. 18; KA MslWkg, Allg. Nr. 98, pp. 25, 48; Conrad, *Dienstzeit*, IV, pp. 109-110, 122; Holsti, *Crisis, Escalation, War*, p. 32.
24. Conrad, *Dienstzeit*, IV, p. 272; KAAOKEBB, fasz. 4119, 24 Juli; Ratzenhofer, "Aufmärsche gegen B und R," Folge 30, p. 2, and KA MslWkg,Allg. Nr. 99, p. 191; KA MslWkg, Allg. Nr. 103, p. 3.
25. KAAOKEBB, fasz. 4119, 25 Juli; KA MslWkg, Allg. Nr. 103, p. 3.
26. KA MslWkg, Allg. Nr. 103.
27. Conrad, *Dienstzeit*, IV, pp. 267, 271.
28. *OUA*, VIII, Nr. 10685; KA MslWkg, Allg. Nr. 98, pp. 17, 25; KANC, fasz. B-12, Nr. 10/123 reservat.
29. KANC, B-12, 25 Juli, AOK Gstb. Nr. 2659.
30. KAAOK, fasz. 867; *OUA*, VIII, Nr. 10687; Pourtales, *Meine letzten Verhandlungen*, Nr. 22; *DD*,I, Nr. 216; IV, Anhang und Nr. 9.

31. KA Ms1Wkg, Nr. 99, p. 196, and Ratzenhofer, "Die Festsetzung der ersten Mobilisierungstage in Österreich-Ungarn im Sommer 1914, *Berliner Monatshefte* 14 (1936), p. 804; Stone, "Mobilmachung," p. 78.
32. Conrad, *Dienstzeit*, IV, pp. 131-132; KA Ms1Wkg, Allg. Nr. 98, pp. 25-26; KA Ms1Wkg, Allg. Nr. 99, p. 230; Max Hoen, "Mobilmachung," *Der Grosse Krieg*, edited by Max Schwarte, V. *Der österreichisch-ungarische Krieg* (Berlin: E. S. Mittler und Sohn, 1922), p. 19.
33. KA Ms1Wkg, Nr. 98, p. 18, and Ms1Wkg, A65; see KAAOK, fasz. 4119; Ratzenhofer, "Festsetzung der ersten Mobilisierungstage," p. 804.
34. KAAOKEBB, fasz. 4119, 26 Juli; Conrad, *Dienstzeit*, IV, p. 273.
35. Conrad, *Dienstzeit*, IV, p. 272, and KANC, B-12, 26 Juli.
36. Conrad, *Dienstzeit*, IV, p. 132; KA Ms1Wkg Allg. Nr. 103.
37. KAAOK, fasz. 867, varia; Conrad, *Dienstzeit*, IV, pp. 136, 137, 274; KA Ms1Wkg, Allg. Nr. 98, p. 26, and KA Nachlass B/8:8-15.
38. Conrad, *Dienstzeit*, IV, pp. 272, 274.
39. *OUA*, VIII, Nr. 10633; Conrad, *Dienstzeit*, IV, p. 109; KA Ms1Wkg, Allg. Nr. 98, p. 20, and Ms1Wkg, Allg. Nr. A-65.
40. KA Ms1Wkg, Allg. Nr. 98, pp. 18, 26, and KA Ms1Wkg, Allg. A-65; KAAOK, fasz. 867, varia; KA Nachlass B-8:8-15; KA Ms1Wkg, Nr. 99, p. 190; and Ratzenhofer, "Die Festsetzung der ersten Mobilisierungstage," p. 804; KA Nachlass B/61, Nr. 11, p. 37; Rudolf Kiszling, "Die praktische Undurchführbarkeit eines Handstreiches auf Belgrad," *Berliner Monatshefte* (1927), p. 236; Stone, "Mobilmachung," pp. 78, 82, 98.
41. Ratzenhofer, "Die Festsetzung der ersten Mobilisierungstage," p. 805, but see KA Ms1Wkg, Allg. Nr. 98, pp. 18, 21; Conrad, *Dienstzeit*, IV, p. 110; Hoen, "Mobilmachung," p. 19.
42. Ratzenhofer, "Die Festsetzung der ersten Mobilisierungstage," pp. 804, 805, but see KA Ms1Wkg, Allg. Nr. 98, p. 19, and KA Ms1Wkg, Allg. Nr. A-65; KA Nachlass B/61, footnote p. 35.
43. *DD*, II, Nrs. 271, 293; Geiss, *Juli*, II, p. 486; Albertini, *Origins*, II, pp. 468-469.
44. KANC B-12; Conrad, Dienstzeit, IV, pp. 137, 142; KAAOK, fasz. 867, Nr. 1860, Nr. 3/R, 4/R; KA Nachlass B/8:8-15; KAAOKEBB, fasz. 4119, 29 Juli; KA Ms1Wkg, Allg. Nr. 103, p. 4.

45. *OUA,* VIII, Nrs. 11002-11134; KANC B-12; see Conrad, *Dienstzeit,* IV, p. 146; KAAOK, fasz. 867, Nr. 178; Ratzenhofer, "Aufmärsche gegen B und R," Folge 39, p. 2.

46. *OUA,* VIII, Nr. 10717; Conrad, *Dienstzeit,* IV, pp. 132-133; *OSTA-OULK,* I, pp. 18-19; *DD,* I, Nrs. 194, 216, 291; Pourtales, *Verhandlungen,* p. 22, and Nrs. 16, 22, 39.

47. *OUA,* VIII, varia; *DD,* I, Nrs. 204, 217, 246, II, Nr. 412; Pourtales, *Verhandlungen,* Nrs. 19-23.

48. KAAOKEBB, fasz. 4119, 30 Juli; Conrad, *Dienstzeit,* IV, pp. 155,158; KA Ms1Wkg, Allg. Nr. 99, pp. 201-202; KA Ms1Wkg, Allg. Nr. 103, p. 5.

49. Conrad, *Dienstzeit,* IV, p. 275. See Stone, "Mobilmachung," p. 85.

50. KOOAK, fasz. 867, Nrs. 172, 178, 5/R, 6/R, 8/12; KAAOK, Gruppenregistratur fasz. 495, R Gruppe, Op. Nr. 1-1417 August 1914, Reservat (Res.) Nr. 1; Conrad, *Dienstzeit,* IV, pp. 148, 275; KA Ms1Wkg, Allg. Nr. 99, p. 231; Stone, "Mobilmachung," pp. 78, 85.

51. KAAOK, R Gruppe, fasz. 495, Nr. 1; KAAOK, fasz. 867, Nrs. 8/R, 172; KA Nachlass B/61, Nr. 11, p. 33; KA Nachlass B/8:8-15; Conrad, *Dienstzeit,* IV, pp. 18, 275; KA Ms1Wkg, Allg. Nr. 99, pp. 190, 231.

52. KA Ms1Wkg, Allg. Nr. 99, pp. 159, 196. See KAAOKEBB fasz. 4119; KA Ms1Wkg, Allg. Nr. 103, p. 5; Hoen, "Mobilmachung," p. 19.

53. KA Ms1Wkg, Allg. Nr. 98, p. 34, and Nr. A-65.

54. KA Nachlass B/405 (Regenauer).

55. Conrad, *Dienstzeit,* IV, pp. 148, 149-150, 151.

56. KAAOK, R Gruppe, fasz. 495, Moltke Reserve Nr. 221; *DD,* I, Nr. 257; *OUA,* VIII, Nrs. 10783, 10792, 10855; Conrad, *Dienstzeit,* IV, pp. 132, 152.

57. Conrad, *Dienstzeit,* IV, p. 152; Holsti, *Crisis, Escalation, War,* pp. 128-129.

58. *OUA,* VIII, Nr. 11118; *DD,* II, Nr. 482; III, Nrs. 502, 503; *RAWK,* II, p. 29; Ratzenhofer, "Aufmärsche gegen B und R," Folge 39, p. 2.

59. Conrad, *Dienstzeit,* IV, p. 276; Ratzenhofer, "Aufmärsche gegen B und R," Folge 40, p. 2; KA Ms1Wkg, Allg. Nr. 103, p. 24.

60. KAAOKEBB, fasz. 4119; KA Ms1Wkg, Allg. Nr. 103, p. 6.

61. *OSTAOULK,* I, p. 94; KA Ms1Wkg, Allg. Nr. 103, p. 6. See Conrad, *Dienstzeit,* IV, p. 276.

62. Conrad, *Dienstzeit*, IV, pp. 156, 158; KANC, B-12; KA Ms1Wkg, Allg. Nr. 99, p. 206; KAAOK, R Gruppe, fasz. 495, Fleischmann Res., Nrs. 9, 11; KAAOK, Verbindungsoffiziere fasz. 6180, Bevollmächtigter Generalstabsoffizier beim (deutschen) Oberbefehlshaber Ost (Fleischmann), Res. Nr. 1-512, 30.7.-30.9.1914, Nr. 38-14; KA Ms1Wkg, Allg. Nr. A-65; Stone, "Mobilmachung," pp. 69, 87.

63. Conrad, *Dienstzeit*, IV, pp. 112, 156; KAAOKEBB, fasz. 4119, 31 Juli; KA Ms1Wkg, Nr. 99, pp. 107, 109, 214; KA Ms1Wkg, Allg. Nr. 98, p. 4 and KA Ms1Wkg, Allg., Nr. A-65; KA Nachlass B/61, Nr. 11, p. 36; Stone, "Mobilmachung," pp. 79, 82.

64. KAAOKEBB, fasz. 4119, 31 Juli; KA Ms1Wkg, Allg. Nr. 103, p. 6; Ratzenhofer, "Aufmärsche gegen B und R," Folge 40, p. 2.

65. KAAOKEBB, fasz. 4119; KA Ms1Wkg, Allg. Nr. 103, p. 8.

66. KANC B-12, 31 Juli, Op. Nr. 86; Conrad, *Dienstzeit*, IV, p. 276.

67. KAAOKEBB, fasz. 4119; KA Ms1Wkg, Allg. Nr. 103, p. 7; Conrad, *Dienstzeit*, IV, p. 312.

68. KAAOKEBB, fasz. 4119, 1 August; KA Ms1Wkg, Allg. Nr. 103, p. 7.

69. KAAOKEBB, fasz. 4119. See Hoen, "Mobilmachung," p. 20.

70. KAAOKEBB, fasz. 4119; KA Ms1Wkg, Allg. Nr. 99; Allg. Nr. 103. See Conrad, *Dienstzeit*, IV, p. 157.

71. KAAOK, R Gruppe, fasz. 495; KA Ms1Wkg, Nr. 99, pp. 203, 204, 209.

72. Conrad, *Dienstzeit*, III, pp. 534, 535; KA Ms1Wkg, Nr. 98, p. 36, and KA Ms1Wkg, Nr. A-65; KA Nachlass B/61, Nr. 11, pp. 45, 51-52; KA Ms1Wkg, Nr. 103, pp. 1, 72. 74.

73. KA Ms1Wkg, Allg. Nr. 103, pp. 2, 90-91; KA Nachlass B/61, Nr. 23, pp. 51-52 (Res. Gstb. Nr. 5601/I); Nr. 11, Vorwort, p. 45; KA Ms1Wkg, Allg. Nr. 98; Conrad, *Dienstzeit*, III, p. 535.

74. KA Ms1Wkg, Nr. 103, p. 90.

75. KA Ms1Wkg, Allg. Nr. 103, p. 90; KA Ms1Wkg, Nr. 99, p. 215; and "Aufmärsche gegen B und R," Folge 40, p. 2; *OSTAOULK*, I, p. 323.

76. KA Nachlass B/61, Nr. 11, p. 37; Ratzenhofer, "Aufmärsche gegen B und R," Folge 40, p. 2.

77. KA Nachlass B/61, Nr. 11, p. 27; Stone, "Mobilmachung," p. 82; Kiszling, "Mobilisierung," p. 282.

78. KA Ms1WKG, Allg. Nr. 98, p. 90; KA Ms1Wkg, Nr. 99 , pp. 209-210; Ratzenhofer, "Aufmärsche gegen B und R," Folge 41, p. 2; Stone, "Mobilmachung," p. 82.
79. KA Ms1Wkg, Allg. Nr. 103, p. 90; KA Ms1Wkg, Nr. 99, pp. 209, 215; Stone, "Mobilmachung," p. 82.
80. KAAOKEBB, fasz. 4119; KA Ms1Wkg, Allg. Nr. 98, pp. 32, 33, 39; KA Ms1Wkg, Nr. 99, pp. 7, 202; KA Nachlass B/61, Nr. 11, p. 46; OSTAOULK, I, pp. 20, 322; Stone, "Mobilmachung," pp. 79, 80.
81. KA Ms1Wkg, Nr. 99, p. 203.
82. KA Ms1Wkg, Allg. Nr. 103; KA Ms1Wkg, Nr. A-65; see KA Nachlass B/61, Nr. 11, pp. 23, 51, and Nr. 23, p. 17; KA Ms1Wkg, Nr. 99, p. 7; Ratzenhofer, "Aufmärsche gegen B und R," Folge 39, p. 2.
83. KA Nachlass B/61, Nr. 11, pp. 11, 37-38; Krauss, Theorie, p. 39.
84. KA Ms1Wkg, Allg. Nr. 98, pp. 9, 41; KA Ms1Wkg, Allg. Nr. A-65; KA Ms1Wkg, Allg. Nr. 103, p. 78.
85. KA Ms1Wkg, Allg. Nr. 98, pp. 32, 36; KA Ms1Wkg, Allg. Nr. A-65; KA Ms1Wkg, Allg. Nr. 103, pp. 2, 72, 74; KA Nachlass B/61, Nr. 11, pp. 45, 51-52.
86. KA Ms1Wkg, Allg. Nr. 103, p. 90.
87. KA Ms1Wkg, Allg. Nr. 98, pp. 43-44; KA Ms1Wkg, Allg. Nr. A-65.
88. Enderes, "Die österreichischen Eisenbahnen," pp. 159, 160; KA Ms1Wkg, Allg. Nr. 103, pp. 88, 89; Stone, "Mobilmachung," p. 83.
89. Enderes, "Die österreichischen Eisenbahnen," pp. 61, 161; KA Nachlass B/151 (Theodor Zeynek), Das Leben eines österreichisch-ungarischen Generalstabesoffizeres, p. 11; Carl Freiherr von Bardolff, Soldat im alten Österreich. Erinnerungen aus meinem Leben (Jena, 1943), pp. 190-191.
90. KANFA 3. Armee, fasz. 42, pp. 6-8; KA Ms1Wkg, Allg. Nr. 103, p. 92; Stone, The Eastern Front, 1975, p. 78.
91. Enderes, "Die österreichischen Eisenbahnen," pp. 57, 158; Stone, Eastern Front, p. 77, and "Mobilmachung," p. 83.
92. Enderes, "Die österreichischen Eisenbahnen," pp. 57, 58, 59; KA Ms1Wkg, Allg. Nr. 103, p. 89, see pp. 88-92.
93. KA Ms1Wkg, Allg. Nr. 103, pp. 72, 89, 92.
94. KA Ms1Wkg, Allg. Nr. 103; Enderes, "Die österreichischen Eisenbahnen," pp. 57, 58, 59.

Chapter VIII
The Historiography of Mobilization, the Railroad Bureau, the Creation of a Habsburg Command Conspiracy

1. Stone, *The Eastern Front 1914-1917;* Kurt Peball, "Der Feldzug gegen Serbien und Montenegro im Jahre 1914", *Österreichische Militärische Zeitschrift,* 1965, 18-31.

2. Wolfgang Doppelbauer, *Zum Elend noch die Schande. Das altöster-reichische Offizierskorps am Beginn der Republik,* Vienna: Österreichischer Bundesverlag, 1988; Emil Ratzenhofer, "Gerichtliche Verfolgung militärischer Führer in Österreich," *Vierteljahresschrift für Politik und Geschichte* 1 (1929), pp. 137-151.

3. Conrad, *Dienstzeit,* IV, p. 146-152; 157-303; KA Ms1Wkg, Allg. Nr. 99, p. 203; KA Ms1Wkg, Allg. Nr. 98, p. 26; KA Nachlass B/61, Nr. 11, p. 45: Stone, "Mobilmachung," pp. 68,77, 80, 84, 85.

4. Conrad, *Dienstzeit,* IV, pp. 200+; *OSTAOULK,* I, pp. 321-322; KA Ms1Wkg, Allg. Nr. 99, p. 202; KA Ms1Wkg, Allg. Nr. 98, p. 17; Pitreich, *1914,* pp. 36, 80; KA Nachlass B/61, Nr. 11, pp. 21, 23; KA Ms1Wkg, Allg. Nr. 103, p. 75; Stone, "Mobilmachung," pp. 72, 74, 89.

5. KA Ms1Wkg, Allg. Nr. 98, pp. 10, 25, 27, and Ms1Wkg, A-65; See Stone, "Mobilmachung," p. 84; KA Nachlass B/151.

6. Conrad, *Dienstzeit,* IV, pp. 157, 303; Stone, "Mobilmachung," pp. 68, 80. But see KA Ms1Wkg, Allg. Nr. 98, pp. 10, 25, 27, 31, and Ms1Wkg, A-65; KA Nachlass B/151, Zeynek; Kurt Peball, "Der Feldzug gegen Serbien und Montenegro im Jahre 1914," *Österreichische Militärische Zeitschrift* (Sonderheft, I/65), pp. 18-31.

7. Rudolf Pfeffer, *Zum 10. Jahrestag der Schlachten bei Zloczów und Prezemyslany 26.30. August 1914. Eine Entgegnung auf die Angaben des Feldmarschalls Conrad über die Führung der 3. Armee in diesen Schlachten im vierten Band Aus meiner Dienstzeit* (Vienna: Im Selbstverlage, 1924); Pitreich, *1914.*

8. August Urbanski von Ostrymiecz, *Conrad von Hötzendorf. Soldat und Mensch. Dargestellt von seinem Mitarbeiter Feldmarschalleutnant August* (Vienna: Ulrich Mosers Verlag, 1938).

9. Ludwig von Pastor, *Conrad von Hötzendorf: Ein Lebensbild nach originalen Quellen und persönlichen Erinnerungen entworfen* (Vienna; B. Herder, 1916); Karl Friedrich Nowak, *Der Weg zur Katastro-*

phe, mit Briefen, Gesprächen, Dokumenten und Karten (Berlin: Verlag für Kulturpolitik, 1919).

10. Ferdinand Stoller, *Feldmarschall Franz Graf Conrad von Hötzendorf* (Leipzig: Friedrich Brandstetter, 1942); Friederich von Cochenhausen, "Conrad von Hötzendorf. Eine Studie über seine Persönlichkeit" (Berlin: Junker und Dunnhaupt Verlag, 1934).

11. Kurt Peball, "The Official Military History: Austria-Hungary's Last War (*Österreich-Ungarns letzter Krieg*) in *Official Histories: Essays and Bibliographies From Around the World*, Series 9, Ed. Robin Higham (Lawrence: University of Kansas 1970).

12. Peter Broucek, "Militärgeschichte in Österreich von 1918 bis 1938/45," *Verträge zur Militärgeschichte*, Vol. 6 *Militärgeschichte in Deutschland und Österreich vom 18. Jahrhundert bis in die Gegenwart* (Bonn: Verlag E.S. Mittler & Sohn GMBh, 1985), p. 97; Kurt Peball, "Literarische Puklikationen des Kriegsarchivs im Weltkrieg 1914 bis 1918," *Mitteilungen des österreichischen Staatsarchivs*, XIV (1961), pp. 240 footnote, 241. Edmund Glaise von Horstenau and Rudolf Kiszling led the preparation of the first volume covering 1914. The official group included Maximilian Ehnl, Gustav Hubka, Eduard Steinitz, and Rudolf Kiszling. Others involved in preparing the official history included Eduard Czegka, Maximilian Hoen and Ernest Wisshaupt.

13. Peball, "The Official Military History: Austria-Hungary's Last War 1914-1918," pp. 64,65.

14. Generalleutnant Max Schwarte, *Der Grosse Krieg*, Vol. V, *Der österreichisch-ungarische Krieg* (Leipzig: Barth in Auslg, 1922).

15. Rudolf Kiszling, *Die hohe Führung der Heere Habsburg im Ersten Weltkrieg* (Bundesministerium für Landesverteidigung, 1984). Kiszling's other book, *Österreich-Ungarns Anteil am ersten Weltkrieg* (Graz: Stiasny Verlag, 1958). The principle articles, "Feldmarschall Conrad und der Aufmarsch der Mittelmächte 1914" in 1926; "Feldmarschall Conrads Kriegsplan gegen Russland," 1925; "Kriegspläne und Aufmärsche der k.u.k. Armeen sowie der Feindheere im Sommer 1914," 1964; "Die Mobilmachung der europäischen Mächte im Sommer 1914: Österreich-Ungarn," 1936; and very significant "Österreich-Ungarns Kriegsvorbereitungen. Mobilisierung, Aufmarsch und Operationspläne im Sommer 1914," *MTM*, 1922. These are examples from numerous articles, the most significant for our purposes.

16. KA Nachlass B/61, Nr. 11, pp. 39, 40, 41, 43, 48, 51.
17. Broucek, "Militärgeschichte in Österreich von 1918 bis 1938/45," p. 98. KA MsWkg, Allg. Nr. 98, pp. 15, 16; KA Nachlass B/61, Nrs. 23, 11.
18. KA Nachlass B/61, Nr. 11, p. 37.
19. KA Nachlass B/198, Maximillian Csiscerics, Nr. 13, Feldmarschall Graf Conrad. Ein Charakterbild.
20. KA Nachlass B/198
21. See KA Nachlass, B/60 Fa; Peter Broucek, "Militärgeschichte in Österreich von 1918 bis 1938/45," p. 97.
22. KA Nachlass B/60 Fa; see Alfred Krauss, *Theorie und Praxis in der Kriegskunst* (Munich: J.F. Lehmanns Verlag, 1938), and *Die Ursachen unserer Niederlage. Erinnerungen und Urteile aus dem Weltkrieg* (Munich: J.F. Lehmanns Verlag, 1920).
23. KA Nachlass, B/60 Fa.
24. Max Freiherr von Pitreich *1914:* see footnote Nr. 3, and *Lemberg 1914,* (Vienna: Adolph Holzhausens, 1929); KA, Ms1Wkg, Allg. Nr. 98, 1914. "Unterlagen zur Beurteilung des damaligen Kriegsbeginnes an der österreichisch-ungarischen Front." Oberst Max Freiherr von Pitreich.
25. KA Ms1Wkg A-65.
26. Conrad, *Dienstzeit*, III, p. 535; see *KA* Ms1Wkg, Allg. Nr. 98, p. 36, and Ms1Wkg A-65; *KA* Ms1Wkg, Allg. Nr. 103, p. 74.
27. Conrad, *Dienstzeit*, III, p. 14; KA Ms1Wkg, Allg. Nr. 98, p. 36.
28. KA Ms1Wkg, Allg. Nr. 98, p. 34, and Ms1Wkg A-65.
29. Pitreich, *1914*, p. 125.
30. Pitreich, *1914*, p. 122-123.
31. Pitreich, *1914*, pp. 122-123, 125-127.
32. KA Nachlass B/61, Nr. 11; Der kritische Monat Juli 1914; Nr. 23, "Licht ohne Schatten. Über eine Biographie Feldmarschall Conrads."
33. Josef Steiner, "Gustav Hubka (1873-1962). Sein Wirken als k. u. k. Militärattaché und Schriftsteller." University of Vienna: 1975 Dissertation, pp. 83-85, 141, 220, 228, 229-230.
34. KA Nachlass B/61, Nr. 23; see KA Nachlass B/151, Nr. 2.
35. KA Nachlass B/61, Nr. 23, pp. 27, 28; Conrad, *Dienstzeit*, IV, pp. 72, 94-95.
36. Conrad, *Dienstzeit*, IV, pp. 37-38, 40-72, 94-95; KA Nachlass B/61, Nr. 23, pp. 27, 28; Nr. 11. p. 59.

37. Oscar Regele, *Feldmarschall Conrad. Auftrag und Erfüllung, 1906-1918* (Vienna: Verlag Herold, 1955).

38. Manfred Rauchensteiner, "Die Militärgeschichtsschreibung in Österreich nach 1945," *Vorträge zur Militärgeschichte,* Vol. 6, *Militärgeschichte in Deutschland und Österreich vom 18. Jahrhundert bis in die Gegenwart* (Bonn: Verlag E.S. Mittler & Sohn GmbH, 1985), pp. 147, 152.

39. Peter Fiala, *Feldmarschall Conrad von Hötzendorf (1825-1925)* (Vienna: Bundesministerium für Landesverteidigung, 1972).

40. KA Ms1Wkg, Allg. Nr. 103, p. 86.

41. KA Ms1Wkg, Allg. Nr. 103, pp. 72, 74, 98. See *OSTAOULK,* I, pp. 20-21.

42. KA Ms1Wkg, Allg. Nr. 103, pp. 40, 68, 78, 86. See KA Nachlass B/61, Nr. 11, p. 47; Kiszling, "Österreich-Ungarns Kriegsvorbereitungen. Mobilisierung, Aufmarsch und Operationspläne im Sommer 1914," p. 282, and Stone, "Mobilmachung," p. 82.

43. KA Ms1Wkg, Allg. Nr. 103, p. 86. For the remaining Keri material, see pp. 86, 91-92, 94, 20, 21, 23, 2, 7, 24, 8, 14-15, 17-18.

44. Albertini, *Origins.*

Chapter IX
The War: Failure of the Schlieffen Plan

1. HHSTA:PA, I, fasz, 506, Nr. 481 Pallavinci; fasz. 512, Nrs. 228, 246 Tarnowski, Nr. 41452; fasz. 513, Liasse XLVII, 6b-d, Geheime Verhandlungen mit Bulgarien über einen geheimen Vertrag mit Bulgarien August-September 1914, Nr. 459 Tarnowski; fasz. 516, Nrs. 296, 308, 316 Czernin; Conrad, *Dienstzeit,* IV, pp. 158, 312. For German pressure on Italy, Bulgaria, Rumania and Turkey, Geiss, *Juli 1914,* II, p. 529 and Nrs. 805, 877, 982, 988, 994, 998, 1078.

2. HHSTA:PA, I, fasz. 496, Nr. 345; fasz. 521, Liasse XLVII, 8, Geheime Verhandlungen mit der Türkei 1914-1918, Nr. 55-P, A-E, and Nrs. 338, 391; fasz. 522, Haltung der Türkei (Korrespondenz) Juli 1914, Vom Gesandten Flotow verfasste Darstellung der Vertragsverhandlungen mit der Türkei August 1914-März 1915, Document Nr. 338; Silberstein, *The Troubled Alliance,* pp. 28, 73, and "The High

Command and Diplomacy in Austria-Hungary, 1914-1916," JMH, 42 (1970), p. 587.

3. HHSTA:PA, I, fasz. 512, Liasse XLVII, 6, Geheime Verhandlungen mit Bulgarien Juli 1914-1917, a, Haltung Bulgariens, Juli-November 1914, varia; fasz. 513, varia; fasz. 515, Liasse XLVII, 7, Geheime Verhandlungen mit Rumänien Juli 1914-August 1916, varia; fasz. 522, Nr. 232 Tarnowski, 253 Czernin; fasz. 905, Krieg 9: Diverse Kriegs- und Zeitungsnachrichten, Nr. 286 Pallvinci.

4. Conrad, *Dienstzeit*, IV, pp. 158-159.

5. For 3 August, HHSTA:PA, I, fasz. 496, Adalia-Kleinasiatische Interressenphäre 1913-1914, Liasse XLVII: Korrespondenz aus dem Komplexe der Verhandlungen während des Kriegs 1914-1918, Nr. 289 Czernin; fasz. 506, Liasse XLVII, 5, Geheime Verhandlungen mit Italien Juli 1914-Mai 1915, Nr. 576 Merey; *DD*, IV, Nrs. 614, 664, 694, 745, 748, 756, 757, 759, 838, 840, 850; Fellner, *Dreibund*, pp. 82-83.

6. *DD*, IV, Nrs. 755, 766, 862; Stürgkh, *Im Deutschen Grossen Hauptquartier*, p. 83.

7. *DD*, IV, Nr. 827; *RAWK*, I, p. 23; II, pp. 45, 50-51, 203, 238-240, 253, 258, 451, 457, 607; Elze, *Tannenberg*, p. 100; Schäfer, "Conrad in den Anfangsoperationen," pp. 129-130, 138; Stürgkh, *Im Deutschen Grossen Hauptquartier*, p. 83. The actual promise, Conrad, *Dienstzeit*, II, pp. 248-249.

8. *DD*, III, Nr. 662; quoted in Geiss, *July 1914*, p. 352.

9. KANC, B fasz. 6; *DD*, III, Nrs. 544, 597; Conrad, *Dienstzeit*, IV, pp. 167-168. For the diplomatic side, HHSTA:PA, I, fasz. 522, Liasse XLVII 8b.

10. HHSTA:PA, I, fasz. 516, Document Nr. 358; *DD*, III, Nrs. 506, 582, 646; *DD*, IV, Nrs. 795, 830, 870; Conrad, *Dienstzeit*, IV, p. 167; Silberstein, *The Troubled Alliance*, p. 38; Verosta, *Bündnissen*, p. 517.

11. HHSTA:PA, I, fasz. 522, Nr. 3736 Tagesbericht Berchtold; Pribam, *Austrian Foreign Policy*, p. 70. On 4 August General Conrad pressured Count Berchtold to promise Romania Bessarabia and certain Serbian territory for active participation in the war. Conrad, *Dienstzeit*, IV, p. 175; *DD*, III, Nrs. 506, 507, 582, 597, 646, 761, 864, 865. For Austro-German pressure on Romania to declare war on Russia from St. Petersburg's viewpoint, see *IB*, I, 5, Nr. 502; Geiss, *Juli 1914*, II, Nrs. 1071, 1128. On 5 September Kaiser Wilhelm

telegraphed King Carol asking Romanian active intervention and support for the Austrian army hard pressed at Lemberg. HHSTA:PA, I, fasz. 515 and 516, Czernin Nr. 514 and Nr. 278-P. For Russia, HHSTA:PA, I, fasz. 516, Czernin; fasz. 521, Czernin Nr. 357; *IB*, I, 5, Nr. 411; Geiss, *Juli 1914*, II, Nrs. 920, 1030, 1149; Glenn E. Torrey, "Rumania and the Belligerents 1914-1916," *JCH* (1966), p. 166 and Silberstein, *The Troubled Alliance*, p. 38.

12. For the exchanges, KAAOK, R Gruppe, fasz. 495, Op. Nr. 7 vom 1914; fasz. 868, Evidenzbüro Nachrichten; *Österreichisch-ungarisches Rotbuch, Diplomatische Aktenstücke betreffend die Beziehungen Österreich-Ungarns zu Rumänien in der Zeit vom 22. Juli bis 27. August 1916* (Vienna: Manzsche Buchhandlung, 1916), pp. 5, 7, Nrs. 8, 12; HHSTA:PA, I, fasz. 515, Czernin Nr. 527; Conrad, *Dienstzeit*, IV, p. 189; Torrey, "Rumania and the Belligerents," pp. 167-168; Silberstein, *The Troubled Alliance*, pp. 68, 181.

13. HHSTA: PA, I, fasz. 516, Nrs. 284, Z74-P; fasz. 521, Tarnowski Nr. 489; fasz. 515, Czernin Nr. 531; KAAOK, fasz. 867; *DD*, IV, Nrs. 761, 811, 841, 847, 864.

14. KAGOB, fasz. 34.

15. KAAOK, R Gruppe, fasz. 495; Conrad, *Dienstzeit*, IV, p. 172.

16. HHSTA: PA, I, fasz. 498, Liasse XLVII: Korrespondenz aus dem Komplexe der Verhandlungen während des Kriegs 1914-1918, 2, Geheime Korrespondenzen mit militärischen Behörden, Geheime Situationsberichte über die Operationen 18.8.1914-22.8.1915; fasz. 499, Liasse XLVII/b: Diverse geheime Korrespondenzen mit dem Armee-Ober-Kommando und unserem Vertreter bei demselben, August 1914-Oktober 1918, 3, Auskünfte über die Haltung Italiens, Rumäniens und Bulgariens September 1914, Baron Giesl, Nrs. 12 and 13; fasz. 522, Tarnowski, Nrs. 633, 488, 536; fasz. 516, Szögyeny Nr. 414; fasz. 512, Mittag Nrs. 849, 853, Tarnowski Nr. 468, 472, Nrs. 561, 640; *OSTAOULK*, I, pp. 95, 97; *DD*, IV, Nr. 854.

17. HHSTA: PA, I, fasz. 499, Nr. 305 Conrad to Berchtold; KAAOK, fasz. 1, AOK Op. Nr. 443; *DD*, III, Nr. 729; IV, Nr. 873; *OSTAOULK*, I, p. 107. Conrad knew that Bulgarian entry against Serbia would assure him of his victory over Serbia. Conrad, *Dienstzeit*, IV, pp. 195, 200, 204, 364.

18. Alfred Tirpitz, *Erinnerungen* (Leipzig: Verlag von K. F. Koehler, 1920), pp. 242-243; Moltke, *Erinnerungen*, pp. 19-20; Zwehl, *Falkenhayn*, pp. 58-59; Geiss, *Juli 1914*, II, p. 610 and Nrs. 1070, 1073,

1079, 1117, 1140, 1141, 1161; Jarausch, *Bethmann Hollweg*, p. 175. *RAWK*, II, pp. 41-42, 53, 64, 66, 113, 114, 117-118; General Max Hoffman, *Der Krieg der versäumten Gelegenheiten* (Munich: Verlag für Kulturpolitik, 1956), p. 23.

19. Conrad, *Dienstzeit*, IV, pp. 134, 158, 231, 280, 282 and footnote, 285, 321; Sturgkh, *Im Deutschen Grossen Hauptquartier*, p. 157.

20. KAAOK, R Gruppe, fasz. 495; Conrad, *Dienstzeit*, IV, pp. 252, 280; Stürgkh, *Im Deutschen Grossen Hauptquartier*, p. 30; Leppa, *Conrad und Moltke*, p. 47; Theobald von Schäfer, "Der Feldherr Conrad. Ein Beitrag zum Kapitel: Herrführung und Politik," *Deutscher Offizierbund*, 7 (1930) p. 224; Beck, "Besass Deutschland 1914 einen Kriegsplan," p. 103; Verosta, *Bündnissen*, pp. 346, 347-348, 363, 501, 558.

21. Frantz, *Russlands Eintritt*, pp. 24-25, and "Strategische Eisenbahnnetz Russland 1914," *BM* (1930), p. 274; Suchomlinow, *Erinnerungen*, pp. 240, 243; Kiszling, "Entwicklung operativer Ideen," *MTM* (1932), p. 643; Ratzenhofer, "Österreich-Ungarns und Russlands Aufmarschkraft, ein Prüfstein des Willens zum Angriffskrieg," *BM*, 5 (1928), pp. 441-452; Generalmajor A.D. Hugo Kerchnawe, "Die unzureichende Kriegsrüstungen der Mittelmächte," *MTM* (1932) - *OSTAOULK*, Ergänzungs-Heft Nr. 4, pp. 150-208. Between 1888-1913 France poured twelve billion gold francs into Russia. In 1890 Russia possessed 30,000 kilometers of railroad lines; in 1913 the number had increased to 73,000 kilometers. _____, "Französische Milliarden und Russische Bahnen in der Vorkriegzeit," *BM* (1930), p. 497.

22. For Tannenberg, see *RAWK*, II, pp. 148-244; Theobald von Schäfer, *Tannenberg. Schlachten des Weltkrieges [In Einzeldarstellungen bearbeitet und herausgegeben im Auftrage des Reichsarchivs]* (Berlin: Verlag Gerhard Stalling, 1928), especially pp. 100-110; Churchhill, *Unknown War*, pp. 215-231; Gunther Frantz, "Die russische 1. Armee unter Rennenkampf während der Schlacht bei Tannenberg," *DOB* (1925), pp. 779-782; Hoffman, *Krieg der versäumtem Gelegenheiten*, pp. 26-60. Masurian Lakes, *RAWK*, II, pp. 245-292; Churchill, *Unknown War*, pp. 215-231; Alexander Horace Cyril Kearsey, *A Study of the Strategy and Tactics of the East Prussian Campaign 1914* (London: Sifton Praed & Co., Ltd., 1932), pp. 10-19, 25-37; Stone, *The Eastern Front*, pp. 44-69; Dennis E. Showalter, *Tannenberg. Clash of Empires* (Connecticut: Anchor Books, 1991).

23. KAGOB, fasz. 34, k.u.k. Chef Gstbs.-Directiven für E.B.B. zu Be-
arbeitung Aufmarschelaborates für Kriegsfall "R," gültig 1.Apr.1914;
KAAOKEEB, fasz. 4108, Kriegsfall "R" für das Jahr 1914-1915,
Res. Gstb. Nr. 4600-I, 28.3.1914, and Verbesserung der Aufmarsch-
verhältnisse gegen "R" durch Ausgestaltung der Bahnen, auf Grund-
lage des Aufmarsches 1914-1915; Pitreich, *1914*, pp. 123-125; Ratzenhofer, "Aufmärsche gegen B und R," p. 2.
24. KAGOB, fasz. 34 and 53, Kriegsfall "R", Skizzen mit der Grenzbe-
wachung N.O. (Nordost); Bardolff, *Soldat im alten Österreich*, p.
193.
25. Conrad, *Dienstzeit*, IV, p. 282. General Conrad decided to field
30-1/2 infantry divisions on the San-Dniester line; by the end of
August the total deployment, after the Second Army had been redirected to Galicia from the Serbian theater, would be 38 1/2 infantry
divisions, 2 replacement brigades, 8 reserve brigades and 10 cavalry
divisions, or 670 battalions, 330 squadrons. *OSTAOULK*, I, pp. 157-
158.
26. KAGOB, fasz. 34; Kiszling, "Österreich-Ungarns Kriegsvorbereitungen," p. 285.
27. Metzger, "Krieg gegen Russland," p. 25 (Metzger served in the
higher echelon in the k.u.k. Operations Bureau); Kiszling, "Kriegspläne und Aufmarsch Österreich-Ungarn," p. 7.
28. KAAOKETB, fasz. 13, Eintreffübersichten Verlegung "B" nach "R";
KAGOB, fasz. 34 and 35, Konkreter Aufmarschbehelf "R" 1914-
1915; fasz. 53; *RAWK*, II, p. 248; Pitreich, *1914*, p. 124; Leppa,
Conrad und Moltke, p. 12; Ratzenhofer, "Aufmarsch gegen B und
R," p. 2 and "Die österreichisch-ungarischen Aufmärsche," p. 107.
29. Russia possessed five two-rail, four one-rail deployment railroads,
which did not have to overcome the difficulties the Austrians would
have to in traversing the Carpathian Mountains to attain their deployment areas. The Russian lines had the capacity of sending 260 trains
daily. On the Austrian side, seven rail lines, two having to overcome
the Carpathians, had the capacity to dispatch 153 trains daily. Conrad, *Dienstzeit*, III, p. 605; IV, Anlage 13; KAGOB, fasz. 34; Ratzenhofer, "Russlands Aufmarschkraft gegen Österreich-Ungarn,"
Österreichische Wehrzeitung (*OW*), 15 (1928), p. 2. For the threat
of the Russian cavalry masses, KAGOB, fasz. 27, Kavallerie Alarm-
verlegungen 1913-1914, 1914-1915; Ratzenhofer, "Die österreichi-
sche-ungarischen Aufmärsche, Friedenspläne, Durchfuhrung,"

Schweizerische Monatsschrift für Offiziere aller Waffen, 2 (1930), p. 74; Bardolff, *Soldat im alten Österreich*, p. 191.

30. KAGOB, fasz. 53, Aufmarsch gegen "R" 1914 (13 Juli 1914); KAAOKETB, fasz. 13; Conrad, *Dienstzeit*, III, p. 605; Pitreich, *Lemberg*, p. 5.

31. Conrad, *Dienstzeit*, IV, p. 283; Leppa, *Conrad und Moltke*, p. 12. For the deployment see KAGOB, fasz. 10, 30, 33-35, 37, 49; KAAO-KEBB, fasz. 4107, 4108, 41119; KAAOKETB, fasz. 2, 3, 5, 41, 42; KANFA, 1. A. Operierendes Armeekommando, fasz. 29, 135-137; 2. A. Operierendes Armeekommando, fasz. 1, 2, 4, 5, 7, 9: 3. A. Operierendes Armeekommando, fasz. 1, 2, 18, 61; 4. A. Operierendes Armeekommando, fasz. 1, 1a, 1b, 2, 3, 34, 70.

32. KAGOB, fasz. 37, 43, 53a, 221, 223-224; KAAOKEEB, fasz. 4119; KAAOKETB, fasz. 13, 41; Conrad *Dienstzeit*, IV, pp. 122-225, 269; *OSTAOULK*, I, pp. 7, 23.

33. Conrad, *Dienstzeit*, IV, p. 313; AOK Op. Nr. 122 to the 2nd and 5th Armies and the VII Corps, and Op. Nr. 123 to the 6th Army Commander that in spite of the general mobilization the deployment against Serbia remained in force. Also KANFA, 2.A., fasz. 4, Präs. Nr. 2941/M: Op. Nr. 25; *OSTAOULK*, I, p. 94; Ritter, *SK*, p. 312.

34. Pourtales, *Verhandlungen*, pp. 70-72, II, Nr. 96; *DD*, III, Nr. 540A; Geiss, *Juli 1914*, II, Nrs. 910, 985, 1004, 1023; *IB*, I, 5, Nr. 398; Fischer, *KI*, p. 724. For the German twelve-hour ultimatum to Russia to halt her mobilization *IB*, I, 5 Nr. 385; Geiss, *Juli 1914*, II, Nrs. 892, 1021, 1024; KAAOK, fasz. 867, Fleischmann Res. Nr. 13.

35. KAAOK, R Gruppe, fasz. 495; KAAOKEBB, fasz. 4119; *DD*, III, Nr. 601; Conrad, *Dienstzeit*, IV, pp. 154-165; quoted in Churchill, *The Unknown War*, pp. 123-124; Albertini, *Origins*, III, pp. 49-50; Ritter, "Anteil," p. 88, and *SK*, p. 326.

36. Conrad, *Dienstzeit*, IV, pp. 318-319; quoted in Albertini, *Origins,* III, p. 50; KAAOK, fasz. 6180, Res. Nr. 11-1.

37. The telegram was in reply to Wilhelm's demand that Austria direct her main forces against Russia. For Franz Joseph's message, *DD*, III, Nr. 601; *Ö. Rotbuch*, III, Nr. 816; Geiss, *Juli 1914*, II, Nr. 978; Conrad, *Dienstzeit*, IV, p. 160; quoted in Schmit, *Coming of the War*, II, p. 331.

38. Conrad, *Dienstzeit*, IV, p. 319; quoted in Albertini, *Origins*, III, p. 50. From 29 July Moltke had considered war inevitable and after 31 July pushed forcefully for general mobilization and war.

39. KAAOK, fasz. 1, Nr. 15; Conrad, *Dienstzeit*, IV, pp. 318-321, Aufmarschanweisung 1914-1915; *OSTAOULK*, I, pp. 157, 159; *RAWK*, II, pp. 248-249; quoted in Churchill, *The Unknown War*, pp. 133-134; Ritter, "Zusammenarbeit," p. 545; Schafer, "deutsche offensive," p. 12, and "Conrad in den Anfangs Operationen," p. 129; Stone, "Moltke-Conrad," p. 224.

40. *OSTAOULK*, I, pp. 158-159; Pitreich, *1914*, p. 140.

41. For the question see *IB*, I, 5, Nr. 496; Geiss, *Juli 1914*, II, Nr. 1125; *DD*, IV, Nrs. 722, 814, 860, 870, 871, 874, 875, 877-879. Conrad did, however, suggest that hostilities with Russia could commence as early as 2 August, KAAOK, fasz. 1, Op. Nr. 125; Conrad, *Dienstzeit*, IV, p. 314.

42. KAAOK, R Gruppe, 495; fasz. 6180, Res. Nr. 12; Conrad, *Dienstzeit*, IV, p. 324.

43. *OSTAOULK*, I, p. 160; Conrad, *Dienstzeit*, IV, p. 208; Churchill, *The Unknown War*, pp. 134-135; Ritter, "Zusammenarbeit," p. 535; Kiszling, "deutsche[s] Ostheer," pp. 389-390.

44. Conrad, *Dienstzeit*, IV, p. 195; quoted in Churchill, *The Unknown War*, p. 136.

45. KAAOK, R Gruppe, fasz. 495, Res. Nr. 34 for Conrad's calculations; *OSTAOULK*, I, pp. 96-97; Stone, "Moltke-Conrad," p. 224; Redlich, Politisches Tagebuch, I, p. 245; Barldoff, *Soldat im alten Österreich*, p. 107.

46. KAAOK, R Gruppe, fasz. 495; Pitreich, *1914*, p. 141.

47. For the reconnaissance see KAAOK, fasz. 34, R Gruppe, fasz. 495, fasz. 867, 868; KAAOKEBB, fasz. 4119; Conrad, *Dienstzeit*, IV, pp. 386, 877; Auffenberg-Komarów, *Österreich-Ungarns Teilnahme*, pp. 116-117, and *Aus Österreichs Hohe und Niedergang*, p. 280; *OSTAOULK*, I, pp. 8, 10, 12, 168; Pitreich, *Lemberg*, pp. 9, 11, 12; L. V. Fabini, "Die Feuertaufe des Eisernen Korps, (III ö-u): Der erste Tag der Schlacht von Zloczów am 26. August 1914," *MTM*, p. 789; Heinrich Mast, "Die Aufklärungstätigkeit der österr.-ung. Kavallerie bei Kriegsbeginn 1914," *Österreichische Militärische Zeitung* (*OMZ*) (1/1965), pp. 8-17; Konrad Leppa, "Der Aufmarsch der Reiterei," *Wissen und Wehr* (*WW*) (1932), pp. 195-214; Alfred von Dragoni, "Die österreichisch-ungarische Heereskavallerie beim Nordost-Aufmarsch und Kriegsbeginn 1914," *MTM* (1934), pp. 3-10; Alphons Bernhard, "Die Wandlung in der Verwendung und Organi-

sation der Kavallerie-divisionen während des Weltkrieges, *MTM* (1928), pp. 1-22.

48. KANFA, 1.A. fasz. 137, and 4.A. fasz. 3; Pitreich, *Lemberg*, p. 26.

49. KAAOK, R Gruppe, fasz. 495; *OSTAOULK*, I, p. 160; *RAWK*, II, pp. 8, 250; Conrad, *Dienstzeit*, IV, p. 210; Pitreich, *1914*, pp. 141, 224; Ritter, "Zusammenarbeit," p. 545 footnote.

50. KAAOK, R Gruppe, fasz. 495, fasz. 867 and 6180, Res. Nr. 48, Evidenz Nr. 49-K. See KAAOK, fasz. 868, Fleischmann Reservat Nr. 58 (18.8.); Conrad, *Dienstzeit*, IV, pp. 388-389, 390; *OSTA-OULK*, I, p. 160; Pitreich, *1914*, pp. 141-142; Elze, *Tannenberg*, pp. 95-96, 99, 100.

51. KAAOK, R Gruppe, fasz. 495, Op. Nr. 710; *OSTAOULK*, I, pp. 159, 160, 162; Conrad, *Dienstzeit*, IV, pp. 392-393, 709; Elze, *Tannenberg* Nr. 109, Conrad to Prittwitz, Churchill, *The Unknown War*, p. 138; Pitreich, *1914*, pp. 141-143; Schäfer, "Conrad in den Anfangsoperationen," p. 130, and Kiszling, "Deutsche Ostheer Sommerfeldzuge," pp. 389, 393.

52. KAAOK, R Gruppe, fasz. 495, AOK Op. Nrs. 822, 823; fasz. 6180, Res. Nr. 57; Conrad, *Dienstzeit*, IV, p. 419; *OSTAOULK*, I, p. 150; Pitreich, *1914*, p. 199.

53. KAAOK, fasz. 789, 867, 6180, Res. Nr. 54 stated that strong enemy forces advanced towards the area Stalluponen-Biala and south; Res. Nr. 58, where it is stated that at least seven Russian corps and eight cavalry divisions advanced. Elze, *Tannenberg*, Nrs. 29, 108a; Conrad, *Dienstzeit*, IV, p. 434; *RAWK*, II, p. 114.

54. KAAOK, R Gruppe, fasz. 495; fasz. 868, Res. Nrs. 62, 63, 64; fasz. 6180, Res. Nrs. 61, 65; *RAWK*, II, pp. 79-101, 253-254; Elze, *Tannenberg*, pp. 93-110, 221, Nrs. 43, 62; Schäfer, "Conrad in den Anfangsoperationen," p. 131; Leppa, *Conrad und Moltke*, pp. 43, 48, and "Die beste Strategie," pp. 624-625; Hoffmann, *Krieg der versäumten Gelegenheiten*, pp. 26, 28; General Erich von Ludendorff, *Das Marne Drama* (Munich: Lundendorff's Verlag GmbH, 1935), p. 11; E. Kabisch, "Ein Beitrag zum Problem Gumbinnen," *DOB*, 17 (1927), pp. 721-725; Kearsey, *East Prussian Campaign 1914*, pp. 8-10, 22-23.

55. For the reports, KAAOK, fasz. 867, Nr. 651; fasz. 868, Nachrichten bis 16.8.; Conrad, *Dienstzeit*, IV, p. 374.

56. HHSTA:PA, I, fasz. 498, Baron Giesl Nr. 4; KAAOK, R Gruppe, fasz. 495; Pitreich, *Lemberg*, p. 24.

57. KAAOK, R Gruppe.fasz. 868, varia; fasz. 869, Op. Nr. 111 (3.A. Kdo.), Nr. 114; fasz. 789, k.u.k. 3. A.Kdo. Op. Nr. 126; KANFA, 3. A. fasz. 2; Conrad, *Dienstzeit*, IV, p. 443; *OSTAOULK*, I, p. 169; Ronge, *Kriegs-und Industrie-Spionage*, pp. 107, 109.

58. KANFA, 2. A. fasz. 9; Conrad, *Dienstzeit*, IV, p. 420; *OSTAOULK*, I, p. 166;. Schäfer, "Conrad in den Anfangsoperationen," p. 132.

59. KAAOK, fasz. 868 for the intelligence bureau reports 18.-21.8.; KANFA, 4. A. fasz. 3. The Russian forces (Third and Eighth Armies) marched at night and camouflaged themselves during the day in the forests.

60. KAAOK, R Gruppe, fasz. 495, Nr. 93; Conrad, *Dienstzeit*, IV, pp. 452, 457, 607; *RAWK*, II, pp. 253, 258, 451, 457, 607; Elze, *Tannenberg*, p. 100 and Nrs. 113, 113a; *RAWK*, II, pp. 253, 258, 451, 457, 507; Schäfer, "Conrad in den Anfangsoperationen," pp. 129-130; Freytag-Loringhoven, *Menschen und Dinge*, pp. 196-197; Stürgkh, *Im Deutschen Grossen Hauptquartier*, p. 39.

61. Conrad, *Dienstzeit*, IV, p. 467; *OSTAOULK*, I, p. 147; *RAWK*, II, pp. 253-254; Pitreich, *Lemberg*, p. 28.

62. KAAOK, fasz. 789, Op. Nr. 175/I, AOK Op. Nr. 161; Conrad, *Dienstzeit*, IV, p. 471.

63. KAAOK, R Gruppe, fasz. 495, AOK Op. Nrs. 975, 1000, 1004, 1063; KANFA, 3. A. fasz. 2, Op. Nrs. 181, 193 (AOK Op. Nr. 1077); 4.A. fasz. 4. AOK Op. Nr. 117; Conrad, *Dienstzeit*, IV, pp. 473, 490-491; Pitreich, *1914*, pp. 154, 158 and *Lemberg*, pp. 27, 32; Auffenberg-Komarów, *Österreich-Ungarns Teilnahme*, pp. 113-132, 135-136; Stürgkh, *Im Deutschen Grossen Hauptquartier*, p. 12; Fabini, "Feuertaufe des Eisernen Korps," p. 788.

64. KANFA, 2.A. fasz. 4, Op. Nr. 273; 2.A. fasz. 5, 2. Op. A.Kdo., Nr. 455, k.u.k. AOK, Op. Nr. 243; Conrad, *Dienstzeit*, IV, pp. 344, 359, 363; *OSTAOULK*, I, p. 118.

65. For the Second Army see KAAOK, fasz. 1, k.u.k. A.Kdo., Op. Nr. 619; KANFA, 2.A. fasz. 4, AOK Op. Nr. 380 auf Op. Nrs. 143, 178, 182 auf 171; 2. Op. Kdo., Op. Nr. 380; fasz. 5, 2. Op. Kdo., Op. Nr. 308/2, 353, 392, 509, 519; fasz. 7, Weisungen für Abtransport 2. Armee und VII Korps; Conrad, *Dienstzeit*, IV, pp. 344-346, 347-348, 363, 367, 369, 370, 396, 413, 431-433, 460. KAAOKEBB, fasz. 4119; Conrad, *Dienstzeit*, IV, pp. 396 (AOK Op. Nr. 692), 370. For the orders, KAAOK, R Gruppe, fasz. 495, AOK Op. Nr. 852, 1150; KANFA, 2.A. fasz. 5, Op. Nrs. 308/2. 353 (IV Corps); 390 (VII

Corps and 23 Militia division); 392; AOK Op. Nr. 692; fasz. 7;
Conrad, *Dienstzeit*, IV, pp. 367, 396, 407; *OSTAOULK*, I, p. 127.

66. KANFA, 2.A. fasz. 5, 2.A. Op. A.Kdo., Op. Nrs. 378, 383, 386, 398,
402; Conrad, *Dienstzeit*, IV, p. 431. For Berchtold's interference in
this military question, MKSM, Res. Nrs. 18, 20; Conrad, *Dienstzeit*,
IV, p. 500.

67. KAAOK, fasz. 867, Nachrichten 22.8. and k.u.k. 3 A.Kdo., Op. Nrs.
181, 789; *OSTAOULK*, I, pp. 171-178; Conrad, *Dienstzeit*, IV, pp.
489-490.

68. KAAOK, fasz. 495; AOK Op. Nrs. 1063, 1075; fasz. 6180, Res. Nr.
60; Conrad, *Dienstzeit*, IV, p. 492; *RAWK*, II, pp. 253, 258, 451, 457,
607; Elze, *Tannenberg*, p. 100; Schäfer, "Conrad in den Anfangsoperationen," pp. 129-130.

69. The Russian armies were composed of 44 infantry and 18-1/2 cavalry
divisions. Pitreich, *1914*, p. 156, and *Lemberg*, pp. 41-42; *RAWK*,
II, pp. 36, 255, 256; General Jury N. Danilov, *Russland im Weltkriege 1914-1915* (Jena: Verlag Frommann, 1925), p. 110.

70. KAAOK, fasz. 868, Kriegs Nr. 10; Pitreich, *1914*, pp. 154-155, and
Lemberg, pp. 32, 167, but see Conrad, *Dienstzeit*, IV, p. 505; Ronge,
Kriegs-und Industrie-Spionage, p. 110.

71. KAAOK, fasz. 789; KAAOKEBB, fasz. 4119; Ronge, *Kriegs-und
Industrie-Spionage*, pp. 106, 107, 110; Pitreich, *1914*, p. 154, and
Lemberg, p. 35.

72. HHSTA:PA, I, fasz. 499, Kriegs Nr. 305; Conrad, *Dienstzeit*, IV, pp.
511, 520; Silberstein, *The Troubled Alliance*, varia.

73. For the debate, HHSTA:PA, I, fasz. 498, Kriegs Nr. 326; fasz. 499;
KAMKSM Res., Res. Nrs. 18, 20; KAAOK, R Gruppe, fasz. 495,
AOK Op. Nrs. 1085, 1097, 1182; fasz. 789; AOK Op. Nr. 1167;
KANFA, 2.A. fasz. 9; Conrad, *Dienstzeit*, IV, pp. 469, 484, 495,
499, 500, 501, 518; Freytag-Loringhoven, *Menschen und Dinge*, p.
209.

74. KAAOK, R Gruppe, fasz. 495, AOK Op. Nrs. 1150, 1157, 1161,
1180, 1214; fasz. 789, AOK Op. Nrs. 1667, 1130, 3. Op. Nr. 218;
KAMKSM, Res. Nrs. 20, 21/I, 22. For Berchtold's concern about
shifting Austrian forces northward to Galicia, particularly the IV
Corps, see *OSTAOULK*, I, p. 207; Conrad, *Dienstzeit*, IV, p. 500,
above all, KAAOKEBB, fasz. 4108; MKSM Res. fasz. 100, Res. Nr.
20; KAAOK, fasz. 4119.

Chapter X
Epilogue: The Battles of Lemberg

1. KANFA, 4. A. fasz. 3, Op. Nrs. 228, 230, 235; *OSTAOULK*, I, pp. 189-190; Auffenberg-Komarów, *Österreich-Ungarns Teilnahme*, pp. 149 (Op. Nr. 235, 4. A. Kdo.), 150-151.
2. KAAOK, R Gruppe, fasz. 495, AOK Op. Nrs. 1095, 1102; KANFA, 3. A. fasz. 2, Op. Nr. 209; Conrad, *Dienstzeit*, IV, p. 509; *OSTA-OULK*, I, pp. 187-188; Pitreich, *Lemberg*, p. 74.
3. KAAOK, R Gruppe, fasz. 495, AOK Op. Nrs. 1127, 1147; KANFA, 3. A. fasz. 2, AOK Op. Nr. 1147; 3. A. Op. Nr. 220; Conrad, *Dienstzeit*, IV, pp. 473, 489-491, 505, 509, 513, 516, 517. See *OSTA-OULK*, I, pp. 187-188, 206, 207; Pitreich, *1914*, pp. 155, 198.
4. KAAOK, R Gruppe, fasz. 495, AOK Op. Nrs. 1182, 1191, 1200; fasz. 868, 3. A. Kdos., Kriegs Nr. 11 and reports of 27.8.; HHSTA:PA, I, fasz. 498, Baron Giesl Nr. 33; Conrad, *Dienstzeit*, IV, p. 528; *OSTAOULK* I, p. 209; *Pitreich, 1914*, p. 181.
5. KAAOK, R Gruppe, fasz. 495; Conrad, *Dienstzeit*, IV, pp. 522, 525, 527 and footnote; Stabbs, *Aufmarsch nach zwei Fronten*, pp. 50-51.
6. KAAOK, fasz. 868; fasz. 6180, Res. Nr. 80; Conrad, *Dienstzeit*, IV, pp. 355, 457.
7. KAAOK, R Gruppe, fasz. 495, AOK Op. Nrs. 1182, 1208, 1209; Conrad, *Dienstzeit*, IV, pp. 529, 532, 534, 547, 548; *OSTAOULK*, I, pp. 202, 213; Pitreich, *Lemberg*, p. 74.
8. Conrad, *Dienstzeit*, IV, p. 542; *OSTAOULK*, I, pp. 214, 219; Pitreich, *Lemberg*, p. 50; Auffenberg-Komarow, *Österreich-Ungarns Teilnahme*, pp. 274, 275; Bardolff, *Soldat im alten Österreich*, p. 194.
9. KAAOK, fasz. 868; fasz. 6180, Res. Nr. 81; *RAWK*, II, pp. 202, 203-204, 207, 259; Pitreich, *1914*, pp. 200-201.
10. Conrad, *Dienstzeit*, IV, p. 563; Ritter, "Zusammenarbeit," p. 545 footnote.
11. KAAOK, R Gruppe, fasz. 495; fasz. 6180, Res. Nr. 95.
12. KAAOK, fasz. 6180, Res. Nr. 101; Conrad, *Dienstzeit*, IV, pp. 561, 564, 568; *OSTAOULK*, I, p. 221; *RAWK*, II, p. 259; Pitreich, *1914*, pp. 201, 225.
13. HHSTA:PA, I, fasz. 498; *OSTAOULK*, II, pp. 201, 217; Redlich, *Politisches Tagebuch*, pp. 257-258; Pitreich, *1914*, p. 182.

14. KAAOKEBB, fasz. 4119; KAAOK, fasz. 6180, Res. Nr. 101; KAN-
    FA, 4.A. fasz. 3; Pitreich, *1914*, pp. 171, 173; *Lemberg*, p. 53;
    Conrad, *Dienstzeit*, IV, p. 567. The ratio of forces at the Third
    Army's front was:

	battalions	squadrons	artillery
Third Army	115	91	376
Enemy	292	162	720

    OSTAOULK, I, p. 217; Pitreich, *Lemberg*, pp. 76, 78.

15. KAAOK, R Gruppe, fasz. 495, AOK Op. Nrs. 1267, 1343; Conrad,
    Dienstzeit, IV, pp. 542, 554; *OSTAOULK*, I, pp. 201, 223; Pitreich,
    1914, pp. 173, 183, *Lemberg*, p. 57; Bardolff, *Soldat im alten Öster-
    reich*, p. 194.
16. Conrad, *Dienstzeit*, IV, p. 576; Redlich, *Politisches Tagebuch,* p.
    263.
17. KAAOK, fasz. 868, Res. Nrs. 77, 82, 87, 94; fasz. 869, Res. Nr. 97;
    fasz. 6180, Res. Nrs. 80, 82, 85, 87, 101; Conrad, *Dienstzeit*, IV, pp.
    573, 574, 578; *OSTAOULK*, I, p. 221; *RAWK*, V, p. 402.
18. KAAOK, fasz. 869, Res. Nr. 101; fasz. 6180; Stürgkh, *Im Deutschen
    Grossen Hauptquartier*, pp. 40, 41, 158; Conrad, *Dienstzeit*, IV, pp.
    527, 574.
19. HHSTA:PA, I, fasz. 498, Baron Giesl Nr. 35; KAAOK, fasz. 6180,
    Res. Nr. 85; Conrad, *Dienstzeit*, IV, pp. 572, 577; *OSTAOULK*, I, p.
    243; Pitreich, *Lemberg*, p. 59.
20. For the Second Army see HHSTA:PA, I, fasz. 498; KAAOK, R
    Gruppe, fasz. 495, AOK Op. Nrs. 1150, 1346, 1410, 1431; fasz. 868,
    3. A. Kdos. Kriegs Nr. 23, 29; KAAOKEBB, fasz. 4119; KANFA,
    2. A. fasz. 10, Op. Nrs. 83, 84, 85; Conrad, *Dienstzeit*, IV, pp.
    584-590; *OSTAOULK*, I, pp. 244, 250, 251; Pitreich, *Lemberg*, p.
    60.
21. Conrad, *Dienstzeit*, IV, p. 582; Pitreich, *1914*, pp. 185, 186; Auffen-
    berg-Komarów, *Österreich-Ungarns Teilnahme*, p. 172.
22. KAAOK, R Gruppe, fasz. 495, AOK Op. Nrs. 1376, 1412; fasz.
    6180, Res. Nr. 95; Conrad, *Dienstzeit*, IV, pp. 595, 596, 597-598;
    Pitreich, *1914*, p. 183, *Lemberg*, p. 85.
23. KAAOK, R Gruppe, fasz. 495, AOK Op. Nr. 1286; R Gruppe, fasz.
    496, AOK Op. Nr. 1459, k.u.k. A. Kdo., Russische Streitkräfte gegen
    Österreich-Ungarn; fasz. 869, Evidenz Gruppe "R," September 1914,

Die Verteilung der russischen Streitkräfte; fasz. 6180, Kraftgruppie-
rung an 31.8.1914.

24. KAAOK, R Gruppe, fasz. 495, AOK Op. Nr. 1376; Conrad, *Dienstzeit*, IV, pp. 593-594; *OSTAOULK*, I, p. 252; Pitreich, *1914*, pp.
185-186, 201, *Lemberg*, p. 85.

25. HHSTA:PA, I, fasz. 498, Baron Giesl Nr. 39; KAAOK, R Gruppe,
fasz. 496, AOK Op. Nr. 1466 (R 305); fasz. 869, 4. Op. A. Kdo.,
Kriegs Nr. 50; fasz. 6180, Res. Nrs. 100, 102; KANFA, 1. A. fasz.
137, Op. Nrs. 570, 572, 598; Conrad, *Dienstzeit*, IV, p. 609; *OSTA-
OULK*, I, pp. 192-201, 204, 224-231, 241, 252; *RAWK*, II, pp. 168-
173, 190-193, 196-197, 260; Bardolff, *Soldat im alten Österreich*,
pp. 139, 202; Ronge, *Kriegs-und Industrie-Spionage*, pp. 113-114;
Leppa, *Die Schlacht bei Komarów*; Pitreich, *Lemberg*, p. 86; Auffenberg-Komarów, *Österreich-Ungarns Teilnahme*, pp. 147-238,
248, and *Aus Österreichs Höhe und Niedergang*, p. 321; Freytag-
Loringhoven, *Menschen und Dinge*, p. 222. At the battle of Komarów, the ratio of forces was:

	battalions	squadrons	artillery
Russian	152	150	600
Austrian	194	102	610

OSTAOULK, I, p. 240.

26. KAAOK, R Gruppe, fasz. 496, AOK Op. Nrs. 1463, 1523, 1543,
1565 (R 342), 1568 (R 343); fasz. 790, 1914 AOK Evidenz der
eigenen Situation aus Op. Nrs. 1425-2700, 1.9.-30.9. 1914 russ.
Krieg, AOK Op. Nr. 1467-28; KANFA, 4. A. fasz. 3, 4. A. Op. Nr.
335; KANFA, 2. A. fasz. 11, Nr. 168; Conrad, *Dienstzeit*, IV, pp.
606, 609, 617; *OSTAOULK*, I, p. 253; Pitreich, *1914*, p. 208, *Lemberg*, p. 86; Auffenberg-Komarów, *Aus Österreichs Höhe und Niedergang*, pp. 326, 329; August Urbanski von Ostrymiecz, *Das Tornisterkind: Lebenserinnerung des Feldmarschalleutnants August von
Urabnski*, Unpublished (1948), p. 114; Bardolff, *Soldat im alten
Österreich*, p. 203.

27. HHSTA:PA, I, fasz. 498; Baron Giesl Nr. 46; KAAOK, fasz. 496;
AOK Op. Nrs. 1465, 1473; fasz. 6180, Res. Nr. 100; Conrad, *Dienstzeit*, IV, pp. 607-608; *RAWK*, II, p. 261; *OSTAOULK*, I, p. 251. For
the actual retreat order see KANFA, 3. A. fasz. 2, AOK Op. Nr.
1747 and Op. Nr. 367/Op; 2. A. fasz. 11, AOK Op. Nr. 1475; Conrad,
Dienstzeit, IV, pp. 607-608, 620, 622; Pitreich, *Lemberg*, p. 88;

Freytag-Loringhoven, *Menschen und Dinge*, p. 222; Bardolff, *Soldat im alten Österreich*, p. 203.

28. KAAOK, fasz. 6180, Res. Nr. 104; Conrad, *Dienstzeit*, IV, p. 626; *OSTAOULK*, I, p. 273; *RAWK*, II, p. 262; Pitreich, *1914*, p. 208.

29. *OSTAOULK*, I, p. 273; *RAWK*, II, p. 340; Pitreich, *1914*, p. 208. Until 10 September the German Eastern Army had tied down thirty-six and one-half Russian divisions. If one recalls the Conrad-Moltke "agreements," the German eastern forces were to bind nineteen and one-half enemy divisions. The charges and countercharges of infidelity by the Germans in not attacking towards Siedlce are purely semantic exercises, although the debate raged in the inter-war years.

30. KAAOK, R Gruppe, fasz. Nr. 496, AOK Op. Nr. 1576; fasz. Nr. 790, k.u.k. 3. A. Kdo., Op. Nr. 385, AOK Op. Nr. 1510-14; fasz. 6180, Res. Nrs. 102, 104, 110, Op. R 334a; KANFA, 4. A. fasz. 3, Op. Nrs. 381, 403, and AOK Op. Nr. 1454; Conrad, *Dienstzeit*, IV, pp. 629, 631; *OSTAOULK*, I, pp. 254, 262; Pitreich, *1914*, pp. 209, 213, *Lemberg*, p. 90; Auffenberg-Komarow, *Österreich-Ungarns Teilnahme*, p. 281.

31. HHSTA:PA, I, fasz. 498, Res. Nr. 53; KAAOK, R Gruppe, fasz. 495, Op. Nr. R 334a; fasz. 790, AOK Op. Nr. 1510 (3. A. Op. Nr. 385); KANFA, 3. A. fasz. 2, Op. Nrs. 385, 391; 2. A. fasz. 11, Op. Nr. 168 (AOK Op. Nr. 1523); Auffenberg-Komarow, *Österreich-Ungarns Teilnahme*, pp. 254, 289, 315; Conrad, *Dienstzeit*, IV, p. 638.

32. HHSTA:PA, I, fasz. 498; KAAOK, fasz. 869, Baron Giesl Nr. 56; KANFA, 2. A. fasz. 11, Op. Nr. 202; Conrad, *Dienstzeit*, IV, p. 640; *OSTAOULK*, I, p. 264, 265, 267; KAAOK, "R Gruppe," fasz. 496, AOK Op. Nrs. 1501, 1779; fasz. 6180, Res. Nr. 12. For the overall situation see KANFA, 4. A. fasz. 3, 4. A. Op. Nr. 399; fasz. 869, 3. A. Kdo. Kriegs Nr. 35; AOK Op. Nr. 1561, 4. A. Op. Nr. 397; k.u.k. 3. A. Kdo., Op. Nr. 386; Auffenberg-Komarow, *Aus Österreichs Höhe und Niedergang*, p. 337. A Russian radio message gave away the danger. See KAAOK, fasz. 869; fasz. 790, AOK Op. Nr. 1550/4; Pitreich, *1914*, pp. 207, 210, 213; Auffenberg-Komarow, *Österreich-Ungarns Teilnahme*, pp. 252-253. The Austrian First Army, consisting of thirteen infantry, two cavalry divisions, and five reserve brigades, faced two enemy armies totalling twenty-two infantry and six and one-half cavalry divisions. *OSTAOULK*, I, p. 265.

33. KAAOK, fasz. 869, 3. A. Kdo. Kriegs Nr. 35; fasz. 6180, Res. Nr. 112; Conrad, *Dienstzeit*, IV, p. 652; Pitreich, *1914*, pp. 210, 213,

Lemberg, p. 90; Auffenberg-Komarow, *Österreich-Ungarns Teilnahme*, pp. 253, 288.

34. KAAOK, fasz. 790, AOK Op. Nr. 150-19 and 1. A. Op. Nr. 640; *OSTAOULK*, I, pp. 273, 312; *RAWK*, II, p. 263; Stürgkh, *Im Deutschen Grossen Hauptquartier*, pp. 40, 41, 71; Pitreich, *1914*, pp. 207-208.

35. For the attack orders see KAAOK, R Gruppe, fasz. 496, AOK Op. Nrs. 1620, 1675 (R 379); fasz. 869, Telegraph 6.9.; KANFA, 2. A. fasz. 11, 2. A. Kdo. Op. Nrs. 232, 248; 4. A. fasz. 3, AOK Op. Nrs. 1620, 4. A. Kdo. Op. Nr. 426/I; Conrad *Dienstzeit*, IV, pp. 642, 644, 652, AOK Op. Nr. 1655; *OSTAOULK*, I, p. 272; *RAWK*, II, pp. 331, 332; Pitreich, *1914*, pp. 214-215, 219, *Lemberg*, p. 99.

36. Conrad, *Dienstzeit*, IV, pp. 656, AOK Op. Nr. 3558; Stürgkh, *Im Deutschen Grossen Hauptquartier*, pp. 41, 42. Stürgkh had requested twice the number promised.

37. Conrad, *Dienstzeit*, IV, pp. 657, 658-660; *OSTAOULK*, I, p. 273; Stürgkh, *Im Deutschen Grossen Hauptquartier*, p. 40.

38. KAAOK, R Gruppe, fasz. 496, AOK Op. Nrs. 1712, 1716 (R 390); fasz. 869, Nachricht 7.9, air reconn report 8.9.; KANFA, 2 A. fasz. 11, 2. A. Kdo. Op. Nr. 248; 4. A. fasz. 3, 3. A. Kdo. Op. Nr. 464; HHSTA:PA, I, fasz. 498, Baron Giesl Nr. 60; fasz. 6180, Res. Nr. 112; Conrad, *Dienstzeit*, IV, pp, 662 (AOK Op. Nr. 1745), 666, 672; *OSTAOULK*, I, pp. 282, 283; Freytag-Loringhoven, *Menschen und Dinge*, p. 223; *RAWK*, II, p. 331; Pitreich, *1914*, pp. 210-211, 215-216, 218, *Lemberg*, p. 100. Conrad hurled twenty-nine and one-half infantry and seven cavalry divisions at Lemberg in his effort to regain it.

39. HHSTA:PA, I, fasz. 500; Conrad, *Dienstzeit*, IV, p. 681. This exchange occurred as the German offense began against General Rennenkampf's First Russian Army. Redlich, *Politisches Tagebuch*, p. 264; Ritter, "Zusammenarbeit," p. 547.

40. HHSTA:PA, I, fasz. 500, Nr. 7880; fasz. 498, Tisza to Berchtold; Ritter, "Zusammenarbeit," p. 547; Redlich, *Politisches Tagebuch*, pp. 265, 274.

41. HHSTA:PA, I, fasz. 500, Nr. 7880, Conrad to Berchtold, and Nr. 551, Berchtold to Berlin; KANC, B fasz. 6; Redlich, *Politisches Tagebuch*, p. 270; Pitreich, *1914*, p. 226.

42. For the military situation see KAAOK, R Gruppe, fasz. 496; Conrad, *Dienstzeit*, IV, p. 689; *OSTAOULK*, I, p. 299; Pitreich, *1914*, p. 226.

This date, 9 September, was the German fortieth mobilization day, the day the German General Staff had assumed they would have defeated France. Conrad, *Dienstzeit*, I, pp. 370, 383, 384, 395, 396; III, pp. 610, 673.

43. KAAOK, fasz. 6180, Res. Nr. 133; HHSTA:PA, I, fasz. 500.
44. HHSTA:PA, I, fasz. 500, Document Nr. 508.
45. HHSTA:PA, I, fasz. 500, Pro domo Nr. 4315.
46. HHSTA:PA, I, fasz. 500; Silberstein, *The Troubled Alliance*, p. 184.
47. For 8 September see HHSTA:PA, I, fasz. 498, Baron Giesl Nr. 61; Conrad, *Dienstzeit*, IV, p. 681; *OSTAOULK*, I, pp. 282, 283; *RAWK*, II, pp. 331-332; KAAOK, R Gruppe, fasz. 496, AOK Op. Nrs. 1776 (R 413), 1782 (R 415), 1785 (R 409); fasz. 869, Vermutliche Gruppierung der feindlichen Kräfte 8.9.; Pitreich, *1914*, p. 218.
48. KAAOK, R Gruppe, fasz. 496, AOK Op. Nrs. 1791, 1796, 1799 (R 417), 1850 (R 424); Conrad, *Dienstzeit*, IV, p. 668; *OSTAOULK*, I, p. 284; Freytag-Loringhoven, *Menschen und Dinge*, pp. 223-224. The enemy forces attacking from the Zbrucz River region were the Russian forces reputedly defeated at the battle of Komarow, but which were now approaching the battlefields north of Lemberg. At the same time massive Russian reinforcements from the Lublin area threatened the First Army with encirclement. HHSTA:PA, I, fasz. 500; *OSTAOULK*, I, p. 299; *RAWK*, II, p. 332; Pitreich, *1914*, p. 218, and *Lemberg*, p. 112. A Russian cavalry corps had maneuvered into the forty-mile gap between the First and Fourth Austrian Armies. *RAWK*, II, pp. 332, 335.
49. KANFA, 1. A. fasz. 138, 1. A. Kdo., Op. Nr. 768; *OSTAOULK*, I, p. 299.
50. KAAOK, R Gruppe, fasz. 496, AOK Op. Nr. 1791, 1796 (R 418), 1850.
51. KAAOK, R Gruppe, fasz. 496, Conrad to Moltke, AOK Op. Nrs. 1937, 1940; fasz. 6180, Res. Nr. 125; KANFA, 1. A. fasz. 137, 1. A. Kdo., Op. Nr. 853; 2. A. fasz. 9, k.u.k. 2. A. Kdo., Op. Nr. 341; HHSTA:PA, I, fasz. 498, Baron Giesl Nr. 67; *RAWK*, II, pp. 332, 333, 335, 403; Conrad, *Dienstzeit*, IV, varia between 697-734; Ronge, *Kriegs-und Industrie-Spionage*, p. 114; Pitreich, *Lemberg*, pp. 112, 113. One of the key factors in the retreat: General Conrad had no reserves to plug the gap between his armies. Pitreich, *Lemberg*, pp. 104, 113.

52. HHSTA:PA, I, fasz. 498, von Wiesner Nr. 68; KANFA, 2. A. fasz. 9, 2. A. Kdo. Op. Nr. 355; Conrad, *Dienstzeit*, IV, p. 752; Bardolff, *Soldat im alten Österreich*, p. 206; *OSTAOULK*, I, p. 342. The armed ratios between the Vistula and Dniester Rivers were:

	battalions	squadrons	artillery
Russia	824	694	2,888
Austria	770	356	2,098
	54	338	790

   Of the battalions, 100 Austrian consisted of non-regular forces. Pitreich, *1914*, p. 221.

53. HHSTA:PA, I, fasz. 500; KAAOK, R Gruppe, fasz. 496, Conrad to Moltke, Stürgkh to Conrad, Res. Nr. 28; fasz. 869, Res. Nrs. 118, 124, 141, Hindenburg report; Conrad, *Dienstzeit*, IV, varia between 647-731; *RAWK*, V, pp. 403-404; *OSTAOULK*, I, pp. 312, 342, 343; Pitreich, *1914*, p. 226. Austrian intelligence sources placed forty Austrian divisions of thirteen battalions each (526 battalions) versus forty-seven Russian divisions of sixteen battalions each (752 battalions). Thus the Russians had an advantage of 226 battalions (200,000 men) or seventeen infantry divisions. Conrad, *Dienstzeit*, IV, pp, 698, 707.

54. HHSTA:PA, I, fasz. 500, Nr. 2404, Baron Giesl Nr. 66.

55. HHSTA:PA, I, fasz. 500, Pro domo Nr. 4360, telegram Nr. 520 (the barb was inserted that according to German calculations Austria battled with only an enemy numerical advantage of two divisions).

56. KAAOK, R Gruppe, fasz. 496; Torrey, "Rumania and the Belligerents," p. 170; Silberstein, *The Troubled Alliance*, pp. 185, 187.

57. HHSTA:PA, I, fasz. 500; KAMKSM, fasz. 100, Nr. 39 Res. 1914; Conrad, *Dienstzeit*, IV, p. 725; *OSTAOULK*, I, p. 312.

58. HHSTA:PA, I, fasz. 500, Pro domo Nrs. 4392, 6792, 9280, and Franz Joseph to Wilhelm; Czernin Nr. 474, Hohenlohe Nr. 588; see KAAOK, R Gruppe, fasz. 496, AOK Op. Nrs. 1957, 2054 (R 494).

59. HHSTA:PA, I, fasz. 500, Hohenlohe Nr. 7814.

60. Conrad, *Dienstzeit*, IV, pp. 740-741.

61. KAAOK, R Gruppe, fasz. 496, AOK Op. Nr. 1957; HHSTA:PA, I, fasz. 500, Pro domo Nr. 9280; Conrad, *Dienstzeit*, IV, p. 731.

62. KAAOK, R Gruppe, fasz. 496, AOK Op. Nrs. 2352, 2354; Conrad, *Dienstzeit*, IV, p. 811; Redlich, *Politisches Tagebuch*, pp. 277, 278.

63. KAMKSM, fasz. 100, Nrs. 44, 52 Res.; Conrad, *Dienstzeit*, IV, p. 814; Stürgkh, *Im Deutschen Grossen Hauptquartier*, p. 51; HHSTA:PA, I, fasz. 500, Pro domo Nr. 4392, Czernin Nr. 474, Hohenlohe Nr. 588; Wilhelm to Franz Joseph, 16 September.

64. Conrad, *Dienstzeit*, IV, pp. 795-799.

65. Conrad, *Dienstzeit*, IV, pp. 796, 797; *OSTAOULK*, I, pp. 345-346.

66. HHST:PA, I, fasz. 500.

67. HHSTA:PA, I, fasz. 500, Hohenlohe Nr. 534.

68. KAAOK, R Gruppe, fasz. 496, AOK Op. Nr. 2267, Res. Nr. 164, AOK Op. Nr. 2375; Conrad, *Dienstzeit*, IV, pp. 824-827, 838-839.

69. KAAOK, R Gruppe, fasz. 496, Conrad to Moltke; Conrad, *Dienstzeit*, IV, pp. 818, 819. Conrad in wiring Moltke was not aware that General Falkenhayn had assumed the Supreme Command on 14 September.

70. KAAOK, fasz. 6180, Res. Nrs. 169, 181.

71. Conrad, *Dienstzeit*, IV, p. 821. Many of the best Austro-Hungarian officers and non-commissioned officers were lost on the battlefield. Almost one-third of the entire army was dead, wounded, or prisoners. Bardolff, *Soldat im alten Österreich*, p. 208.

72. Conrad, *Dienstzeit*, IV, pp. 810-811; I, pp. 398, 399, 402 and 404 for the 1909 "agreements." At the same time the transferral of two German corps to the eastern theater before the battle of the Marne negatively affected the outcome of that battle.

73. KAAOK, R Gruppe, fasz. 496, AOK Op. Nr. 2375; fasz. Nr. 869, Res. Nr. 355; Conrad, *Dienstzeit*, IV, p. 826; *OSTAOULK*, I, pp. 346-347.

74. KAAOK, fasz. 6180, Res. Nrs. 223, 234; Conrad, *Dienstzeit*, IV, p. 836; *OSTAOULK*, I, p. 347.

75. For the planning see KAAOK, R Gruppe, fasz. 496, AOK Op. Nr. 2645; Conrad, *Dienstzeit*, IV, pp. 845, 858, 866-867; *OSTAOULK*, I, p. 347; Freytag-Loringhoven, *Menschen und Dinge*, p. 241. Conrad agreed that five divisions would cooperate with the German offensive. Conrad, *Dienstzeit*, IV, p. 837; Auffenberg-Komarow, *Aus Österreichs Höhe und Niedergang*, p. 378.

76. Conrad, *Dienstzeit*, IV, pp. 890 (Res. Nr. 226), 892 (Kriegs Nr. 876).

Bibliography

Unpublished Documents

Austria: Österreichisches Staatsarchiv — Kriegsarchiv

Generalstab, Operationsbüro:
Faszikel   1-38, 44-54, 61, 67-68, 70-73, 79-80, 87-88,89a, 90-91, 94-95, 105-105a, 108, 110-112, 115-117, 147-153, 155-156, 159, 161, 176, 178-179, 181, 183, 221, 223-224, 235.

AOK (Armeeoberkommando), Allgemeine Registratur:
Faszikel   1-5.

Gruppenregistratur:
Faszikel   495-496.

Deutsche Westfront:
Faszikel   600.

Evidenz der eigenen Situation:
Faszikel   789-790.

Evidenz der feindlichen Situation:
Faszikel   867-869.

Verbindungsoffiziere:
Faszikel   6180.

Armeeoberkommando: Eisenbahnbüro:
Faszikel   4107, 4108, 4119.

Etappenbüro
Faszikel   1-5, 11, 13, 30, 34, 37-39, 41-42, 45, 54, 56-60.

Neue Feldakten

1. Armee: Operierendes Armeekommando:
   Faszikel   29, 30, 135-139, 172-174, 202, 226, 245, 248.

2. Armee: Operierendes Armeekommando:
   Faszikel   1-7, 9-11, 35-38, 66, 94, 137, 226, 245, 248.

3. Armee: Operierendes Armeekommando
   Faszikel   1, 2a, 3, 18-20, 36, 38, 42, 44, 61.

4. Armee: Operierendes Armeekommando:
   Faszikel   1, 1a, 1b, 2-4, 32, 34-35, 70, 73, 90, 94-95, 104.

Nachlässe

Archiv Conrad von Hötzendorf
    A Faszikel 6, B Faszikel   1-6, 12.
Archiv Beck-Rzikowski
    Faszikel   241-242.
General
    B/23, 58, 60, 61, 75, 96, 109, 151, 198, 203, 269, 327, 366,
    405, 527, 691, 700, 800, 1041.
Kriegsministerium Präs.:
    Varia: 1913 Documents Nrs. 40-29-1, 46-16-6, 47-4-9, 47-4-35,
    47-5-5, 47-8-2, 47-8-3, 47-8-51, 51-2-11, 51-2-30, 51-2-33, 51-
    2-39, 51-2-59, 51-7-131-5, 51-8-5, 51-8-14, 56-8-14, 54-4-2.
Militärkanzlei Franz Ferdinand
    Faszikel   194, 194-1, 202. Varia: Document Nrs. 41-25, 45-10-
    17, 41-25-6, 40-3-9, 40-3-8, 40-1-13, 41-25-6, 14-24-11, 14-24-
    5, 40-3-3.
Militärkanzlei Seiner Majestät des Kaisers:
    Faszikel   100 res. Varia: Document Nrs. 18-2:3-1, 56-2-5R
    (1914), 18-2-9-1(1914).

Austria. Haus-, Hof- und Staatsarchiv

Politisches Archiv I
    487, 496-500, 506-507, 512-513, 515-516, 521-522, 534-536,
    829, 837, 842, 880, 905, 983.
Politisches Archiv XII
    357, 365, 424-425, 440-450.

Published Documents and Official Collections

Austria-Hungary. *Diplomatische Aktenstücke zur Vorgeschichte des Kriegs 1914: Ergänzungen und Nachträge zum Österreichisch-Ungarischen Rotbuch.* 4 vols. Vienna: Staatsdruckerei, 1919.
Austria-Hungary. *Österreich-Ungarns Aussenpolitik von der Bosnischen Krise 1908 bis zum Kriegsausbruch 1914. Diplomatische Aktenstücke des österreichisch-ungarischen Ministeriums des Äussern.* 8 vols. Selected by L. Bittner, A. F. Pribam, H. Srbik and H. Uebersberger, edited by L. Bittner und H. Uebersberger. Vienna: 1930.

Austria-Hungary. *Österreichisch-ungarisches Rotbuch. Diplomatische Aktenstücke betreffend die Beziehungen Österreich-Ungarns zu Italien in der Zeit vom 20. Juli bis 23. Mai 1915.* Vienna: Manzsche k.u.k. Hof-Verlags-und Universitäts-Buchhandlung. 1915.

Austria-Hungary. *Österreichisch-ungarisches Rotbuch. Diplomatische Aktenstücke betreffend die Beziehungen Österreich-Ungarns zu Rumänien in der Zeit vom 22. Juli bis 27. August 1916.* Vienna: Manzsche k.u.k. Hof-Verlags-und Universitäts-Buchhandlung. 1916.

Austria-Hungary. *Protokolle des gemeinsamen Ministerrates der österreichisch-ungarischen Monarchie (1914-1918).* Editor Miklós Komjáthy. Budapest: Akadémiai Kiadó, 1966.

Germany. *Die Grosse Politik der europäischen Kabinette 1871-1914.* Edited by Johannes Lepsius, Albrecht Mendelssohn-Bartholdy and Friedrich Thimme. 40 vols. Deutsche Verlagsgesellslchaft für Politik.

Germany. *Reichstag. Untersuchungsausschuss über die Weltkriegsverantwortlichkeit. Zur Vorgeschichte des Weltkrieges.* Heft 2: *Militärische Rüstungen und Mobilmachung.* Berlin: Verlag von Reimer Hobbing in Berlin, 1921.

Russia. Hoetzsch, Otto (ed.). *Die Internationalen Beziehungen im Zeitalter des Imperialismus. Dokumente aus den Archiven der zarischen und der provisorischen Regierung. Reihe 1. Band 4 and 5.* Berlin: Verlag von Reimar Hobbing, 1932.

Prussia. *Grosser Generalstab. Dienstschriften des Chefs des Gene-ralstabes der Armee, Generalfeldmarschall Graf von Schlieffen.* Herausgegeben vom Generalstab des Heeres 7 (Kriegswissenschaftliche) Abteilung. 2 vols. Berlin: E. S. Mittler & Sohn, 1937.

Official Military Histories

Österreich-Ungarns letzter Krieg 1914-1918. Erster Band Das Kriegsjahr 1914. Herausgegeben vom österreichischen Bundesministerium für Heereswesen und vom Kriegsarchiv. Vienna: Verlag Militärwissenschaftlicher Mitteilungen, 1929, 1931.

Der Weltkrieg 1914 bis 1918. Vols. 1 and 2. *Die militärischen Operationen zu Lande.* Bearbeitet im Reichsarchiv. Berlin: E. S. Mittler & Sohn, 1925.

Monographs

Alberti, A. *General Falkenhayn. Die Beziehungen zwischen den General-stabschefs des Dreibundes.* Translated by Walter Weber. Berlin: E.S. Mittler & Son, 1924.

Albertini, Luigi. *The Origins of the War of 1914.* Translated and edited by Isabella M. Massey. 3 vols. New York: Oxford University Press, 1957.

Arz Straussenburg, Generaloberst von. *Zur Geschichte des Grossen Krie-ges 1914-1918. Aufzeichnungen.* Vienna: Rikola Verlag, 1924.

_____. *Kampf und Sturz der Kaiserreiche.* Vienna: Johannes Gunther Verlag, 19?.

Asprey, Robert B. *The German High Command. Hindenburg and Luden-dorff Conduct World War 1.* New York: William Morrow and Com-pany, Inc., 1991.

Auffenberg-Komarow, General M. *Aus Österreich-Ungarns Teilnahme am Weltkriege.* Berlin: Ullstein Verlag, 1920.

_____. *Aus Österreichs Höhe und Niedergang. Eine Lebensschilderung.* Munich: Drei Masken Verlag, 1921.

Baernreither, Joseph M. *Fragmente eines politischen Tagebuches: Die südslawische Frage und Österreich-Ungarn vor dem Weltkrieg.* Editor Joseph Redlich. Berlin: Verlag für Kulturpolitik, 1928.

Bardolff, Carl Freiherr von. *Deutsch-österreichisches Soldatentum im Weltkrieg.* Jena: E. Diederichs Verlag, 1937.

_____. *Soldat im alten Österreich. Erinnerungen aus meinen Leben.* Jena: E. Diederichs Verlag, 1943.

Belt, Oberst J.C. van den. *Die ersten Wochen des grossen Krieges. Lut-tich, Marne-Ource, Tannenberg, Lemberg.* Berlin: E.S. Mittler & Sohn, 1922.

Bethmann-Hollweg, Theobald von. *Betrachtungen zum Weltkrieg.* 2 vols. Berlin: Reimer Hobbing, 1919-1922. (*Reflections on the World War.*) Translated by George Young. 2 vols. New York: Harper and Bros., 1920.

Boetticher, Friedrich von. *Graf Alfred Schlieffen. Sein Werden und Wirken.* Berlin: Schlieffen Verlag, 1933.

Brandenburg, Erich. *From Bismarck to the World War: A History of German Foreign Policy, 1870-1914.* 3rd Edition. Translated by Annie Elizabeth Adams. New York: Oxford University Press, 1938.

Bridge, F.R. *From Sadowa to Sarajevo. The Foreign Policy of Austria-Hungary, 1866-1914.* Boston: Routledge & Kegan Paul, 1971.
_____.*The Habsburg Monarchy.* New York: Oxford University Press, 1967.

Brussilov, General A.A. *A Soldiers Notebook 1914-1918.* Westport, Connecticut: Greenwood Press Publishers, 1971.

Buat, General. *Die deutsche Armee im Weltkrieg.* Munich: Verlag Wieland, 1921.

Bundesministerium für Landesverteidigung. Militärwissenschaftliche Abteilung. *Der österreichisch-ungarische Aufmarsch im Juli/August 1914.*

Burian von Rajecz, Stephan. *Austria in Dissolution. (Being the Personal Recollections of Stephen, Count Burian.)* Translated by Brian Luna. London: Ernest Benn Limited, 1925.

Choucri, Nazli and North Robert C. *Nations in Conflict. National Growth and International Violence.* San Francisco: W.H. Freeman and Company, 1974.

Churchill, Winston. *The Unknown War: The Eastern Front .* New York: Charles Scribner's Sons, 1931.

Cochenhausen, Friedrich Generalleutnant. *Conrad von Hötzendorf. Eine Studie über seine Persönlichkeit.* (Schriften der kriegsgeschichtlichen Abteilung im historischen Seminar der Friedrich-Wilhelms Universität). Berlin: Junker and Dunnhaupt Verlag, 1934.

Collenberg, Ludwig Frh. Rudt. von. *Die deutsche Armee von 1871 bis 1914.* Berlin: E.S. Mittler & Sohn, 1922.

Conrad, Feldmarschall Franz von Hötzendorf. *Aus meiner Dienstzeit, 1906-1918.* 4 vols. Vienna: Rikola Verlag, 1921-1925.

Corti, E. C. and Sokol, Hans. *Der Alte Kaiser Franz Joseph I. vom Berliner Kongress bis zu seinem Tode.* Graz: Verlag Styria, 1955.

Craig, Gordon A. *The Politics of the Prussian Army, 1640-1945.* New York: Oxford University Press, 1956.

Cramon, August und Fleck, Paul von. *Deutschlands Schicksalsbund mit Österreich-Ungarn. Von Conrad von Hötzendorff zu Kaiser Karl.* Berlin: Verlag für Kulturpolitik, 1932.

_____. *Unser österreich-ungarischer Bundesgenosse im Weltkriege: Erinnerungen aus meiner vierjährigen Tätigkeit als bevollmächtigter deutscher General beim k.u.k. Armeeoberkommando.* Berlin: E.S. Mittler & Sohn, 1920.

Csicerics, von Bacsany. *Die Schlacht. Studie auf Grund des Krieges in Ostasien 1904-1905*. Vienna: L.W. Siedel & Sohn, 1908.

Czernin, Ottokar, *Im Weltkriege*. Vienna: Ullstein Verlag, 1919.

Danilov, General Jury N. *Russland im Weltkriege 1914-1915*. Jena: Verlag Frommann, 1925.

_____. *Grossfürst Nikolai Nikolajewitsch. Sein Leben und Wirken*. Berlin: Verlegt bei Richard Schroeder, 1930.

Dedijer, Vladimir, *The Road to Sarajevo*. New York: Simon & Schuster, 1966.

Das deutsche Feldeisenbahnwesen. Vol. 1, *Die Eisenbahnen zu Kriegsbeginn*. Berlin: E.S. Mitler & Sohn, 1928.

Dieterich, Rudolf von. *Berichtigung zu Österreich-Ungarns letztem Krieg 1914-1918. Erste Schlacht bei Lemberg am 29., 30. und 31. August 1914*. Vienna: 1933.

Dobrorolskij, General Sergej. *Die Mobilmachung der russischen Armee, 1914. Beiträge zur Schuldfrage*. Berlin: Verlag für Politik, 1922.

Eggeling, Bernhard Friedrich. *Die russische Mobilmachung und der Kriegsausbruch. Beiträge zur Schuldfrage am Weltkriege*. Berlin: E. Stalling, 1919.

Elze, Walter. *Der strategische Aufbau des Weltkrieges 1914-1918. Betrachtungen und Anregungen*. Berlin: Junker & Dunnhaupt, 1933.

_____. *Tannenberg, Das deutsche Heer von 1914. Seine Grundzüge und deren Auswirkung an der Ostfront*. Breslau: Verlag Hirt, 1928.

Enderes, Bruno. *Verkehrswesen im Kriege. Die österreichischen Eisenbahnen*. Wirtschaft und Sozialgeschichte des Weltkrieges. Österreichische und Ungarische Serie, Editor James T. Shotwell. Vienna: Holder-Pichler-Tempsky A-G, 1931.

Evans, R.J.W., and Strandmann, Hartmut Pogge von. *The Coming of the First World War*. Oxford: Clarendon Press, 1988.

Falkenhayn, Erich von. *Die oberste Heeresleitung 1914-1916 in ihren wichtigsten Entscheidungen*. Berlin: E.S. Mittler & Sohn, 1920.

Farrar, L.L., Jr. *The Short-War Illusion. German Policy, Strategy and Domestic Affairs August-December 1914*. Santa Barbara, California: ABC Clio, Inc., 1973.

Fay, Sidney Bradshaw. *The Origins of the World War*. 2 vols. New York: Macmillan & Co., 1928, 1930.

Fellner, Fritz. *Der Dreibund. Europäische Diplomatie vor dem ersten Weltkriege*. Vienna: Verlag für Geschichte und Politik, 1960.

Fiala, Wisskmar Peter. *Feldmarschall Conrad von Hötzendorf (1852-1925)*. Vienna: Bundesministerium für Landesverteidigung, 1972.

Fischer, Dr. Eduard. *Krieg ohne Heer. Meine Verteidigung der Bukowina gegen die Russen*. Vienna: Franz Schubert, 1935.

Fischer, Fritz. *Griff nach der Weltmacht: Die Kriegszielpolitik des kaiserlichen Deutschland 1914-1918*. Düsseldorf: Droste Verlag und Drukkerei GmbH., 1964.

———. *Krieg der Illusionen. Die deutsche Politik von 1911 bis 1914*. Düsseldorf: Droste Verlag und Druckerei GmbH., 1969.

Foerster, Wolfgang. *Aus der Gedankenwerkstatt des deutschen Generalstabes*. Berlin: E.S. Mitler & Sohn, 1931.

———. *Graf Schlieffen und der Weltkrieg*. Berlin: E.S. Mittler & Sohn, 1925.

Förster, Gerhard; Helmert, Heinz: Otto, Helmut; Schnitter, Helmut. *Der preussisch-deutsche Generalstab 1640-1965. Zu seiner politischen Rolle in der Geschichte*. Berlin: Dietz Verlag, 1966.

Francois, Hermann von. *Marneschlacht und Tannenberg*. Berlin: August Scherl GmbH., 1920.

Franek, F. *Die Entwicklung der österreich-ungarischen Armee in den ersten zwei Kriegsjahren*. Berlin: Verlag für Militärwissenschaft, 1933.

Frantz, Günther. *Russland auf dem Wege zur Katastrophe*. Berlin: Deutsche Verlagsgesellschaft für Politik und Geschichte, 1926.

———. *Russlands Eintritt in den Weltkrieg: Der Ausbau der russischen Wehrmacht und ihr Einsatz bei Kriegsausbruch*. Berlin: Deutsche Verlagsgesellschaft für Politik und Geschichte, 1924.

———. *Die Vernichtungsschlacht in kriegsgeschichtlichen Beispielen*. Berlin: Mittler & Sohn, 1928.

Freytag-Loringhoven, Freiherr Hugo von. *Generalfeldmarschall Graf von Schlieffen. Sein Leben und die Verwertung seines geistigen Erbes im Weltkriege*. Leipzig: Historia-Verlag Paul Schragsler, 1920.

———. *Heerführung im Weltkriege. Vergleichende Studien*. Vols. I & II. Berlin: E.S. Mittler & Sohn, 1923.

———. *Menschen und Dinge, wie ich sie in meinem Leben sah*. Berlin: E.S. Mittler & Sohn, 1923.

Galántai, Jószef. *Die österreichisch-ungarische Monarchie und der Weltkrieg*. Budapest: Akadémiai Kiadó 1979.

Gehre, Ludwig, *Die deutsche Kräfteverteilung während des Weltkrieges: Eine Clausewitzstudie*. Berlin: E.S. Mittler & Sohn, 1928.

Geiss, Imanuel. *Julikrise und Kriegsausbruch 1914: Eine Dokumenten-sammlung.* 2 vols. Hanover: Verlag für Literatur und Zeitgeschehen GmbH., 1963. (*July 1914 The Outbreak of the First World War: Selected Documents.* New York: Charles Scribner's Sons, 1967).

Gianni Baj Macario. *Unser Heer. 300 Jahre österreichisches Soldatentum in Krieg und Frieden.* Vienna: Herbert St. Furlinger, 1963.

Glaise-Horstenau, Edmund von. *Die Katastrophe. Die Zertrümmerung Österreich-Ungarns und das Werden der Nachfolgestaaten.* Vienna: Amalthea-Verlag, 1929.

_____. *Franz Josephs Weggefährte. Das Leben des Generalstabchefs Grafen Beck.* Vienna: Amalthea-Verlag, 1930.

Golovin, Nikolai. *The Russian Army in the World War.* New Haven: Yale University Press, 1931.

_____. *The Russian Campaign of 1914. The beginning of the War and Operations in East Prussia.* Translated by A.G.S. Muntz. Fort Leavenworth, Kansas: The Command and General Staff School Press, 1938.

Groener, Wilhelm. *Das Testament des Grafen Schlieffen. Operative Studien über den Weltkrieg.* Berlin: E.S. Mittler & Sohn, 1927.

_____. *Der Feldherr wider Willen. Operative Studien über den Weltkrieg.* Berlin: E.S. Mittler & 1930.

_____. *Graf Schlieffen und der Weltkrieg.* Berlin: E.S. Mittler & Sohn, 1925.

_____. *Lebenserinnerungen. Jugend. Generalstab Weltkrieg.* Edited by Hiller von Gaertingen. Göttingen: Vandenhoeck & Ruprecht, 1957.

Hantsch, Hugo. *Leopold Graf Berchtold. Grandseigneur und Staatsmann.* 2 vols. Graz-Vienna-Cologne: Verlag Styria, 1963.

Hantsch, Hugo, Wagner, Anton, et al. *Österreich am Vorabend des ersten Weltkrieges.* (Institut für Österreichkunde). Graz-Vienna: Stiasny Verlag, 1964.

Hat der deutsche Generalstab zum Kriege getrieben. Dokumente des deutschen Generalstabes über die militärpolitische Lage vor dem Kriege. (Urkunden des deutschen Generalstabs uber die militärpolitische Lage vor dem Kriege). Berlin: Gedruckt in der Reichsdruckerei, 1919.

Heller, Eduard. *Das deutsch-österreichisch-ungarische Bündnis in Bismarcks Aussenpolitik.* Berlin: E.S. Mittler & Sohn, 1925.

Helmreich, E.C. *The Diplomacy of the Balkan Wars 1912-1913.* Cambridge: Harvard University Press, 1938.

Herzfeld, Hans. *Der erste Weltkrieg.* Munich: Deutscher Taschenbuch Verlag GmbH & Co., 1968

_____. *Die deutsche Rüstungspolitik vor dem Weltkrieg*. Bonn and Leipzig: Kurt Schroeder Verlag, 1923.

Hindenburg, Paul von. *Aus meinem Leben*. Leipzig: Hirzel, 1920.

Holsti, Ole R. *Crisis, Escalation, War*. London: McGill-Queen's University Press, 1972.

Hoeniger, Robert. *Russlands Vorbereitung zum Weltkrieg auf Grund unveröffentlichter russischer Urkunden*. Berlin: E.S. Mittler & Sohn, 1919.

Hoffman, General Max. *Der Krieg der versäumten Gelegenheiten*. Munich: Verlag für Kulturpolitik, 1924.

_____. *Tannenberg, wie es wirklich war*. Berlin: Verlag für Kulturpolitik, 1926.

_____. *War Diaries and Other Papers*. Translated by Eric Sutton. London: M. Secker, 1929.

Holzle, Erwin. *Der Geheimnisverrat und der Kriegsausbruch 1914*. Historisch-Politische Hefte Der Ranke-Gesellschaft. Heft 23. Göttingen: Musterschmidt Verlag, 1973.

Horstenau, Edmund Glaise von. *Ein General im Zwielicht: Die Erinnerungen Edmund Glaises von Horstenau*. Editor Peter Broucek. Volume 1. Vienna: 1980.

_____. *Franz Josephs Weggefährte: Das Leben des Generalstabschefs Grafen Beck*. Vienna, 1930.

Gina Gräfin Conrad von Hötzendorf. *Mein Leben mit Conrad von Hötzendorf. Sein Vermächtnis*. Leipzig: Grethlein & Co., 1935.

Janssen, Karl Heinz. *Der Kanzler und der General. Die Führungskrise um Bethmann Hollweg und Falkenhayn (1914-1916)*. Göttingen: Musterschmidt-Verlag, 1966.

Jarausch, Konrad H. *The Enigmatic Chancellor. Bethmann-Hollweg and the Hubris of Imperial Germany*. New Haven: Yale University Press, 1973.

Johnson, Douglas Wilson. *Topography and Strategy in the War*. New York: Henry Holt & Co., 1917.

Joll, James. *The Origins of the First World War*. New York: Longman, Inc., 1992.

Justrow, Karl. *Feldherr und Kriegstechnik: Studien über den Operationsplan des Grafen Schlieffen*. Munich: Oldenburg, Gerhard Stalling, 1933.

Kaebisch, Generalleutnant Ernst. *Streitfragen des Weltkrieges, 1914-1918*. Stuttgart: Bergers Literarisches Bureau, 1924.

Kann, Robert. *Dynasty, Politics and Culture. Selected Essays.* Editor Stanley B. Winters. Highland Lakes, NJ: Atlantic Research and Publications, 1991.

_____. *Erzherzog Franz Ferdinand-Studien.* Vienna: Verlag für Geschichte und Politik, 1976.

Kanner, Heinrich. *Kaiserliche Katastrophen-Politik: Ein Stück zeitgenössischer Geschichte.* Vienna: Verlag, E.P. Tal & Co., 1922.

_____. *Der Schlüssel zur Kriegsschuldfrage: Ein verheimlichtes Kapitel der Vorkriegsgeschichte.* Munich: Südbayer. Verlags-Ges. 1926.

Kearsey, Alexander Horace Cyril. *A Study of the Strategy and Tactics of the East Prussian Campaign.* London: Sifton, Praed and Co., Ltd. 1932.

Kennan, George. F. *The Fateful Alliance. France, Russia and the Coming of the First World War.* New York: Pantheon Press, 1984.

_____. *The Decline of Bismarck's European Order. France-Russian Relations.* Princeton: Princeton University Press, 1980.

Kennedy, Paul M., ed.. *The War Plans of the Great Powers 1880-1914.* London: 1979.

Kessel, Eberhard, *Moltke.* Stuttgart: K.F. Koehler Verlag, 1957.

Kielmansegg, Peter Graf. *Deutschland und der erste Weltkrieg.* Frankfurt am Main: Akademische Verlagsgessellschaft Athenaion, 1968.

Kisch, Egon Erwin. *Der Fall des Generalstabschefs Redl.* Berlin: Die Schmiede, 1924.

Kiszling, Rudolf. *Österreich-Ungarns Anteil am ersten Weltkrieg. Historische Schriften des Arbeitskreises für österreichische Geschichte.* Graz: Stiasny Verlag, 1958.

_____. *Erzherzog Franz Ferdinand von Österreich-Este. Leben, Pläne und Wirken am Schicksalsweg der Donaumonarchie.* Graz-Cologne: Hermann Bohlaus Nachf. GmbH, 1953.

_____. *Die Hohe Führung der Heere Habsburg im Ersten Weltkrieg.* Bundesministerium für Landesverteidigung, Büro für Wehrpolitik, 1984.

Koch, H.W., ed. *The Origins of the First World War. Great Power Rivalry and German War Aims.* New York: Macmillan, 1972, 1991.

Krauss, General d.Infanterie Alfred. *Theorie und Praxis in der Kriegskunst.* Munich: J.F. Lehmanns Verlag, 1930.

_____. *Die Ursachen unserer Niederlage. Erinnerungen und Urteile aus dem Weltkrieg.* Munich: J.F. Lehmanns Verlag, 1920.

Krumpelt, Ihno, ed. *Die grossen Meister der Kriegskunst: Clausewitz, Moltke, Schlieffen.* Frankfurt/Main: E.S. Mittler & Sohn, 1960.

Kühl, General Hermann von. *Der deutsche Generalstab in Vorbereitung und Durchführung des Weltkrieges.* Berlin: E.S. Mittler & Sohn, 1920.

_____. *Der Weltkrieg, 1914-1918*, Vol. 1. Berlin: Wilhelm Kolk, 1929.

Lamsdorff, Gustav von. *Die Militärbevollmächtigten Kaiser Wilhelms II. Am Zarenhofe 1904-1914.* Berlin: Schlieffen Verlag, 1926.

Langer, William L. *European Alliances and Alignments 1871-1890.* New York: Alfred A. Knopf, 1931.

_____. *The Franco-Russian Alliance 1890-1894.* Cambridge: Harvard University Press, 1929.

Leppa, Konrad. *General der Infanterie Alfred Krauss. Ein Vorbild für Volk und Heer.* Munich: I.F. Lehmann, 1932.

_____. *Moltke und Conrad. Die Heerführung des Generalobersten von Moltke und des Generals der Infanterie Freiherrn von Conrad im Sommer 1914.* Stuttgart: W. Kohlhammer, 1935.

_____. *Der Sommerfeldzug 1914 in Galizien und Polen. Die Schlacht bei Komarow. Die Kämpfe der k.u.k. 4. Armee und der russ. 5. Armee vom 26. August bis 2. September 1914.* Karlsbad: Dranowitz, 1932.

Lieven, D.C.B. *Russia and the Origins of the First World War.* New York: St. Martins Press, 1983.

Ludendorff, General Erich von. *Meine Kriegserinnerungen 1914-1918.* Berlin: E. S. Mitler & Sohn, 1921.

_____. *Tannenberg.* Munich: Ludendorff Verlag, GmbH, 1939. Mantey, Oberst D. von. *Kartenbild des Sommerfeldzuges im Osten.* Berlin: E.S. Mittler & Sohn, 1930.

Margutti, Albert Freiherr von. *Kaiser Franz Joseph. Persönliche Erinnerungen.* Vienna: Manz'sche Verlags und Universitätsbuchhandlung, 1924.

Markus, Georg. *Der Fall Redl.* Vienna: Amalthea Verlag, 1984.

May, Ernest R. *Knowing One's Enemies. Intelligence Assessment before the Two World Wars.* Princeton: Princeton University Press, 1984.

Meisner, Heinrich Otto, Editor. *Denkwürdigkeiten des General-Feldmarschalls Alfred Waldersee*, Vol. 2, *1888-1890.* Berlin: Deutsche Verlagsanstalt, 1923.

Miller, Steven E., Lynn-Jones, Sean M., and Van Evera, Stephen Van, Editors. *Military Strategy and the Origins of the First World War.* Princeton: Princeton University Press, 1991.

Mohs, Hans (ed.). *General-Feldmarschall Alfred Graf von Waldersee in seinem militärischen Wirken. Auf Veranlassung des Generalleutnants a.D. Georg Grafen von Waldersee.* Vol. 2. Berlin: Verlag R. Eisenschmidt, 1929.

Moltke, Generaloberst Helmuth Graf von. *Erinnerungen, Briefe, Dokumente 1877-1916. Ein Bild vom Kriegsausbruch, erster Kriegsführung und Persönlichkeit des ersten militärischen Führers.* Stuttgart: Der Kommende Tag A.G. Verlag, 1922.

Moser, General Otto von. *Ernsthafte Plaudereien über den Weltkrieg. Eine kritische, militärpolitische Geschichte des Krieges für Fachleute und Nichtfachleute. Zur Rückschau in die Vergangenheit und zur Ausschau in die Zukunft.* Stuttgart: Belser A. G., Verlagsbuchhandlung, 1925, 1937.

_____. *Feldzugsaufzeichnungen als Brigade-Divisionskommandeur und als Kommandierender General 1914-1918.* Stuttgart, Chr. Belsersche Verlagsbuchhandlung, 1920.

Mühlmann, Carl. *Oberste Heeresleitung und Balkan im Weltkrieg 1914-1918.* Berlin: Wilhelm Limpert-Verlag, 1942.

Nicolai, Walter. *Geheime Mächte. Internationale Spionage und ihre Bekämpfung im Weltkriege und heute.* Leipzig: Verlag R.F. Koehler, 1925. (*The German Secret Service.* Translated by George Renurick. London: S. Paul & Co., 1924).

Nitsche, Georg. *Österreichisches Soldatentum im Rahmen deutscher Geschichte.* Berlin-Leipzig: G. Freytag AG., 1937.

Partsch, J. *Die Kriegsschauplätze.* Vol. III: *Der östliche Kriegsschauplatz.* Leipzig-Berlin: Verlag von B.G. Teubner, 1916.

Peball, Kurt. *Conrad von Hötzendorf. Private Aufzeichnungen. Erste Veröffentlichungen aus den Papieren des k.u.k. Generalstabschefs.* Vienna: Amalthea Verlag, 1977.

Pfeffer, Feldmarschalleutnant Rudolf. *Zum 10. Jahrestage der Schlachten von Zloczów und Przemyslany. Eine Entgegnung auf die Angaben des Feldmarschalls Conrad über die Führung der 3. Armee in diesen Schlachten im vierten Bande Aus meiner Dienstzeit.* Vienna: Im Selbstverlage, 1924.

Pitreich, Max Freiherr von. *Lemberg 1914.* Vienna: Verlag von Adolf Holzhausens Nachfolger Universitätsbuchdrucker, 1929.

_____. *1914: Die militärischen Probleme unseres Kriegsbeginnes. Ideen, Gründe und Zusammenhänge.* Vienna: Selbstverlag, 1934.

Pitreich, August. *Der österreichisch-ungarische Bundesgenosse im Sperrfeuer*. Klagenfurt: Arthur Killitsch, 1930.

Pourtales, Graf A. *Meine letzten Verhandlungen in St. Petersburg Ende Juli 1914: Tagesaufzeichnungen und Dokumente*. Berlin: Gessellschaft für Politik und Geschichte, 1927.

Pribam, Alfred Francis. *Austrian Foreign Policy 1908-1918*. London: George Allen and Univer Ltd., 1923.

_____. *The Secret Treaties of Austria-Hungary*. 2 vols. Cambridge: Harvard University Press, 1920-1922.

Redlich, Joseph. *Schicksalsjahre Österreichs 1908-1919: Das politische Tagebuch Joseph Redlichs*. Edited by Fritz Fellner. 2 vols. Graz: Verlag Hermann Bohlaus, 1954.

Regele, Oskar. *Feldmarschall Conrad. Auftrag und Erfüllung, 1906-1918*. Vienna: Verlag Herold, 1955.

Ritter, Gerhard. *The Schlieffen Plan: Critique of a Myth*. Translated by Andrew and Eva Wilson. New York: Frederick A. Praeger, 1958.

_____. *Staatskunst und Kriegshandwerk: Das Problem des Militarismus in Deutschland*. 3 vols. Munich: Verlag H. Oldenbourg, 1954. (*The Sword and the Scepter: The Problem of Militarism in Germany*. 3 vols. Translated by Heinz Norden. Coral Gables, Florida: University of Miami Press, 1969-1971.)

Ronge, Max. *Kriegs-und Industrie-Spionage. Zwölf Jahre Kundsschaftsdienst*. Zurich-Leipzig-Vienna: Amalthen-Verlag, 1930.

_____. *Meister der Spionage*. Leipzig-Vienna: Amalthen-Verlag, 1930.

Ropponen, Risto. *Die Kraft Russlands. Wie beurteilte die politische und militärische Führung der europäischen Grossmächte in der Zeit von 1905 bis 1914 die Kraft Russlands*. Helsinki: Turun Sanomalehte ja Kirjapamo Osakeyhtic, 1968.

Rosinski, Herbert. *The German Army*. Edited by Gordon A. Craig. New York: Frederick A. Praeger, 1966.

Rothenberg, Gunther. *The Army of Francis Joseph*. West Lafayette, Indiana: Purdue University Press, 1976.

Russlands Mobilmachung für den Weltkrieg. Neue Urkunden zur Geschichte des Weltkrieges. Berlin: E.S. Mittler & Sohn, 1919.

Rutherford, Ward. *The Russian Army in World War I*. London: Gordon Cremonesi, 1975.

Sarter, Adolph. *Die deutschen Eisenbahnen im Kriege*. Wirtschafts und Sozialgeschichte des Weltkrieges, Deutsche Serie. Edited by James T. Shotwell. Berlin: Deutsche Verlagsanstalt, 1930.

Schäfer, Theobald D. von. *Tannenberg, Schlachten des Weltkrieges*. (In Einzeldarstellungen bearbeitet und herausgegeben im Auftrage des Reichsarchivs). Vol. 9. Berlin: Verlag Gerhard Stalling, 1928.

Schlieffen, Generalfeldmarschall Graf Alfred von. *Briefe*. Edited and introduced by Eberhard Kessel. Göttingen: Vandenhoeck & Ruprecht, 1958.

_____. *Gesammelte Schriften*. 2 vols. Berlin: E.S. Mittler, 1913.

_____. *Die grossen Generalstabsreisen-Ost. Aus den jahren 1891-1905*. Berlin: E. S. Mittler & Sohn, 1938.

_____. *Die taktisch-strategischen Aufgaben aus den Jahren 1891-1905*. Berlin: E.S. Mittler & Sohn, 1937.

Schmerfeld, Ferdinand von, ed. *Graf Moltke. Die deutschen Aufmarschpläne 1871-1890*. Berlin: E.S. Mittler & Sohn, 1929.

Schmitt, Bernadotte E. *The Annexation of Bosnia 1908-1909*. Cambridge: At the University Press, 1937.

_____. *The Coming of the War 1914*. 2 vols. Charles Scribner's Sons, 1930.

Schroeter, J. Gen. d. Inf. a. D. *Die Bedeutung der Landesbefestigungen im Weltkriege*. Schweidnitz: Selbstverlag des Verfassers, 1927.

Schwarte, Max. *Der grosse Krieg 1914-1918*. Vol. V: *Der österreichisch-ungarische Krieg*. Leipzig: Barth in Auslg., 1922.

_____. ed. *Die militärischen Lehren des grossen Krieges und Kriegslehren in Beispielen aus dem Weltkriege*. Berlin: E.S. Mittler & Sohn, 1925.

Sazonov, Serge. *Fateful Years 1909-1916: The Reminiscences of Serge Sazonov*. London: Butler & Tanner, 1927.

Showalter, Dennis E. *Tannenberg: Clash of Empires*. Hamden: Anchor Books, 1991.

Sieghart, Rudolf. *Die letzten Jahrzehnte einer Grossmacht: Menschen, Völker, Probleme des Habsburgerreiches*. Berlin: Verlag Ullstein, 1932.

Silberstein, Gerard E. *The Troubled Alliance: German-Austrian Relations 1914 to 1917*. Lexington, Kentucky: The University Press of Kentucky, 1970.

Snyder, Jack. *The Ideology of the Offensive: Military Decision Making and the Disasters of 1914*. Ithaca, NY: Cornell University Press, 1984.

Sosnosky, Theodor von. *Franz Ferdinand, der Erzherzog-Thronfolger. Ein Lebensbild*. Munich & Berlin: Verlag von R. Oldenbourg, 1929.

Staabs, H. von. *Aufmarsch nach zwei Fronten: Auf Grund der Operationspläne von 1871-1914*. Berlin: E.S. Mittler & Sohn, 1925.

Stieve, Friedrich. *Die Tragödie der Bundesgenossen: Deutschland und Österreich-Ungarn 1908-1914*. Munich: Verlag F. Bruckmann, 1930.

Stöller, Ferdinand. *Feldmarschall Franz Graf Conrad von Hötzendorf.* Leipzig: Friedrich Brandstetter, 1942.

Stone, Norman. *The Eastern Front 1914-1917*. New York: Charles Scribners Sons, 1975.

Sturgkh, Graf Joseph von. *Im deutschen Grossen Hauptquartier*. Leipzig: Paul List Verlag, 1921.

_____. *Politische und militärische Erinnerungen*. Leipzig: Paul List Verlag, 1922.

Suchomlinow, W.A. *Erinnerungen*. Berlin: Reimer Hobbing, 1924.

_____. *Grossfürst Nikolai Nikolajewitsch*. Berlin: Welt-Export Verlag, 1925.

Szillassy Julius. *Der Untergang der Donau-Monarchie*. Berlin: Verlag Neues Vaterland, 1921.

Taylor, Alan J. P. *War by Timetable: How the First World War Began.* London: Macdonald & Co., 1969.

Uebersberger, Hans, *Österreich zwischen Russland und Entstehung des ersten Weltkrieges*. Cologne-Graz: Verlag Hermann Böhlaus Nachf., 1958.

Urbanski von Ostrymiecz, August. *Conrad von Hötzendorf. Soldat und Mensch. Dargestellt von seinem Mitarbeiter Feldmarschalleutnant August.* Vienna: Ulrich Mosers Verlag, 1938.

_____. *Das Tornisterkind: Lebenserinnerungen des Feldmarschalleutnants August von Urbanski*, 1948 (unpublished).

Vermes, Gábor. *István Tisza*. Boulder, Colorado: East European Monographs, 1985.

Verosta, Stephan. *Theorie und Realität von Bündnissen: Helmrich Lammasch, Karl Renner und der Dreibund (1897-1914)*. Vienna: Europa Verlag, 1971.

Wagner, Anton. *Der erste Weltkrieg. Ein Blick zurück.* (Truppendienst-Taschenbücher Band 7). Vienna: Verlag Carl Ueberreuter, 1968, 1981.

Wagner, Rudolf. *Hinter den Kulissen des Grossen Haupt-quartiers*. Berlin: Verlag Adalbert Schultz, 1931.

Waldersee, Alfred Graf von. *Denkwürdigkeiten des General-Feldmarschalls Alfred Grafen von Waldersee*. Edited by Heinrich Otto Meisner. 2 vols. Stuttgart-Berlin: Deutsche Verlagsanstalt, 1922-1923.

332 Graydon A. Tunstall

_____. *Aus dem Briefwechsel des Generalfeldmarschalls Alfred von Waldersee.* Edited by Heinrich Otto Meisner. Berlin: Deutsche Verlagsanstalt, 1928.

Wallach, Jehuda I. *Das Dogma der Vernichtungsschlacht. Die Lehren von Clausewitz und Schlieffen und ihre Wirkung in zwei Weltkriegen.* Munich: Deutscher Taschenbuch-Verlag, 1970.

Walter, Oberst d. R. Anton. *Am Ostflügel der 4. Armee (Auffenberg) in der Schlacht von Komarow. Beobachtungen und Erkenntnisse eines Truppenführers.* Austria: Im Selbstverlag, 1933.

Wandruszka, Adam, and Urbanitsch, Peter, Editors. *Die Habsburger-Monarchie, 1848-1918.* Vol. V: *Die bewaffnete Macht.* Vienna: Österreichische Akademie der Wissenschaft, 1987.

Weber, Frank G. *Eagles on the Crescent. Germany, Austria, and the Diplomacy of the Turkish Alliance 1914-1918.* Ithaca, New York: Cornell University Press, 1971.

Wendt, Hermann. *Der italienische Kriegsschauplatz in europäischen Konflikten. Seine Bedeutung für die Kriegführung an Frankreichs Nordostgrenzen.* Berlin: Junker und Dunnhaupt Verlag, 1936.

Wetzell, General d.Inf. *Der Bündniskrieg, Eine militärpolitisch-operative Studie des Weltkrieges.* Berlin: E.S. Mittler & Sohn, 1937.

Williamson, Samuel R., Jr.and Peter Paster, eds. *Austria-Hungary and the Origins of the First World War.* New York: St. Martin's Press, 1991.

Winkler, Dr. Wilhelm. *Die Totenverluste der österreichisch-ungarischen Monarchie nach Nationalitäten. Die Altersgliederung der Toten.* Vienna: Verlag von L.W. Seidl & Sohn, 1919.

Wittich, Alfred von. *Conrad von Hötzendorf.* Colemens Kleine Biographien 58. Lubeck: Verlag Charles Coleman, 1934.

Zechlin, Egmont. *Krieg und Kriegsrisiko. Zur deutschen Politik im ersten Weltkrieg. Aufsätze.* Düsseldorf: Verlag Droste, 1979.

Zeman, A. B. *The Break-up of the Hapsburg Empire, 1914-1918.* London: Oxford University Press, 1961.

_____. *A Diplomatic History of the First World War.* London: Weidenfeld and Nicobon, 1969.

Zwehl, Hans von. *Erich von Falkenhayn, General der Infantrie: Eine biographische Studie.* Berlin: Verlag K.F. Koehler, 1926.

Articles

Aleksic-Pejkovic, "Political and Diplomatic Importance of the Balkan Wars." *War and Society in East Central Europe*, XVIII. New York: Columbia University Press, 1987, 371-385.

Allmayer-Beck, Joh. Christoph. "Der Sommerfeldzug von 1914 gegen Russland." *Österreichische militärische Zeitschrift* (1965), 31-39.

Bach, August. "Die November- und Dezemberkrise 1912. Vorspiel zum Weltkrieg." *Berliner Monatshefte*, (1935), 101-122.

Battha, kgl.ung.Hptm. des Generalstabes a.D. Zoltan von. "Strategische Durchfuhrung eines Zweifrontenkrieges." *Deutsche Wehr*, 2 (1930), 25-27.

Beck, Ludwig. "Besass Deutschland 1914 einen Kriegsplan?" In *Studien*, ed. Hans Speidel (1955), 89-112.

_____. "West- oder Ost-Offensive 1914?" In *Studien*, ed. Hans Speidel (1955), 141-189.

"Berchtolds Erlass nach Berlin, vom 1. August 1913." *Berliner Monatshefte*, 8 (1930), 361-368.

Bernhard, Alphons. "Die österreichisch-ungarische Kavallerie." *Militärwissenschaftliche und technische Mitteilungen* (1931), 638-653.

Boetticher, Friedrich von. "Der Lehrmeister des neuzeitlichen Krieges." D. von Cochenhausen. *Von Scharnhorst zu Schlieffen 1806-1906: Hundert Jahre preussisch-deutscher Generalstab*. Berlin: E.S. Mittler, 1933, 249-319.

_____. "Graf Schlieffen als Lehrmeister und Wegweiser." *Wissen und Wehr*, (1933), 71-83.

Bredt, Joh. Victor. "Italien als Bundesgenosse." *Preussische Jahrbücher*, 216 (1929), 1-29.

_____. "Italien und der Dreibund 1914." *Die Kriegsschuldfrage*, 6 (1928), 281-296.

Brettner-Messler, Horst. "Die Balkanpolitik Conrad von Hötzendorfs von seiner Wiederernennung zum Chef des Generalstabes bis zum Oktober-Ultimatum 1913," *Sonderdruck: Mitteilungen des österreichischen Staatsarchivs*, 20 (1967), 180-276.

_____. "Die militärischen Absprachen zwischen den Generalstäben Österreich-Ungarns und Italiens vom Dezember 1912 bis Juni 1914." *Mitteilungen des österreichischen Staatsarchivs*, 23 (1970), 225-249.

334 Graydon A. Tunstall

Broucek, Peter. "Literaturberichte. Ungedruckte Prüfungsarbeiten aus Österreich zur österreichischen Militärgeschichte." *Mitteilungen des österreichischen Staatsarchivs*, 34 (1981), 463-479.

_____. "Der Nachlass Conrads und des Kriegsarchivs." *Mitteilungen des österreichischen Staatsarchivs*, 28 (1975), 164-182.

_____. "Militärgeschichte in Österreich von 1918 bis 1938/45." *Vorträge zur Militärgeschichte*, vol. 6: *Militärgeschichte in Deutschland und Österreich vom 18. Jahrhundert bis in die Gegenwart.* Bonn: Verlag E. S. Mittler & Sohn GmbH, (1985), 87-107.

_____. "Taktische Erkenntnis aus dem russisch-japanischen Krieg und deren Beachtung in Österreich-ungarn." *Mitteilungen des österreichischen Staatsarchiv*, 30 (1977), 191-220.

Craig, Gordon A. "The World War Alliance of the Central Powers in Retrospect. The Military Cohesion of the Alliance." *Journal of Modern History*, 37 (1965), 336-344.

Czegka, Eduard. "Die Mobilmachung der europäischen Mächte im Sommer 1914. Serbien und Montenegro." *Berliner Monatshefte*, 14 (1936), 3-23.

_____. "Die Wandlungen in der Verwendung und Organisation der Kavalleriedivisionen während des Weltkrieges." *Militärwissenschaftliche und technische Mitteilungen* (1928), 1-22.

Demus-Moran, Ferdinand von. "Erinnerungen an die Mobilisierung des k.u.k. I. Korps." *Militärwissenschaftliche und technische Mitteilungen* (1934), 718-724.

_____. "Tagebuchaufzeichnungen über die Massnahmen des österreichisch-ungarischen I. k.u.k. Korpskommandos vor Beginn der allgemeinen Mobilisierung." *Die Kriegsschuldfrage*, 4 (1926), 549-552.

Djordjevic, Jojvoda. "The Serbian High Command and Strategy in 1914. *East Central European Society in World War I.* Volume 19 of *War and Society in East Central Europe* (1985), 569-89.

Dobrorolski, General Sergie. "Die Kriegsbereitschaft der russischen Armee im Jahre 1914." *Berliner Monatshefte*, 3 (1925), 27-38.

Dragoni, Oberst Alfred von. "Die österreichisch-ungarische Heereskavallerie beim Nordost-Aufmarsch und Kriegsbeginn 1914." *Militärwissenschaftliche und technische Mitteilungen* (1934), 3-10.

_____. "Die Organisation der österreichisch-ungarischen Wehrmacht in ihren letzten Friedensjahren" *Militärwissenschaftliche und technische Mitteilungen* (1932), 481-486.

_____. "Studie über den österreichisch-ungarischen Aufmarsch und Kriegsbeginn," *Militärwissenschaftliche und technische Mitteilungen* (1933), 2-8.

Ehnl, Maximilian. "Die österreichisch-ungarische Landmacht nach Aufbau, Gliederung, Friedensgarnison, Einteilung und nationaler Zusammensetzung im Sommer 1914." *Österreich-Ungarns letzter Krieg*, Erganzungs-Heft.9.

Enderes, Bruno. "Die österreichischen Eisenbahnen." *Verkehrswesen im Kriege*. In *Wirtschafts und Sozialgeschichte des Weltkrieges, Österreichische und ungarische Serie*. Vienna: Holder-Pichler-Tempsky A-6, 1931.

Evans, R.J.W. "The Habsburg Monarchy and the Coming of War."Editors R.J.W. Evans and Hartmut Pogge von Strandmann/eds. *The Coming of the First World War*. Oxford: Clarendon Press, 1988, 33-55.

Fabini, L. V. "Die Feuertaufe des Eisernen Korps (III.-ö.-u.): Der erste Tag der Schlacht von Zloczów am 26. August 1914." *Militärwissenschaftliche und technische Mitteilungen* (1930), 785-843.

Fellner, Fritz. "Die Mission Hoyos." *Les grandes puissances et la Serbie a la veille de la Premiere guerre mondiale. Assissee scientifique de l'Academie serbe des sciences et des arts.* v. IV, Class des sciences historiques N. 1, Beograd, 1976.

Foerster, Wolfgang. "Die deutsch-italienische Militärkonvention." *Berliner Monatshefte*, 5 (1927), 395-416.

_____. "Der deutsche und der italienische Generalstab vor dem Weltkrieg." *Deutscher Offizier-Bund*, 19 (1926), 837-842; 20 (1926), 874-878.

"Fragen der grossen Kriegsführung. Die Aufmärsche und Anfangsoperationen Österreich-Ungarns 1914 in Süd und Nord. Eine kritische Betrachtung von einem Offizier des ehemaligen k.u.k. Generalstabes." *Deutsche Wehr*, 40, 41 (1929), 869-872; 895-899.

Franek, Major Dr. Fritz. "Die Entwicklung der österreich-ungarischen Wehrmacht in den ersten zwei Kriegsjahren." *Militärwissenschaftliche und technische Mitteilungen*, (1933), 15-31, 98-111.

_____. "Probleme der Organisation im ersten Kriegsjahre." *Militärwissenschaftliche und technische Mitteilungen*, (1930), 977-990.

Frantz, Gunther. "Die Entstehung der Mobilmachungsbefehle in Petersburg am 29. und 30. Juli 1914." *Wissen und Wehr* (1923), 275-284.

_____. "Die Entwicklung des Befestigungssystems in Westrussland von 1880 bis 1914." *Deutsche Wehr*, 23 (1930), 573-576.

_____. "Die Entwicklung des Offensivgedankens im russischen Opera-
tionsplan." *Wissen und Wehr* (1924), 373-392.

_____. "Ost- oder Westaufmarsch." *Deutscher Offizier-Bund*, 11 (1925),
435-438.

_____. "Die russischen Operationen an der Weichsel 1914." *Deutscher
Offizier-Bund*, 11 (1925), 259-261.

_____. "Russlands Westaufmarsch seit 1880." *Wissen und Wehr* (1930),
235-255.

_____. "Das strategische Eisenbahnnetz Russlands 1914 unter besonderer
Berücksichtigung des Bündnisses mit Frankreich." *Berliner Monatshefte*, 8 (1930), 259-280.

_____. "Die Wandlung des operativen Gedankens in Russland 1908-
1912." *Deutscher Offizier-Bund*, 28 (1930), 1010-1013.

_____. "Wie Russland 1914 mobilmachte. "*Berliner Monatshefte*, 14
(1936), 277-319.

Frantz, Rudolf. "Der Sommerfeldzug in Ostpreussen 1914." *Der Grosse
Krieg*. Edited by Max Schwarte. Volume I, *Der deutsche Landkrieg
I: Vom Kriegsbeginn bis zum Frühjahr 1915*. Berlin: E.S. Mittler &
Sohn, 1921, 277-338.

Fuller, William C., Jr. "The Russian Empire." *Knowing One's Enemies*.
ed. Ernest R. May Princeton: Princeton University Press, 1988, 98-126.

Gall, Franz. "Adjustierung, Rüstung und Waffen der österreich-ungarischen Armee im Jahre 1914. Ein kurzgefasster Überlick." *Österreichische militärische Zeitschrift*. Sonderheft II, 1964. *Zur Vorgeschichte
des ersten Weltkrieges*, 37-43.

Geyer, Michael. "German Strategy in the Age of Machine Warfare, 1914-
1945." *Makers of Modern Strategy from Machiavelli to the Nuclear
Age*. Ed. Peter Paret. Princeton: Princeton University Press, 1971,
527-597.

Goiginger, Feldmarschalleutnant. "Betrachtungen über die anfänglichen
Operationspläne der Mittelmächte." *Militärwissenschaftliche und technische Mitteilungen* (1927), 171-181.

_____. "Komarow und Lemberg." *Österreichische Wehrzeitung*, 30, 31
(1928), 3-4; 2.

Golovin, N. "The Great Battle of Galicia (1914): A Study in strategy."
Salvonic Revue (1926), 25-47.

Groener, Wilhelm. "Das Testament des Grafen Schlieffen." *Wissen und
Wehr* (1925), 193-217.

Hantsch, Hugo. "Die kritischen Wochen vom Thronfolgerattentat bis zum 28. Juli 1914." *Österreichische Militärische Zeitschrift* (Sonderheft II/1964 *Zur Vorgeschichte des Ersten Weltkrieges*), 22-29.

_____. "Die Spannungen zwischen Österreich-Ungarn und Serbien-Russland 1908 bis 1914." *Österreich am Vorabend des Ersten Weltkrieges.* Graz: Stiasny Verlag, 1964, 7-18.

Helmreich, E.C. "Russlands Einfluss auf den Balkanbund im Oktober 1912." *Berliner Monatshefte*, XI (1933), 217-234.

_____. "Die tieferen Ursachen der Politik Berchtolds im Oktober 1912." *Berliner Monatshefte*, 10 (1932), 218-244.

_____. "An Unpublished Report on Austro-German Military Conversations of November 1912." *Journal of Modern History*, 5 (1933), 197-207.

Herwig, Holger H. "The Dynamics of Necessity: German Military Policy during the First World War." In Allan R. Millett and Murray Williamson, *Military Effectiveness*, Vol. 1: *The First World War.* Boston: Allen and Unwin, 1988, 80-115.

_____. "Imperial Germany." *Knowing One's Enemies.* Ed. Ernest R. May, Princeton: Princeton University Press, 1988, 62-97.

Hobelt, Lothar. "Österreich-Ungarn und das deutsche Reich als Zweibundpartner." *Österreich und die deutsche Frage im 19. und 20. Jahrhundert. Probleme der politisch-staatlichen und soziokulturellen Differenzierung im deutschen Mitteleuropa*, ed. Lutz, Heinrich und Rumpler, Helmut. Vienna: Verlag für Geschichte und Politik, 1982.

_____. "Schlieffen, Beck, Potiorek und das Ende der gemeinsamen deutsch-österreichisch-ungarischen Aufmarschpläne im Osten." *Militärgeschichtliche Mitteilungen*, 36 (1984).

Hoen, Max. "Mobilmachung." *Der Grosse Krieg.* Edited by Max Schwarte, V. *Der österreichisch-ungarische Krieg.* Berlin: E.S. Mittler und Sohn, (1922), 17-21.

_____. "Österreich-Ungarns Wehrmacht." *Der Grosse Krieg.* Edited by Max Schwarte. V *Der österreichisch-ungarische Krieg.* Berlin: E.S. Mittler & Sohn, 1922, 1-16.

Holborn, Hajo. "Moltke and Schlieffen: The Prussian-German School." *Makers of Modern Strategy: Military Thought From Machiavelli to Hitler.* Ed. Edward Meade Earle. New York: Atheneum, 1967, 172-205.

Hoffmeister, E. "Von Moltke zu Falkenhayn: Eine kriegsgeschichtliche Studie." *Wissen und Wehr* (1938), 513-536.

338 Graydon A. Tunstall

Horetzky, General Ernst von. "1914. Die militärischen Probleme unseres Kriegsbeginnes." *Militärwissenschaftliche und technische Mitteilungen* (1934), 902-926.

Howard, Michael. "Europe on the Eve of the First World War."Ed. R.J.W. Evans and Hartmut Pogge von Strandmann. *The Coming of the First World War*. Oxford: Clarendon Press, 1988, 1-17.

_____. "Men Against Fire: The Doctrine of the Offensive in 1914." *Makers of Modern Strategy from Machiavelli to the Nuclear Age*. Ed. Peter Paret. Princeton: Princeton University Press, 1971, 510-526.

Jannen, William Jr. "The Austro-Hungarian Decision for War in 1914." *Essays on World War I: Origins and Prisoners of War*. New York: Brooklyn College Press, 1983, 55-81.

Jones, David R. "Imperial Russia's Forces at War." In Allan R. Millett and Williamson Murray, *Military Effectiveness*, Volume 1: *The First World War*. Boston: Allen and Unwin, 1988, 249-328.

Kann, Robert A. "Erzherzog Franz Ferdinand and Graf Berchtold als Aussenminister, 1912-1914." *Mitteilungen des österreichischen Staatsarchivs*, 22 (1969), 245-278.

_____. "Emperor William II and Archduke Francis Ferdinand in their Correspondence." *American Historical Review*, 57 (1952), 323-351.

Kennedy, Paul. "The First World War and the International Power System." *Military Strategy and the Origins of the First World War*. Princeton: Princeton University Press, 1985, 7-40.

Kerchnawe, Generalmajor a.D. Hugo von. "Die unzureichende Kriegsrüstung der Mittelmächte." *Militärwissenschaftliche und technische Mitteilungen* 10 (1932), 151-208.

Kiszling, Rudolf. "Das deutsche Ostheer im Sommerfeldzug 1914: Ein Beitrag zur Geschichte des Koalitionskrieges der Mittelmächte." *Militärwissenschaftliche und technische Mitteilungen* (1924), 385-394.

_____. "Die Entwicklung der operativen Idee vor Ausbruch des Weltkrieges." *Militärwissenschaftliche und technische Mitteilungen* 10 (1932), 625-647.

_____. "Entwicklung der österreichisch-ungarischen Wehrmacht seit der Annexionskrise 1908." *Militärwissenschaftliche und technische Mitteilungen*, 12 (1934), 789-802.

_____. "Feldmarschall Conrad von Hötzendorf." *Österreich in Geschichte und Literatur*, 8 (1954), 157-167.

_____. "Feldmarschall Conrads Kriegsplan gegen Russland." *Militärwissenschaftliche und technische Mitteilungen* (1925), 469-475.

_____. "Generalfeldmarschall Graff Schlieffen und die Kriegsvorbereitungen Österreich-Ungarns." *Militärwissenschaftliche und technische Mitteilungen* 11 (1933), 153-159.

_____. "Die Kriegserklärung Österreich-Ungarns an Serbien." *Berliner Monatshefte*, 8 (1930), 1130-1141.

_____. "Kriegspläne und Aufmärsche der k.u.k. Armeen sowie der Feindheere im Sommer 1914." *Österreich am Vorabend des ersten Weltkrieges*. Graz: Stiasny Verlag, 1954, 83-96.

_____. "Kriegspläne und Aufmärsche der k.u.k. Armeen und der Feindheere im Sommer 1914." *Österreichische Militärische Zeitschrift*, Sonderheft I/1965, 2-8.

_____. "Die militärischen Beziehungen und Bindungen zwischen Österreich-Ungarn und dem Deutschen Reiche vor dem Weltkriege." *Die Kriegsschuldfrage*, 4 (1926), 820-835.

_____. "Die Mobilmachung der europäischen Mächte im Sommer 1914: Österreich-Ungarn." *Berliner Monatshefte*, 14 (1936), 189-224.

_____. "Ost- oder Westaufmarsch." *Militärwissenschaftliche und technische Mitteilungen* (1925), 97-109.

_____. "Die österreichische-ungarische Armee in den letzten Dezennien vor 1914." *Österreichische militärische Zeitschrift* (Sonderheft II/1964), 29-34.

_____. "Österreich-Ungarns Kriegsvorbereitungen. Mobilisierung, Aufmarsch und Operationspläne im Sommer 1914." *Militärwissenschaftliche und technische Mitteilungen* (1922), 273-288.

_____. "Die österreichisch-ungarischen Kriegsvorbereitungen und die Mobilisierungsmassnahmen gegen Russland 1914." *Die Kriegsschuldfrage* 4 (1936), 365-377.

_____. "Die praktische Undurchführbarkeit eines Handstreiches auf Belgrad." *Berliner Monatshefte*, 5 (1927), 231-238.

_____. "Russlands Kriegsvorbereitungen im Herbst 1912 und ihre Rückwirkungen auf Österreich-Ungarn." *Berliner Monatshefte*, 13 (1935), 181-192.

_____. "Die serbische Mobilmachung im Juli 1914." *Berliner Monatshefte*, 10 (1932), 674-686.

Kuhl, General des Inf. Hermann. "Graf Schlieffen und der Weltkrieg." *Wissen und Wehr* (1923), 1-8.

Lehmann, Konrad. "Conrad von Hötzendorf und die deutsche oberste Heeresleitung im ersten Kriegshalbjahre." *Archiv für Politik und Geschichte*, 10/11 (1926), 521-556.

340 Graydon A. Tunstall

Lengyel, Bela von. "Die österreichisch-ungarische Heeresleitung 1914." *Allgemeine Schweizer Militärische Zeitung* (1964), 503-510.

Leppa, Konrad. "Der Aufmarsch der Reiterei." *Wissen und Wehr*, 19 (1932), 196-214.

_____. "Die beste Strategie." *Wissen und Wehr* (1926), 611-633.

_____. "Der Entschluss zur Schlacht bei Grodek-Lemberg." *Wissen und Wehr* (1929), 22-40.

_____. "Die galizische Schlacht: Die Heerführung des Feldmarschalls Conrad in russicher Beurteilung." *Militärwissenschaftliche und technische Mitteilungen* (1931), 618-637.

_____. "General von Conrads Kampf um die Balkanstreitkräfte 1914." *Wissen und Wehr* (1930), 483-503.

_____. "Die Heerführung des Feldmarschall Conrad im Jahre 1914." *Allgemeine Schweizerische Militär-Zeitschrift* (1956), 679-689, 756-789.

_____. "Das Hirn des Heeres. Feldmarschall Conrad und der k.u.k. Generalstab im Urteil des russischen Generalstabschefs." *Militärwissenschaftliche und technische Mitteilungen* (1929), 753-772.

_____. "Lehren aus der Kriegsgeschichte. 'Komarow: Eine Studie über den Vernichtungsgedanken in der Schlacht.'" *Deutsche Wehr*, 38 (1928), 821-824.

Levy, Jack S. "Preferences, Constraints, and Choices in July 1914." Ed. Steven E. Miller, Sean M. Lynn-Jones, Stephen Van Evera, *Military Strategy and the Origins of the First World War*, Revised and Expanded Edition. Princeton: Princeton University Press (1991), 226-261.

Lutz, Herman. "Moltke und der Präventivkrieg." *Berliner Monatshefte*, 5 (1927), 1107-1120.

Mantey, Oberst a.D. von. "Betrachtungen über den deutschen Aufmarsch 1914." *Wissen und Wehr* (1926), 234-250.

Mast, Heinrich. "Die Aufklärungstätigkeit der österreichisch-ungarischen Kavallerie bei Kriegsbeginn 1914." *Österreichische Militärische Zeitung,* Sonderheft I (1965), 8-17.

Metzger, Josef. "Der Krieg 1914 gegen Russland." *Der Grosse Krieg*. Ed. M. Schwarte, 5 (*Der österreichisch-ungarische Krieg*). Leipzig: Johann Ambrosius, 1922, 22-53.

Otto, Helmut. "Zum strategisch-operativen Zusammenwirken des deutschen und österreichisch-ungarischen Generalstabes bei den Vorbereitungen des Ersten Weltkrieges." *Zeitschrift für Militärgeschichte*, 2 (1963), 423-440.

Palumbo, Michael. "Italian-Austro-Hungarian Military Relations Before World War I." *Essays on World War I: Origins and Prisoners of War*. New York: Brooklyn College Press, 1983, 37-53.

Peball, Kurt. "Briefe an eine Freudin: Zu den Briefen des Feldmarschalls Conrad von Hötzendorf an Frau Walburga von Sonnleithner während der Jahre 1905 bis 1918." *Mitteilungen des österreichischen Staatsarchivs* 25 (1972), 492-503.

_____. "Der Feldzug gegen Serbien und Montenegro im Jahre 1914." *Österreichische Militärische Zeitschrift* Sonderheft I 1965, 18-31.

_____. "Literarische Publikationen des Kriegsarchivs im Weltkrieg 1914 bis 1918." *Mitteilungen des österreichischen Staatsarchivs*, 14, (1961), 240-260.

_____. "Österreichische militärhistorische Forschung zum ersten Weltkrieg zwischen 1918 und 1968." *Die Auflösung des Habsburgerreiches. Zusammembruch und Neuorientierung im Donauraum*, Ed. Richard Georg Plaschka and Karlheinz Mack. Vienna: Verlag für Geschichte und Politik, 1970, 308-317.

Pohl, R.R. von. "Der Feldzug gegen Serbien und Montenegro." *Der Grosse Krieg*. Ed. M. Schwarte. Volume V (*Der Österreichisch-ungarische Krieg*). Leipzig: Johann Ambrosius, 1922, 54-89.

Ratzenhofer, R.E. (General). "Deutsches und österreichisch-ungarisches Feldeisenbahnwesen. Vergleiche." *Wissen und Wehr* (1928), 47-55.

_____. "Die Festsetzung der ersten Mobilisierungstage in Österreich-Ungarn im Sommer 1914." *Berliner Monatshefte*, 14 (1936), 801-805.

_____. "Zum Kampf Conrads um die Balkanstreitkräfte." *Wissen und Wehr* (1931), 236-238.

_____. "Das Kriegseisenbahnwesen." *Militärwissenschaftliche und technische Mitteilungen* (1928), 56-63.

_____. "Die österreichisch-ungarischen Aufmärsche, Friedenspläne, Durchführung." *Schweizerische Monatsschrift für Offiziere aller Waffen*, 1; 2; 3 (1931), 31-38; 73-77; 103-108.

_____. "Österreich-Ungarns und Russlands Aufmarschkraft, ein Prüfstein des Willens zum Angriffskrieg." *Die Kriegsschuldfrage*, 5 (1928), 441-452.

_____. "Die Österreichisch-ungarischen Aufmärsche gegen Balkan und Russland: Einfluss der Aufmarschtechnik." *Österreichisch-Wehrzeitung*, 39; 40; 41 (1927), 2-3; 2; 2.

_____. "Russlands Aufmarschkraft gegen Österreich-Ungarn." *Öster-reichische-Wehrzeitung*, (1928), 2-3.

_____. "Truppentransporte zu Kriegsbeginn." *Militärwissenschaftliche und technische Mitteilungen* (1930), 231-244.

Rauchensteiner, Manfred. "Die Militärgeschichtsschreibung in Österreich nach 1945." *Vorträge zur Militärgeschichte.* Vol. 6. *Militärgeschichte in Deutschland und Österreich vom 18. Jahrhundert bis in die Gegen-wart.* Bonn: Verlag E.S. Mittler GmbH, 1985, 134-161.

Remak, Joachim. "1914 - The Third Balkan War: Origins Reconsidered." *Journal of Modern History*, (1971), 353-366.

_____. "The Healthy Invalid: How Doomed the Habsburg Empire." *Jour-nal of Modern History*, (1969), 127-143.

Ritter, Gerhard. "Der Anteil des Militärs an der Kriegskatastrophe von 1914." *Historische Zeitschrift*, 193 (1961), 72-91.

_____. "Die Zusammenarbeit der Generalstäbe Deutschlands und Öster-reich-Ungarns vor dem Ersten Weltkrieg." *Zur Geschichte und Proble-matik der Demokratie. Festgabe für Hanz Herzfeld.* Berlin: Duncker & Humbolt, 1958, 523-549.

Rothenberg, Gunther E. "The Habsburg Army in the First World War: 1914-1918." *The Habsburg Empire in World War I.* Edited by Robert Kann, Béla Király, Paula S. Fichtner, 1977, 73-85.

_____. "Moltke, Schlieffen, and the Doctrine of Strategic Envelopment." *Makers of Modern Strategy from Machiavelli to the Nuclear Age.* Ed. Peter Paret. Princeton: Princeton University Press, 1986, 296-325.

Sagan, Scott D. "1914 Revisited. Allies, Offense, and Instability." *Military Strategy and the Origins of the First World War.* Ed. Steven E. Miller, Sean M. Jones, Stephen Van Evera, Revised and Expanded Edition. Princeton: Princeton University Press, 1991, 109-133.

Schäfer, Theobald von. "Betrachtungen zum Bündniskrieg." *Wissen und Wehr* (1938), 373-392.

_____. "Der Casus foederis zwischen Deutschland und Österreich-Un-garn." *Deutscher Offizier-Bund*, 24; 25; 26 (1930), 1001-1003; 1037-1040; 1047-1050.

_____. "Die deutsche Mobilmachung von 1914." *Berliner Monatshefte*, 14 (1936), 597-639.

_____. "Deutsche Offensive aus Ostpreussen über den Narew auf Siedlce." Ergänzungsheft 1 zum Werke *Österreich-Ungarns letzter Krieg*, 1930, 961-976.

_____. "Der Feldherr Conrad. Ein Beitrag zum Kapitel: Heerführung und Politik." *Deutscher Offizier-Bund*, 7; 8 (1930), 223-226; 262-264.

_____. "General von Conrad in den Anfangsoperationen des Weltkrieges." *Wissen und Wehr* (1924), 115-141.

_____. "Generaloberst von Moltke in den Tagen vor der Mobilmachung und seine Einwirkung auf Österreich-Ungarn." *Die Kriegsschuldfrage*, 4 (1926), 514-549.

_____. "Generaloberst von Moltke und der Präventivkrieg." *Deutscher Offizier-Bund*, (1926), 1510-1512.

_____. "Hat Deutschland seinen Verbündeten bei den Anfangsoperationen gegen Russland im Stich gelassen?" *Deutscher Offizier-Bund*, (1924), 1-4.

_____. "Das Kriegsjahr 1914 im Osten und die Frage einer einheitlichen Oberbefehls." *Wissen und Wehr* (1930), 137-148.

_____. "Nochmals: Ost- oder Westaufmarsch." *Deutscher Offizier-Bund*, 21 (1925), 631-633.

_____. "Operationen gegen Übermacht dargestellt an den Ostfeldzügen des Jahres 1914." *Wissen und Wehr* (1926), 257-276.

_____. "Der österreichisch-ungarische Bundesgenosse im Sperrfeuer." *Deutscher Offizier-Bund*, 25 (1931), 282-283.

_____. "Die russischen Angriffsoperationen unter dem Grossfürsten Nikolaus Nikolajewitch." *Wissen und Wehr* (1925), 481-499.

_____. "Wollte Generaloberst von Moltke den Präventivkrieg?" *Berliner Monatshefte*, 5 (1927), 543-550.

Shimshoni, "Technology, Military Advantage, and World War I." *Military Strategy and the Origins of the First World War*. Ed. Steven E. Miller, Sean M. Jones, Stephen Van Evera. Revised and Expanded Edition. Princeton: Princeton University Press (1991), 134-162.

Snyder, Jack. "Civil-Military Relations and the Cult of the Offensive, 1914 and 1984." *Military Strategy and the Origins of the First World War*. Ed. Steven E. Miller. Princeton: Princeton University Press, 1991, 108-146.

Steinitz, Eduard Ritter von. "Berchtolds Politik während des ersten Balkankrieges." *Berliner Monatshefte*, 9 (1931), 229-248.

_____. "Berchtolds Politik während des Waffenstillstands auf dem Balkan." *Berliner Monatshefte*, 9 (1931), 723-746.

_____. "Berchtolds Politik während des zweiten Balkankrieges." *Berliner Monatshefte*, 10 (1932), 660-674.

_____. "Berchtolds Politik zu Beginn der Balkankrise 1912." *Berliner Monatshefte*, 9 (1931), 45-57.

_____. "Krasnik-Lublin 1914." *Militärwissenschaftliche und technische Mitteilungen* (1937), 685-711.

Stokelle, D. Gustav. "Der Kampf in Osten." in Gianni, Baj-Macario. *Unser Heer. 300 Jahre österreichisches Soldatentum in Krieg und Frieden.* Vienna: Herbert St. Furlinger, 1963,

Stone, Norman. "Austria-Hungary." *Knowing One's Enemies*. Ed. Ernest R. May. Princeton: Princeton University Press, 1988, 37-61.

_____. "Die Mobilmachung der österreichisch-ungarischen Armee 1914." *Militärgeschichtliche Mitteilungen*. 2, (1974), 67-95.

_____. "Moltke-Conrad: Relations between the Austro-Hungarian and German General Staffs, 1909-1914." *The Historical Journal*, 9 (1966), 202-228.

Torrey, Glenn E. "Rumania and the Belligerants 1914-1916." *Journal of Contemporary History*, 3 (1966), 165-185.

Trachtenberg, Marc. "The Meaning of Mobilization in 1914." *Military Strategy and the Origins of the First World War*. Ed. Steven E. Miller, Sean M. Lynn-Jones, Stephen Van Evera. Revised and Expanded Edition. Princeton: Princeton University Press (1991), 195-225.

Trumpener, Ulrich von. "War Premeditated? German Intelligence Operations in July 1914." *Central European History*, 9 (1976).

Turner, L.C.F. "The Russian Mobilization in 1914." *Journal of Contemporary History*, III (1968), 65-88.

_____. "The Russian Mobilization in 1914." *The War Plans of the Great Powers. 1880-1914*. Ed. Paul M. Kennedy. London: George Allen and Unwin, 1978, 252-267.

_____. "The Significance of the Schlieffen Plan." *The War Plans of the Great Powers, 1880-1914*. Ed. Paul M. Kennedy. London: George Allen and Unwin, 1978, 199-221.

Van Evera, Stephen. "The Cult of the Offensive and the Origins of the First World War." *Military Strategy and the Origins of the First World War*. Ed. Steven E. Miller. Princeton: Princeton University Press, 1985, 81.

Wagner, Anton. "Zur Entwicklung der Kriegspläne Deutschlands und Österreich-Ungarns gegen Russland bis 1914." *Österreich am Vorabend des Ersten Weltkrieges*. Herausgegeben vom Institut für Österreichkunde. Graz: Stiasny Verlag, 1964, 73-82.

Waldersee, Graf. "Von Deutschlands militärpolitischen Beziehungen zu Italien." *Berliner Monatshefte*, 7 (1929), 636-664.

_____. "Über die Beziehungen des deutschen zum österreichisch-ungarischen Generalstab vor dem Weltkriege." *Berliner Monatshefte*, 8 (1930), 103-142.

Williamson, Samuel R., Jr. "Military Dimensions of Habsburg-Romanov Relations During the Era of the Balkan Wars." *War and Society in East Central Europe*. Volume XVIII. Ed. Béla Király and Dimitrije Djordjevic. New York: Columbia University Press, 1987, 317-337.

_____. "Vienna and July 1914: The Origins of the Great War Once More." *Essays on World War I: Origins and Prisoners of War*. New York: Brooklyn College Press, 1983, 9-36.

Wittich, Alfred von. "Feldmarschall Conrad." *Sonderabdruck aus der Schweizerischen Monatsschrift für Offiziere aller Waffen* (1930), 1-32, 171-176, 247-254, 286-294, 362-366, 456-460.

_____. "Feldmarschall Conrad in der Kriegsvorbereitung." *Wissen und Wehr* (1936), 631-640.

_____. "Die Rüstungen Österreich-Ungarns von 1866 bis 1914." *Berliner Monatshefte*, 10 (1932), 861-880.

_____. "Vor zwanzig Jahren. Der Krieg gegen Serbien 1914-1915. Eine operative Betrachtung." *Militärwissenschaftliche und technische Mitteilungen* (1935), 661-679.

_____. "Vor zwanzig Jahren, Serbien." *Militärwissenschaftliche und technische Mitteilungen* (1936), 677-701.

Dissertations

Artner, Gerhard. Die österreichischen Eisenbahnen im Ersten Weltkrieg. University of Vienna: 1973.

Deutschmann, Wilhelm. Die militärischen Massnahmen in Österreich-Ungarn während der Balkankriege 1912-1913. University of Vienna: 1966.

Geyer, Gerhard. Der Ausbau des nordöstlichen Eisenbahnnetzes der österreichisch-ungarischen Monarchie unter Berücksichtigung von Krisenzeiten. University of Vienna: 1954.

Hecht, Rudolf. Fragen zur Heeresergänzung der gesamten bewaffneten Macht Österreich-Ungarns während des Ersten Weltkrieges. University of Vienna: 1969.

Kas, Ferdinand. Versuch einer zusammenfassenden Darstellung der Tätigkeit des österreichisch-ungarischen Generalstabes von 1905 bis 1914 unter besonderer Berücksichtigung der Aufmarschpläne und Mobilmachung. University of Vienna: 1962.

Mann, Josef. Feldmarschalleutant Blasius Schemua. Chef des Generalstabes am Vorabend des Weltkrieges, 1911-1912. University of Vienna: 1978.

Krieger, Rudolf. Die Entwicklung des Conradschen Offensivgedankens. Friedrich Wilhelms University (Stuttgart: Druck von X. Kohlhammer, 1934).

Seyfert, Gerhard. *Die militärischen Beziehungen und Vereinbarungen zwischen dem deutschen und dem österreichischen Generalstab vor and bei Beginn des Weltkrieges*. University of Leipzig (Leipzig: Buchdrukkerei Joh. Moltzlen, 1934).

Steiner, Josef. Gustav Hubka (1873-1962). Sein Wirken als k.u.k. Militärattache und Schriftsteller. University of Vienna: 1975.

Maps

1. Total Strategy. Austria-Hungary and Germany 1908-1914.

2. Deployment Area 1908-1914 with Austro-Hungarian Deployments 1912 and 1913.

3. Austro-Hungarian Deployment against Russia 1914.

4. Austro-Hungarian Deployment against Serbia 1914.

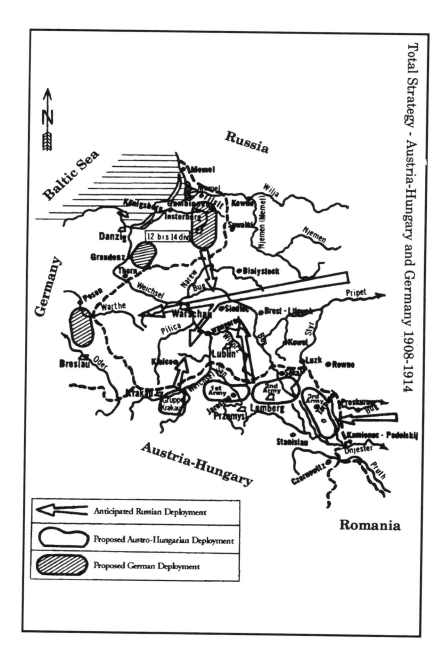

Total Strategy - Austria-Hungary and Germany 1908-1914

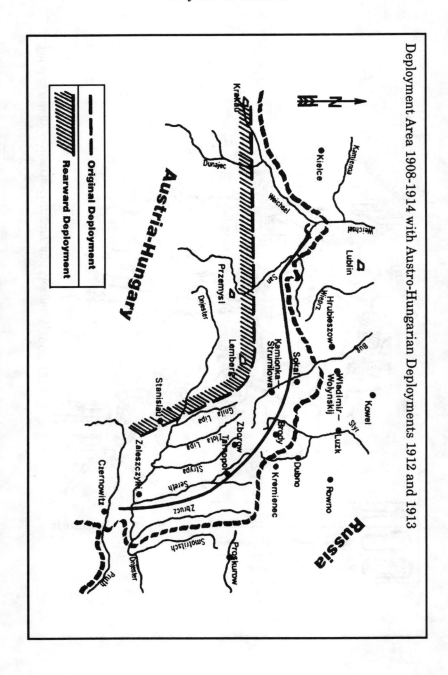

Deployment Area 1908–1914 with Austro-Hungarian Deployments 1912 and 1913

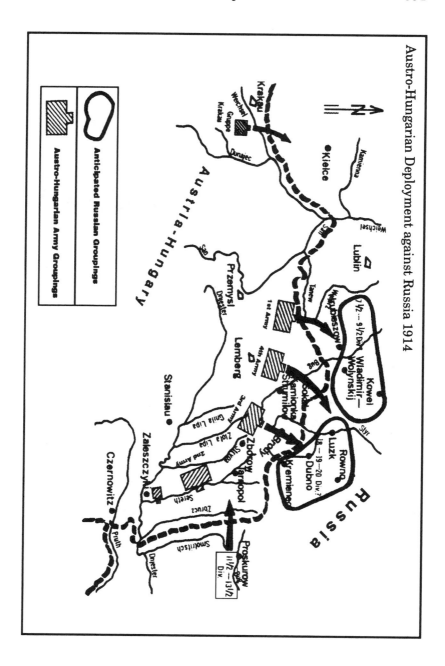

Austro-Hungarian Deployment against Russia 1914

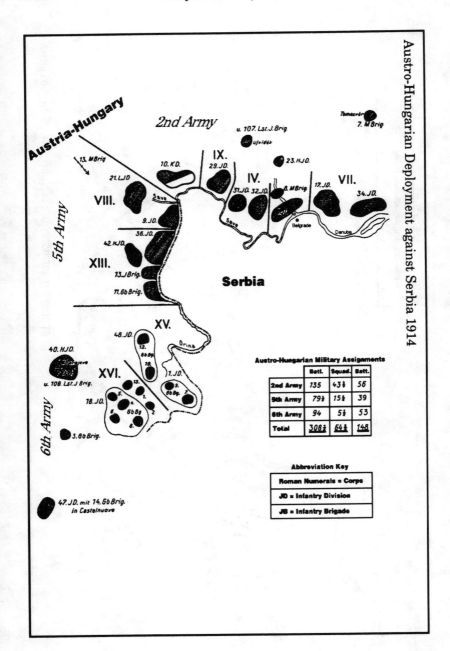

Austro-Hungarian Deployment against Serbia 1914

Austria-Hungary

2nd Army

u. 107. Lst.J.Brig.

Temesvár
7. M.Brig.

13. M.Brig.

Ujvidér

23. H.J.D.

10. K.D.

IX.
29. J.D.

IV.

8. M.Brig.

17. J.D.

VII.

21. LJD.

VIII.

Save

31.J.D. 32.J.D.

34. J.D.

5th Army

9. J.D.

36. J.D.

Save

Belgrade

Danube

42. H.J.D.

XIII.

13. J.Brig.

Serbia

11. Gb.Brig.

XV.

48. J.D.

Drina

40. H.J.D.

12. Gb.Bg.

XVI.

18.

1. J.D.

u. 108. Lst.J.Brig.

13.

9. Gb.Bg.

18. J.D.

5.

4.

5.

6.Gb.Bg.

2.

6th Army

3.

3. Gb.Brig.

Austro-Hungarian Military Assignments

	Batl.	Squad.	Batt.
2nd Army	135	43½	56
5th Army	79½	15½	39
6th Army	94	5½	53
Total	308½	64½	148

Abbreviation Key

Roman Numerals = Corps
JD = Infantry Division
JB = Infantry Brigade

47. J.D. mit 14. Gb.Brig.
in Castelnuovo

Name Register

AEHRENTHAL, ALOIS, Graf. Lexa von (1854-1912)
Austro-Hungarian Ambassador in St. Petersburg 1899-1906; Foreign Affairs Minister 1906-1912.

ALEXANDER II, NIKOLAIEVICH (1818-1881)
Father of Alexander III; Tsar of Russia (1855-1881); Signer of the Treaty of the Three Emperors (1872).

ALEXANDER III, ALEKSANDROVICH (1845-1894)
Tsar of Russia (1881-1894).

ANDRÁSSY, Gyula, Graf (1823-1890)
Austro-Hungarian Foreign Minister (1871-1887); Hungarian Prime Minister; Created the Three Emperors' Union with Bismarck and Gortschakov.

ARZ, STRAUSSENBURG von, ARTHUR, Baron (1857-1935)
Chief of the Austro-Hungarian General Staff (1917-1918).

AUFFENBERG-KOMAROW, MORITZ, Freiherr (1852-1928)
War Minister (1911-1912); Army Inspector; Fourth Army Commander (1914) at the battle of Komarov.

AVERESCU, ALEXANDRU (1859-1938)
Minister of War in 1907, Chief of the Romanian General Staff (1912-1913).

BECK-RZIKOWSKY, FRIEDRICH, Graf (1830-1920)
Chief of the Austro-Hungarian General Staff (1881-1906); Close military confidant of Emperor Franz Joseph.

BERCHTOLD, LEOPOLD, Graf (1862-1942)
Austro-Hungarian Ambassador in St. Petersburg (1907-1911); Foreign Minister (1912-1915).

BETHMANN HOLLWEG, THEOBALD von Graf (1856-1921)
German Conservative Chancellor (1909-1917).

BISMARCK, OTTO, von, Prince (1815-1898)
Foreign Minister (1862-1890); Chancellor (1871-1890).

BOLFRAS, ARTHUR, Baron (1838-1922)
General Adjutant and Chief of the Military Chancellory of Franz Joseph (1899-1916).

BOROEVIC, von BONJA, SVETOZAR von (1856-1920)
VI Corps Commander (1914), Fourth Army; Third Army Commander (1914); Field Marshal (1918), Italian front.

BRUDERMANN, RUDOLF R., von (1851-1941)
Third Army Commander, removed 3 September 1914 after the first battle of Lemberg.

BRUSILOV, ALEKSANDR ALEKSANDREVICH (1853-1926)
Commander of the Russian Eighth Army in Galicia (1914-1915); Commander of the South-West Russian front (March 1916); Supreme Commander (May-July 1917).

BÜLOW, BERNHARD (1849-1929)
German Reichs Chancellor (1900-1909).

CAROL I (1839-1914)
Prince of Romania (1866-1881); King of Romania (1881-1914).

CONRAD von HÖTZENDORF, FRANZ Freiherr (1852-1925)
Chief of the Austro-Hungarian General Staff (1906-1911 and 1912-1917).

CSICERICS, von BACSÁNY MAXIMILIAN (1865-1948)
General of Infantry; Military observer Russo-Japanese War; 1918 Corps Commander on the Italian front.

CZERNIN, OTTOKAR Graf Chudenitz (1872-1932)
Ambassador in Bucharest (1913-1914); Foreign Minister (1916-1918).

EMMANUEL VICTOR, III (1869-1947)
King of Italy (1900-1946).

FALKENHAYN, ERICH von (1861-1922)
Prussian War Minister (1913), replaces Moltke after the battle of the Marne; Chief of the German General Staff (1914-1916) until after the battle of Verdun.

FERDINAND II (1861-1948)
Prince of Bulgaria (1887-1908); King of Bulgaria (1908-1918).

FRIEDRICH MARIA ALBRECHT, ERZHERZOG von AUSTRIA (1856-1936)
Field Marshall, nominal Commander of the Austro-Hungarian forces (1914-1916).

FRIEDRICH III (1831-1888)
Former Crown Prince Friedrich Wilhelm; Prussian Kaiser for 99 days in 1888.

FRANZ FERDINAND, Archduke (1863-1914)
Heir apparent to the Austro-Hungarian throne; Assassinated leading to the outbreak of World War I.

FRANZ JOSEPH I (1830-1916)
Kaiser of Austria (1848-1916); King of Hungary (1848-1916).

GOLUCHOWSKI, von GOLUCHOWA, AGENOR, Graf (1849-1921)
Austro-Hungarian Foreign Minister (1895-1906).

HINDENBURG, PAUL von (1847-1934)
German General, victor at Tannenberg and Masurian Lakes; Commander-in-Chief of the Eastern front; Chief of the German General Staff (1916-1918).

ISVOLSKII, ALEKSANDR PETROVICH (1856-1919)
Russian Foreign Minister (1906-1910); Ambassador in Paris (1910-1917).

IANUSHKEVICH, NIKOLAI NIKOLAEVICH (1864-1918)
Chief of the Russian General Staff March 1914 to August 1915.

JOSEPH FERDINAND, ERZHERZOG von AUSTRIA (1872-1942)
Army Group Commander, Fourth Army (August and September 1914); Commander of the Austro-Hungarian Fourth Army (1914-1916); General Inspector of the Air Force (1917-1918).

KIDERLEN-WAECHTER, ALFRED von (1852-1912)
State Secretary of the German Foreign Office (1910-1912).

KISZLING, RUDOLF (1872-1976)
Lieutenant Colonel in the Austro-Hungarian General Staff; Director of the Vienna War Archives (1938-1945); One of the key contributors to the official General Staff series *Österreich Ungarns letzter Krieg.*

KÖVESS, von KÖVESSHÁZA, HERMANN, Baron (1854-1924)
Group Commander in eastern Galicia until 26 August 1914; Field

Marshal; 3 November 1918 given High Command of dissolving Austro-Hungarian Army.

KRAUSS, ALFRED (1882-1938)
Commandant of the War School (1910-1914); Author of books criticizing 1914 strategy against Serbia; 1918 Commander of the East Armies.

LICHNOWSKY, KARL MAX (1860-1928)
German Ambassador in London (1912-1914).

LIMAN, von SANDERS, OTTO (1855-1929)
Commander of the German military mission to Turkey (1913-1914); prominent in the Dardanelles campaign.

LUDENDORFF, ERICH von (1865-1937)
Prussian General; Hindenburg's Chief of Staff on the Eastern front; Chief Quartermaster (1916).

MILAN, KING OF SERBIA (1854-1901)
King of Serbia (1882-1901); Unsuccessful in war against Bulgaria (1885).

MOLTKE, HELMUTH, Graf von (1800-1891)
Chief of the German General Staff (1871-1888).

MOLTKE, HELMUTH von (1848-1916)
Chief of the German General Staff (1906-1914) succeeding General Schlieffen; Modified the Schlieffen Plan; Removed after the defeat at the Marne.

NICHOLAS II (1868-1918)
Tsar of Russia (1894-1918); Abdicated in March 1917 in the Russian Revolution.

PETER I (1844-1921)
King of Serbia (1903-1918); First King of Serbia, Croatia, Slovenia (1918-1921).

PITREICH, MAXIMILIAN (1877-1945)
Colonel in the General Staff of the Austro-Hungarian Third Army (1914); Author of several critical books and manuscripts on 1914 concerning strategy and Railroad Bureau mobilization measures.

POINCARÉ, RAYMOND (1860-1934)
President of the French Republic (1913-1920); Foreign Minister (1913-1914).

POLLIO, Baron ALBERTO (1852-1914)
Chief of the Italian General Staff (1908-1914).

POTIOREK, OSKAR von (1853-1933)
Landeschef for Bosnia and Herzegowina (1911-1914); Commander of the Balkan front forces (1914); Dismissed after failure of invasions of Serbia (1914).

PUTNIK, RADOMIR (1847-1917)
Commander of the Serbian forces 1914-1915.

PRITTWITZ-GAFFRON MAXIMILLIAN von (1848-1929)
Commander of the German Eighth Army until replaced by General Hindenburg (late August 1914).

RATZENHOFER, EMIL (1877-1964)
Major in Austro-Hungarian Railroad Bureau of the General Staff (1908-1918); Major figure in the "Command Conspiracy"; Became editor of *Militärwissenschaftliche und technische Mitteilungen* after the war; A leader of the "official history" (OULK) school.

RENNENKAMPF, PAVEL KARLOVICH (1854-1918)
Russian General defeated at the Masurian Lakes Battle; Executed in 1918.

SAZONOV, SERGEI DMITIEVICH (1860-1927)
Russian Foreign Minister 1910-1916.

SCHEMUA, BLASIUS (1856-1920)
Chief of the Austro-Hungarian General Staff (1911-1912); Commander of the II. Corps during the battle of Komarov; Removed from command on 24 September 1914.

SCHLIEFFEN, ALFRED Graf von (1833-1913)
Chief of German General Staff (1891-1905); Creator of the Schlieffen Plan, which, modified by the Younger Moltke, became the basis of German operations in 1914.

STRAUB, JOHANN (1866-1929)
Major General; Section leader of the Austro-Hungarian Railroad Bureau (1914-1918); Key figure in the July and August military railroad planning.

SZÖGYÉNY-MARICH, LÁSZLÓ, Graf (1840-1916)
Austro-Hungarian Ambassador to Germany (1892-1914).

TISZA, ISTVÁN, Graf (1861-1918)
Hungarian Minister President (1903-1905, 1913-1917).

TSCHIRSCHKY-BÖGENDORFF, HEINRICH LEONARD von (1858-1916)
German Ambassador to Austria-Hungary (1907-1916).

URBANSKI, AUGUST (1866-1950)
Officer in the Intelligence Bureau during the Redl Affair; Chief of the Intelligence Bureau (1909-1913); Wrote a "command conspiracy" biography of Conrad von Hötzendorf (1938).

VIVANI, RENÉ (1863-1925)
Socialist leader, French Prime Minister at the outbreak of the war.

WALDERSEE, ALFRED, Graf (1832-1904)
Chief of the German General Staff (1888-1891); Prussian General Field Marshal (1900); Close relations with the Austro-Hungarian General Staff.

WILHELM I (1797-1888)
Kaiser of Germany (1871-1888); Unifier of Germany.

WILHELM II (1859-1941)
Kaiser of Germany (1888-1914).

Name Index

Place Index

363

Volumes Published in
"Atlantic Studies on Society in Change"

No. 1   *Tolerance and Movements of Religious Dissent in Eastern Europe.* Edited by Béla K. Király. 1977.

No. 2   *The Habsburg Empire in World War I.* Edited by R. A. Kann. 1978

No. 3   *The Mutual Effects of the Islamic and Judeo-Christian Worlds: The East European Pattern.* Edited by A. Ascher, T. Halasi-Kun, B. K. Király. 1979.

No. 4   *Before Watergate: Problems of Corruption in American Society.* Edited by A. S. Eisenstadt, A. Hoogenboom, H. L. Trefousse. 1979.

No. 5   *East Central European Perceptions of Early America.* Edited by B. K. Király and G. Barány. 1977.

No. 6   *The Hungarian Revolution of 1956 in Retrospect.* Edited by B. K. Király and Paul Jónás. 1978.

No. 7   *Brooklyn U.S.A.: Fourth Largest City in America.* Edited by Rita S. Miller. 1979.

No. 8   *Prime Minister Gyula Andrássy's Influence on Habsburg Foreign Policy.* János Decsy. 1979.

No. 9   *The Great Impeacher: A Political Biography of James M. Ashley.* Robert F. Horowitz. 1979.

No. 10
Vol. I[*]   *Special Topics and Generalizations on the Eighteenth and Nineteenth Century.* Edited by Béla K. Király and Gunther E. Rothenberg. 1979.

---

[*]Volumes Nos. I through XXXI refer to the series *War and Society in East and Central Europe.*

No. 11 Vol. II	*East Central European Society and War in the Pre-Revolutionary 18th-Century.* Edited by Gunther E. Rothenberg, Béla K. Király, and Peter F. Sugar. 1982.
No. 12 Vol. III	*From Hunyadi to Rákóczi: War and Society in Late Medieval and Early Modern Hungary.* Edited by János M. Bak and Béla K. Király. 1982.
No. 13 Vol. IV	*East Central European Society and War in the Era of Revolutions: 1775-1856.* Edited by B. K. Király. 1984.
No. 14 Vol. V	*Essays on World War I: Origins and Prisoners of War.* Edited by Samuel R. Williamson, Jr. and Peter Pastor. 1983.
No. 15 Vol. VI	*Essays on World War I: Total War and Peacemaking, A Case Study on Trianon.* Edited by B. K. Király, Peter Pastor, and Ivan Sanders. 1982.
No. 16 Vol. VII	*Army, Aristocracy, Monarchy: War, Society and Government in Austria, 1618-1780.* Edited by Thomas M. Barker. 1982.
No. 17 Vol. VIII	*The First Serbian Uprising 1804-1813.* Edited by Wayne S. Vucinich. 1982.
No. 18 Vol. IX	*Czechoslovak Policy and the Hungarian Minority 1945-1948.* Kálmán Janics. Edited by Stephen Borsody. 1982.
No. 19 Vol. X	*At the Brink of War and Peace: The Tito-Stalin Split in a Historic Perspective.* Edited by Wayne S. Vucinich. 1982.
No. 20	*Inflation Through the Ages: Economic, Social, Psychological and Historical Aspects.* Edited by Edward Marcus and Nathan Schmuckler. 1981.
No. 21	*Germany and America: Essays on Problems of International Relations and Immigration.* Edited by Hans L. Trefousse. 1980.
No. 22	*Brooklyn College: The First Half Century.* Murray M. Horowitz. 1981.

No. 23   *A New Deal for the World: Eleanor Roosevelt and American Foreign Policy.* Jason Berger. 1981.

No. 24   *The Legacy of Jewish Migration: 1881 and Its Impact.* Edited by David Berger. 1982.

No. 25   *The Road to Bellapais: Cypriot Exodus to Northern Cyprus.* Pierre Oberling. 1982.

No. 26   *New Hungarian Peasants: An East Central European Experience with Collectivization.* Edited by Marida Hollos and Béla C. Maday. 1983.

No. 27   *Germans in America: Aspects of German-American Relations in the Nineteenth Century.* Edited by Allen McCormick. 1983.

No. 28   *A Question of Empire: Leopold I and the War of Spanish Succession, 1701-1705.* Linda and Marsha Frey. 1983.

No. 29   *The Beginning of Cyrillic Printing — Cracow, 1491. From the Orthodox Past in Poland.* Szczepan K. Zimmer. Edited by Ludwik Krzyzanowski and Irene Nagurski. 1983.

No. 29a   *A Grand Ecole for the Grand Corps: The Recruitment and Training of the French Administration.* Thomas R. Osborne. 1983.

No. 30   *The First War between Socialist States: The Hungarian*
Vol. XI   *Revolution of 1956 and Its Impact.* Edited by Béla K. Király, Barbara Lotze, Nandor Dreisziger. 1984.

No. 31   *The Effects of World War I, The Uprooted: Hungarian*
Vol. XII *Refugees and Their Impact on Hungary's Domestic Politics.* István Mócsy. 1983.

No. 32   *The Effects of World War I: The Class War after the Great*
Vol. XIII *War: The Rise Of Communist Parties in East Central Europe, 1918-1921.* Edited by Ivo Banac. 1983.

No. 33   *The Crucial Decade: East Central European Society and*
Vol. XIV *National Defense, 1859-1870.* Edited by Béla K. Király. 1984.

No. 35 Vol. XVI	*Effects of World War I: War Communism in Hungary, 1919.* György Péteri. 1984.
No. 36 Vol. XVII	*Insurrections, Wars, and the Eastern Crisis in the 1870s.* Edited by B. K. Király and Gale Stokes. 1985.
No. 37 Vol. XVIII	*East Central European Society and the Balkan Wars, 1912-1913.* Edited by B. K. Király and Dimitrije Djordjevic. 1986.
No. 38 Vol. XIX	*East Central European Society in World War I.* Edited by B. K. Király and N. F. Dreisziger, Assistant Editor Albert A. Nofi. 1985.
No. 39 Vol. XX	*Revolutions and Interventions in Hungary and Its Neighbor States, 1918-1919.* Edited by Peter Pastor. 1988.
No. 40 Vol. XXI	*East Central European Society and War, 1750-1920. Bibliography and Historiography.* Complied and edited by László Alföldi. Pending.
No. 41 Vol. XXII	*Essays on East Central European Society and War, 1740-1920.* Edited by Stephen Fischer-Galati and Béla K. Király. 1988.
No. 42 Vol. XXIII	*East Central European Maritime Commerce and Naval Policies, 1789-1913.* Edited by Apostolos E. Vacalopoulos, Constantinos D. Svolopoulos, and Béla K. Király. 1988.
No. 43 Vol. XXIV	*Selections, Social Origins, Education and Training of East Central European Officers Corps.* Edited by Béla K. Király and Walter Scott Dillard. 1988.
No. 44 Vol. XXV	*East Central European War Leaders: Civilian and Military.* Edited by Béla K. Király and Albert Nofi. 1988.
No. 46	*Germany's International Monetary Policy and the European Monetary System.* Hugo Kaufmann. 1985.
No. 47	*Iran Since the Revolution — Internal Dynamics, Regional Conflicts and the Superpowers.* Edited by Barry M. Rosen. 1985.

No. 48
Vol. XXVII

The Press During the Hungarian Revolution of 1848-1849. Domokos Kosáry. 1986.

No. 49

The Spanish Inquisition and the Inquisitional Mind. Edited by Angel Alcala. 1987.

No. 50

Catholics, the State and the European Radical Right, 1919-1945. Edited by Richard Wolff and Jorg K. Hoensch. 1987.

No. 51
Vol. XXVIII

The Boer War and Military Reforms. Jay Stone and Erwin A. Schmidl. 1987.

No. 52

Baron Joseph Eötvös, A Literary Biography. Steven B. Várdy. 1987.

No. 53

Towards the Renaissance of Puerto Rican Studies: Ethnic and Area Studies in University Education. Maria Sanchez and Antonio M. Stevens. 1987.

No. 54

The Brazilian Diamonds in Contracts, Contraband and Capital. Harry Bernstein. 1987.

No. 55

Christians, Jews and Other Worlds: Patterns of Conflict and Accommodation. Edited by Phillip F. Gallagher. 1988.

No. 56
Vol. XXVI

The Fall of the Medieval Kingdom of Hungary: Mohács, 1526, Buda, 1541. Géza Perjés. 1989.

No. 57

The Lord Mayor of Lisbon: The Portuguese Tribune of the People and His 24 Guilds. Harry Bernstein. 1989.

No. 58

Hungarian Statesmen of Destiny: 1860-1960. Edited by Paul Bödy. 1989.

No. 59

For China: The Memoirs of T. G. Li, former Major General in the Chinese Nationist Army. T. G. Li. Written in collaboration with Roman Rome. 1989.

No. 60

Politics in Hungary: For A Democratic Alternative. János Kis, with an Introduction by Timothy Garton Ash. 1989.

No. 61

Hungarian Worker's Councils in 1956. Edited by Bill Lomax. 1990.

No. 62   *Essays on the Structure and Reform of Centrally Planned Economic Systems.* Paul Jonas. A joint publication with Corvina Kiadó, Budapest. 1990.

No. 63   *Kossuth as a Journalist in England.* Éva H. Haraszti. A joint publication with Akadémiai Kiadó, Budapest. 1990.

No. 64   *From Padua to the Trianon, 1918-1920.* Mária Ormos. A joint publication with Akadémiai Kiadó, Budapest. 1990.

No. 65   *Towns in Medieval Hungary.* Edited by László Gerevich. A joint publication with Akadémiai Kiadó, Budapest. 1990.

No. 66   *The Nationalities Problem in Transylvania, 1867-1940.* Sándor Bíró. 1992.

No. 67   *Hungarian Exiles and the Romanian National Movement, 1849-1867.* Béla Borsi-Kálmán. 1991.

No. 68   *The Hungarian Minority's Situation in Ceausescu's Romania.* Edited by Rudolf Joó and Andrew Ludanyi. 1993.

No. 69   *Democracy, Revolution, Self-Determination. Selected Writings.* István Bibó. Edited by Károly Nagy. 1991.

No. 70   *Trianon and the Protection of Minorities.* József Galántai. A joint publication with Corvina Kiadó, Budapest. 1991.

No. 71   *King Saint Stephen of Hungary.* György Györffy. A joint publication with Corvina Kiadó, Budapest. Pending.

No. 72   *Dynasty, Politics and Culture. Selected Essays.* Robert A. Kann. Edited by Stanley B. Winters. 1991.

No. 73   *Jadwiga of Anjou and the Rise of East Central Europe.* Oscar Halecki. Edited by Thaddeus V. Gromada. A joint publication with the Polish Institute of Arts and Sciences of America, New York. 1991.

No. 74   *Hungarian Economy and Society During World War II.*
Vol. XXIX   Edited by György Lengyel. 1992.

No. 75   *The Life of a Communist Revolutionary, Béla Kun.* György Borsányi. 1993.

No. 76   *Yugoslavia: The Process of Disintegration.* Laslo Sekelj. 1993.

No. 77
Vol. XXX   *Wartime American Plans for a New Hungary. Documents from the U.S. Department of State, 1942-1944.* Edited by Ignác Romsics. 1992.

No.78
Vol. XXXI   *Planning for War against Russia and Serbia. Austro-Hungarian and German Military Strategies, 1871-1914.* Graydon A. Tunstall, Jr. 1993.

No. 79   *American Effects on Hungarian Imagination and Political Thought, 1559-1848.* Géza Závodszky. 1993.